The Religion & Family Connection:

Social Science Perspectives

The Religion & Family Connection:

Social Science Perspectives

Edited with an Introduction and Summary by
Darwin L. Thomas

Volume Three
in the Religious Studies Center
Specialized Monograph Series

Religious Studies Center
Brigham Young University
Provo, Utah

Copyright © 1988 by
Religious Studies Center
Brigham Young University

Library of Congress Catalog Card Number; 87-71826
ISBN 0-88494-636-3

First Printing, 1988

Produced and Distributed by
BOOKCRAFT, INC.
Salt Lake City, Utah

Printed in the United States of America

Contents

Preface

This volume had its beginning in March 1984 at the Conference on Religion and the Family sponsored by the Family and Demographic Research Institute at Brigham Young University. All of the nineteen chapters were prepared especially for this volume. Twelve were initially presented at the conference. Six presentations from the conference were chosen for publication in the *Journal of Marriage and the Family*, May 1985, in a special section on religion and the family, and are reprinted in this volume.

The editor and the authors appreciate the encouragement given this project by Professor Stephen J. Bahr, Director of the Family and Demographic Research Institute, and the financial support received from that institute. They are grateful also for financial aid from two other sources: the College of Family, Home, and Social Sciences, under Dean Stan L. Albrecht, and the Department of Sociology, under its Chairman, James T. Duke. Without the continual encouragement of Professor Kent S. Brown of the Religious Studies Center at Brigham Young University, this volume would never have been completed. Last, and most important, Norene Petersen arranged the conference, contacted authors, typed and edited manuscripts, and in general made my editorial role manageable.

The authors of the various chapters were selected because of their interest and expertise in family and religious studies. They represent not only various perspectives in the social sciences (sociology, psychology, anthropology, and so on), but also various perspectives from a variety of Judaeo-Christian backgrounds (Jewish, Catholic, Mormon, Protestant, and so forth). The chapters are not official statements of any religious organization, but they are social scientists' best efforts at describing the religion and family interface in various religious denominations.

Part I of the book introduces the discussion of the religion and family interface by placing the current heightened interest in the social sciences in historical context and identifying areas in which research and theory can make significant contributions. Part II develops the central message of the volume, namely, how to understand change and constancy in both religion and family in an ever-changing social order. Part III looks specifically at socialization processes and outcomes, emphasizing how religion and family combine to influence the child in the family. Part IV develops a broader perspective on the religion and family interface by presenting contrasting typologies and raising questions about how an investigator's own presuppositions about religion and family might influence the questions asked and answers suggested. Part V uses research on the Mormon family to illustrate some potential contributions of future research and theory which take as their mandate the study of religion and family simultaneously.

If this volume adds to our current understanding of the religion and family connection by stimulating more and better comparative research and theory, then the editor and the authors will be more than amply rewarded for their work.

DARWIN L. THOMAS

I. Introduction

The Religion and Family Connection: Increasing Dialogue in the Social Sciences

Darwin L. Thomas, Gwendolyn C. Henry

Introduction

In October 1984 the National Council of Family Relations began a new section on religion. The group of NCFR members committed to furthering the cause of the study of religion and the family met to elect officers and chart their course. The group was told that it was an auspicious moment. First, the future looked bright because the recent interest in the religion and family connection was part of a larger movement within the social sciences of focusing on things religious. Second, the current postpositivist era in the social sciences probably would generate fewer dogmatic statements than had occurred earlier in the sometimes heated dialogue between science and religion. Third, the coming

Darwin L. Thomas is Professor of Sociology and former Director of the Family and Demographic Research Institute at Brigham Young University. He has authored and/or edited four books and published numerous journal articles. His research interests have focused on the social-psychological dimensions of family interaction, with his latest work attempting to unravel the independent and combined effects of religion and family variables on attitudes and behavior. He received his Ph.D. from the University of Minnesota.

Gwendolyn C. Henry received her Ph.D. in Family Studies with an emphasis in Gerontology and Family Life Education from Brigham Young University (August 1987). Other research interests include intergenerational relationships, life-span issues in the family, and parenting.

TABLE 1. NCFR SECTION ON RELIGION AND THE FAMILY, 1952–1961

Conference Dates	No. of Section Meetings	No. of Presentations	Chairperson			Presenters			Discussants		
			A[a]	C	P	A	C	P	A	C	P
8/30–9/02/52	1	2	1				1			3	
8/31–9/02/53	1	2	1							7	
7/07–7/10/54	2	7		1			7		1	3	
8/24–8/27/55	2	4		1			4		1	1	1
8/16–8/18/56	2	2		1			8	1		1	1
8/21–8/24/57	2	2		1		1	1				
8/20–8/23/58	3	5		1		2	3				
8/19–8/21/59	2	2		1			1	2	1	1	1
8/23–8/26/60	2	6		1			5	1			
8/23–8/25/61	2	4	1				3	1			
Totals	19	36	3	7		3	33	5	3	16	3

[a]A = Academic, C = Clergy, P = Private practice.

together of researchers, theologians, and practitioners concerned with the religion and family interface had the potential of producing significant payoffs in society's larger effort to understand the human condition. (Thomas and Sommerfeldt, 1984.)

One irony noticed by the NCFR group was that this was really not a *new* NCFR section in the sense of creating something that had never existed but rather was new in the sense of resurrecting that which had been born, lived a few short years, and died. In 1952 a religion section in NCFR began holding meetings. That section ended in 1962. Table 1 presents some of our findings in an effort to understand some of the characteristics of that first religion section.

The data point to a number of conclusions. First, it appears as though the section remained relatively small, with few meetings and relatively few people presenting or otherwise participating. We were unable to come up with section attendance figures; but in examining the yearly programs, we could not detect a sense of periodic or sustained growth. Second, section participants from the clergy were largely responsible for the content and activities of the section. Third, the academic researchers and theoreticians, along with private practice participants, were minimally involved. Of the few academicians who did participate, they tended to do so only for one year, whereas many clergy were repeat participants.

Our sense is that the current interest in religion within NCFR is different from that which emerged in the 1950s. Our judgment is that the larger milieu which currently exists within the social sciences is more open to investigation into things of a religious nature, and therefore makes a dialogue focusing on the interface between religion and family much more promising. Recent attempts to assess the social scientists' perspectives on the religion and family connection conclude that up through the late 1970s the two had remained largely independent of one another. Only two of the fifty-seven family texts surveyed had a chapter on religion, and only two religious texts published before 1978 had a chapter on the family (D'Antonio, Newman and Wright, 1982).

This is obviously changing. Two universities, traditionally having close ties with religious institutions, recently held conferences on religion and family. The Notre Dame Seminar during the summer of 1981 produced the D'Antonio and Aldous volume (1983) on families and religions. The Twelfth Annual Family and Demographic Research Conference at Brigham Young University in 1984 generated a series of presentations on religion and the family, some of which are published in this volume. Last, the aforementioned creation of the religion section in the fall of 1984 at NCFR promises to continue to emphasize the religion and family connection.

We think this increased interest in the 1980s is just now beginning to be reflected in the basic family texts. For example, one of the most widely used texts over the last twenty years, Leslie's *The Family in Social Context*, now has appeared in its sixth edition (Leslie and Korman, 1985) with, for the first time ever, a chapter on the influence of religion on families. None of the first five editions (1967, 1973, 1976, 1979, 1982) had one entry under religion in the indexes. The advertisements for the 1985 edition highlight the new chapter on religion, along with new material on working women, female-headed households, ethnicity, delayed parenting, etc., as evidence for the text's timeliness.

Even though the foregoing signs argue for recent increased interest in religion by those studying the family, our optimism is determined more by what we see occurring in the social sciences in general with respect to religion. We see the study of the family as an interdisciplinary field which traditionally has been nourished by methodological developments and theoretical formulations in related disciplines. We expect that trend to continue. We see those relevant disciplines as calling attention to the significance of the study of religion; thus, we think that the increased interest in religion in the mother disciplines will encourage study of the family and religion connection.

The Social Science Setting

By the time the social sciences were born in the last half of the 1800s, the centuries-old dialogue between philosophy and theology, which in large measure had determined the basic parameters of Western intellectual heritage, was significantly altered by the rise of science. Within Western culture, scientific knowledge was highly valued and scientific discoveries had forever changed humankind's perception of and encounters with the natural order. Philosophy more easily integrated and built upon scientific worldviews than did theology, with the major lines of dialogue gradually shifting from the philosophy/theology axis to the science/religion axis—especially any discussions focusing on the natural order. As many have noted (Merton, 1957:579; Martindale, 1960:425–27, 1962:424–58; and Thomas and Wilcox, 1987), the rise of scientific thought occurred concomitantly with the union of rationalism and empiricism. Martindale (1962) argued that the social order had to value empirical evidence equal to or perhaps even higher than rational proof for scientific knowledge to become so widely valued. Thus, by 1850 a naturalistic emphasis informed many Western thinkers.

With Darwin's important work at midcentury came the evolutionary perspective that would also influence much social science thought emerging later, during the last half of the nineteenth century. Hinkle (1980) has labeled the underlying philosophical orientation of much of the early social science work as evolutionary naturalism. The social order was seen as part of the natural order; and scientific procedures, following the lead of the physical sciences, offered the best approach for understanding the social order. The social order was seen as evolving into more complex and better adapted social forms.

Many of the early works in the social sciences showed an explicit interest in religion. For example, the psychology of religion is generally described as a flourishing area of interest within psychology during the closing decades of the 1800s and the first two decades of the twentieth century. The work of W. James and G. S. Hall, along with their students and colleagues, is cited as typical of this early work (Beit-Hallahmi, 1974). Similarly, in sociology many of the early founders explicitly focused on the religious institutions in their theoretical and empirical works. Weber, Durkheim, and Marx are illustrative.

Just as there is general agreement that religion as an area of study emerged quickly in the social sciences, there is agreement that from the 1920s to the 1950s there was a marked decline in the number and quality of studies in the religious realm. In psychology, the reviews of published research showed that few studies were carried out after 1933. The few studies being done came mostly from German and French social scientists, thus emphasizing even more the relatively few studies of the psychology of religion in the United States. The survey of courses on the psychology of religion at American universities in 1938 showed a marked decline from the previous decades, with only 24 out of 154 colleges offering them. The decline was so sharp that some observers pronounced the psychology of religion movement dead (Beit-Hallahmi, 1974). While the sociology of religion apparently did not show the rapid swells and declines observed in psychology, it too experienced a noticeable drop from the 1920s on. Demerath and Roof (1976:19) observe that "despite the classic statements of Emile Durkheim, Max Weber, and Ernst Troeltsch, and others, there emerged very few works on religion in the years between 1920 and 1955."

Many observers have offered a variety of reasons for the decline. The following are some of the typical reasons given.

1. [The field] failed to separate itself from theology, philosophy of religion, and the general dogmatic and evangelistic tasks of religious institutions.
2. The desperate effort to be recognized as "scientific" [led to] an emphasis on collecting discrete facts without integrating them into a comprehensive theory.
3. Public opinion was changing away from religion and towards a behavioristic and positivistic world view.
4. "Subjective" phenomena were avoided by . . . social science which tried to be "empirical" and "objective." [The above four came from Douglas (1963), cited in Beit-Hallahmi, 1974:87.]
5. Psychoanalytic approaches to religion seemed more promising.
6. The influence of behaviorism led to the neglect of complex human behaviors. [Items 5 and 6 come from Strunk, 1957:287, 289.]
7. Inside academic psychology in the 20's and 30's, interest in religion began to be perceived as evidence of unscientific orientation.
8. As early as 1921 . . . it was shown that scientists, especially psychologists, were less religious than most of the American population. Scientists in the 30's might have felt that the long war between science and religion was won by science and there was not much left to study in religion. [Items 7 and 8 came from Beit-Hallahmi, 1974:88, 89.]

Just as there seems to be widespread agreement about the decline of social scientific interest in religion beginning in the 1920s, there seems to be considerable agreement among social science observers that the 1960s and 1970s saw an unusual revival of interest in religion. Part of the increased interest came from research generated, paid for, and/or conducted by churches or church-related organizations. Many of these organizations had social scientists design, conduct, and report the research in an effort to better understand the challenges that faced churches desiring to deal more effectively with individuals and families. This outpouring of research from Catholic, Protestant, Mormon, Jewish and other non-Christian churches contributed significantly to the religious literature in the social sciences. The book *Understanding Church Growth and Decline: 1950–1978* (Hoge and Roozen, 1979) is illustrative of this emphasis.

In addition to church-related research, increased interest in religion appears to have occurred generally within the social sciences. Demerath and Roof (1976:19) argue that "beginning in the middle 1950's, the field [sociology of religion] has undergone what can only be described as an accelerating revival." Robbins and Anthony (1979:75) review sociological research on new religions in the United States and conclude that "during the last decade the West has witnessed an explosion of heterodox religiosity." Bergin (1980:96) discusses the remarkable growth of interest in the psychology of religion over the past few decades and observes that "the present phenomenon has all the aspects of a broad-based movement with a building momentum." He observes that psychologists are part "of this developing zeitgeist" and are influenced by these larger cultural forces all generating renewed interest in things religious. After identifying a number of the basic trends in this increased interest in religion, Demerath and Roof (1976:31) conclude: "In sum, the last decade of research and theory may well be judged as the most exciting since the first decade of the twentieth century and new developments in the making signal even more excitement and fruition in the decade to come."

In a further attempt to investigate the increased interest in religion that the many observers had noticed, we attempted to identify any organization created by social scientists with the purpose of focusing on religion. Our purpose was to identify when the organization was founded, what its purpose was, whether it produced any publications, and what the approximate membership was. Since we were unable to locate a directory that already had prepared such a compilation of organizations, our strategy was to call any organizations that we knew, obtain the above information from them, and then ask for names of other organizations. Table 2 presents a summary of our efforts. We do not take this to be an exhaustive list since our methodology of following the informal lines probably resulted in incomplete data. Even so, we think our efforts are informative.

The conclusion of increased activity since the late 1950s through the decade of the 1970s is obvious. Up to 1959 there were four organizations involving social scientists that focused on religion. Over the next 20 years, 1959 to 1978, 11 such organizations formed. Ten of the fifteen organizations are identified specifically as Christian in nature (Mormons are here categorized as Christians). We suspect that this preponderance of Christian organizations reflects a preponderance of Christian affiliation among social scientists; however, it also may reflect the failure of our informal network to lead us to the non-Christian social sicence organizations, since we are Christians doing the research. We need more and better research to identify whether or not non-Christian social scientists feel the need to organize and are organizing along religious lines. We also need research to study the durability of these religious organizations within social science to determine whether the current heightened interest in religion is ephemeral or a more lasting phenomenon. Given our view of the underlying cultural milieu, we expect this to be a more long-lasting interest in religion than that occurring in the early years of the social sciences or in NCFR during the 1950s.

We are not sure that the reasons for increased interest in religion within the social sciences have been adequately explained; nevertheless, a number of observers have posited possible causes for this recent renaissance of interest. The reasons given generally include a reevaluation of the role of science in making truth claims, crises of values and sense of community in the larger social order, the role of families and religions in meeting social and psychological needs, and the need to include the spiritual realm in attempts to understand human behavior. The following are illustrative:

1. "General psychology is gradually being made conscious of its narrowly-conceived science" (Andrews, 1979:36–37).
2. The current spiritual ferment is linked to a crisis of values which in turn is seen as linked to the erosion of a cultural tradition of moral absolutism in a highly differentiated and pluristic society.
3. The present upsurge of interest in religion (especially unconventional movements) is linked to a crisis of community because the traditional mediating structures between the individual and the social order such

9

TABLE 2. SOME SOCIAL SCIENCE ORGANIZATIONS FOCUSING ON RELIGION

Organization	Year Founded	Purpose	Publications	Approximate Membership
The American Catholic Sociological Society (ACSS—changed to the Association for the Sociology of Religion [ASR] in 1971)	1936	To stimulate research in sociology and religion	*The American Catholic Sociological Review* (1940)[a]	
The American Catholic Psychological Association (ACPA—changed to Psychologists Interested in Religious Issues [PIRI] in 1965)	1948	To study psychology of religion and its application	*Catholic Psychological Record* (1960)	600
The Society for the Scientific Study of Religion (SSSR)	1949	To stimulate/communicate significant scientific research on religious institutions and experience	*Journal for the Scientific Study of Religion* (1961)	1,400
The National Association of Christians in Social Work (NACSW—changed to North American Association of Christians in Social Work [NAACSW] in 1984)	1950	To bring together Christians in social work for discussion of common concerns and to interest Christians in entering the profession	*Catalyst* (bimonthly newsletter); *The Paraclete*	1,125
Religion Research Association (RRA)	1959	To understand the role of religion in contemporary life	*Review of Religious Research* (1959)	500
The Christian Association for Psychological Studies (CAPS)	1960	Professional association to try to relate Christian faith to psychological concepts	*Psychology and Christianity*(1980) *CAPS Bulletin and Proceedings*	1,500
The LDS Personnel and Guidance Association (LDSPGA—changed to the Association of Mormon Counselors and Psychotherapists [AMCAP] in 1975)	1964	To promote fellowship	No publications	
Psychologists Interested in Religious Issues (PIRI was formerly the American Catholic Psychological Association [ACPA] from 1948 to 1965; changed to Division 36 of the American Psychological Association [APA] in 1976)	1965	To study psychology of religion and its application	No publications	450

Organization	Year[a]	Purpose	Publication (year)	Membership
Christian Anthropological Association	1969	Fellowship	The Christian Anthropological Association Newsletter (1969)	500
Association for the Sociology of Religion (ASR—formerly called the American Catholic Sociological Society from 1936 to 1971)	1971	To stimulate research in sociology of religion	Sociological Analyses (1964)	
Association for the Sociological Study of Jewry (ASSJ)	1971	To engage in the scientific study of Jewish life/forum for discussion	Newsletter (1973) Journal of Contemporary Jewry (annual) (1973)	350
The Christian Sociological Society (CSS)	1972	To witness for Christ in sociological areas	Newsletter (1972) (no meetings)	650
Association of Mormon Counselors and Psychotherapists (AMCAP—formerly called the LDS Personnel and Guidance Association from 1964 to 1975)	1975	To promote fellowship, communication, professional development/leadership—a forum for LDS professionals	AMCAP Journal (1975)	796
The Association for Christians Teaching Sociology (ACTS)	1975	A forum where Christian sociologists can explore Christianity and sociology, explore professional and personal development and Christian fellowship within a supportive network	Annual Conference with program (1976); no publications	125
Society for the Sociological Study of Mormon Life (SSSML)	1978	Research/study of Mormon life	Newsletter (1979)	140

Note: Our attempt was to list any organization whose focus was religion and whose membership and purpose appeared to be related to the social sciences. Some organizations, such as the American Philosophical Association and the American Scientific Association, include a focus on religion; but most of the members are either philosophers or physical scientists, rather than social scientists. Another organization that has existed since 1960—the American Jewish Committee—emphasizes religion but was designed for broad political reasons and involves many people other than social scientists. Some organizations, such as the American Sociological Association and the American Psychological Association, provide a forum for presentations on religious issues as part of their annual meeting programs. In addition, some specifically religious organizations, such as The Council on the Study of Religion, have sections on "religion and the social sciences" at their annual meetings. Papers presented at these meetings would be another important source for analysis of trends in religious research in the social sciences.

[a]Year when publication or other activity such as meetings began is shown in parentheses.

as families, homogeneous neighborhoods, and personalistic work settings are being supplanted increasingly by social inventions. (Items 2 and 3 are paraphrased from Robbins and Anthony, 1979:76, 78).

4. "The current evangelical revival evidently meets not only emotional but also moral and cognitive needs of vast sectors of the population, needs that are going unmet by competing systems" (Warner, 1979:8).

5. Part of the new religious consciousness of many within the countercultural movement is linked to changing family patterns (paraphrased from D'Antonio, 1980:99).

6. "Science has lost its authority as the dominating source of truth it once was. . . . The ecological, social and political consequences of science and technology are no longer necessarily viewed as progress. Although a belief in the value of the scientific method appropriately persists, there is widespread disillusionment with the way it has been used and loss of faith in it as a cure for human ills."

7. "Psychology, in particular, has been dealt blows to its status as a source of authority for human action because of its obsession with "methodolitry," its limited effectiveness in producing practical results, its conceptual incoherence, and its alienation from the mainstream of the culture."

8. "The emergence of studies of consciousness and cognition which grew out of disillusionment with mechanistic behaviorism has . . . set the stage for a new examination of the possibility that presently unobservable realities—namely spiritual forces—are at work in human behavior." (Items 6–8 are from Bergin, 1980:95, 96.)

The current climate in the social sciences is considerably different from that of the 1940s and 1950s when NCFR first began its religion section. While we cannot trace the rise of family theory here (see Thomas and Wilcox, 1987, for a discussion), suffice it to say that those researchers and theorists focusing on the family in the 1950s began a strong emphasis on theory building with a decidedly positivist view of its subject matter during the 1960s and 1970s. This theory-building emphasis drew from the positivist theory-building tradition in general sociological theory (Thomas and Wilcox, 1987) and set the theory agenda in family study through the 1970s even though there were some who argued for a different course. For example, Robert G. Ryder recalls that he argued at those first "theory" meetings "that the task being urged was a mistaken idea—grand synthesis of propositions derived along positivist lines was a mistaken one tried by psychologists to their sorrow, and not a good idea for us" (Ryder, personal communication, Feb. 5, 1985). Those few voices crying in the wilderness went unheard as social scientists concerned about the study of the family sought to improve its scientific respectability by doing better research and building better theory.

In the research and theory rush of the 1960s and 1970s, the place of religion in the study of the family went almost unnoticed. Of the 1,006 pages in Christensen's *Handbook of Marriage and the Family* (1964), "religion and the family" appears in only three entries of the index, as does "religious groups." This separation of religion and family is also seen in the two volumes of *Contemporary Theories about the Family* (Burr et al., 1979). These two volumes were designed to summarize research and theory in important substantive areas in family study, and they have no religion chapter or even an extended discussion of religion within a chapter. There are only two insignificant references to religion in the index in each of the two volumes.

Beginning in 1971 NCFR's Theory Construction and Research Methodology Workshop has been held annually and has become an important forum for family researchers to present ongoing research and theory projects. At present, 268 presentations have been given. It was not until 1984 that the first presentation on religion and the family appeared in the workshop. Two presenters addressed issues related to the Jewish family. (LaRossa, 1985.)

We suspect that the general tendency of family researchers to avoid religion in their studies was a continuation of the general climate that existed in the preceding decades in the social sciences. The psychology of religion generally was seen as unscientific and sociology had reduced its study of the religious institution beginning in the 1920s.

Possible Payoffs

If the above treatise has some basis in fact and the current intellectual milieu augurs well for research, theory, and practical application directed towards the family and religion connection, so what? So what if we are moving into a time when more psychologists, sociologists, therapists, and family life educators may be more inclined to focus on family and religion? What might we come to understand better about the human condition than we currently do?

Although predicting the future is risky business—be it in economics, politics, or social/psychological projections on the human condition—we think some useful clues can be found in recent efforts focusing on religion and the family simultaneously. The articles in this volume are illustrative of the areas of investigation in the social sciences which we think will greatly benefit from the simultaneous study of religion and the family.

We expect current and future research to add significantly to our understanding of the role that religion and family institutions play in social change. Thornton's chapter (1985) carefully lays out the reciprocal relationship between the family institution and the religious institution in the West's recent past. While explaining social change wherein the political, economic, and religious institutions influence family patterns, Thornton also argues convincingly that the family institution reciprocally influences other institutions, specifically the religious institution. His general treatise leads to an appreciation of the interconnectedness among social institutions and the importance of looking at the family and religious institutions as both independent and dependent variables in one's analysis.

The issue about when family and religion are seen as independent (source of change) or dependent (that which has been changed) variables, is further discussed in the chapter on the Jewish family. In much of the analysis, the family variables are treated as independent variables accounting for transmission of "Jewish identity and survival of the group." As Brodbar-Nemzer (1988) notes, those who would understand social change within Judaism must be prepared for the very difficult task of trying to separate out the effects of family and religion from those of ethnicity. This is no easy task, but one that must be addressed by researchers/theorists who would understand the religion and family connection to social change within Judaism.

D'Antonio's more specific analysis (1985) of the relationship between the Catholic family and its church focuses on the interplay between these institutions. He notes that Catholic families vary in how they adapt to directives from the religious institution relative to family functioning. Just as families adapt to religious institutions, so too do religious institutions adapt to changing families. He argues that, in the case of the Catholic church, continued failure to modify some teachings with respect to contraceptive use and perhaps abortion undoutedly will lead to a more general loss of influence and authority by the religious institution in the lives of Catholic families. From his position, given the current realities of the social situation, it is likely that the religious institution will modify some positions in order to be more effective with its constituent families.

We suspect that one of the more important issues in the general area of social change is that related to how much the religious institution and the institution of the family are changing over time. In the absence of good baseline data, it is very easy for social scientists and the general public to conclude that there has been a great amount of change in the recent past. With respect to both religion and family, it is easy to see the "good old days" as significantly different and significantly better than the present conditions. Some of the best data available to assess the amount of and direction of change in these institutions come from the Middletown research (Caplow et al., 1982, 1983). As Bahr and Chadwick (1985) argue, the myths of radical change, within both the religious institution and the institution of the family, ought to be laid to rest. Looking at their data from a number of different angles, they conclude persuasively that both institutions have remained remarkably stable over the last fifty years in Middletown America. They wonder about how stability and change in one of these institutions is related to stability and change in the other, and they urge the necessity and utility of research focusing on the interface between these two institutions.

Heaton (1988) looks at the interface between the two institutions and argues convincingly for the distinctiveness of some Mormon family patterns because of theological underpinnings. What is not well understood, however, is just how distinctive some of the patterns are. For example, Heaton points to the fact that the more educated Mormons have larger families and he sees a possible cause in theological teachings. Brodbar-Nemzer (1988) points to the same relationship occurring among Jews but assumes that it only occurs among Jews. Is it only the more educated Mormons and Jews who have more children, or is that relationship true for any familistic religion? How does social change alter education-fertility dynamics among various religions?

When the issues of the connection between religion and the family are enlarged to include a historical perspective, even more caution is warranted in drawing conclusions. It is common to point to the Amish family (Olshan, 1988) as the example of a religious group that has successfully withstood change from the larger social order for centuries. But as Olshan argues in his chapter (1988), the Amish, according to what they write, are not that separate from the larger social order. Even the Amish exhibit a modern mentality in their daily struggle to live the Amish way. Hynes's discussion (1988) of religious and familial change in mid-nineteenth-century Ireland is a sobering reminder of the necessity to take into account local conditions in order to better understand how both the church and family change when confronting a catastrophe of such enormous proportions as the Great Hunger of 1845–49. An increase in attendance at Mass from about 30 percent in 1830 to over 90 percent in 1870 is remarkable, but, as Hynes reminds us, that change was only brought about because of the way the stem family functioned. Likewise, the religion that flourished during the devotional revolution was Catholicism of a particular type—an extremely puritanical variety that meshed with the needs of the times.

The Brinkerhoff and MacKie chapter (1988) addresses the area of gender identity and sex-role attitudes and behavior related specifically to religion and the family. There are perhaps few issues as important as gender identity and sex-role attitudes as they relate to social change. A significant portion of Scanzoni's chapter (1988) discusses gender roles from the Protestant woman's perspective. Religion and family are the two institutions most often discussed in the contemporary literature. While all the relevant questions obviously have not been asked and the relevant data are not currently in, there is enough evidence available to conclude that the religious and family institutions are perhaps two of the most important institutions in society with respect to understanding changes in sex-role attitudes and behavior. Clearly there is much important work remaining to be done.

Out of research designed to study two or more social institutions simultaneously, we think answers will be fashioned allowing us to understand better the similarities and differences among institutions. For example, important research in the neglected social-psychological area of commitment to institutions shows that the commitment patterns are more similar in the political, economic, and educational institutions than they are in the religious and familial institutions. The latter two institutions appear to be quite different from the other three (Abrahamson and Anderson, 1984). This further evidences the need to study the religion and family institutions simultaneously.

The second area where we see the prospects for considerable increase in our current knowledge is the general area of how the religious and family institutions are related to the personal well-being of various members within those institutions. From the work of Freud and others, much of the early history of the social sciences is characterized by the expectation that involvement in and reliance upon the religious institution will be associated with people who have a low sense of personal well-being. The assumption is that the psychological and sociological misfits, those having difficulty in establishing meaningful social relationships in the larger social context, turn to religion. As reviews (Stark, 1971; Lea, 1982; Bergin, 1983; Donahue, 1985) have shown, this negative relationship between religiosity and personal well-being is more an article of faith than a social fact. The research findings are ambiguous. Some research supports the negative relationship, while other research argues for a positive relationship between religiosity and personal well-being.

After reviewing a number of studies, Bergin (1983:176) concludes that his meta-analysis of the reported results "provide no support for . . . [the negative relationship] and they also do not provide much more than marginal support for a positive effect on religion." When he considers only those studies reporting statistically significant relationships, he notes that, of the seven, five support the positive relationship and two the negative relationship. Most positive relationships tend to be reported in more recent studies. This impression is corroborated by Judd (1985) who analyzed studies published since 1980 not encountered in any of the before-mentioned reviews; he found that most reported a positive relationship, some reported no relationship, while none reported a negative relationship.

The Stack chapter (1985), which reports his findings of the influence of familial and religious integration on suicide, comes down clearly on the side of the positive argument, showing religious and family integration to be associated with lower suicide rates. In addition to stressing the significance of the Durkheimian perspective that integration into basic societal institutions such as family and religion enhances personal well-being, an important aspect of the Stack research is that the effects of the family and religious institutions appear to be very similar—so similar, in fact, that Stack argues that he cannot really separate one effect from another in his data. Thus, he must analyze the effects of integration in both institutions simultaneously. In short, he is arguing that there is some underlying dimension common to both family and religious institutions that is being tapped by his measurement strategies.

One of the real payoffs in helping to reduce the ambiguity as to religion's effect on personal well-being will come, we suspect, when more studies treat religiosity as a multidimensional construct and then relate various dimensions to personal well-being. We expect that some aspects of religiosity are likely to be associated with problems and difficulties within a person's life, while other dimensions of religiosity may be related to personal well-being. Some recent progress along these lines is reported by Donahue (1985) in his meta-analyses of numerous studies. He takes Allport's very influential concepts of intrinsic and extrinsic religiosity and shows that extrinsic religiosity is positively associated with socially devalued characteristics such as anxiety, fear, prejudice, and dogmatism, while it is unrelated to prosocial behaviors such as altruism. Donahue's most important contribution comes as he further demonstrates the increased utility of his conceptualization wherein intrinsic and extrinsic are seen as distinct dimensions of religiosity rather than opposite poles on a single continuum. His resultant fourfold classification system allows him to test for interaction effects between the two dimensions and accounts much better for the observed patterns in the data. By treating religiosity as multidimensional, researchers then will be able to understand better the relationships to personal well-being. At that point family variables could be used along with multiple dimensions of religiosity to see how family variables may combine with these various combinations to better account for personal well-being.

The focus on personal well-being points to a common concern encountered in the literature on religion. Our third potential payoff area is an increase in social/psychological studies of religion and family. A number of reviewers have noted an absence of social/psychological studies of religion. Demerath and Roof (1976:31) observe that "while it is too much to expect the field to discard its primary reference to institutional religion, increasing concern with belief systems and ritual activities as part of a broader pursuit of meaning and integration are critical if the field is to fulfill its promise." Robbins and Anthony (1979:85) observe that the consequences of involvement in today's religious movements will never be understood "without additional information regarding the long-term social adjustment and attitudinal and personality transformations." In D'Antonio, Newman and Wright's (1982) research on social scientists' view of the connection between religion and family, the authors note that most of the work emphasizes the social control aspect of religious institutions and so the structural characteristics of religion. What is glaringly absent is a concern by the social scientists of the social support functions of religious institutions, which are more social-psychological in nature. D'Antonio and his colleagues conclude that there is a "substantial need for . . . more social psychological research focusing . . . on the cognitive links between family . . . and religious institutions" (1982:222).

This lack of emphasis on social support functions is ironical because the religious and familial institutions are clearly more intricately involved with mechanisms of emotional love and support than are all other social institutions. The religious functionaries preach a great deal about love in this world as well as other-worldly love; and almost by definition families are based upon marital, parental, and sibling emotional bonds.

D'Antonio's (1980) research on love clearly indicates that, for many, love in the social realm cannot clearly be separated and differentiated from love that contains a vertical or a divine element. From his research findings he concludes that "young people see love as the central aspect of the meaning of life; they believe that love is the most important ingredient in religion; they believe that religion is still important in helping to form judgments and attitudes, and they are dubious about a religion that doesn't help people to love others." (1980:102.)

Increased social/psychological studies add to our understanding of socialization processes and outcomes. Cornwall's chapter (1988) makes it possible for the social scientist to begin to specify how the family, church, and peers influence religious identity. Parents and the church offer to children a meaningful system within which to interpret religious experience, model relevant religious behavior, and channel their children into peer groups which share similar familial and religious values. Stott's chapter (1988) underscores the influence on religious involvement of the group (family, peer) which the respondent currently belongs to. Socialization is thus a lifelong process and not just something that happens during the childhood years. Clayton's chapter (1988) shows that parents' beliefs about the moral dimensions of human nature have to be studied along with parental attitudes about child-rearing to more fully understand socialization processes in the family.

We see the increased concern for social/psychological investigations of religion and family to be very important. We suspect that out of that coming research will flow a greater appreciation of the role of spiritual influences in the lives of people (Thomas and Sommerfeldt, 1984). This increased study of spiritual influences in religion and family studies is the fourth area of potential contribution. Our own judgment is that the human condition is very much concerned about meaning; that meaning is intricately involved with one's perception of emotionally bonding relationships with others in the social world; and that, for a large proportion of the American population, such relationships with others are inextricably connected with their view of the basic relationship with Deity (D'Antonio, 1980). For us, therefore, family and religion will become inextricably involved in these studies of social/psychological processes that attempt to understand better the spiritual element in the human condition.

The final area of payoff addressed here is one identified in McNamara's chapter on presuppositions. Unlike the foregoing concerns, this issue addresses social science research and theory endeavors, rather than family or religious institutions in particular. We agree with McNamara (1985) and Alexander (1982) that the postpositivist era in the social sciences has underscored the necessity of asking questions about the researchers' presuppositions informing their effort to acquire reliable knowledge. Since, for us, any acquisition of knowledge simultaneously involves a reading of meaning *into* the data well as a reading of meaning out of the data, it becomes important for social scientists to look carefully at their presuppositions. McNamara's work (1985), along with Warner's (1979) earlier treatise, clearly shows that the social scientist's presuppositions are related to the conclusions drawn from studies of families and religions. We see this as a healthy occurrence in the social sciences and expect that the concern for presuppositions will help illuminate the social scientists' role in producing the knowledge that is generated in any research endeavor. In this context it becomes important for social scientists to make apparent their own value positions. We see some movement occurring in that direction.

Bergin (1980) argues that therapists are engaged in instituting value systems and, therefore, need to become aware of how their own values interfere with or facilitate their ability to work with particular people having similar or different values. McNamara (1985) asserts that social scientists analyzing conservative Christian families tend to see them from a particular point of view, given their own presuppositions about the nature of the religious institutions. These presuppositions blind some social analysts to alternative sources of data and information about particular families. When this blind spot is illuminated, a very different view of family roles, family functioning, and meaning structures within those families emerges. Questions about a social scientist's presuppositions ought to be asked frequently in our current postpositivist era.

Schroll's chapter (1988) traces the rise of postpositivist views in the physical sciences and argues for their relevance to social science. If modern physics emphasizes an observer-created reality, social scientists ought not to back away from questions about how their own conceptual systems along with measurement devices combine to influence the meaning they see in their data. The chapters by Spickard (1988) and Helle (1988) illustrate the very different typologies of families and religions created by the social scientist, depending upon the particular conceptual system he chooses to use in constructing the typology.

If the central thesis of this treatise has some validity—namely, that the familial and religious institutions need to be studied simultaneously in our efforts to understand the human condition better—we think that the thesis applies equally well in our collective efforts to understand the role of the social scientist in investigating that basic human creation, the family. We will need to study simultaneously the influence of presuppositions coming from either religious or nonreligious worldviews, along with the characteristics of the data and how the two interact as the social scientist reads meaning into and out of the data. Then, perhaps, through these reciprocal acts of knowing, we will better understand the human condition. The prospects are exhilarating.

Bibliography

Abrahamson, M. and W. P. Anderson. 1984. "People's Commitments to Institutions." *Social Psychology Quarterly* 47(4):371-81.

Alexander, J. C. 1982. *Theoretical Logic in Sociology* (Vol. 1). Berkeley, Los Angeles: University of California Press.

Andrews, A. R. 1979. "Religion, Psychology, and Science: Steps Toward a Wider Psychology of Religion." *Journal of Psychology and Theology* 7(1):31-38.

Bahr, H. M. and B. Chadwick. 1985. "Religion and Family in Middletown, USA." *Journal of Marriage and the Family* 47 (May): 407-14.

Beit-Hallahmi, B. 1974. "Psychology of Religion in 1880-1930: The Rise and Fall of a Psychological Movement." *Journal of the History of the Behavioral Sciences* 10:84-94.

Bergin, A. E. 1980. "Psychotherapy and Religious Values." *Journal of Consulting and Clinical Psychology* 48 (1):95-105.

Bergin, A. E. 1983. "Religiosity and Mental Health: A Critical Reevaluation and Meta-analysis." *Professional Psychology: Research and Practice* 14(2):170-84.

Brinkerhoff, M. B. and M. MacKie. 1985. "Religion and Gender: A Comparison of Canadian and American Student Attitudes." *Journal of Marriage and the Family* 47 (May):415-29.

Burr, W. R., R. Hill, F. I. Nye, and I. L. Reiss. (Eds.) 1979. *Contemporary Theories About the Family* (2 vols.). New York: The Free Press.

Caplow, T., H. M. Bahr, B. A. Chadwick, R. Hill, and M. H. Williamson. 1982. *Middletown Families: Fifty Years of Change and Continuity*. Minneapolis: University of Minnesota Press.

Caplow, T., H. M. Bahr, and B. A. Chadwick. 1983. *All Faithful People: Change and Continuity in Middletown's Religions*. Minneapolis: University of Minnesota Press.

Christensen, H. T. 1964. "Development of the Family Field of Study." Pp. 3–32 in H. Christensen (ed.), *Handbook of Marriage and the Family*. Chicago: Rand McNally.

D'Antonio, W. V. 1980. "The Family and Religion: Exploring a Changing Relationship." *Journal for the Scientific Study of Religion* 19(2):89–104.

D'Antonio. W. V. 1985. "The American Catholic Family: Signs of Cohesion and Polarization." *Journal of Marriage and the Family* 47(May): 395–405.

D'Antonio, W. V. and J. Aldous. 1983. *Families and Religions: Conflict and Change in Modern Society*. Beverly Hills, CA: Sage Publications.

D'Antonio, W. V., W. M. Newman, and S. A. Wright. 1982. "Religion and Family Life: How Social Scientists View the Relationship." *Journal for the Scientific Study of Religion* 21(3):218–25.

Demerath, N. J., III and W. C. Roof. 1976. "Religion—Recent Strands in Research." *Annual Review of Sociology* 2:19–33.

Donahue, M. J. 1985. "Intrinsic and Extrinsic Religiousness: A Review and Meta-analysis." *Journal of Personality and Social Psychology* (forthcoming).

Douglas, W. 1963. "Religion." Pp. 80–95 in N. L. Farberow (ed.), *Taboo Topics*. New York: Atherton.

Hinkle, R. C. 1980. *Founding Theory of American Sociology 1881–1915*. Boston: Routledge & Kegan Paul.

Hoge, D. R. and D. A. Roozen (Eds.) 1979. *Understanding Church Growth and Decline: 1950–1978*. New York: The Pilgrim Press.

Judd, D. R. 1985. Religiosity and Mental Health. Unpublished master's thesis, Brigham Young University.

LaRossa, R. 1985. Annual Newsletter of the NCFR Theory Construction and Research Methodology Pre-Conference Workshop (January).

Lea, G. 1982. "Religion, Mental Health, and Clinical issues." *Journal of Religion and Health* 21(4):336–51.

Leslie, G. R. and S. K. Korman. 1985. *The Family in Social Context*. New York: Oxford University Press.

Martindale, D. 1960. *The Nature and Types of Sociological Theory*. Boston: Houghton Mifflin.

Martindale, D. 1962. *Social Life and Culture Change*. Princeton, NJ: D. Van Nostrand Company.

McNamara, P. H. 1985. "The New Christian Right's View of the Family and Its Social Science Critics: A Study in Differing Presuppositions." *Journal of Marriage and the Family* 47 (May): 449–58.

Merton, R. 1957. *Social Theory and Social Structure* (rev. and enl. ed.). Glencoe, IL: Free Press.

Robbins, T. and D. Anthony. 1979. "The Sociology of Contemporary Religious Movements." *Annual Review of Sociology* 5:75–89.

Smith, C. B., A. J. Weigert, and D. L. Thomas. 1979. "Self-esteem and Religiosity: An Analysis of Catholic Adolescents from Five Cultures." *Journal for the Scientific Study of Religion* 18:51–60.

Stack, S. 1985. "The Effect of Domestic Religious Individualism on Suicide, 1954–1978." *Journal of Marriage and the Family* 47 (May): 431–47.

Stark, R. 1971. "Psychopathology and Religious Commitment." *Review of Religious Research* 12(3): 165–76.

Strunk, O. 1975. "The Present Status of the Psychology of Religion." *The Journal of Bible and Religion* 25:287–92.

Thomas D. L. and J. E. Wilcox. 1987. "The Rise of Family Theory: An Historical and Critical Analysis." Pp. 81–102 in M. B. Sussman and S. K. Steinmetz (eds.), *Handbook of Marriage and the Family*. New York: Plenum Press.

Thomas, D. L. and V. Sommerfeldt. 1984. "Religion, Family, and the Social Sciences: A Time for Dialogue." *Family Perspective* 18:117–25.

Thornton, A. 1985. "Reciprocal Influences of Family and Religion in a Changing World." *Journal of Marriage and the Family* 47 (May): 381–94.

Warner, R. S. 1979. "Theoretical Barriers to the Understanding of Evangelical Christianity." *Sociological Analysis* 40(1):1–9.

Wright, S. A. and W. V. D'Antonio. 1980. "The Substructure of Religion: A Further Study." *Journal for the Scientific Study of Religion* 19(3):292–98.

Chapters Cited from This Volume

Brodbar-Nemzer, J. Y. 1988. "The Contemporary American Jewish Family."

Clayton, L. O. 1988. "The Impact of Parental Views of the Nature of Humankind upon Child-Rearing Attitudes."

Cornwall, M. 1988. "The Influence of Three Agents of Religious Socialization: Family, Church, and Peers."

Heaton, T. B. 1988. "Four C's of the Mormon Family: Chastity, Conjugality, Children, and Chauvinism."

Helle, H. J. 1988. "Types of Religious Values and Family Cultures."

Hynes, E. 1988. "Family and Religious Change in a Peripheral Capitalist Society: Mid-Nineteenth-Century Ireland."

Olshan, M.A. 1988. "Family Life: An Old Order Amish Manifesto."

Scanzoni, L. D. 1988. "Contemporary Challenges for Religion and the Family from a Protestant Woman's Point of View."

Schroll, M. A. 1988. "Developments in Modern Physics and Their Implications for the Social and Behavioral Sciences."

Spickard, J. V. 1988. "Families and Religions: An Anthropological Typology."

Stott, G. N. 1988. "Familial Influence on Religious Involvement."

II. Religion and Family in the Changing Social Order

2

Reciprocal Influences of Family and Religion in a Changing World

Arland Thornton

Introduction

During the last two centuries changes in family structure and relationships have been dramatic and pervasive in Western societies, with the trends of the past two decades being particularly significant, well publicized, and controversial. Religious institutions and values have influenced the course of family change and are involved in many of the current controversies. At the same time many family changes have evoked debate and controversy within and between churches and have been the catalyst for changes in the doctrines and programs of religious groups.

This paper considers family change during the last two centuries and examines several interrelationships between family and religion. The paper investigates *both* the influence of religious institutions and values on changing family structure *and* the impact of family trends on religious teachings and

Arland Thornton is Research Scientist, Institute for Social Research, at the University of Michigan, where he is Associate Professor of Sociology, and Faculty Associate at the Population Studies Center. His research interests focus on family and demographic issues, with particular interest in the causes and consequences of marriage, divorce, fertility, gender roles, intergenerational relations, and adolescent sexuality and pregnancy. He has written numerous articles on these topics in the United States and Taiwan and is initiating similar research in Nepal. He received his Ph.D. from the University of Michigan.

programs. The discussion of these issues has been organized around three basic themes:

1. In all Western societies and within virtually every subgroup within these societies, the structure and dynamics of families and households have been modified substantially over the past two centuries. Many of these family trends are intricately interwoven with several fundamental transformations of Western societies, including long-term economic growth, industrialization, urbanization, increased school attendance, lower mortality, and the growth of scientific knowledge and technology.

2. Religious institutions and values had significant effects on family life in societies of the past and are important factors in family structure and relationships today. Religion and its changing role in the lives of individuals also has influenced the course of family change over the last century.

3. Changes in family life have had substantial effects on the religious doctrines, teachings, and programs of religious institutions; and the varying responses of the churches to these family changes have modified the influence of religion in the lives of individuals and their families.

The Changing Western Family

In Western societies before 1800, there were few economic enterprises outside the home; and the family was the basic organizational unit for many important activities, including production and consumption. In this family economy the household organized and managed its resources, including the labor of its members, to produce its means of existence. Individual family roles—such as husband, wife and child—implied and overlapped economic roles, such as master, helper, and servant. (Demos, 1970; Laslett, 1965; Lesthaeghe and Wilson, 1986; Greven, 1970; Shorter, 1975; Tilly and Scott, 1978.)

There was an important division of labor in Western families of the past. The husband generally directed the economic activity of the family which was often, but not always, an agricultural enterprise. While the wife maintained a primary role in caring for the home and children, she often made an important contribution to the family economic enterprise. Children also were involved in the productive activities of the family. (Demos, 1970; Greven, 1970; MacFarlane, 1979; Tilly and Scott, 1978; Gillis, 1974; Kett, 1977; Vanek, 1980.)

Traditionally, the older generations maintained control over the family economy as long as they were able to organize and direct its operation (Berkner, 1972). The younger generations could not become economically independent until the fathers passed the family economic organization on to them or they obtained the financial ability to acquire another economic unit. This type of family structure and a scarcity of economic alternatives outside the family limited the independence of young people. (Katz and Davey, 1978; Kett, 1977; Modell et al., 1976; Tilly and Scott, 1978.)

Educational institutions were not an important part of societies of the past. School attendance was not widespread and was subservient to the needs of the family's economic endeavors. Consequently, the educational attainments of children were limited—certainly by the standards of today (U.S. Bureau of the Census, 1980).

Disease and death were omnipresent in the past and had crucial implications for family life. Many children died in infancy, many mothers died in childbirth, and families were often disrupted by the death of one of the parents. (Uhlenberg, 1980; Sullivan, 1983.) High mortality required high fertility to ensure the replacement of the population. In addition, although relatively effective techniques of contraception have been known for thousands of years (Himes, 1970), there was no extensive practice of family limitation in the past because birth control was not known or not acceptable to the majority of people. Consequently, the number of children born averaged around seven in many European countries and in the United States. (Knodel, 1977; van de Walle and Knodel, 1980; Coale and Zelnik, 1963.)

School enrollment and educational achievement have expanded over the last two centuries with dramatic implications for the lives of individuals and their families (Caldwell, 1982; Schultz, 1973; Thornton, 1980). The amount of time parents and young children spend together is likely to decline when children enter school careers at a young age. The availability of children to work in the family economy decreases, and the direct costs of rearing children increases. School attendance also represents a shift in the locus of control from parents to a public institution, and peer relationships are modified. In those instances in which educational systems are coeducational, the pattern of interactions between the sexes is modified, with implications for mate selection.

When there are rapid increases in educational attainment, an educational generation gap develops. Since educational systems transmit technological and cultural innovations, children often have more access than their parents to the latest ideas and skills (Ogburn and Nimkoff, 1976). The superior levels of education and knowledge provide children with resources for interacting with their parents at home and superior opportunities in the developing labor market. This may allow them more autonomy in relationships with parents, greater independence in living arrangements, and more freedom in mate selection.

Over the last two centuries the household production economy has been slowly replaced by the family wage economy in which people work outside the boundaries of the households where they reside (Tilly and Scott, 1978; Anderson, 1971). Families and individuals responded to the shifting structure of employment in terms of the patterns of behavior and role allocations already familiar to them (Hareven, 1982). Fathers, who had always specialized primarily in economic production, followed the economic opportunities outside the home; and young adult sons and daughters also became active in the new wage economy. The shift of the primary locus of employment from the household to the market place, however, substantially reduced the opportunity for mothers to combine economic production with the care of the home and children. Consequently, as recently as 1940 only 14 percent of married women were in the paid labor force in the United States. (Oppenheimer, 1970; U.S. Bureau of Labor Statistics, 1982.) The result of these differential responses of individual family members to market employment was a separation of the locus of activities of family members—with a large majority of mothers emphasizing their domestic roles in the home and fathers and young adult sons and daughters working outside the household.

In recent years many mothers have entered the labor force and are again combining economic production with the care of the home and children. For example, in the United States between 1948 and 1982 the fraction of married mothers with children under six who were working increased from 1 in 10 to 1 in 2 (U.S. Bureau of Labor Statistics, 1982). This increase in female labor-force participation, however, is not simply a return to earlier patterns, because their economic production now occurs outside the household, with implications for child-care arrangements and decisions about family size (Oppenheimer, 1970; U.S. Bureau of Labor Statistics, 1982; Smith, 1979).

During the early stages of industrialization, both parents and children continued to view the economic activities of family members as contributions to the family economy. Although individual family members increasingly participated in the labor market, it was common for them to pool their money into a family budget. (Early, 1982; Dublin, 1979; Tilly and Scott, 1978; Hareven, 1982.) However, children's control of their earnings has expanded during recent years, and now there is little expectation of children contributing substantially to their parental households even when they are living with their parents (Tilly and Scott, 1978; Bachman, 1983). This gives young people a source of independence and autonomy that was uncommon in the past. Similarly, paid employment of married women provides them with an independent source of income, which can be particularly important when considering alternatives to unsatisfactory marriages.

Since many jobs outside the family involve large-scale activities and the concentration of workers, industrialization often is accompanied by urbanization and rural-to-urban migration. A number of families moved as entire units from agricultural to urban areas; but often it was young people who took jobs outside the family as wage laborers and migrated to urban areas while their parents maintained the existing rural economic unit. (Hareven, 1982; Hareven and Tilly, 1979; Tilly and Scott, 1978; Modell and Hareven, 1973.) In cities these migrant young people often lived with other relatives or with nonrelatives as boarders and lodgers. The importance of this phenomenon for industrializing America is illustrated by the fact that 15 to 20 percent of all urban homes contained lodgers in the nineteenth century. (Modell and Hareven, 1973.) In addition, in the early period of industrialization many companies developed dormitories to house single workers (Dublin, 1979; Hanlan, 1981; Tilly and Scott, 1978; Hareven, 1982). Although extensive efforts were made by the older generation to provide structure and supervision for lodgers and boarders, it was probably impossible to provide supervision and control comparable to that received at home (Dublin, 1979; Hanlan, 1981; Thornton, 1984).

During the twentieth century, as the urbanization process was generally completed and as living standards increased, boarding and lodging in the United States nearly disappeared (Modell and Hareven, 1973). In recent years, however, single persons have used their independence and rising incomes to take an additional step toward residential separation and are increasingly maintaining their own households (Kobrin, 1976; Michael et al., 1980; Thornton and Freedman, 1983). Just between 1950 and 1982 the percentage of never-married men and women age twenty-five to thirty-four maintaining their own households in the United States more than quadrupled (Thornton and Freedman, 1983).

Working and living outside of family households provide young people with opportunities for independence and autonomy, since it is more difficult for parents to observe, supervise, and socialize them. Urban living also brings access to many ideas and opportunities that are unavailable in rural areas.

Improvements in mortality during the last two centuries made it possible for families to replace themselves with a lower birthrate. At the same time contraceptive usage became nearly universal; and during recent decades there have been important advances in the effectiveness of contraception, including sterilization, the oral contraceptive pill, and the intrauterine device (Mosher, 1982; Mosher and Westoff, 1982). Abortion also has become an important form of fertility control in the United States since its nationwide legalization by the Supreme Court in 1973 (Henshaw and O'Reilly, 1983).

Modern birth control not only has helped to reduce the incidence of unplanned fertility but probably has altered orientations toward childbearing. While traditional contraceptive methods were effective in reducing overall fertility, their substantial failure rates made it difficult for couples to plan confidently the timing and number of their children. Motherhood now has become a matter of choice for most women, so that couples can rationally integrate their childbearing decisions with education and career plans. (Bumpass, 1973.)

There was a sustained decline in the fertility rate in the United States from 1800 to 1930, when the average number of children born per woman dropped from about seven to just over two (Heuser, 1976; Coale and Zelnik, 1963). Then came the postwar baby boom, bringing a sharp rise in fertility, followed by an equally sharp drop during the 1960s and 1970s. The birthrates of the early 1980s imply that women will have, on average, fewer than two children each. (Heuser, 1976; U.S. National Center for Health Statistics, 1984.)

Marriage patterns in the United States have gone through a wave of change since World War II. Except for relatively minor fluctuations, first marriage rates were quite steady during the first four decades of this century, but after World War II there was a substantial increase. The rates remained high through the 1950s and 1960s and then fell sharply again during the 1970s and now may be similar to levels of the first few decades of the century. (Rodgers and Thornton, 1985.)

Although marital incompatibility and divorce are old phenomena, the divorce rate increased gradually and steadily in the United States, with some fluctuations, from 1860 to the early 1960s. Then came two decades of sustained and rapid increase, with the rate more than doubling by the end of the

1970s. (U.S. National Center for Health Statistics, 1983.) If the current divorce rates were to continue, approximately one-half of all recent marriages will end in divorce, as compared with about 5 percent of the marriages of the 1860s (Preston and McDonald, 1979; Weed, 1980).

Accompanying the decline in marriage and the increase in divorce during the 1970s was an expansion of the number of unmarried American adults sharing households with unrelated persons of the opposite sex. The number of unmarried people living together more than tripled from 1970 to 1982, and the increase may have been as much as sixfold. By 1983 nearly two million American couples—4 percent of all couples maintaining separate households— were living together without marriage. (Sweet, 1979; U.S. Bureau of the Census, 1983.)

Premarital sexual activity in the United States already was widespread by 1970 and increased steadily during the 1970s. By 1979 just less than half of all never-married women between the ages of fifteen and nineteen living in metropolitan areas reported that they had had sexual intercourse, and the figure for nineteen-year-old single women was just over two-thirds. (Zelnik and Kantner, 1980.)

Although the usage of contraceptives among sexually active young people increased during the 1970s, the premarital pregnancy rate doubled beween 1971 and 1979 (Zelnik and Kantner, 1980). Moreover, even though the abortion rate increased during the 1970s, the birthrate among unmarried teenagers continued its long-term increase (Zelnik and Kantner, 1980; Henshaw and O'Reilly, 1983). In fact, the increased fertility among unmarried women, the decline in the marriage rate, and the decline in childbearing among married couples combined to increase the percentage of all children born out of wedlock from about 5 percent in 1960 to 19 percent in 1982 (U.S. National Center for Health Statistics, 1984).

Families maintained by single mothers also have increased because of increased divorce and out-of-wedlock childbearing, lower marriage rates, and an increased tendency of single mothers to live on their own. In 1982 nearly one-fifth of all households containing minor children were maintained by single mothers (U.S. Bureau of the Census, 1983).

Attitudinal and value shifts have been generally consistent with these behavioral trends. Americans increasingly have accepted the legitimacy of remaining single, the appropriateness of divorce, the expansion of the roles of women, the use of contraception, the legitimacy of childlessness, and premarital sexual relations (Thornton and Freedman, 1983). A general theme in most of these attitudinal trends is a greater willingness among Americans to allow others to choose their own behavior and family relationships without imposing personal standards or preferences. The acceptance of alternative family styles and arrangements is now quite widespread in America.

Although these trends have been interpreted by some as signaling disintegration of the family, predictions about the demise of the family are premature. Having a happy marriage and a good family life are consistently singled out by Americans as the two most important domains of their lives, and most Americans continue to be embedded in a significant network of kin, where they receive substantial physical and emotional support. About four-fifths of all married Americans report their marriages as being very happy or above average, while only about 2 percent say their marriages are not happy. Ninety percent of young people say they plan to marry and have children, and most are optimistic about the success of their marriages. These data suggest that despite, or perhaps because of, changes in family life, families continue to play a vital role in today's world. (Bane, 1976; Cherlin and Furstenberg, 1983; Caplow et al., 1982; Veroff et al., 1981; Thornton and Freedman, 1982, 1983.)

While this discussion of family trends has focused on the American experience, the same basic outline of trends could be repeated in virtually every country of western and central Europe as well as in overseas European populations. When the broad sweep of family trends in European populations is examined, the pervasiveness of the changes and fluctuations in marriage, divorce, childbearing, women's work, premarital sexuality, and household composition are very impressive, although there are important differences both in family structure and behavior and in the timing and tempo of changes. (van de Walle and Knodel, 1980; Roussel and Festy, 1979; Chester, 1977; Hajnal, 1953; Kiernan, 1983; Lesthaeghe, 1983; McDonald, 1981.)[1]

The trends observed for the United States as a whole also generally apply to specific subgroups within the society. Particularly important for the topic of religion and family is that virtually every religious group in the United States has experienced the same basic trends in marriage, divorce, childbearing, and women's employment. Although there have been and continue to be important differences among religious groups, the available evidence suggests that virtually every religious group in the United States today—whether they be Catholic, Jewish, Protestant, or Mormon—has experienced the same general trends in family behavior, structure, and attitudes. (Goldscheider, 1971; Jones and Westoff, 1979; Thornton, 1979, 1985; Thornton et al., 1983; Greeley, 1977; Bahr, 1981.[2] The uniformity of these trends attests to the strength of the factors modifying family life.[3]

The Influence of Religion on Family Change

It is useful to consider the role of religion in family change in the Western world within the context of the teachings and authority of the Christian church. The Roman Catholic church developed the view that, while marriage was inferior to celibacy, it was a sacrament that could be dissolved only by death. Within marriage, procreation was seen as the primary purpose of sexual relations; and intentional interference with this purpose, by either contraception or abortion, was prohibited. The Protestant reformers adopted a somewhat different view of marriage but continued to hold the ideal of a lifetime marriage, although they allowed divorce for a limited set of serious causes. Celibacy was de-emphasized during the Reformation, but the prohibitions against contraception remained strong. In fact, the proscriptions against divorce and birth control remained fairly monolithic in the Christian churches well into the twentieth century. (Noonan, 1966; Fagley, 1960; Chester, 1977; O'Neill, 1967; Kennedy, 1970; Hoyt, 1968; McGregor, 1957; Bush, 1976.)

Of course, the Protestant Reformation only marked the beginning of religious pluralism in the western European world. Over the centuries the number of religious organizations and viewpoints has proliferated, resulting in many different centers of religious authority. Many of these religious groups had different opinions concerning family forms. Consequently, the ability of the churches to speak in a unified voice on family issues diminished, and there was more latitude for diverse opinions and behavior.

Although religion continues to be an important element in the lives of many men and women today, there have been important changes in relationships between the churches and individuals, and the moral authority of the churches has been modified. New institutions exist independently of the churches; science has expanded its domain; the autonomy of the individual has been emphasized; rationalization and abstract thought have expanded; technology has progressed; and human relationships have become more complex. (Greeley, 1972.)

In recent years individuals increasingly have interpreted their religious commitments and beliefs in individualistic terms and less in terms of institutional loyalty and obligation. They are now looking to religion more for its personal meaning and less for its moral rules and are feeling more confidence in their own ability to define standards of conduct independently of the doctrines and teachings of church hierarchies.[4] This trend in the definition of religious commitment and meaning gives individuals more opportunity to choose new family structures. As a result of these many trends in religious beliefs and definitions, the power of the churches over individual thought and behavior probably has declined, giving individuals more opportunity and freedom for making decisions. (Greeley, 1972.) The increased autonomy of individuals in making family decisions has become especially important during the last few decades as diversity of life-style, family structure, and individual behavior has become more accepted. (Thornton and Freedman, 1982, 1983; Veroff et al., 1981; Caplow et al., 1982.)

It is likely that the weakening of church influence was instrumental in permitting individuals to adopt new family strategies, including the use of contraception. The fertility decline in several western European countries—including Belgium, Holland, Switzerland, Germany, Sweden, and Italy—occurred earliest and most rapidly in areas where the influence of the churches was weakest and secularization strongest. (Lockridge, 1983; Lesthaeghe, 1977, 1980; Lesthaeghe and Wilson, 1986.) Multivariate statistical analyses also suggest that these relationships are not merely the result of both secularization and fertility decline being joint products of economic and social change. The weakening of Catholic authority in France also may help to explain why the fertility decline began in France about the time of the Revolution—significantly earlier than in other countries of Europe. (Noonan, 1966; Lesthaeghe, 1980.)

The declining ability of churches to influence public opinion, governmental policy, and the actions of individuals probably has been a factor in other areas of family change as well. Lesthaeghe (1983) has shown that, in the areas of Belgium where there was historically widespread support for secularized political parties, the incidence of divorce was also high. Similarly, in Switzerland both the support for abortion and the incidence of divorce in the 1970s were related to support for secularized parties early in the century. Apparently, political secularization and the weakening of the authority of the churches are related to the adoption of family values and behaviors that have been historically opposed by the churches.

Although the authority of churches over the decisions and behavior of individuals may have declined, religion still influences family behavior, as witnessed by the continuing differentials in family structure and behavior associated with different religious groups. Although a full review of religious differentials in family structure is beyond the scope of this paper, a few examples will illustrate this point. The fertility of Jewish populations is an important example of a long-standing and continuing religious effect. The fertility decline in several European countries occurred earlier among Jews than among Catholics and Protestants. (Knodel, 1974; Livi-Bacci, 1977.) In addition, relatively low fertility for Jewish populations has been documented throughout the twentieth century in several countries (Goldscheider, 1971; DellaPergola, 1980).

Although family behavior among Catholics is hard to characterize simply—as illustrated by the fact that the European fertility decline began earlier in Catholic France than elsewhere in Europe—in many countries, including the United States, Catholic fertility has been substantially higher than average. In addition, Catholics consistently have used more traditional or less modern contraceptives than others in the United States. Comparisons between Catholics and other Americans also have shown behavioral and attitudinal differences in other areas of family life. (Westoff, 1979; Lenski, 1963; McCarthy, 1979; Greeley, 1977.)

Because of the traditional differences between Catholics and Protestants, one of the most interesting developments of the last two decades has been the convergence of Catholic and Protestant attitudes and behavior in a number of important areas. Just a few years ago an article entitled "The End of 'Catholic' Fertility" was published (Jones and Westoff, 1979). While the announcement that the uniqueness of Catholic fertility had disappeared may have been somewhat premature, there is substantial evidence that Catholic fertility is not substantially different from the United States average (Mosher and Hendershot, 1983; Blake, 1984). Catholic couples have also increasingly adopted modern contraceptives in recent years, so that their usage patterns now maintain little uniqueness (Westoff and Jones, 1977; Westoff, 1979). In the early 1960s Catholics, as compared with others, held substantially higher family size preferences, were more insistent that everyone should have children, and were slightly more negative about divorce; but by 1980 the only difference between Catholics and nonfundamentalist Protestants on these dimensions was in the area of fertility, and this difference was much smaller than earlier.[5] The uniqueness of Catholics in other areas of family life, including child rearing values, also has diminished during recent years (Alwin, 1984).

At the same time that Catholics have become less unique, fundamentalist Protestants have become more distinct. During the last two decades—when there were important trends toward more egalitarian sex-role attitudes, more acceptance of divorce, more acceptance of childlessness, and a desire for smaller families—fundamentalist Protestants changed along with the rest of the American population, but the extent of their change was smaller. The result is that they are now generally more traditional than other Americans on many aspects of family life. (Thornton et al., 1983; Thornton and Camburn, 1983; Thornton, 1985.) This group of Protestants also continues to have somewhat higher fertility than others (Marcum, 1981).

Another example of the influence of religion on family structure and behavior is Mormonism. Utah is the home of one of the most significant and well-publicized familial innovations in American history: "plural marriage" or polygyny. For half a century many Mormon women and men accepted the teachings and exhortations of their leaders to form polygynous unions—all the while enduring the moral condemnation of the country and, during the later years, risking the possibility of prison sentences.

Although polygyny was abandoned by the Mormon church nearly a century ago, Utah family patterns continue to depart from national averages in at least two important ways. First, the marriage imperative appears to be somewhat stronger in Utah, with mean age at marriage now being nearly a year younger than in the nation as a whole. (Mason and Brockert, 1981.) Second, although Mormon fertility declined substantially over the last century, it continues to be higher than the national averages in Canada and the United States (Thornton, 1979). In 1981 the Utah birthrate was approximately 70 percent higher than the national rate (Mason et al., 1983).

Although the continuing relevance of religion for family structure and values has been emphasized here, this point should not obscure two equally important considerations. First, although many of the differences in family behavior currently existing among religious groups in the Western world are important, they are generally substantially smaller than the differences existing between behavior today and that observed two centuries ago. That is, time differences in family behavior are larger than religious differences. Second, there are areas of family life where one might expect differences among religious groups but where the data indicate that family structure is fairly unresponsive to religious affiliation. Two examples of important family areas where religious differences are relatively minor today are divorce and the labor-force participation of women. (Bumpass and Sweet, 1972; Bahr and Goodman, 1981; Bahr, 1979.)

The Influence of Family Change on Religion

Given the historically strong interests and doctrines of the Christian churches concerning family matters, it is difficult to imagine how far-reaching family changes of the last two centuries could have occurred without provoking fundamental reexamination of theology, doctrine, and programs. Heated and extensive debates concerning family changes and appropriate responses to them are not new phenomena but have been endemic for a century in the Western world. These debates have occurred both within and between churches and have spilled over into the political arena. Changes in family structure and behavior also have been the source of numerous shifts in the doctrines and policies of the Christian churches, although both the pace and the extent of modifications among the religious groups have varied. It now appears that the responses of the churches to these familial changes have had important ramifications for the ability of those churches to maintain moral authority and credibility among their constituencies.

Given the traditional positions of Western religions concerning family issues, church leaders throughout the Western world responded to the emerging evidence of family change with concern and opposition. From all sides—be it Rome, London, or Salt Lake City—the churches responded to the issue of birth control with opposition. (Noonan, 1966; Fagley, 1960; Bush, 1976.) Although we now think of Catholicism as being rather strict and Protestantism as permissive on the issue of birth control, "in the 19th century, official Protestant opposition was only less severe than that of Roman Catholicism" (Fagley, 1960:193), and the Mormon reaction mirrored that of the larger society (Bush, 1976). Laws were passed prohibiting the advertising and distribution of contraceptives in many countries, including the United States, as well as in several individual American states (Himes, 1970; Kennedy, 1970; Noonan, 1966; Fagley, 1960; Lesthaeghe, 1977). Many of these laws stayed on the books until well past World War II, and although prosecutions were not numerous, there were several important and well-publicized trials in the nineteenth and twentieth centuries that probably served primarily to expand knowledge concerning contraception (Himes, 1970; Kennedy, 1970).

Although there were important declines in fertility, extensive increases in the use of contraception, and the development of organizations devoted to making birth control more widely accessible at the end of the nineteenth century, the overwhelming opposition to birth control among the churches remained very solid until the late 1920s. Finally, however, the changes in family behavior caused all the churches to examine their traditional positions. During the last half century, one by one the churches have reexamined their positions on the birth control issue, and one by one they have modified those positions. The first major modification among the Christian churches occurred in 1930 when a conference of Anglican bishops gave their reluctant approval to birth control. This was followed across the next several decades by the approval of birth control among numerous other Protestant groups. (Noonan, 1966; Fagley, 1960; Kennedy, 1970.) The opposition enunciated most clearly by the Mormon church during World War I was modified in 1968, and Jewish groups also have accepted birth control (Bush, 1976; Fagley, 1960). In most cases the process of change can best be described as evolutionary; the individual changes were generally small, but the cumulation of several small changes produced significant long-term trends (Fagley, 1960; Kennedy, 1970; Bush, 1976). In many cases the justification given for the approval of birth control centered on the protection of the family unit in a changing world (Kennedy, 1970). However, while change has been nearly universal among the Western churches, there have been variations in the timing, tempo, extensiveness, and structure of changes.

Although the Catholic position has been modified toward the acceptance of nonprocreative purposes of sex and the use of the rhythm method to prevent conception, the overall position of the Catholic church has been less flexible than that observed among other churches (Noonan, 1966; Moore, 1973; Hoyt, 1968; D'Antonio and Cavanaugh, 1983). As the Protestant churches began to reevaluate their positions in 1930, the Catholic position was reemphasized by a new papal encyclical, *Casti Connubii*. Nevertheless, by the early 1960s the issue of birth control was being debated vigorously within the church, and a papal commission extensively studied the issue. Although the majority report of the commission recommended modification of the historical position, the papal encyclical *Humanae Vitae* issued in 1968 maintained the earlier position against artificial prevention of conception. (Hoyt, 1968.) This decision was not received well by many Catholics (Hoyt, 1968) and probably has contributed to what one observer has described as a "crisis in the church" (Greeley, 1979).

Divorce and remarriage also have been subjects of serious debates within and between churches for more than a century. Of central concern have been the legitimate grounds for divorce, if any, and the question of remarriage, with the trend being toward the expansion of the accepted reasons for divorce and the recognition of remarriage. Although the opposition of the Catholic church towards divorce and remarriage has been strongest and most persistent, even its overall position has been modified recently by the broadening of the grounds for annulment and the weakening of the sanctions against divorce and remarriage. (O'Neill, 1967; Chester, 1977; Preister, 1982; D'Antonio, 1983, 1984; Ripple, 1978.)

Of course, divorce, remarriage, and contraception are only a few of the family changes to challenge and modify the traditional wisdom and policies of the churches. Changing patterns of women's employment, appropriate roles for women and men, premarital sexuality, teenage childbearing, abortion, and cohabitation also have provoked debates among the churches and initiated the reexamination and modification of traditional positions (D'Antonio and Aldous, 1983).

The process of religious accommodation to significant shifts in family structure and behavior is facilitated by the fact that religious leaders and policymakers experience the forces of change directly in their own personal lives and indirectly through sharing the experiences of their relatives. As clergyman are faced directly with such issues as the appropriate roles for men and women, the resolution of unhappy marriages, and decisions about childbearing, they are better able to understand and empathize with the decisions lay members face. In this process church leaders may come to modify or reinterpret official teachings for their personal lives, and these considerations then can become input to the official decision-making process.

Mormonism provides an example of the reflection of societal trends in the behavior of church leaders. The average family sizes of Mormon leaders has declined substantially; whereas wives of the top hierarchy of Mormon leaders born during the early part of the nineteenth century averaged about nine children, the average for those born early in this century was just over four. (Thornton, 1979.) The personal experiences and adaptations of these church leaders probably made it easier subsequently to modify the official pronouncement of the church on family size and contraception.

Although this discussion has focused primarily on the role of religion as lawgiver, religious organizations also can play an important supportive and helping role for individuals and their families. In recent years there has been a widespread recognition among religious groups of the need for church programs and policies to strengthen family life. There has been a substantial growth in family ministries and programs designed to assist families, and some groups devote considerable effort to ensure maximum congruence between family and religious goals. Although the nature of these programs vary, virtually all recognize the changing structure of families in today's world and attempt to be responsive to the changed patterns of behavior. Of course, as religious groups try both to support traditional values and behavior and to assist individuals who are experiencing nontraditional living arrangements, they are likely to experience continual strain and ambivalence.

Changing family relations also have had direct implications for church organization. One important example of this is the relationship between men and women in the churches. Just as gender has become a suspect basis for making distinctions and discriminations within the larger society, it has become increasingly suspect in the churches. Consequently, the role of women in many churches has expanded, and the issue of women in the clergy and holding the priesthood has risen everywhere. (Hargrove, 1983; D'Antonio and Cavanaugh, 1983; Aldous, 1983.) It is likely that the pressure to treat men and women totally equally within the churches will continue to mount with time, and where this pressure is strongly resisted, significant controversy is likely.

A constant theme of this paper has been the significant number of important linkages among societal, familial, and religious changes. One additional feedback loop merits comment: the responses of the churches to societal and familial change have important ramifications for the role of religion in the lives of individuals and their families. Intimate family and personal relationships are of such significance in the lives of individuals that the programs, guidance, and policies that churches provide on these issues can affect the total relationships between individuals and their churches.

Perhaps the strongest and most relevant evidence for the influence of family doctrine on the religious activity and commitment of individuals can be found in the Catholic experience of the past twenty years. In 1968, when the papal encyclical *Humanae Vitae* was issued, it was justified by its supporters as a reaffirmation of the church's commitment to ethical values. Nevertheless, the encyclical met with immediate, widespread, and public dissent in the United

States; it was criticized as being out of touch with modern circumstances, the authority of the papacy was questioned, and the right of individual dissent was emphasized. The strong traditional reaffirmation of the church's teachings on family issues and the accompanying decline in church authority also may have contributed to rather substantial declines in religious devotion, belief, and activity among Catholics. Thus, the family doctrine and policy of the church may have eroded both the commitment of individual Catholics to the institutional church and the ability of the church to influence the lives of individual Catholics on nonfamily issues. (Greeley et al., 1976.)[6]

If the recent impact of Catholic family policy on the religious commitment and activity of American Catholics is as strong as the evidence suggests, this same kind of influence could have been operating in both Catholic and non-Catholic groups in less dramatic ways throughout the last century. The relatively slow and reluctant adaptations of the doctrines and programs of the churches to the changes in family life may have operated to decrease both the moral authority of the churches and the religious commitment and activity of individuals. That is, the long-term decline in the moral authority of the churches, which is often decried in religious circles, may have been accelerated by the rigidity and slowness of the churches in adapting to the changes occurring in family life. Of course, the churches also have had to be concerned about the reactions of individuals who look to religion as a source of unchanging values and proscriptions. It is possible that some individuals have been alienated from their churches because the adaptations that were made were interpreted as an abandonment of fundamental religious principles. Thus, there are constant pressures for religious groups to adhere to a narrow line between tradition and change.

Summary

This paper has documented an intricate web of interrelationships between religious institutions and values and family structure and behavior. Religious teachings and doctrine influence family structure and relationships, and family trends have an impact on religious programs and doctrine. In addition, the interrelationships between family and religion are not static but dynamic and changing, with the relationship being constantly modified as both institutions are changed by larger societal forces.

Three general themes have permeated this paper. The first has dealt with the substantial changes that have occurred in family structure and relationships in the Western world during the last two centuries. These changes have been observed across virtually every Western society and within virtually every population subgroup within those societies. Many of these family changes are interwoven with changes in the larger society, including increases in school attendance and achievement, declines in mortality, the growth of scientific knowledge, long-term economic growth, industrialization, and urbanization. Because of the central place of the family in historical social structures, these transformations have been instrumental in modifying the organization of the family and household unit, the activities of individual family members, and the nature of interaction within the family and household.

Second, the timing and pace of family change were influenced by religion and the changing place of religion and religious beliefs in the social fabric. Although the precise influence of religion and religious affiliation has been modified over the years, religion continues to influence family structure and behavior. Differences among religious groups today, however, are smaller than the changes that have occurred in family life.

Third, changes in family structure and behavior have led to substantial modifications in the teachings and policies of the Western churches. All religions have had to examine their traditional positions, and all have modified their stances on specific issues, although the extent and timing of religious changes have varied. The ways in which the churches respond to these issues also have ramifications for the moral authority and credibility of the churches themselves.

Although this paper has been able to provide only a brief overview of the interrelationships among the economic, social, religious, and familial dimensions of society, it demonstrates the intricacy and complexity of those relationships. All of these dimensions of society are bound together in an interlocking web of reciprocating causal influences. Changes, especially those of the magnitude experienced during the past two centuries, of necessity have implications throughout the system. The result has been centuries of adapting existing norms and patterns of behavior to new circumstances. Because of the unevenness of change across the institutions of society, there has been a century of dynamic tension among individuals and their institutions. These changes have occurred in central areas of human concern, with the consequence that they have generated great debates, political controversy, and difficult decisions by individuals, families, and institutions. Although a number of issues appear to be resolved, many are not; and it is likely that the next century will also be characterized by important family change, intense debate, political controversy, and religious adjustment.

Notes

1. Although the thrust of this discussion is limited to the Western experience, it is of some interest to note that a number of the same processes and trends also can be observed among non-European populations (Knodel, 1977; van de Walle and Knodel, 1980; Thornton, 1984).

2. An important exception to this conclusion of relatively uniform trends is represented by the fertility of the Hutterites in Canada. As recently as 1971 their fertility levels resembled those existing in the United States during the nineteenth century (Statistics Canada, 1973). Their uniqueness probably can be attributed both to their strong religious beliefs about childbearing and contraception and to their commitment to a rural, agricultural life-style.

3. The above discussion is not meant to be an exhaustive examination of family trends or their causes. Instead, its purpose is to highlight some of the major trends and to suggest some of the ways in which these changes were linked to the transformations of society brought about by increased school attendance, industrialization, urbanization, the decline of mortality, and the increase in scientific knowledge and technology. This discussion also emphasizes the American experience, although fundamental changes in family life also have occurred among the populations of other Western countries.

4. This view is based on longitudinal research being conducted by W. C. McCready of the University of Chicago and summarized in personal communication with the author (see also "Religious Feeling . . . ," 1984).

5. These unpublished data are derived from a panel study of women conducted between 1962 and 1980. Also see Thornton (1985).

6. Of course, the task of linking complex behavioral and value changes to institutional events and decisions is a difficult one, and alternative explanations are possible. Consequently, as Greeley and his colleagues (1976:143) themselves suggest, they "have not made a completely unchallengeable case in favor of the encyclical explanation for the decline in Catholic religiousness." Nevertheless, they present a substantial amount of information that is consistent with this explanation.

Bibliography

Aldous, J. 1983. "Problematic Elements in the Relationship Between Churches and Families." In W. V. D'Antonio and J. Aldous (eds.) *Families and Religions: Conflict and Change in Modern Society*. Beverly Hills, CA: Sage Publications.

Alwin, D. F. 1984. "Trends in Parental Socialization Values: Detroit, 1958 to 1983." *American Journal of Sociology* 90 (September):359–82.

Anderson, M. 1971. *Family Structure in Nineteenth Century Lancashire*. London: Cambridge University Press.

Bachman, J. G. 1983. "Premature Affluence: Do High School Students Earn Too Much?" *Economic Outlook USA* 10(3):64–67.

Bahr, H. M. 1979. "The Declining Distinctiveness of Utah's Working Women." *Brigham Young University Studies* 19(Summer):525–43.

Bahr, H. M. 1981. *Utah in Demographic Perspective: Regional and National Contrasts*. Provo, UT: Brigham Young University, Family and Demographic Research Institute.

Bahr, H. M. and K. Goodman. 1981. "Divorce." In H. M. Bahr (ed.), *Utah in Demographic Perspective: Regional and National Contrasts*. Provo, UT: Brigham Young University, Family and Demographic Research Institute.

Bane, M. J. 1976. *Here to Stay*. New York: Basic Books.

Berkner, L. K. 1972. "The Stem Family and the Developmental Cycle of the Peasant Household: An 18th-century Austrian Example." *American Historical Review* 77:398–418.

Blake, J. 1984. "Catholicism and Fertility: On Attitudes of Young Americans." *Population and Development Review* 10(June):329–40.

Bumpass, L. L. 1973. "Is Low Fertility Here to Stay?" *Family Planning Perspectives* 5 (Spring):67–69.

Bumpass, L. L. and J. A. Sweet. 1972. "Differentials in Marital Instability, 1970." *American Sociological Review* 37:754–66.

Bush, L. E., Jr. 1976. "Birth Control Among the Mormons: Introduction to an Insistent Question." *Dialogue: A Journal of Mormon Thought* 10 (Autumn):12–44.

Caldwell, J. C. 1982. *Theory of Fertility Decline*. New York: Academic Press.

Caplow, T., H. M. Bahr, B. A. Chadwick, R. Hill, and M. H. Williamson. 1982. *Middletown Families: Fifty Years of Change and Continuity*. Minneapolis: University of Minnesota Press.

Cherlin, A. and F. F. Furstenberg, Jr. 1983. "The American Family in the Year 2000." *The Futurist* (June):7–14.

Chester, R. 1977. *Divorce in Europe*. Leiden, The Netherlands: Martinus Nijhoff.

Coale, A. J. and M. Zelnik. 1963. *New Estimates of Fertility and Population in the United States*. Princeton, NJ: Princeton University Press.

D'Antonio, W. V. 1983. "Family Life, Religion, and Societal Values and Structures." In W. V. D'Antonio and J. Aldous (eds.), *Families and Religions: Conflict and Change in Modern Society*. Beverly Hills, CA: Sage Publications.

D'Antonio W. V. 1984. "Religion and the Catholic Family: Trends Toward Cohesion and Disintegration." Paper presented at Conference on Religion and the Family, Brigham Young University, Provo, UT.

D'Antonio, W. F. and J. Aldous. 1983. *Families and Religions: Conflict and Change in Modern Society*. Beverly Hills, CA: Sage Publications.

D'Antonio, W. V. and M. J. Cavanaugh. 1983. "Roman Catholicism and the Family." In W. V. D'Antonio and J. Aldous (eds.), *Families and Religions: Conflict and Change in Modern Society*. Beverly Hills, CA: Sage Publications.

DellaPergola, S. 1980. "Patterns of American Jewish Fertility." *Demography* 17 (August):261–73.

Demos, J. 1970. *A Little Commonwealth: Family Life in Plymouth Colony*. New York: Oxford University Press.

Dublin, T. 1979. *Women at Work*. New York: Columbia University Press.

Early, F. H. 1982. "The French-Canadian Family Economy and Standard-of-living in Lowell, Massachusetts, 1870." *Journal of Family History* 7:180-99.

Fagley, R. M. 1960. *The Population Explosion and Christian Responsibility*. New York: Oxford University Press.

Gillis, J. R. 1974. *Youth and History*. New York: Academic Press.

Goldscheider, C. 1971. *Population, Modernization, and Social Structure*. Boston: Little, Brown.

Greeley, A. M. 1972. *Unsecular Man*. New York: Schocken Books.

Greeley, A. M. 1977. *The American Catholic*. New York: Basic Books.

Greeley, A. M. 1979. *Crisis in the Church*. Chicago: Thomas More.

Greeley, A. M., W. C. McCready, and K. McCourt. 1976. *Catholic Schools in a Declining Church*. Kansas City, MO: Sheed and Ward.

Greven, P., Jr. 1970. *Four Generations*. Ithaca, NY: Cornell University Press.

Hajnal, J. 1953. "The Marriage Boom." *Population Index* 19 (February):80-103.

Hanlan, J. P. 1981. *The Working Population of Manchester, New Hampshire, 1840-1886*. Ann Arbor, MI: University Microfilms.

Hareven, T. K. 1982. *Family Time and Industrial Time*. New York: Cambridge University Press.

Hareven, T. K. and L. Tilly. 1979. "Solitary Women and Family Mediation in Two Textile Cities: Manchester, New Hampshire and Roubaix, France." Unpublished paper of the University of Michigan (December).

Hargrove, B. 1983. "Family in the White American Protestant Experience." In W. V. D'Antonio and J. Aldous (eds.), *Families and Religions: Conflict and Change in Modern Society*. Beverly Hills, CA: Sage Publications.

Henshaw, S. K. and K. O'Reilly. 1983. "Characteristics of Abortion Patients in the United States, 1979 and 1980." *Family Planning Perspectives* 15 (January/February):5-16.

Heuser, R. L. 1976. *Fertility Tables for Birth Cohorts by Color: United States, 1917-73*. Washington, D.C.: U. S. Government Printing Office.

Himes, N. E. 1970. *Medical History of Contraception*. New York: Schocken Books.

Hoyt, R. G. 1968. *The Birth Control Debate*. Kansas City, MO: National Catholic Reporter.

Jones, E. F. and C. F. Westoff. 1979. "The End of 'Catholic' Fertility." *Demography* 16 (May):209-17.

Katz, M. B. and I. E. Davey. 1978. "Youth and Early Industrialization in a Canadian City." In J. Demos and S. S. Boocock (eds.), *Turning Points: Historical and Sociological Essays on the Family*. Chicago: University of Chicago Press.

Kennedy, D. M. 1970. *Birth Control in America*. New Haven, CT: Yale University Press.

Kett. J. F. 1977. *Rites of Passage*. New York: Basic Books.

Kiernan, K. E. 1983. "The Structure of Families Today: Continuity or Change." Paper presented at British Society for Population Studies Conference on the Family (September).

Knodel, J. 1974. *The Decline of Fertility in Germany, 1871-1939*. Princeton, NJ: Princeton University Press.

Knodel, J. 1977. "Family Limitation and the Fertility Transition: Evidence from the Age Patterns of Fertility in Europe and Asia." *Population Studies* 31 (July):219-49.

Kobrin, F. E. 1976. "The Fall of Household Size and the Rise of the Primary Individual in the United States." *Demography* 13 (February):127–38.

Laslett, P. 1965. *The World We Have Lost*. New York: Charles Scribner's Sons.

Lenski, G. 1963. *The Religious Factor*. New York: Anchor Books.

Lesthaeghe, R. J. 1977. *The Decline of Belgian Fertility. 1800–1970*. Princeton, NJ: Princeton University Press.

Lesthaeghe, R. J. 1980. "On the Social Control of Human Reproduction." *Population and Development Review* 6 (December):527–48.

Lesthaeghe, R.J. 1983. "A Century of Demographic and Cultural Change in Western Europe: An Exploration of Underlying Dimensions." *Population and Development Review* 9 (September):411–35.

Lesthaeghe, R. and C. Wilson. 1986. "Modes of Production; Secularization and the Pace of the Fertility Decline in Western Europe, 1870–1930." In A. J. Coale and S. C. Watkins (eds.), *The Decline of Fertility in Europe*, pp. 261–92. Princeton, NJ: Princeton University Press.

Livi-Bacci, M. 1977. *A History of Italian Fertility During the Last Two Centuries*. Princeton, NJ: Princeton University Press.

Lockridge, K. A. 1983. *The Fertility Transition in Sweden: A Preliminary Look at Smaller Geographic Units, 1855–1890*. Umea, Sweden: The Demographic Data Base.

MacFarlane, A. 1979. *The Origins of English Individualism*. New York: Cambridge University Press.

Marcum, J. P. 1981. "Explaining Fertility Differences Among U.S. Protestants." *Social Forces* 60 (December):532–43.

Mason, J. and J. E. Brockert. 1981. *Utah Marriage and Divorce, 1979*. Salt Lake City, UT: Utah Dept. of Health, Bureau of Health Statistics (May).

Mason, J. O., M. J. Stapley, and J. E. Brockert. 1983. *Utah Vital Statistics: Annual Report 1981*. Salt Lake City, UT: Utah Dept. of Health, Bureau of Health Statistics (May).

McCarthy, J. 1979. "Religious Commitment, Affiliation, and Marriage Dissolution." In R. Wuthnow, *The Religious Dimension: New Directions in Quantitative Research*. New York: Academic Press.

McDonald, P. 1981. *Marriage and Divorce in Australia*. Canberra: Australian National University.

McGregor, O. R. 1957. *Divorce in England: A Centenary Study*. London: William Heinemann.

Michael, R. T., V. R. Fuchs, and S. R. Scott. 1980. "Changes in the Propensity to Live Alone: 1950–1976." *Demography* 17 (February):39–56.

Modell, J., F. Furstenberg Jr., and T. Hershberg. 1976. "Social Change and Transitions to Adulthood in Historical Perspective." *Journal of Family History* 1 (Autumn):7–32.

Modell, J. and T. K. Hareven. 1973. "Urbanization and the Malleable Household: An Examination of Boarding and Lodging in American Families." *Journal of Marriage and the Family* 35 (August):467–79.

Moore, J. J. 1973. *Death of a Dogma?* Chicago: Community and Family Studies Center, The University of Chicago.

Mosher, W. D. 1982. "Fertility and Family Planning in the 1970's: The National Survey of Family Growth." *Family Planning Perspectives* 14 (November/December):314–20.

Mosher, W. D. and G. E. Hendershot. 1983. "Religion and Fertility Reexamined." Paper presented at the annual meetings of the Population Associaton of America, Pittsburgh.

Mosher, W. D. and C. F. Westoff. 1982. "Trends in Contraceptive Practice: United States, 1965-1976." *Vital and Health Statistics*, Series 23, No. 10. Washington, D.C.: U.S. Government Printing Office.

Noonan, J. T., Jr. 1966. *Contraception: A History of Its Treatment by the Catholic Theologians and Canonists*. Cambridge, MA: Harvard University Press.

Ogburn, W. F. and M. F. Nimkoff. 1976. *Technology and the Changing Family*. Westport, CT: Greenwood Press.

O'Neill, W. L. 1967. *Divorce in the Progressive Era*. New Haven, CT: Yale University Press.

Oppenheimer, V. 1970. *The Female Labor Force in the United States*. Population Monograph Series, No. 5. Berkeley, CA: Institute of International Studies, University of California.

Preister, S. 1982. "Social Change and the Family: An Historical Perspective with Family Impact Assessment Principles for Catholic Charities." *Social Thought* 8 (Summer):3-21.

Preston, S. H. and J. McDonald. 1979. "The Incidence of Divorce Within Cohorts of American Marriages Contracted Since the Civil War." *Demography* 16 (February):1-26.

"Religious Feeling Seen Strong in U.S." 1984. *The New York Times* 134 (December 9):30.

Ripple, P. 1978. *The Pain and the Possibility: Divorce and Separation Among Catholics*." Notre Dame, IN: Ave Maria Press.

Rodgers, W. and A. Thornton. 1985. "Changing Patterns of First Marriage in the United States." *Demography* 22 (2):265-79.

Roussel, L. and P. Festy. 1979. "Recent Trends in Attitudes and Behavior Affecting the Family in Council of Europe Member States." *Population Studies* No. 4. Strasbourg, France: Council of Europe.

Schultz, T. W. 1973. "The Value of Children: An Economic Perspective." *Journal of Political Economy* 81:502-13.

Shorter, E. 1975. *The Making of the Modern Family*. New York: Basic Books.

Smith, R. E. 1979. *The Subtle Revolution: Women at Work*. Washington, D.C.: The Urban Institute.

Statistics Canada. 1973. *1971 Census of Canada (Vol. 1): Population*. Ottawa: Information Canada.

Sullivan, T. A. 1983. "Family Morality and Family Mortality: Speculations on the Demographic Transition." In W. V. D'Antonio and J. Aldous (eds.), *Families and Religions: Conflict and Change in Modern Society*. Beverly Hills, CA: Sage Publications.

Sweet, J. A. 1979. "Estimates of Levels, Trends, and Characteristics of the 'Living Together' Population from the Current Population Survey." *Center for Demography and Ecology Working Paper 79-49*. Madison, WI: University of Wisconsin (December).

Thornton, A. 1979. "Religion and Fertility: The Case of Mormonism." *Journal of Marriage and the Family* (February):131-42.

Thornton, A. 1980. "The Influence of First Generation Fertility and Economic Status on Second Generation Fertility." *Population and Environment* 3 (Spring):51-72.

Thornton, A. 1984. "Modernization and Family Change." Paper prepared for presentation at the Seminar on Social Change and Family Policies, The Australia Institute of Family Studies, Melbourne, Australia (August).

Thornton, A. 1985. "Changing Attitudes Toward Separation and Divorce: Causes and Consequences." *American Journal of Sociology* 90 (January):856–72.

Thornton, A., D. F. Alwin, and D. Camburn. 1983. "Causes and Consequences of Sex-role Attitudes and Attitude Change." *American Sociological Review* 48 (April):211–27.

Thornton, A. and D. Camburn. 1983. "The Influence of the Family on Premarital Sexual Attitudes and Behavior." Paper presented at annual meeting of the American Sociological Association.

Thornton, A. and D. Freedman. 1982. "Changing Attitudes Toward Marriage and Single Life." *Family Planning Perspectives* 14 (November/December):297–303.

Thornton, A. and D. Freedman. 1983. "The Changing American Family." *Population Bulletin* 38 (October):1–44.

Tilly, L. A. and J. W. Scott. 1978. *Women, Work, and Family*. New York: Holt, Rinehart, and Winston.

Uhlenberg, P. 1980. "Death and the Family." *Journal of Family History* 5 (Fall):313–20.

U.S. Bureau of Labor Statistics. 1982. *Labor Force Statistics Derived from the Current Population Survey: A Databook*. Washington, D.C.: U.S. Government Printing Office.

U.S. Bureau of the Census. 1980. "Educational Attainment in the United States: March 1979 and 1978." *Current Population Reports*, Series P-20, No. 356. Washington, D.C.: U.S. Government Printing Office.

U.S. Bureau of the Census. 1983. "Households, Families, Marital Status and Living Arrangements: March 1983 (advance report)." *Current Population Reports*, Series P-20, No. 382. Washington, D.C.: U.S. Government Printing Office.

U.S. National Center for Health Statistics. 1983. "Annual Summary of Births, Deaths, Marriages, and Divorces: United States, 1982." *Monthly Vital Statistics Report*, Vol. 31, No. 13 (October). Hyattsville, MD: Public Health Service.

U.S. National Center for Health Statistics. 1984. "Advance Report of Final Natality Statistics." *Monthly Vital Statistics Report*, Vol. 33, No. 6 Suppl. (September). Hyattsville, MD: Public Health Service.

van de Walle, E. and J. Knodel. 1980. "Europe's Fertility Transition: New Evidence and Lessons for Today's Developing World." *Population Bulletin* 34 (February):1–44.

Vanek, J. 1980. "Work, Leisure, and Family Roles on U.S. Farms," *Journal of Family History* 5 (Winter):422–31.

Veroff, J., E. Douvan, and R. A. Kulka. 1981. *The Inner American: A Self-Portrait from 1957 to 1976*. New York: Basic Books.

Weed, J. A. 1980. "National Estimates of Marital Dissolution and Survivorship: United States." *Vital and Health Statistics*, Series 3, No. 19. Washington, D.C. U.S. Government Printing Office.

Westoff, C. F. 1979. "The Blending of Catholic Reproductive Behavior." In R. Wuthnow, *The Religious Dimension: New Directions in Quantitative Research*. New York: Academic Press.

Westoff, C. F. and E. F. Jones. 1977. "The Secularization of U.S. Catholic Birth Control Practices." *Family Planning Perspectives* 9:203–7.

Zelnik, M. and J. F. Kantner. 1980. "Sexual Activity, Contraceptive Use and Pregnancy Among Metropolitan Area Teenagers: 1971-1979." *Family Planning Perspectives* 12 (September/October):230–37.

3

Religion and Family in Middletown, USA

Howard M. Bahr, Bruce A. Chadwick

Introduction

This paper considers the relationship between religion and family life in Middletown (Muncie, Indiana). Specifically, we discuss the association between religiosity and several types of family behavior. The analysis is grounded in a comparison of indicators of family life and religious practices in Middletown in 1925 and 1977–1978.

Since 1976 we have participated in the Middletown III Project, an interdisciplinary research program whose primary objective has been to compare Middletown in the late 1970s with the Middletown of the 1920s. This research

Howard M. Bahr is Professor of Sociology, Brigham Young University. His research interest in a distinguished social science career has centered on the Middletown Studies. The analysis of data from the Middletown Studies continues with two recent publications, *Middletown Families* and *All Faithful People,* highlighting his interest in both religion and family. His numerous books and articles have made significant contributions toward understanding the contemporary social order. He received his Ph.D. from the University of Texas.

Bruce A. Chadwick is Professor of Sociology at Brigham Young University. He is the author or coauthor of ten books and of numerous articles in professional journals. His books include *All Faithful People,* a report of religious change and the lack thereof in Middletown U.S.A. He is studying the dynamics of marital satisfaction in American and German families. He served as chairman of the Department of Sociology at Brigham Young University for six years and is Director of the Family Studies Doctoral Program. He received his Ph.D. from Washington University, St. Louis.

has produced some notable, though not astounding, findings about the importance of families and religious life. For one thing it appears that, although Middletown families have changed in some ways, they remain central to the life of Middletown people and are perhaps more remarkable in their similarities to families of fifty years ago than in their differences. (Caplow et al., 1982.)

Another major conclusion is that religion in Middletown is at least as strong as it ever was, and local observers affirm its promise and positive future rather than lament its decline, as did Middletown ministers in the 1920s and 1930s. Middletown people—judging from their statements about what they believe, how much money they donate to churches, and how often they attend church meetings—take their religion at least as seriously as did their grandfathers. In terms of the percentage of income they contribute to churches, they are more religious than their forebearers of the 1920s. (Caplow et al., 1983.)

Religiosity, Family Solidarity, and the Myths of Decline

These generalizations about the stability, continuity, and vitality of family and religious life in Middletown have not been greeted with wild enthusiasm by many students of family and religious behavior. For example, one critic suggests that we have accentuated the positive and neglected the negative:

> But has the challenge to one myth created another, such as the generalized image of an "ever harmonious, successful family life?" The authors pronounce the Middletown family to be in "exceptionally good condition" and note along the way that even the "demanding role of working mother is performed with every appearance of ease and comfort by the majority of Middletown's married women." One wonders where all the stress has gone. (Elder, 1982:856.)

As in any study there were things in Middletown that we might have studied but did not, and there are data in hand that remain to be fully analyzed. Nevertheless, the sheer bulk and consistency of the evidence—different kinds of data from different samples of Middletown, combined with data from elsewhere revealing similar patterns—is compelling. Middletown is not America, and we may quibble about what is meant by family strength or religiosity; however, the myths that American families are mere shadows of their former selves, and that organized religion in America is an anachronistic hulk shambling into oblivion, are demonstrably false.

Howard M. Bahr, Bruce A. Chadwick

The Myth of the Declining Family

To affirm that American families are at least as strong as they were sixty years ago flies in the face of a conventional wisdom supported by evidence of high—and apparently rising—rates of divorce, family violence, single parenthood, and voluntary childlessness. In the 1980s American families clearly are not what they might be. Even so, they are better than they used to be.

To appreciate the comparison of a miserable past with a flawed, but fairly comfortable present, one needs a long-range perspective, including a firm hold on the realities of the past. John Mack Faragher's (1979) *Women and Men on the Overland Trail* and Otto Bettmann's (1974) *The Good Old Days: They Were Terrible* are among the works by other researchers that corroborate the findings of the Middletown III Project. Bettmann, who has created the most widely known photograph archive in the nation, writes in his introduction (1974:xii) to *The Good Old Days*:

> My post at "the picture window of history" has given me a more optimistic if less fashionable vista. I have concluded that we have to revise the idealized picture of the past and turn the spotlight on its grimmer aspects. This more realistic approach will show us Gay Nineties man (man in the street, not in the boardroom), as one to be pitied rather than envied.... Compared with him we are lucky—even if dire premonitions darken our days and we find much to bemoan in our society.... Even if we cast but a cursory glance at the not so good old days and bring them into alignment with our own, we will find much to be grateful for. We are going forward, if but slowly.

Surely there is no more depressing portrait of normal, everyday family life in twentieth-century America than Robert and Helen Lynd's description of blue-collar families in *Middletown* (1929) and *Middletown in Transition* (1937). In these accounts most of Middletown's citizens are pictured in stark poverty, trapped in perpetual insecurity and hopelessness. The Lynds show the families of the 1920s practicing a strict separation of the sexes even in social activities, affirming the subordination of women, and committed to an economic system that allowed—even encouraged—ten-year-old children to work full-time in the factories. The Middletown of the 1920s, by contrast with the Middletown we came to know both statistically and personally in the late 1970s, was a bleak and brutish place. Concern for the maladies of the modern family need not blind us to the less visible—but no less pernicious—liabilities, limitations and aberrations of the American family in the first decades of this century.

Contemporary families have their strains and their tragedies, but that does not mean that the families of the 1920s were any less likely to stifle, thwart, or maim their members. Nor should concern over the faults and failures of modern families blind us to their strengths and successes.

The Secularization Myth

A major finding of the Middletown III Project is that the city has not experienced a decline in religiosity over the past fifty years. To some, that finding is a surprise that flies in the face of what almost everyone "knows" about secularization in Western society. Secularization is supposed to be an irreversible process accompanying modernization. It is generally treated as continuous, starting from an unspecified point in the past—somewhere between the Renaissance and 1900—and proceeding inexorably into the future, affecting Middletown no less predictably than Manchester or Moscow.

According to Peter Berger, secularization is a fact of life in Western societies:

> By secularization we mean the process by which sectors of society and culture are removed from the domination of religious institutions and symbols. . . . As there is a secularization of society and culture, so is there a secularization of consciousness. Put simply, this means that the modern West has produced an increasing number of individuals who look upon the world and their own lives without the benefit of religious interpretations. (Berger, 1967:107-8.)

Berger said that the impact of secularization varies from group to group— having more effect on men than on women, on the middle-aged than on the young or the old, in the city than in the country, on industrial workers than on shopkeepers, and on Protestants than on Catholics. In Europe, according to Berger, only marginal individuals and populations have resisted secularization, while in America the churches have survived "only by becoming highly secularized themselves."

In another work Berger told of the "demise of the supernatural," as reflected in the "available evidence":

> Whatever the situation may have been in the past, *today* the supernatural as a meaningful reality is absent or remote from the horizons of everyday life of large numbers, very probably of the majority, of people in modern societies, who seem to manage to get along without it quite well. This means that those to

whom the supernatural is still, or again, a meaningful reality find themselves in the status of a minority. (Berger, 1969:6, 7.)

Bryan Wilson (1982:53–54) also has concluded that secularization is an accomplished fact:

> In western countries, the process of secularization is well documented. Men's diminished concern with the supernatural, and its reduced significance for the organization of contemporary society, illustrates the growing irrelevance to modern life both of conceptions of a transcendent order and concern with ultimate values.

It was this kind of overgeneralization from "available evidence" that first sensitized us to the possibility that secularization might be as much myth as march of historical process. There is abundant evidence, from surveys and secondary analysis of records, that the supernatural is present as a meaningful reality to most of the residents of Middletown and to most people in the United States (for example, see Greeley, 1972).

Church attendance in Middletown increased dramatically between 1924 and 1978. In 1924 slightly over 20 percent of Middletown's citizens attended church regularly, at least once a week. By 1978 the number of regular attenders had increased to over 50 percent. The number of church buildings increased correspondingly: in 1924 there were twelve churches for every 10,000 residents; in 1978 there were nineteen. Tithing, giving one-tenth of the family income to the church, was virtually unknown in the 1920s. The Lynds discovered only one full tithepayer among the 100 families whose budgets they recorded. In 1978 nearly one-third of the church members in our samples said that they tithed.

Church weddings (that is, weddings at which a minister or priest officiates) are more frequent today, having increased from 63 percent of all weddings in 1924 to 79 percent in 1978. Finally, the religious beliefs that prevail in Middletown today have not changed appreciably in the past two generations. The terms and phrases that people used to describe their inner religious experiences in 1978 were so similar to the language of their grandparents that we cannot tell them apart. (Caplow et al., 1981, 1983.)

We do not say there have been no changes in organized religion during the past half century. Much of *All Faithful People* (Caplow et al., 1983), the second book-length report of the Middletown III Project, tells of changes in religious beliefs, churchgoing, and piety in Middletown and in the United States.

Liturgies, attitudes, and doctrines *have* changed. There are some new things in Middletown's religion; however, we did not find much trace of the massive modernizing trend supposedly moving us all irresistibly from an age of mysticism and faith into a millennium of pragmatism and technological rationality. What has happened instead is a persistence and renewal of religion in a changing society.

We are not the first students of religion to label secularization a myth. Andrew Greeley did so more than a decade ago. His *Unsecular Man* (1972) showed that the available statistical data did not reveal a decline of religion in the United States and that, considered in absolute terms, the levels of religious belief and participation in the country were extraordinarily high.

Other contemporary observers have pointed to signs of renewed religious vigor (Riche, 1982; Gallup, 1981). The 1981 annual report in America by the Gallup organization identified seven "key dimensions in people's religious lives" and concluded with a strong statement on "the remarkable stability of religion in America." Also, figures on book sales compiled in the U.S. Census of Manufacturers show that Americans buy more Bibles and testaments than they did in the past. In 1939, 7.2 million Bibles and testaments (.06 per capita) were purchased in the United States, the corresponding figure for 1977 was 19.4 million volumes (.09 books per capita). (Bahr, 1982:63.)

It has been suggested to us that much of the organized religion of the 1970s and 1980s is a "secularized" Christianity, a weak shadow of the "old-time religion" of previous generations. The ministers are able to fill their churches, the argument goes, because they demand little of their people. There *are* indications that much current religious activity is superficial, but so was much religious activity in former times. To their main conclusion that religion is on the upswing, Gallup and his associates added some "worrisome findings" about the depth or salience of American religiosity:

> The more one probes into the religious and spiritual lives of Americans, through surveys, the more concerned one becomes about what may lie beneath the often impressive outward signs of religion in America today. . . . Many Americans believe but apparently without strong convictions. They want the fruits of faith, but seem to dodge the responsibilities and obligations. Most Americans say they are Christians, but often without visible connection to a congregation of religious fellowship. (Gallup, 1981:4.)

We lack the empirical data to show conclusively how the religiosity of today's churchgoers compares with that of their parents and grandparents, or whether today's church members are more hypocritical than their predecessors. However, a review of the available indicators suggests that religion is at least as demanding today as it was in the 1920s.

Perhaps there *have* been changes in the definitions of piety, in the range of behavior deemed "religious" or "moral," and in the demands religious organizations make on their members. More important, however, we believe that it misses the point to argue that modern religion is a watered-down version of an earlier, perhaps more fervent religion. Whatever is going on now in the churches of Middletown and the United States, what the clergy teach and the people do constitute the organized religion of today. To paraphrase W. I. Thomas, that which is perceived as religion is religious in its consequences. Judging from many indicators—from attendance at religious services to percentage of income contributed, from frequency of prayers to self-monitored religious fervor, from hours of Bible reading to hours of exposure to religious television programming—contemporary religion involves in active participation a wider segment of the population, in Middletown and America generally, than did the organized religion of the 1920s and 1930s. By such indicators, the religions of the 1970s and 1980s "work" for more of the people than did the organized religions of yesteryear.

The findings that Americans remain religious and that their family ties are surprisingly strong may be related. The clergy continue to emphasize that religion is essential to the maintenance of strong families. In Middletown, one of the few communities where systematic data are available for half a century or more, it appears that today's people are as religious and as firmly integrated in families as their grandfathers and grandmothers. Might the apparent vitality of religion in Middletown be related to the continuity of family ties there, and perhaps in American society generally? We cannot infer a causal relationship from our cross-sectional survey data, but some correlational evidence may be informative. First, we examine some work of other researchers on the religious faith/family connection.

Research on Religion and Family

The doctrines of Christianity and Judaism explicitly link marriage, family life, and religiosity. Among Christian denominations the Catholic church anchors one extreme with its insistence on indissoluble marriage and anti-birth-control teachings. At the other extreme are "liberal" Protestant denominations that do not prohibit premarital sex, encourage contraception, and support abortion and no-fault divorce. Despite the diversity in the extent to which churches attempt to control (or interfere in) sexual intimacy and reproductive behavior, even the most permissive denominations foster marital stability and family harmony.

That religiosity and a healthy family life go hand in hand is an article of faith among religious conservatives. Hadden and Swann's (1981) warning about the growing power of "prime time preachers" shows how people in the "moral majority" link religion and family as cause and consequence:

> TV religion . . . has developed and refined a set of battle cries, an agenda for the 1980s to conquer the sins of society and restore to America the strength it needs to fight the Anti-Christ. . . .
>
> The first of these battle cries is against the threatened destruction of the family by the forces of ungodliness. TV preachers seem to have a heightened sense of the utility of "glad words" and "bad words." *Family* is a glad word, and to be pro-family is to be in favor of everything that is good and decent and commendable. According to the more political stream of TV religion, the family is under attack by the forces of secular humanism, ungodliness, homosexuality, and the Equal Rights Amendment.
>
> To most fundamentalists, the traditional concept of the male-dominated nuclear family is sacrosanct. The family is, of course, the basic unit of society. . . . An equal rights amendment for women is anathema to the fundamentalists. (Hadden and Swann, 1981:97–98.)

There is evidence that religious affiliation and activity have a modest positive impact on marriage and family life (Burgess and Cottrell, 1939; Burchinal, 1957; Gurin et al., 1960; Carey, 1967; Kunz and Albrecht, 1977; Hunt and King, 1978; Glenn and Weaver, 1978; Albrecht, 1979; and Shrum, 1980). Williams (1983:3–14) concluded that the relatively small body of empirical research linking religiosity and marital satisfaction pointed to a positive linear relationship between them. To be precise, of seventeen studies published between 1938 and 1980, thirteen reported a direct, positive relationship between religiosity and marital satisfaction. Williams's (1983:40–53) contribution to this literature was a comparison of the explanatory power of several antecedents of marital satisfaction including current religiosity, socioeconomic status, and certain attributes of the marriage. She found that for both men and women a composite measure of religiosity proved to be a stronger predictor of marital

satisfaction than any of the other independent variables. Accordingly, we anticipated that the religious people in Middletown would be more likely than the
nonreligious to manifest profamily patterns and to report happy marriages.
Specifically, we compared the marital status, stability, happiness, and fertility
of Catholics, Protestants, and the unchurched.

Research Methods

The data derive from several surveys, both mail questionnaire and interview, of residents of Middletown in 1977 and 1980. Data collection procedures
are described in detail elsewhere (Caplow et al., 1982). The analysis reported
here involved combining respondents from several surveys in order to obtain a
sizable sample of married respondents with no religious preference.

Findings

Religiosity and Marital Status

Perhaps the most basic question about religiosity and family is whether
there are denominational differences in marital status. The relevant results are
presented in Table 1. The modest differences between Catholics and Protestants are not significant. The major association between religion and marital
status appears in the differences between persons who report a church preference and those with no preference. The latter are overrepresented among the
single/never married, the remarried, and the divorced/separated, and are correspondingly underrepresented in the married (first marriage) category.

There are many ways to define and measure religiosity. Here we have
opted for the simplest measure of participation, namely, church attendance.
The relationship between church attendance and marital stability among Catholics and Protestants is shown in Table 1. Seventy percent of persons attending
church services at least monthly were still in their first marriages, compared
with 60 percent of those attending less often. In Middletown at least, having a
religious preference and attending church are related to the disposition to marry
and to stay married; or perhaps being divorced and/or separated is associated
with low church attendance. The cross-sectional data do not allow us to clearly
identify cause and effect. Justifiable rationales can be given for both interpretations. Religiosity does give greater value to marriage and family values, thereby

reducing divorce. Likewise, those who divorce may find it less rewarding to attend church, thereby scoring lower on this measure of religiosity.

Religiosity and Marital Satisfaction

Do denominational identification and church attendance make a difference in reported marital happiness? We measured marital satisfaction with the item, "How do you feel about your relationship with your wife/husband?" (Response options were "very satisfied," "satisfied," "neutral," "dissatisfied," and "very dissatisfied.") Previous use of this and similar items on perceived happiness of one's marriage had revealed a consistent response bias: usually between two-thirds and three-fourths of married people say they are "satisfied" or "very satisfied" with their marriages. Even taking this bias into account, we expected to find that people who belonged to and attended church would be more likely than others to say that their marriages were happy.

Judging from the results (Table 2) in Middletown, religious affiliation is positively associated with marital satisfaction. The differences between respondents with a church identification and those with no preference are statistically significant but not large; the nonreligious are more apt to say that they are "dissatisfied" or "very dissatisfied." Apparently religious affiliation per se, and not type of religion, is the characterisitc related to marital satisfaction. The minor differences between Catholics and Protestants are insignificant.

Church attendance also is positively associated with reported marital satisfaction. Attendance is significantly correlated to marital happiness, especially at the upper extreme of "very satisfied." As can be seen in the last two columns of Table 2, 60 percent of the more frequent attenders perceive their marriages as "very satisfactory," compared with 43 percent of the others. This finding is not limited to the item reported in Table 2. On other indicators of marital happiness and willingness to marry the same person again, the distribution of responses is comparable to those shown in Table 2. In Middletown at least, churchgoing and marital satisfaction seem to go together.

Religiosity and Fertility

Do the profamily values of Middletown's churches carry over into fertility? Catholic teachings on birth control and abortion have been seen as leading to higher fertility rates. However, considerable research of the past few decades

TABLE 1. RELIGIOSITY AND MARITAL STATUS: MIDDLETOWN, 1977–1978

| | Indicators of Religiosity | | | | |
| | Religious Preference | | | Church Attendance[a] | |
Marital Status	Catholics (n = 130)	Protestants (n = 760)	None (n = 154)	At Least Monthly (n = 398)	Less Often (n = 473)
Single/never married	16%	10%	18%	10%	14%
First marriage	68	68	59	77	60
Remarried	2	6	8	3	8
Divorced or separated	6	9	12	4	12
Widowed	7	6	2	7	6
Total	99%	99%	99%	101%	100%

Sources: Middletown III men's and women's occupational surveys, religion survey, community survey, and government services survey, 1978.

Note: Differences between Catholics and Protestants are not statistically significant; differences between the affiliated (Catholics and Protestants) and no-preference respondents and between high and low attenders are significant at the .01 level.

[a]Figures on attendance do not include no-preference respondents.

TABLE 2. RELIGIOSITY AND MARITAL SATISFACTION AMONG THE CURRENTLY MARRIED: MIDDLETOWN, 1977–1978

| | Indicators of Religiosity | | | | |
| | Religious Preference | | | Church Attendance | |
Marital Satisfaction	Catholics (n = 88)	Protestants (n = 540)	None (n = 70)	At Least Monthly (n = 319)	Less Often (n = 320)
Very satisfied	56%	60%	50%	60%	43%
Satisfied	34	36	34	31	44
Neutral	6	3	9	8	11
Dissatisfied or very dissatisfied	3	2	7	2	3
Total	99%	101%	100%	101%	101%

Sources: Middletown III men's and women's occupational surveys, religion survey, community survey, and government services survey, 1978.

Note: Differences between Catholics and Protestants are not statistically significant; differences between the affiliated (Catholics and Protestants) and no-preference respondents are significant at the .05 level, and those between high and low attenders are significant at the .01 level.

has shown Catholic and Protestant differences to be steadily decreasing. D'Antonio and Cavanaugh (1983:153) conclude that, with respect to birth control and family size in the United States, "differences between Protestants and Catholics have all but disappeared."

TABLE 3. RELIGIOSITY AND FERTILITY AMONG MARRIED ADULTS: MIDDLETOWN, 1977–1978

| | Indicators of Religiosity | | | | |
| | Religious Preference | | | Church Attendance | |
Number of Children	Catholics (n = 107)	Protestants (n = 621)	None (n = 117)	At Least Monthly (n = 397)	Less Often (n = 472)
0	41%	31%	43%	27%	38%
1	4	15	15	10	16
2	19	21	23	22	19
3	14	17	10	18	14
4 or more	22	17	9	22	13
Total	100%	101%	100%	99%	100%

Sources: Middletown III men's and women's occupational surveys, religion survey, community survey, and government services survey, 1978.

Note: Differences between Catholics and Protestants are significant at .01 level; differences between the affiliated (Catholics and Protestants) and no-preference respondents are significant at the .05 level, and those between high and low attenders are significant at the .01 level.

Our respondents are classified by religiosity and number of children in Table 3. Catholics and Protestants do not differ much in family size, but parents of either persuasion have more children than people who claim no religious preference. The mean number of children for Catholics is 2.0, compared with 1.9 for Protestants and 1.4 for no-preference respondents. Thirty-six percent of the married Catholics have 3 or more children, but so do 34 percent of the Protestants. The sharp differences are between the Catholics or Protestants and the no-preference respondents. Fewer than one-fifth of the latter have three or more children, and they are only half as likely as the religiously affiliated to have four or more children.

The relationship between church attendance and family size also is shown in Table 3. As anticipated, regular churchgoers have larger families than those who attend infrequently or never. Married respondents who say they attend church at least once a month have an average of 2.2 children, compared with 1.6 children among those who attend less often. The finding applies to Catholics and Protestants alike: in both populations the regular churchgoers have more children. There is a slight association between age and church attendance, with religious attenders being slightly older; but this modest age difference is not sufficient to account for the fertility differentials.

The Lynds said that in 1935, Middletown's churches were only partially filled and that most regular attenders were women and old people. Our survey data and our personal observations during two years of residence in Middletown indicated that, if that were ever so, it is so no longer. In the late 1970s

Middletown's churches—Catholic and Protestant—catered to youth and young families, as well as to the middle-aged and older citizens. Programs for children, for teenagers, and for young adults were prominent in most of the churches, and young children were much in evidence in most worship services. From our perspective the profamily values of Middletown churches include the having and rearing of children; and the rearing of children includes a variety of church-related activities.

Summary

The research literature suggests a positive relationship between religiosity and familism. Previous reports of the Middletown III Project noted the surprising vitality of Middletown's churches and the continued strength of Middletown's families. In this paper we have argued that there is a relationship between family solidarity—family "health" if you will—and church affiliation and activity. We have shown that the more religious residents of Middletown were more likely to be married, to remain married, to be highly satisfied with their marriages, and to have more children.

A comparison of the Middletown data with the NORC public use surveys for 1977–1978 suggests that the relationship between religion and family life in Middletown also applies to the rest of the country. In the United States as a whole, churchgoers are more likely to be married, less likely to be divorced or single, more likely to manifest high levels of marital satisfaction, and less likely to have very small families.

The small differences between Middletown Catholics and Protestants are noteworthy. Traditionally there have been sizable differentials between American Catholics and Protestants in educational attainment, occupational status, and income, all favoring Protestants. Catholics usually have been found to divorce less frequently and to have higher fertility. In Middletown, as we have seen, the differences between Catholics and Protestants in marital status, perceived marital satisfaction, and family size are insignificant. Andrew Greeley (1977:212) wrote that "Catholic ethnics are still different in the fundamental matter of family structure and they are likely to continue to be different." There may be some Catholic ethnic groups in America that reflect traditional Catholic-Protestant differences, but such is not the case with Middletown Catholics. For the few indicators of family life considered above, the Catholic-Protestant differences are minuscule or nonexistent. Thus, our Middletown research agrees with other recent research which underscores Catholic-Protestant similarity. The great divide in marital status, marital satisfaction, and family size is not between Catholics and Protestants but between those who identify with a church or denomination and those who do not.

Not only do religion and family life in Middletown seem as vigorous as they were fifty years ago, but it appears that the vitality of these two institutions is related. The limited statistical data we have presented are congruent with qualitative material from in-depth interviews and participant observation in Middletown. People often reaffirmed their religious faith and devotion to their families in the same conversation, many times explicitly linking the two. Although the relationship between family life and religiosity remains a relatively unstudied topic in the social sciences in general and in the more specific areas of family and religion (D'Antonio et al., 1982), the message from Middletown is clear. There is more than pious platitude in the cliche, "the family that prays together, stays together"; and for many, the relationship may run the other way, with the staying preceding the praying. There is little doubt, however, that the institutions are intertwined. The nature and intensity of the connections between these two basic institutions remain to be charted by social scientists.

Bibliography

Albrecht, S. L. 1979. "Correlates of Marital Happiness Among the Remarrieds." *Journal of Marriage and the Family* 41 (November): 857–67.

Bahr, H. M. 1982. "Youth and the Church in Middletown." *Tocqueville Review* 4 (Spring-Summer):31–63.

Berger, P. L. 1967. *The Sacred Canopy: Elements of a Sociological Theory of Religion.* Garden City, NY: Doubleday, Anchor Books.

Berger, P. L. 1969. *A Rumor of Angels: Modern Society and the Rediscovery of the Supernatural.* Garden City, NY: Doubleday.

Bettmann, O. L. 1974. *The Good Old Days: They Were Terrible!* New York: Random House.

Burchinal, L. G. 1957. "Marital Satisfaction and Religious Behavior." *American Sociological Review* 22 (June):307–10.

Burgess, E. W. and L. S. Cottrell, Jr. 1939. *Predicting Success or Failure in Marriage.* Englewood Cliffs, NJ: Prentice-Hall.

Caplow, T., H. M. Bahr, and B. A. Chadwick. 1981. "Piety in Middletown." *Society* 18 (January/February):34–37.

Caplow, T., H. M. Bahr, and B. A. Chadwick. 1982. *Middletown Families: Fifty Years of Change and Continuity.* Minneapolis: University of Minnesota Press.

Caplow, T., H. M. Bahr, and B. A. Chadwick. 1983. *All Faithful People: Change and Continuity in Middletown's Religion*. Minneapolis: University of Minnesota Press.

Carey, R. G. 1967. "Religion and Happiness in Marriage." *Review of Religious Research* 8 (Winter):104-12.

D'Antonio, W. V. and M. J. Cavanaugh. 1983. "Roman Catholicism and the Family." In W. V. D'Antonio and J. Aldous (eds.), *Families and Religions: Conflict and Change in Modern Society*. Beverly Hills, CA: Sage Publishing.

D'Antonio, W. V., W. Newman, and S. Wright. 1982. "Religion and Family Life: How Social Scientists View the Relationship." *Journal for the Scientific Study of Religion* 21 (September):218-25.

Elder G. H., Jr. 1982. "A Third Look at Middletown." *Science* 216 (May 21):854-57.

Faragher, J. M. 1979. *Women and Men on the Overland Trail*. New Haven, CT: Yale University Press.

Gallup Organization, Inc. 1981. *Religion in America: 1981*. The Gallup Opinion Index, Report No. 184. Princeton, NJ: The Gallup Organization and the Princeton Religion Research Center (January).

Glenn, N. D. and C. N. Weaver. 1978. "A Multivariate, Multisurvey Study of Marital Happiness." *Journal of Marriage and the Family* 40 (May:269-80.

Greeley, A. M. 1972. *Unsecular Man: The Persistence of Religion*. New York: Schocken Books.

Greeley, A. M. 1977. *The American Catholic*. New York: Basic Books.

Gurin, G., J. Veroff, and S. Feld. 1960. *Americans View Their Mental Health*. New York: Basic Books.

Hadden, J. K. and C. E. Swann. 1981. *Prime Time Preachers: The Rising Power of Televangelism*. Reading, MA: Addison-Wesley.

Hunt, R. A. and M. B. King. 1978. "Religiosity and Marriage." *Journal for the Scientific Study of Religion* 17 (December): 399-406.

Kunz, P. R. and S. L. Albrecht. 1977. "Religion, Marital Happiness and Divorce." *International Journal of Sociology of the Family* 7 (July-December):227-32.

Lynd, R. S. and H. M. Lynd. 1929. *Middletown*. New York: Harcourt, Brace.

Lynd, R. S. and H. M. Lynd. 1937. *Middletown in Transition*. New York: Harcourt, Brace.

Riche, M. F. 1982. "The Fall and Rise of Religion." *American Demographics* 4 (May):14-19, 47.

Shrum, W. 1980. "Religion and Marital Instability: Change in the 1970's?" *Review of Religious Research* 21 (Spring):135-47.

Williams, C. M. 1983. "Marital Satisfaction and Religiosity." Unpublished masters thesis, Department of Sociology, Brigham Young University.

Wilson, B. 1982. *Religion in Sociological Perspective*. Oxford, England: Oxford University Press.

4

The Contemporary American Jewish Family

Jay Y. Brodbar-Nemzer

Introduction

This volume is but one of several manifestations of a growing desire to better understand the link between religion and the family. In the past several years there has been an increase in interest in encouraging the exploration of this connection by social scientists. Thus, D'Antonio and others (1982) calling for greater attention to religion in the study of the family, the National Council on Family Relations creating a section on religion and family, the publication of a special section on religion and the family in the *Journal of Marriage and the Family* in May of 1985 are but a few examples (see Thomas and Henry [1985] for a fuller treatment of this point). Much of the impetus to this renewed interest has been the perceived role of religion as both buttressing traditional family values and combatting the tide of family instability and dissolution. Thus, family, in causal terms, has been a focus of concern primarily as a dependent variable.

Jay Y. Brodbar-Nemzer is a Jerusalem Fellow, Jerusalem, Israel. He received his Ph.D. from the University of Wisconsin. He has taught at Western Michigan University and Brandeis University. His published research has focused on the American Jewish family. His research interests center on Jewish and family education.

The study of the American Jewish family fits well with this growing interest, and, I argue, can elucidate and augment our understanding of the relationship between family and religion in several ways. First, similar to the growing emphasis on the relationship noted above, a concern with the family has been a dominant feature of the agenda of the Jewish communal institutional world (Rosenman, 1984). It is important to note, as Thornton (1985) reminds us, that the relationship between religion and the family is a reciprocal one. This is underscored by the typical emphases on this relationship in the Jewish communal world. There, the central concern is the role of the family in the transmission of Jewish identity and in the survival of the group (see, for example, Bubis, 1983). Issues of exogamous marriages, fertility and family instability are of more than academic interest. This has been part of the general trend in American Jewry since the late 1960s, shifting the focus of concern from integration—how American Jews can best contribute and be accepted into the mainstream of American society, to survival—how American Jewry can survive as a distinct, committed religious and/or cultural entity (Cohen and Fein, 1985). Thus, complementing the emphasis on the family as the dependent variable, the major focus of those concerned with the issue for Jews has been religion as the dependent variable, with family-related variables chiefly of concern for their impact on group survival.

Second, it is important to note that Jews constitute an ethnic or cultural category as well as a religious one (Parsons, 1975; Zenner, 1985). The disentangling of these two components at a conceptual, behavioral or social-psychological level is difficult and, in terms of the experiences of the vast majority of American Jews, probably futile.[1] However, it is this very comingling of variables that have either been traditionally associated with religion (for example, belief, worldviews, ritual behavior) or ethnicity (institutional infrastructures, for instance) that may prove especially instructive to those who are concerned with the family as a dependent variable. Finally, I shall give various illustrative examples of how the distinctiveness of American Jewish family patterns may serve to advance our theories of religion and family as well as the field of the sociology of the family as a whole.

This chapter, then, will be an overview of the sociological research on the Jewish family with particular emphasis on how that research is suggestive of trends or relationships that will advance our knowledge of the sociology of the family and the relationship between religion and family. Given such a focus, this review is selective rather than comprehensive. The reader is encouraged to consult other recent reviews of the Jewish family in order to construct the most comprehensive understanding of this subfield (Dashefsky and Levine, 1983; Farber et al., 1981; Herz and Rosen, 1982; Waxman, 1982; see Cohen and Hyman, 1986 for a historical perspective).

An Overview

A number of years ago, one of the leading sociologists of American Jewry, Marshall Sklare, observed that much of what is known or believed about the American Jewish family can be traced to its portrayal in contemporary American fiction (Sklare, 1971:73). It is probable that Philip Roth has done more to establish the image of the American Jewish family in the minds of most of us than any social scientist. This is due not only to Roth and his peers' considerable skills with language, but also to the dearth of sophisticated and/or analytically informed sociological research on the American Jewish family. A quick perusal of recent literature reviews on this topic reveals that much of the research in this subfield has been fairly unsophisticated, often guided by unarticulated normative assumptions or goals, with much of the empirical literature suspect (Cherlin and Celebuski, 1983; Brodbar-Nemzer, 1986a). Multivariate analyses with adequate controls are generally lacking (Goldstein, 1985). We are still waiting for an in-depth qualitative observational study of the American Jewish family, though it has figured tangentially in the work of some of our most skilled family ethnographers (e.g., Jules Henry). With a few exceptions, the studies that have been done possess little theoretical or conceptual underpinning.

To be fair, there are special methodological challenges in studying the family patterns of American Jews which make research especially difficult. Any enterprise that seeks to link Jewish commitment, religiosity and so forth with family-related variables runs into problems on both sides of the equation. With respect to the conceptualization and measurement of Jewishness, measurement strategies that are used with other religions (emphasizing statements of belief or creed, frequency of private prayer) often do not tap the full range of Jewish religious commitment which involves ritual and public behavior. As noted, the multidimensional aspect of Jewish identity, with its ethnic as well as religious components adds additional difficulties (see Himmelfarb, 1982, for a review of the issues in measuring Jewish identity).[2]

So too, when we look at the set of variables associated with family (e.g., fertility, household composition, marital formation and dissolution, family-related values), there are many difficulties (see Goldscheider, 1982; Goldstein, 1985, for excellent discussions of the technical problems, especially in demographic research). Much of what we know about family patterns comes from the census and other government studies which do not include religion as a variable. While this is true of other religions as well, the situation is exacerbated for American Jewry, since due to its small size, Jews almost always do not show up in sufficient numbers in general studies that do include the religion variable.[3] Although several creative alternatives have been tried,[4] more and more our knowledge of American Jewry depends upon community surveys undertaken by local Jewish communal organizations. Although the quality and sophistication of these surveys has been improving over recent years, these studies are often undertaken with programmatic and planning but not research issues in mind. Thus, in the main, our sources of data for researching family-related variables among Jews are limited and often inadequate.

Having presented the difficulties involved in the research enterprise, what can we say about family patterns of American Jews beyond the observation that our body of knowledge is problematic? We can paint the broad demographic picture with some confidence, though there is a great deal of controversy over variations in place and time. Thus with respect to intermarriage, there is a broad consensus that the rate has been rising since the 1960s, but the rate itself is a matter of debate. Similarly, there is a recognition that Jewish fertility levels are low but controversy exists over projections for fertility in the near future. Additionally, it is difficult to come up with national estimates of rates based on community studies, especially since the reasons for local variation are not always understood. Let us look at these broad findings in a little more detail.

American Jewry has participated in trends in the larger culture, and this certainly holds for family trends such as increased divorce, single households, lower fertility and so forth. The extent is often hard to determine for the reasons noted above. Indeed, the analytic challenge is to understand where Jewish patterns are similar to the trends in the surrounding culture and where they diverge.[5] I will outline some of these trends, especially where they distinguish Jews from other groups.

American Jews have been historically characterized by high nuptiality. Thus, Schmelz and DellaPergola (1982) report proportions of ever married as high as 98 percent at age forty-five. Jews, especially Jewish men, have tended to marry later than non-Jews. This seems to have been increasing recently, and there is some concern that the proportion of those who will never marry may be equal or even exceed non-Jewish rates. Whether current trends represent deferment or actual forgoing of marriage cannot be determined from the data at hand, and is a matter of some controversy. (See Goldscheider, 1986b; Schmelz and DellaPergola, 1986, for differing views.)

Although not usually conceptualized this way, changing marital patterns are at the core of the issue of fertility as well. Traditionally, American Jews have had relatively low levels of fertility. It is thought that Jews have been at replacement level (2.1) for most of this century. At the present, there are those who argue that the fertility level has decreased to as low as 1.7 or even 1.3 (Schmelz and DellaPergola, 1982). Goldscheider (1986b) and Cohen (1986) argue that the fertility of married Jewish women is still at replacement levels. Thus, as long as marriage is nearly universal, the overall rate should be near that of replacement—though with delays in fertility the spacing of generations can become more extended. However, here again, the debate then shifts toward trends in nuptiality rather than fertility per se.

With respect to marital instability, Jews have had relatively low rates of divorce when compared with Protestants and Catholics (Bumpass and Sweet, 1972; Cherlin and Celebuski, 1983). The divorce rate of all groups has increased over the last twenty-five years, but the gap between Jews and Protestants and Catholics has remained. This difference remains after controlling for education and other socioeconomic variables, though Cherlin and Celebuski (1983) report that the gap is biggest between Protestants and Jews. Marriage, divorce and remarriage patterns lead to Jews being described demographically as a "highly married population" (Kobrin, 1986:179).[6]

The emphasis on marriage translates into differences in household composition. Kobrin (1986) presents a detailed national comparison, working with the Yiddish-mother-tongue subpopulation in the 1970 U.S. Census. She reports that Yiddish households are more likely to be husband-wife and less likely to be single parent, though such families are not exempted from overall societal household compositional trends. She finds that adults without immediate family of procreation ties (spouse or minor children) are less likely to live with other family members. Goldscheider (1986), analyzing data from Boston,[7] finds an exception to this difference among older Jewish women only. He also reports that Jewish and non-Jewish differences persist after controlling for education.

The emphasis on marriage is also reflected in Jewish communal concern over intermarriage. The general trend in the United States has been toward an increase in interfaith marriage, with many homogamous marriages resulting from denominational switching in conjunction with the marriage itself. (Glenn, 1982.) This trend has been seen as important in reflecting a secularization of marriage and the general society (Glenn, 1982) as well as evidence for ethnic assimilation (Hirschman, 1983). Glenn (1982:556) has put the issue well:

> A strong trend away from religious homogamy might reflect a continued secularization of the institution of marriage and a continued diminution of the influence of the church and the extended family on marital choice and on marriage relationships. When and if religious preference becomes no longer an important criterion for spouse selection, the importance of institutionalized religion . . . will almost certainly have declined.

Glenn (1982) presents evidence that such a decline may be in effect. Interestingly, the passage quoted above continues:

> It is true, furthermore, that the continued existence of the American Jewish community and the perpetuation of the Jewish cultural tradition largely depend on Jewish outmarriage being much lower than it would be if marital choice took place without regard to religion or ethnicity.

American Jewry, then, has a special stake in this question. Historically, American Jews have had a lower rate of exogamy than Protestants and Catholics, outmarrying far below what would be expected if their religious ethnic status were not a factor (Glenn, 1982; Heer, 1980). There is evidence that the rate of Jews outmarrying has been increasing since the 1960s, but both the current rate and the amount of change are matters of controversy (Cohen and Ritterband, forthcoming; Schmelz and DellaPergola, 1986). Given the perceived importance of intermarriage to the survival of American Jewry, as the quote from Glenn suggests, there is a tone of urgency in the consideration of this issue in the Jewish community. The problems articulated with respect to research on the Jewish family become exacerbated when studying intermarriage while rigorous methodological research is lacking (Goldscheider, 1986b).

It is difficult to arrive at a national rate, though most responsible estimates range between 24 and 30 percent (Schmelz and DellaPergola, 1986; Silberman, 1985). There is a wide range of local variation, with estimates varying from 11 percent in greater metropolitan New York (Cohen, forthcoming) to 61 percent in Denver (Phillips, 1985). While it is likely that local variation reflects differences in strength of endogamy norms and the strength of the local infra-structure in maintaining such norms, it is also likely that some of this varia-tion is due to differential migration patterns. Moreover, due to the general state of the research, which includes sampling methodology and the lack of comparability across local studies, it is often impossible to know to what degree local variation is spurious. (Goldstein, 1985.) There is also controversy about whether the increase in intermarriage has been leveling off, with some schol-ars noting that the social factors associated with intermarriage, for example, remarriage and migration to areas of lower Jewish concentration, are expected to remain influential (Schmelz and DellaPergola, 1986). These controversies extend to the consideration of the consequences of intermarriage for Jewish commitment, with a number of scholars calling into question the traditional assumption that both those who intermarry and their children are "lost" to the Jewish community (Cohen forthcoming; Goldscheider, 1986).

The Sociology of the American Jewish Family: Issues and Exemplars

As we have seen from this broad overview, the stress on marriage runs through any review of the American Jewish family. Kobrin's (1986:182) con-clusion about Yiddish-mother-tongue differences in family patterns is a good summary of what we know in general:

> The extent and duration of marriage is clearly greater, while fertility is lower. Couple bonds are strong, relative to the U.S. total. Other bonds are less strong, at least in terms of residential decisions, and thus family extension is rarer. Although relationships can be very strong without coresidence, it seems likely that issues of privacy and independence in the relationships between parents and children might be more acute in Jewish households.

Kobrin's observations are instructive in several other ways. First, they are based on Jewish versus non-Jewish comparisons. Although much of the inter-est in Jewish family patterns has been concerned with distinctiveness, precious little research has systematically compared Jews and non-Jews. Second, Kobrin suggests a reason for the difference in coresidence patterns. Lamentably, the general literature suffers from a lack of analytic research and frameworks that try to tackle such issues directly. In this case, there is some indirect evidence that Kobrin may be on a fruitful path. Cherlin and Celebuski (1983), analyzing NORC data, report that Jews are more likely to stress values of independence in their children than are Catholics or Protestants, even after controlling for education. Ironically, the theme of intrafamilial independence has received most consideration by many of the leading American writers of our time as shaped by the experiences of the immigrant generation (Howe, 1976:180–83), recalling Sklare's lament about the dearth of sociological studies on similar themes.

To rectify the situation and to add to our understanding of the American Jewish family vis-à-vis its usefulness for the field as a whole, we need two types of effort. First, there needs to be a greater degree of specification in our studies. Second, there needs to be a broader range of research strategies that sees the study of process as central. Let me deal with the latter first. Many of the types of issues that are central to the evolving concerns of this subfield, such as the consequences of intermarriage on Jewish identity of children, require longitudinal research. Relatedly, the desire to augment the state of qualitative research on the sociology of family as a whole (LaRossa and Wolf, 1985) is especially true for the study of Jewish families. I shall return to this point later, but it is clear that the conceptual issues involved in understanding the relationship between Jewish identity and family processes require in-depth, largely qualitative approaches. In short, the state of the field is such that we require studies that attempt to understand process. Therefore, longitudinal studies, studies that explore the various dimensions of Jewish identity, studies that tackle qualitative issues in a sophisticated manner, are sorely needed. Whether these processes are conceived of at the structural level (Goldscheider, 1986a) or at the social-psychological level (Brodbar-Nemzer, 1986a), much more work needs to be done that places process at its center.

What do I mean by my second concern—my call for greater specification in the study of the American Jewish family? First, as suggested above, we need studies that attempt to specify actual processes at work. What this might mean, by way of example, is specifying *how* Jewish families might be different, examining whether *particular* relationships that are true for families in general exist among Jewish families and whether to the same degree, and inquiring whether such findings are equally true for various *specific* subgroups of American Jewry. What we do not need are general claims about Jewish families that are unsubstantiated by research. Much more useful would be research informed by theory that specifies particular relationships among particular variables relevant to Jewish families. I can probably best illustrate this point by describing several studies that can serve as exemplars of specification in the study of the American Jewish family.

Specification of Distinctiveness

As noted above, much of the sociological concern with the Jewish family has centered around the question of distinctiveness. Unfortunately, there is a lack of cumulative knowledge about that distinctiveness. Some of the reason reflects the conceptual and methodological issues noted earlier.

Additionally, the lack of consensus in the social science literature about whether there are differences between Jewish families and other families is traceable to two factors—a conceptual confusion about what differences ought to exist and a lack of solid empirical research on the topic. On the second point, Cherlin and Celebuski (1983) have recently reviewed the empirical literature on Jewish familial distinctiveness and have correctly concluded that much of this work is flawed. On the conceptual level, analysis is difficult because it is not clear what properties among Jewish families ought to be distinctive. Thus, the putative differences range from queries as to whether Jewish families are "more closely knit" (Balswick, 1966), happier (Cherlin and Celebuski, 1983), more familistic (Bardis, 1961), and so forth. It is clear that this concern with distinctiveness needs specification.

Values

Elsewhere, I have treated in more detail the question of specificity of distinctiveness on a general level (Brodbar-Nemzer, 1986a). There, I have suggested that an exploration of distinctive features would do well to start with the most obvious—that the family as an institution would be of particular import to Jews. Threats to the viability of the family would be perceived as threats to the group. Family stability would be emphasized. Whether families are more closely knit, happier, and so on would depend on particular circumstances of history and place. What would be primary would be a valuing of the family as an institution. Indeed, it could be argued that under certain circumstances the aggregate level of marital happiness could be lower among groups who value the family. Dissatisfaction that might lead to marital dissolution among couples who do not have a similar valuing of the institution might be tolerated by couples who do. Similarly, a perception that one is particularly dependent on the family for nurturance and support might lead one to maintain a stronger commitment to that family and families in general, even in the face of discord and dissatisfaction.

We find that on the normative level, Judaism assigns a major role to the institution of the family (see, for example, Brayer, 1968). Specifically, both the family as a source of support and nurturance and the importance of family stability are especially valued. Indeed, Farber (1984) has recently argued that nurturance "is a central feature in organizing Jewish family life. . . [and] family and kinship norms are continually transformed in ways which are consistent with the nurturance principle." Farber traces this emphasis on nurturance to the fact that Judaism is an ascriptive religion, which therefore relies on the socialization and retention of its progeny rather than wholesale recruitment for its continuity as a group. In terms of their traditional values and their historical experience, Jews would value the family in view of its contribution to group survival and individual support and nurturance.[8]

The issue becomes, then, whether this view of the family still operates normatively in contemporary Jewish American life. That is, how might we empirically test the claim that Jews, in comparison with Protestants and Catholics, are disproportionately likely to value the family as a source of support and value family stability? There is little empirical work that examines this directly. We do know, from the work of Rokeach (1973), that Jews ranked "family security" higher as a terminal value than any other religious group. I examined the valuing of the family on the part of Jews on the social-psychological level, arguing that the incorporation of family values in a person's self-concept structure would result in that person's self-esteem being more tethered to the family. Using a NIMH sample of Chicago, I found that, controlling for education, sex and age, the self-esteem of the Jewish respondents was affected more than the self-esteem of Protestant and Catholic respondents by changes and perceptions of marital support, marital stress, concern about the future of the marriage, seeking professional help for marital problems, being married, and the length of marriage.

Demographic Variables

The specificity of distinctiveness is needed not just with respect to values, but in understanding demographic trends as well. A good example is Goldscheider's (1986) discovery that among Jews, the relationship between education and fertility operates in a specifically distinctive way. In the general population, education has a negative impact on fertility. Thus, those who are concerned about the low level of fertility among Jews have cause for concern in light of the high educational attainment of American Jews (Goldstein, 1981). Goldscheider (1986), however, finds that Jewish women with postgraduate education have higher family size expectations than similarly educated non-Jewish women. Thus, although for the general population it is the less educated women that have the largest family size expectations, among Jewish women the opposite is true—it is the women with the highest levels of educational achievement that have the largest family size expectations. Although this finding needs to be replicated in other communities, Goldscheider has alerted us to a possible process operating uniquely among Jewish women and, by specifying a relationship among variables that operates differently among Jews, has saved us from unwarranted projections based on mistaken assumptions.

Specification of Intra-Group Differences

In addition to specifying the parameters of differences in the comparisons between Jews and non-Jews, it is often useful to specify intra-group differences as well. For example, we have noted that Jewish divorce rates are below the rates for Catholics and Protestants. To further understand the source of this distinctiveness, I analyzed intra-group variation in divorce among the Jews of metropolitan New York, with the specifying variable being group commitment (see Brodbar-Nemzer, 1984, 1986b). Utilizing a wide definition of Jewish commitment, incorporating both religious and ethnic or associational measures, I found that the Jewishly committed were about half as likely to have been ever divorced as Jews with low levels of commitment. Although the differences were most marked for the religiosity measures, it was still the case that among nonreligious Jews, associational measures (such as proportion of friends who were Jewish) halved the ever-divorced rate. The rationale developed to explain such differences, which I will refer to later, concentrated on the networks and associational life of committed Jews—that their commitment to a group attenuates the individualizing tendencies of modern life, of which marital instability is one manifestation. (See Brodbar-Nemzer, 1986b, for a full discussion.)

Another issue which needs specification is the understanding of the causes and consequences of intermarriage. Here too, intra-group analyses specifying the patterns of associations are crucial. For example, similar to his specifying the relationship between education and the fertility expectations of women, Goldscheider (1986a) found that the general positive relationship among Jews between education on the one hand and attitudes of indifference toward inter-marriage on the other did not hold for young adults. In addition, he found that households which are intermarried are not as Jewishly committed as are nonintermarried households. As a general trend, this held across age groups. However, when looking at the nature of the Jewish commitment, he found a pattern reflective of the multidimensional aspect of Jewish identity. Specifically, the differences were most marked for items measuring private worship and formal synagogue membership and least marked for proportion of Jewish friends and neighbors. Such specification is important in times where the bases and manifestation of Jewish commitment may be undergoing transformation. Analyzing these patterns of Jewishness by age, Goldscheider (1986a:26–28) specifies three models of convergence. One type of convergence results from a decrease in Jewishness in younger cohorts of the nonintermarried. This he finds to be the case for the proportion of friends Jewish. A second type of convergence is due to the increase in younger cohorts of the intermarried. This he finds to be true of the proportion of Jewish neighbors. The third type results from the co-occurrence of the two trends together. This he finds to be true of the proportion who endorse Jewish values.

Specification of Changes in Jewishness

Among all American Jews, family variables become an important specifying factor in understanding patterns of religiosity and Jewish commitment. This is especially true of attempts at understanding change in these patterns. In view of the lack of longitudinal data, nearly all such studies use cross-sectional surveys and analyze patterns of Jewishness by age cohort or generation. Practically all such surveys find that young adults are least active Jewishly. One might conclude that there is a diminution over time, with the youngest cohorts becoming less Jewishly active. However, when one further specifies the relationship between age and Jewish involvement by the introduction of family variables, the situation is clarified. Specifically, the relationship is largely a function of family cycle. One of the more in-depth treatments of this topic is to be found in Cohen (forthcoming) in his analysis of the 1982 Greater New York Jewish community study. He finds a very different relationship between age and commitment when he considers family cycle. The basic relationship varies to such an extent that there were instances in which young parents were more Jewishly active than their older counterparts. This relationship was not explained by a possible later marriage by the older parents. In general, by taking family cycle into account, he finds that parents with school-age children are the most active, whereas the never married are the least Jewishly active. Indeed, the differences are striking enough to lead these researchers to suggest that "parental status is a virtual pre-condition for involvement in Jewish communal life." (Cohen and Tenenbaum, forthcoming.) Thus, family cycle specifies the more general relationship between age and Jewish involvement in important ways.

Cohen (forthcoming) also demonstrates the importance of specifying patterns of change in his treatment of the congruence of parent-child Jewish involvement over time. He finds, in keeping with common wisdom, a parent-to-child decline in religiosity. Again, this gives the impression of an overall decline with successive generations of American Jews. However, in specifying the analysis by considering age cohort and the degree and nature of Jewish commitment of the parents of respondents, a more complex picture emerges. A complete discussion is beyond the scope of this paper, but he does find, for example, that among the younger respondents, those whose parents were not very ritually observant actually exceed their parents' observance levels.

The difficulty in understanding change over time is especially true when we try to project into the future. Goldscheider (1986b) cautions us not to project on the basis of straight-line assumptions using period data. This is especially true of groups in which change is occurring and rates are unstable. It appears that fertility and marriage rates are fluctuating, thus projections based on them may be misleading. Another example is the study of the consequences of intermarriage. We know that the grandchildren of intermarrieds are, on the whole, less Jewishly committed than their peers (Cohen, forthcoming). However, projecting a large future decline in Jewish commitment based on rising intermarriage rate may be an unwarranted straight-line prediction (Goldscheider, 1986b; Cohen, 1986). The historical circumstance was sufficiently different that it is likely that the intermarried grandparents of current adults were motivated by a desire to escape from Jewish affiliation. In contrast to those times, today intermarriage is more common, involving the conversion to Judaism of a significant number of non-Jewish spouses (Mayer, 1985). A "flight from Judaism" is less likely a motivator today. Predicting patterns for a future generation of grandchildren based on what appeared to be true for those in similar circumstance two generations earlier (for example, grandchildren of intermarrieds at the time that their own grandparents intermarried) is questionable in general, but more so when the historical conditions are very different.

In this section, I have presented a number of exemplars of analyses which attempt to specify family-related processes at work in contemporary American Jewry. Such specification is necessary to understand best how and why they work. More such analyses are required to advance our level of knowledge about the American Jewish family. In the final section, I will suggest how this greater sophistication might benefit the field as a whole.

The Sociology of the American Jewish Family: Potential Contributions

In this article, I am calling for advances in our understanding of the American Jewish family through studies that specify particular relationships at work as well as research designs (longitudinal designs, observational studies) appropriate to the study of process. Such studies are important, I claim, because our *general* understanding of the American family (including the relationship between the family and religion) will be advanced through such research. At the global level, our theoretical models must account for cultural diversity. Any model of family process or structure or of the role of religion that does not take account of cultural or structural variation is severely limited. Thus, American Jews would be one of the many groups whose variation in family patterns we would explore and analyze. In addition, any general theoretical model, to the extent that it is viable, must also show how different subgroups manifest or reflect the imputed general cultural patterns. In a sense, this view is complementary to Lipset's (1968), who argued that one cannot truly understand patterns of American Jewish life without a conceptual framework which locates those patterns in the dominant social structure. I am arguing that one cannot truly understand dominant or "typical" social patterns without exploring their reflection in the mosaic of subgroup experience. Thus, our understanding of the American Jewish family would serve that goal as well. Indeed, Lipset (1968:27) reports that Robert Park, one of the early giants of American sociology, argued that "the Jews are the most American of all groups in the nation, that they exhibit the predominant American traits in a more integrated fashion than any other group."[9]

In addition, especially promising is work that goes beyond illustrating and elaborating theory, but rather transforms that theory. This is often done by studying phenomena which pose challenges and are often anomalies to the prevailing theoretical models. We have encountered this possibility in the anomaly of the positive relationship between education and fertility expectations among Jewish women. As we better understand the extent and reasons for this reversal, we may gain additional sophistication as to the workings of this relationship in the general society. As another example, the dilemma posed by the Jewish family to the widely held belief of a negative relationship between economic advancement and kinship ties was raised by Lenski (1963) and by Adams (1968) in the 1960s, and still has to be addressed by the mainstream sociological literature. (See Berman, 1976, for an attempt.) This issue can be framed in a larger theoretical question, to which we shall return—why do Jewish Americans, while at the forefront of social innovations often associated with alternative family structures (high level of education, female employment, especially self-employment, egalitarian family values, etc.) still manifest, in their patterns of divorce and childlessness, for example, traditional family patterns?

Finally, studying the American Jewish family is of importance because it may have some unique attributes or emphases which provide a "laboratory" for the development of theory on the family as a whole. Thus, Strodtbeck (1958) saw in American Jewry a unique opportunity to explore the role of values and family patterns in adaptation to the dominant social system. This point is especially salient when one takes a historical perspective. Thus, with respect to fertility, for example, Ritterband (1981:3) has suggested that the onset of the emancipation of Jewish communities in Europe "offers the scholar a unique quasi-experimental design" to study cultural variation in family formation.

I think that the American Jewish family offers a unique opportunity in at least one other way. In the mid-1970s, a telling critique was launched at sociology by such scholars as Scheff, Hochschild and Kemper, among others, of sociology's neglect of emotion.[10] How seriously have sociologists of the family taken emotion as a variable? Very early in the discipline's history, W. I. Thomas suggested that variance in modes of expression of emotions was a sociologically significant phenomenon and used the Jewish family to illustrate his point (Bressler, 1952). Thus, studying the meaning, use of, and rules governing the display of affect in the Jewish family could lead to a greater understanding of cultural variation in families. This focus on affect would also add to our understanding of cross-generational transmission of religious identity. Although the role of the family in this process is crucial, it is poorly understood. This is an important area where sophisticated processually oriented family studies are required. To the extent that researchers combine the study of the sociology of emotion with the study of cross-generational transmission of religious identity, our general understanding of the family's role in socialization and cultural transmission will benefit.

The special contributions that can be made to the affective aspects of family life through the study of the Jewish family have also been noted by the historian Paula Hyman. She calls for scholarly historical study of the affective dimensions of Jewish family life. In addition, in an argument complementary to ours, she argues (1986:231) that, historically, Jews often anticipated "some 'modern' family traits before such characteristics were widespread in the larger population." She singles out the degree of emotional attachment to children, fertility, and attitudes toward marital sexuality as examples of such anticipatory trends. She recommends, as we have, the further exploration of contemporary Jewry in view of its participation in the forefront of social change. In particular, she singles out such issues as the relationship between social mobility and family life and the coping and adaptation of immigrant families.[11] Hyman (1986:233) echoes a theme we have encountered, suggesting that many interesting issues have remained largely unexplored by social scientists:

> Family historians and sociologists have left to novelists such questions as how the Jewish family selectively legitimated values from the larger society, how it perpetuated a measure of assertiveness among its women, how it secularized its values, and how it succeeded in sending forth its children to do battle in the world while keeping them closely attached, not the least by guilt, to the parental hearth.

In conclusion, there are numerous ways in which the study of the American Jewish family can contribute to our general understanding. In particular, in their retention of certain traditional patterns of family life while at the same time being at the vanguard of change, Jewish families may help provide a clue to solving one of the dilemmas of contemporary life: how to maintain individual integrity and human and social connectedness. Naturally, the pattern of Jewish family life does not have a unique answer, but rather, where Jews have been able to balance distinctiveness with accommodation, individualism with group commitment, we would benefit from greater understanding of how or why such processes occur. It is likely that such explanations would be found in the interaction of historical, structural and ideational factors. For example, in appreciating the link between the family and group survival the Jewish tradition has stressed the importance of family stability and cohesion (Brayer, 1968; Bressler, 1952). However, although Judaism emphasizes the importance of family stability, it also recognizes the importance of individual dignity. Thus, historically, Jewish law on marital dissolution has been relatively liberal; divorce has not been proscribed, but rather viewed as a "calamitous necessity." (Brayer, 1968:19.) Goldberg (1968), in a historical demographic analysis, demonstrates that it is likely that as recently as the end of the last century European Jews had a higher divorce rate than other groups. However, non-Jewish divorce rates were climbing faster than Jewish divorce rates, and after World War II the situation reversed to its current status: lower rates for American Jews. This reversal may be best understood in light of Western liberalization of divorce. In the past, a sense of balance required protecting the rights of the individual; today, societal increase in divorce requires greater vigilance on behalf of family and group stability. It is possible that among Jews, in this century of threat and dislocation, it is the valuing of group commitment that is balancing out the dominant forces of individualism.

The concern with individualism and declining social solidarity locates us squarely in the central concern of both family and religion. The work of Bellah and associates (1958) is a good example of an analysis that tries to come to grips with this very concern. They decry the proliferation of a "culture of separation" as the outgrowth of unchecked individualism. This is reminiscent of Bakan's (1966) warning about the dangers of separation ("agency") untempered by integrative forces ("communion"). With respect to the family itself, the implications of this drift toward such individualism have been drawn out by Goode (1984).

Social integration, often manifested both within families and in families' relation to broader institutional structures, stands in opposite relation to the forces of individualism, separation, and fragmentation. As we have seen, American Jews continue to commit themselves to the institution of the family, both on behavioral and social-psychological levels. This makes them theoretically interesting. As Goldscheider (1986a) notes: "Jews have tended in the past to be in the forefront of major socioeconomic revolutions. American Jews are located in social statuses and geographic locations that are most responsive to changes in marriage and the family." They are doubly interesting because of their apparent ability to maintain some traditional patterns (such as nearly universal marriage and relatively lower divorce rates) in spite of their involvement in secular culture. Perhaps it has been this comingling of religious and ethnic variables, noted at the outset, that has made social integration a crucial dynamic of American Jewish life—resulting, in part, in placing religion and group cohesion and perpetuation, as well as family life, at the center. As I have been suggesting, processual studies that specify the links between social integration and the family are sorely needed. By tying together, at conceptual levels, features of religious life such as social integration with various processes and outcomes of family life, we might gain insight into the important question of how to balance the seemingly incessant drive toward individual attainment and separation with interdependence and coherence. To advance our understanding of this and other issues, the further exploration of how religion and family life interrelate among American Jews is a worthy endeavor.

Notes

Assistance for the writing of this chapter was provided by the Center for Modern Jewish Studies, Brandeis University.

1. This can be seen by examining Thornton's treatment (1985) of religion as a dependent variable. His concern is in terms of "religious teachings and programs" whereas the concern here is broader—the perpetuation of a social group.

2. Many researchers try to solve these problems by including a broad variety of ritual, behavioral and attitudinal items in their surveys to assess Jewish identity, including measures of communal affiliation: friendship patterns, charitable giving, organizational involvement, visits to Israel, etc. These are imperfect solutions, since they tend to ignore the largely cognitive and social-psychological aspects of identity as opposed to the more behavioral component of identification. (Himmelfarb, 1982.) In addition, there is not always consensus about the comprehensiveness of such items, their representativeness and their relative weight, especially in an era where the meaning and manifestation of Jewish commitment may be transforming (Goldscheider, 1986a; Silberman, 1985).

3. For example, Gallup no longer routinely reports data on Jews because of the low incidence of Jews in their samples.

4. A number of investigators have attempted strategies to circumvent these limitations, including the use of Yiddish-mother-tongue subgroup in the U.S. Census (Kobrin, 1986) and the concatenation of surveys repeated over time so that the pool of Jews approaches an analyzable number (Cherlin and Celebuski, 1982). Such approaches, though innovative and valuable, are limited.

5. See for example, Cohen (1983), chapter 6, for such a perspective.

6. Traditional Judaism has stressed marriage as a value. It is beyond the scope of this paper to treat the textual and ideational corpus of Jewish tradition. For a brief recent introduction to traditional Jewish values, see Linzer (1986).

7. The Boston community studies are unique in that they systematically surveyed non-Jewish as well as Jewish households for basic demographic comparisons.

8. An analysis of the historical and structural forces underlying these values is beyond the scope of this paper. Although the recent history of the American Jewish experience has been relatively benign, much of that experience is informed by a tradition and circumstances that encompass a larger historical frame. Thus, for example, in the history of American Jewry, which was formed largely within the immigrant experience, the emphasis on the family may also be seen as an extension of the East European experience and applied adaptively to the immigrant experience (Bressler, 1952).

9. Lipset goes on to note that Park "urged more than forty years ago that courses on the history, culture, and behavior of the American Jews should be included as a *required* part of the curriculum of all American high schools, that by studying the American Jews in detail, Americans of all backgrounds could learn to understand their nation and themselves."

10. For a review of the sociology of emotion literature see Gordon (1981).

11. This was one of the main reasons that W. I. Thomas was interested in Jews—as exemplars of coping and adaptation to the immigrant experience. It is this interest in their "definition of the situation" that led him to learn Yiddish and to read and abstract hundreds of letters to the editor requesting advice. (See Bressler, 1952; Metzker, 1971.)

Bibliography

Adams, B. N. 1968. *Kinship in an Urban Setting*. Chicago: Markham Publishing Company.

Bakan, D. 1966. *The Duality of Human Existence: Isolation and Communion in Western Man*. Boston: Beacon.

Balswick, J. 1966. "Are American-Jewish Families Closely Knit?" *Jewish Social Studies* 28:159–69.

Bardis, P. D. 1961. "Familism Among Jews in Suburbia." *Social Science* 36 (June):190–96.

Bellah, R., R. Madsen, W. Sullivan, A. Swidler, and S. Tipton. 1985. *Habits of the Heart: Individualism and Commitment in American Life*. Berkeley, CA: University of California.

Berman, S. 1976. "The Adaptable American Jewish Family: An Inconsistency in Theory." *Jewish Journal of Sociology* 18:5–16.

Brayer, M. M. 1968. "The Role of Jewish Law Pertaining to the Jewish Family, Jewish Marriage and Divorce." Pp. 1–33 in J. Freid (ed.), *Jews and Divorce*. New York: Ktav.

Bressler, M. 1952. "Selected Family Patterns in W. I. Thomas' Unfinished Study of the Bintel Brief." *American Sociological Review* 17:563–71.

Brodbar-Nemzer, J. Y. 1984. "Divorce in the Jewish Community: The Impact of Jewish Commitment." *Journal of Jewish Communal Service* 61:150–59.

Brodbar-Nemzer, J. Y. 1986a. "Marital Relationships and Self-esteem: How Jewish Families Are Different." *Journal of Marriage and the Family* 48:89–98.

Brodbar-Nemzer, J. Y. 1986b. "Divorce and Group Commitment: The Case of the Jews." *Journal of Marriage and the Family* 48:329–40.

Bubis, G. B. 1983. "Strengthening the Jewish Family as an Instrument of Jewish Continuity." *Journal of Jewish Communal Service* 59:306–17.

Bumpass, L. and J. Sweet. 1972. "Differentials in Marital Instability: 1970." *American Sociological Review* 37 (December): 754–66.

Cherlin, A. and C. Celebuski. 1983. "Are Jewish Families Different? Some Evidence from the General Social Survey." *Journal of Marriage and the Family* 45 (4):903–10.

Cohen, S. M. 1983. *American Modernity and Jewish Identity*. New York: Tavistock.

Cohen, S. M. 1986. "Vitality and Resilience in the American Jewish Family." Pp. 221–29 in S. M. Cohen and P. E. Hyman, eds., *The Jewish Family: Myths and Reality*. New York: Holmes and Meier.

Cohen, S.M. Forthcoming. *American Assimilation or Jewish Revival?* Bloomington, IN: Indiana University Press.

Cohen, S. M. and L. Fein., 1985. "From Integration to Survival: American Jewish Anxieties in Transition." *Annals of the American Academy of Political and Social Science* 480:75–88.

Cohen, S. M. and P. E. Hyman. 1986. *The Jewish Family: Myths and Reality*. New York: Holmes and Meier.

Cohen, S. and S. Tenenbaum. Forthcoming. "Age Cohort and Lifestyle Differences in Jewish Education" in S. M. Cohen, *American Assimilation or Jewish Revival?*, Bloomington, IN: Indiana University Press.

D'Antonio, W., W. Newman, and S. Wright. 1982. "Religion and Family Life: How Social Scientists View the Relationship." *Journal for the Scientific Study of Religion* 21:218–25.

Dashefsky, A. and I. M. Levine. 1983. "The Jewish Family." Pp. 163–90 in W. V. D'Antonio and J. Aldous (eds.), *Families and Religions: Conflict and Change in Modern Society*. Beverly Hills, CA: Sage Publishing.

Farber, B. 1984. "The Anatomy of Nurturance: A Structural Analysis of the Contemporary American Jewish Family." Prepared for the National Council on Family Relations Theory and Methods Workshop, San Francisco, October 16.

Farber, B., C. Mindel, and B. Lazerwitz. 1981. "The Jewish American Family." Pp. 350–85 in C. Mindel and R. W. Habenstein (eds.), *Ethnic Families in America: Patterns and Variations* (2nd ed.). New York: Elsevier.

Glenn, N. D. 1982. "Interreligious Marriage in the United States: Patterns and Recent Trends." *Journal of Marriage and the Family*. August:555–66.

Goldberg, N. 1968. "The Jewish Attitude Toward Divorce." In Jacob Freid (ed.), *Jews and Divorce*. New York: Ktav.

Goldscheider, C. 1982. "Demography of Jewish Americans." Pp. 1–55 in M. Sklare (ed.), *Understanding American Jewry*. New Brunswick, NJ: Transaction.

Goldscheider, C. 1986a. *Jewish Continuity and Change: Emerging Patterns in America*. Bloomington, IN: Indiana University Press.

Goldscheider, C. 1986b. "The Demographic Future of American Jewry: Fertility, Marriage and Intermarriage." Paper prepared for the American Jewish Committee Conference on New Perspectives in American Jewish Sociology, New York, May 1986.

Goldstein, S. 1981. "Jews in the United States: Perspectives from Demography." Pp. 31–102 in J. Gittler (ed.), *Jewish Life in the United States*. New York: New York University.

Goldstein, S. 1985. "American Jewish Demography: Inconsistencies That Challenge." Paper presented at the Ninth World Congress of Jewish Studies, Jerusalem, August 1985.

Goode, W. J. 1984. "Individual Investments in Family Relationships over the Coming Decades." *Tocqueville Review* 6:51–83.

Gordon, S. L. 1981. "The Sociology of Sentiments and Emotion." Pp. 562–92 in M. Rosenberg and R. H. Turner (eds.), *Social Psychology*. New York: Basic.

Heer, D. M. 1980. "Intermarriage." Pp. 513–21, in S. Thernstrom, A. Orlov and O. Handlin (eds.), *Harvard Encyclopedia of American Ethnic Groups*. Cambridge, MA: Harvard University Press.

Herz, F. M. and E. J. Rosen. 1982. "Jewish Families." Pp. 364–92 in M. McGoldrick, J. Pierce, and J. Giordano (eds.), *Ethnicity and Family Therapy*. New York: Guilford.

Himmelfarb, H. 1982. "Research on American Jewish Identity and Identification: Progress, Pitfalls, and Prospects." Pp. 56–95 in M. Sklare (ed.), *Understanding American Jewry*. New Brunswick, NJ: Transaction.

Hirschman, C. 1983. "America's Melting Pot Reconsidered." *Annual Review of Sociology* 9:397–423.

Howe, I. 1976. *World of Our Fathers*. New York: Simon and Schuster.

Hyman, P. E. 1986. "Afterword." Pp. 230–35 in S. M. Cohen and P. E. Hyman (eds.), *The Jewish Family: Myths and Reality*. New York: Holmes and Meier.

Kobrin, F. 1986. "Family Patterns Among the U.S. Yiddish-Mother-Tongue Subpopulation: 1970." Pp. 172–83 in S. M. Cohen and P. E. Hyman (eds.), *The Jewish Family: Myths and Reality*. New York: Holmes and Meier.

LaRossa, R. and J. Wolf. 1985. "On Qualitative Family Research." *Journal of Marriage and the Family* 47:531–41.

Lenski, G. 1963. *The Religious Factor*. Revised edition. New York: Anchor Books.

Linzer, N. 1986. "Philosophical Reflections on Jewish Family Life." *Journal of Jewish Communal Service* 62:318–27.

Lipset, S. M. 1968. "The American Jewish Community in a Comparative Context." Pp. 21–32 in P. I. Rose (ed.), *The Ghetto and Beyond*. New York: Random.

Mayer, E. 1985. *Love and Tradition: Marriage Between Jews and Christians*. New York: Plenum.

Metzker, I. 1971. *A Bintel Brief*. Volume 1. New York: Behrman.

Parsons, T. 1975. "Some Theoretical Considerations on the Nature and Trends of Change of Ethnicity." Pp. 53–83 in N. Glazer and D. P. Moynihan (eds.), *Ethnicity: Theory and Experience*. Cambridge, MA: Harvard University Press.

Phillips, B. A. 1985. "Factors Associated with Intermarriage in the Western United States." Paper presented at the ninth World Congress of Jewish Studies. Jerusalem, August.

Ritterband, P. 1981. "Introduction." Pp. 1–17 in P. Ritterband (ed.), *Modern Jewish Fertility*. Leiden: Brill.

Rokeach, M. 1973. *The Nature of Human Values*. New York: Free Press.

Rosenman, Y. 1984. "Research on the Jewish Family and Jewish Education." *Journal of Jewish Communal Service* 60:185–92.

Schmelz, U. O. and S. DellaPergola. 1982. "The Demographic Consequences of U.S. Jewish Population Trends." Pp. 141–87 in M. Himmelfarb and D. Singer, *American Jewish Yearbook 1983*. Philadelphia: Jewish Publication Society.

Schmelz, U. O. and S. DellaPergola. 1986. "Some Basic Trends in the Demography of U.S. Jews: A Re-examination." Paper prepared for the American Jewish Committee Conference on New Perspectives in American Jewish Sociology, New York, May 1986.

Silberman, C. E. 1985. *A Certain People: American Jews and Their Lives Today*. New York: Summit.

Sklare, M. 1971. *America's Jews*. New York: Random House.

Strodtbeck, F. L. 1958. "Family Interaction, Values, and Achievement." Pp. 147–65 in M. Sklare (ed.), *The Jews: Social Pattern of an American Group*. Glencoe, IL: Free Press.

Thomas, D. L. and G. Henry. 1985. "The Religion and Family Connection: Increasing Dialogue in the Social Sciences." *Journal of Marriage and the Family* 47:369–79.

Waxman, C. 1982. "The Family and the American Jewish Community on the Threshold of the 1980s: An Inventory for Research and Planning." Pp. 163–85, in M. Sklare (ed.), *Understanding American Jewry*. New Brunswick, NJ: Transaction.

Zenner, W. P. 1985. "Jewishness in America: Ascription and Choice." Pp. 117–33 in R. Alba (ed.), *Ethnicity and Race in the U.S.A.* London: Routledge & Kegan Paul.

5

The American Catholic Family: Signs of Cohesion and Polarization

William V. D'Antonio

Introduction

In sociological theory religion traditionally is seen as integrative for the group and/or society but also, often, as a cause of conflict between groups and within and between societies. Furthermore, it has been said to be the source of self-identity for the individual and for adherents to a group. In the context of this paper, religion is seen as traditionally being the vital source of norms and beliefs creating family solidarity, defining appropriate behavior within and between families and with individuals and groups external to the family. In turn, the family is viewed as the cross-generational lifeblood for most religious organizations.

I examine the American Catholic family in light of four organizing themes that variously relate to this general theory:

William V. D'Antonio is Executive Officer of the American Sociological Association. During the 1960s he was a member of the Notre Dame Committee on Population and Family Life, which recommended among other things a change in the Catholic church's teachings on birth control. In 1983 he was coeditor of the book *Families and Religions*. He has been president of the Society for the Scientific Study of Religion. He received his Ph.D. from Michigan State University.

1. The process of modernization/rationalization as it has influenced the Roman Catholic church and Catholic families;[1]

2. Within that broader theme, the struggle between personal autonomy and obedience to hierarchical authority;[2]

3. The tensions caused by control versus support mechanisms in developing normative orientations to behavior; and

4. The implications of demographic change for church teachings and family life.

This examination begins with a review of the formal teachings of the Roman Catholic church on marriage and family, touches on the larger societal context in which they have emerged and been framed, and notes the modifications to the present. This is followed by an examination of the changes in attitudes and behavior of the American Catholic population, with particular attention to the impact of Vatican II, "the pill," and the ensuing controversies over birth control and abortion.

In the concluding section, I summarize the shift that has been and is still taking place within Roman Catholicism, away from dogma and unqualified obedience to hierarchy and toward imagery, story, community, and commitment based on love and friendship. However, as anyone following the national news during 1984 is aware, this shift has been met by a strong ideological countershift from the right, in defense of tradition, hierarchy and obedience, with emerging new patterns of cohesion and polarization within the church as an organization and its Catholic family adherents.[3]

Teachings of the Catholic Church from *Casti Connubii* (1933) to "Educational Guidance in Human Love" (1983)

The Roman Catholic church's teachings on marriage and family were formalized in 1933 in the encyclical *Casti Connubii* (On Christian Marriage) by Pope Pius XI (D'Antonio and Cavanaugh, 1983:150–52). To a large degree the encyclical was a response to the new formulations and major changes being made by Protestant church leaders through the Lambeth Conferences held in England during the previous decade. The conferences had led to a reformulation of Protestant church teachings on contraceptive birth control (allowing such practices). They also paved the way for new policies on divorce and remarriage, the role of sexuality in marriage, and the role of women outside the home.

In *Casti Connubii* the Roman Catholic church reaffirmed the traditional teachings: (a) procreation and rearing of children is the prime purpose of marriage; (b) conjugal love is an important purpose of marriage; (c) family size may be limited for licit reasons; (d) periodic abstinence is the only licit means of birth control for married couples (e) total abstinence from any sexual activity is the rule for the unmarried; masturbation is a serious sin; (f) marriage is a sacrament, indissoluble except through annulment; (g) woman's proper place is in the home.

In retrospect, the major thrust of *Casti Connubii* as a teaching document was its focus on birth control and on the bearing and rearing of children. In this regard the key passage of the encyclical was the following: "Any use whatsoever of matrimony exercised in such a way that the act is deliberately frustrated in its natural power to generate life is an offense against the law of God and nature, and those who indulge in such are branded with the guilt of grave sin." Conjugal love took second place, with pastoral reminders that obedience to God's law required self-discipline and self-sacrifice. It was a document severely defining what was moral and what was sinful behavior. Roman Catholics were expected to obey without question. Whatever the intention the result was a primacy of focus on control rather than on support, based on the claim of an authority rooted in tradition. Sunday sermons, articles in diocesan newspapers, and episcopal letters hammered away at the evil of contraception and the virtue of self-discipline through rhythm or abstinence.

The debates that raged within the Vatican halls during Vatican II, and that have raged since then in Rome and throughout the Catholic world, essentially have been efforts to respond to, elaborate on, and/or free the people from the narrow strictures posed by this encyclical.

Vatican II

We know that Roman Catholics did not always live up to the strictures imposed by *Casti Connubii*, but they accepted them as normative. Ultimately, the confessional was the test of obedience to church authority.[4] That there were problems with the teachings became evident during the deliberations of Vatican II, with the creation of the document on "The Church in the Modern World," and with the creation of the special commission to review the church's teachings on birth control. Rapid population growth was acknowledged as a problem, especially in areas with limited food and industrial resources; conjugal love and a woman's right to sexual satisfaction in marriage were explicitly recognized as legitimate expectations of marriage; and birth control became the focal point of the debate, with "the pill" viewed by progressives as the mechanism to free couples from the bind of *Casti Connubii*. The debate became more and more public, and Pope Paul VI vacillated between tradition and change.

In late July 1968, Pope Paul VI issued *Humanae Vitae* (on Human Life), a complex reaffirmation of the traditional teaching on birth control. The encyclical attempted to be more than that, but the sections on the importance of conjugal love and on the need for responsible parenthood were largely ignored in the press and in the minds of church leaders and the laity. The encyclical received strong negative reaction from a majority of the laity in most parts of the Western world and was criticized also by theologians individually and in groups.[5] In reaffirming the church's traditional opposition to contraceptive birth control, Pope Paul VI overrode the proposal of the majority position of the special birth control commission that had been established by the Vatican to consider the question. This action by Paul VI seems to have done more damage to the formal teaching authority of the Pope than any other action in this century. (Greeley, 1976.)

Recent Elucidations by Pope John Paul II

During the early years of his pontificate, Pope John Paul II issued a number of statements about marriage, sexuality, family life, woman's place, all of them essentially reaffirming the traditional teachings, albeit offering a positive orientation to human sexuality as a central and vital component of the human experience, finding its full and appropriate meaning in the context of marital love. At the same time he has denounced divorce, abortion, premarital sexual relations, and the relinquishment of woman's role as central figure in the home. He has actively discouraged discussion about the possibility of ordaining women to the priesthood. Thus, to a great extent, he has tried to shore up the traditional teaching while giving more positive emphasis to marital sexuality. His method has been one of trying to reinvigorate traditional teachings with a warm personal style.

Nevertheless, there is some movement toward change. To show the direction of change that is subtly taking place, and the emphasis on a variety of facets of family life, we need to explore two documents that were released by the Vatican in December 1983. The *first*, entitled "Educational Guidance in Human Love," is meant to provide guidance on matters relating to sex education. In summary: (a) The document encourages sex education (Pope Pius XI had condemned sex education), which is seen as the primary responsibility of parents, but with recognition that educators can help and should do so by working with parents. (b) Authentic sex can be found only in a love relationship, and that relationship can be authentic only within marriage. In turn, the document affirms that sexual communion in marriage leads to personal maturity. (c) Furthermore, the document states that sex education aims "at the harmonious and integral development of the person toward psychological maturity." (d) Sexual intercourse has dual value—it is central to the intimate communion of love, and it leads to the procreation of children.

The document seems to stress conjugal love over procreation, reversing the traditional teaching, albeit not without some equivocation. Moreover, the document goes on to acknowledge how difficult it is to achieve a high level of integration of sexuality and love.

With regard to masturbation (e), the document finds it to be a personal deficiency, since it is not able to foster new life nor serve the love relationship. (f) Homosexuality is presented as an even graver deficiency, since it prevents people from becoming sexually mature, maturation being a function of the heterosexual relationship. (g) The document makes only limited references to contraception, urging that sex education programs provide a full discussion of the natural methods of fertility control and, at the same time, pointing out what is wrong with other methods of birth control. Essentially any method other than rhythm and its correlates simply does not yield a "responsible marriage, full of love and open to life."

The document continues by urging educators and parents to be patient, not coercive; they should avoid laying a heavy burden of guilt on young people but, at the same time, should not act as if the differences between what the church approves and what secular society approves are less than they are. Most scholars and critics have seen in this document a gradual, slow evolution away from norms that threaten and control behavior and toward more supportive norms for behavior.[6]

The *second* document was entitled "The Charter of the Rights of the Family."[7] Addressed to the governments of the world, this document proposed a list of twelve articles basic to family life. Again, it warns about the worldwide danger from contraception, abortion, and divorce, as well as the evils of the media for propounding sex and violence. However, it goes further in some interesting directions: (a) The State should insure that there is a family wage sufficient to provide a decent way of life. (b) Moreover, the family wage should be such that "mothers should not be obliged to work outside the home to the detriment of family life and especially of the education of the children." (Apparently, a father inside the home would not do the job well enough, nor would the sharing of parental tasks.)

The document also (c) speaks to the plight of migrant workers and urges that they be reunited with their families as soon as possible. Taxes on businesses would help defray the costs of such reunions. (d) Another point raised concerns the right of states (India and China, for example) to tell their citizens how many children they should have. It is the contention of the Vatican that the state has no right to intrude in these matters.

This latter point illustrates the tensions created by church leaders when they try to confront modern problems from a traditional orientation. Given what we know about the impact of population growth on all facets of social life within nations, and increasingly between nations, we may ask about the rationale for asserting that the state has no rights in such matters. After all, the Vatican has asserted that the state should provide health, education and jobs, and transportation subsidies for migrant worker families. What criteria, then, will help us determine the proper relationship between the private actions of citizens and their public consequences? The Vatican position seems to limit moral responsibility to one direction—with what larger social impact?

Two other items need to be mentioned in this review of the church's changing and nonchanging teachings on marriage and family. During 1983 Pope John Paul II reprimanded the U.S. hierarchy for giving consideration to discussions on the possibility of women becoming active ministers in church services, eventually even of being ordained to the priesthood. He continues to be adamantly opposed to the possibility; but his opposition has stirred a rift with some laity and many women's religious orders.[8]

While the Pope also continues his denunciation of divorce, the grounds for annulment within the church have been broadened and expanded by the newly revised code of Canon Law. As a result the number of annulments granted annually has jumped dramatically from 338 in 1968 to some 52,000 in 1983 (Farrell, 1984). Even with regard to annulment, however, the Pope warns of abuse. This adherence to traditional teachings may be one of the factors leading Catholics to question and challenge papal authority in many areas of personal morality, a topic to which we now turn our attention.

The Changing Catholic Laity: The Generation of Vatican II and Beyond

Lenski's classic *The Religious Factor* (1963) provided a benchmark portrait and analysis of Catholic, Protestant, and Jewish values, attitudes, and behaviors regarding religion in general and family life and religion in particular. In the late 1950s, when Lenski was completing his study, Catholics were distinguished from Protestants and Jews by their attitudes toward family size, divorce, birth control, the importance of the extended family, the value of personal autonomy versus obedience, and a host of other variables.

Just about all studies in recent years (Heiss, 1977; Westoff and Jones, 1977; McCarthy, 1979; Roof, 1979; Mosher and Goldscheider, 1984; Lane, 1984) show that the differences between Catholics and Protestants on matters like marriage, divorce, birth control, family size, and abortion either have disappeared or have greatly diminished during the period between 1955 and 1982. Studies (Gallup, 1984) also show that age is a strong predictor of attitude and behavior, with young people being more permissive and older people more traditional and conservative. Gallup and other data further show that young Catholics are more like young Protestants in their beliefs and practices than they are like older Catholics. While it is true that as people age they become more conservative, the trend data relating to matters like birth control, divorce, and abortion show that regardless of age the American public is becoming less conservative over time. Even in matters of religious belief, there has been an erosion. For example, in 1970 (Stark and Glock, 1970) 69 percent of Protestants and 86 percent of Catholics declared Jesus to be the Divine Son of God with no doubt about it; in 1984 Gallup reported that only 60 percent of both Protestants and Catholics continued to hold this belief.

While Americans continue to say that they are believers (95 percent), that religion is very important in their lives (56 percent), and that they have more confidence in religion than in any other social institution of American life (62 percent, only 12 percent of the Gallup sample (1984) fell into the category of highly religiously committed.[9] Moreover, only one in four young people expressed a high degree of confidence in organized religion (Gallup, 1984:64), while "overwhelming proportions of Catholics (82 percent) and Protestants

(74 percent) believe that a person can be a good Christian (or Jew) if he or she doesn't go to church." It is in the context of this background that we examine briefly the particular attitudes of young American Catholics.

There are some 52 million people identified in national polls as Roman Catholic in some degree. Catholic youth (18–29) represent about one-third of that total. Conversion to Roman Catholicism has not been a significant factor in church growth in recent years; there were only some 94,000 converts to Roman Catholicism in the U.S. in 1983 (Cullen, 1984). Hence, whether the church remains stable, grows, or declines is, to a large extent, a function of the activities and attitudes of these young people. The young Hispanic population, for instance, may or may not be a significant source of church growth in future years (Fitzpatrick, 1983), since large numbers are still unchurched.

The Younger Generation: Some Findings Related to Religious Beliefs and Practices

The ties of young Catholics to the institutional church have weakened since the days of Vatican II. In 1980, for example, 79 percent of all Catholics identified themselves as members of the church, but only 75 percent of young Catholics (ages 18–29) did so. By contrast, in 1965, at the end of Vatican II but before *Humanae Vitae* and the general social unrest that swept the nation, fully 90 percent of all Catholics declared themselves to be church members (Gallup, 1984).

Just as telling are the figures for regular church attendance. Fee and associates (1980) report that the percentage of young Catholics attending church regularly fell from 35 percent in 1971 to 29 percent in 1979. By contrast, for Catholics in general, 52 percent were attending church regularly in 1979; but this also was a dramatic drop of 22 points from 1958, before Vatican II and *Humanae Vitae*. The church attendance rate for Protestants has remained steady at about 40 percent during the past twenty years, while for young Protestants the rate dropped to 29 percent, mirroring that of the young Catholics.

Young Catholics reflect the general young adult population in their approval of birth control (95 percent), remarriage for divorced people (89 percent), legal abortion in the case of a serious defect in the fetus (85 percent), euthanasia with patient and family support (66 percent), premarital sex (83 percent), and unmarrieds living together (76 percent). They also mirror the general population in their disapproval of homosexuality (77 percent). (Fee et al., 1980:33–40.)

More than anything else, these data reveal that the Roman Catholic church, as represented by the Vatican, has lost its moral authority as teacher on matters of family and sexual morality. Indeed, only 25 percent agreed (Fee et al., 1980) that "the Pope is infallible when he speaks on matters of faith and morals." In a different study of 10,000 Catholics in sixty parishes, Sweetser (1983) has found that only one in three agreed that "Catholics should always follow the teachings of the Pope and not take it upon themselves to decide differently."

While their obedience to Rome and the Vatican has become problematic, three out of four continue to call themselves Catholics. Fee and colleagues explain this phenomenon as follows: these young people retain strong ties to parish organizations, to local units that encourage and are sympathetic to them, are supportive of them. Moreover, within these parish organizations, their ties are strengthened when they are served by priests who empathize and counsel them and offer "well-planned and articulate sermons" (1980:29). The ties, then, are to local parishes, not to the larger, bureaucratic, institutional church located in Rome, with its rules and teachings that seem remote and abstract at best, but increasingly restrictive, unfeeling, and irrelevant now.

In trying to understand further the continuing influence of religion on their lives, Fee and associates (1980) found that the best predictors of young people's continued affiliation with Roman Catholicism were (a) how joyous mother's approach to religion was, (b) coming from an intact family, and (c) the perception that one's family life was happy. While these variables were predictive of continued affiliation with a particular parish or congregation, they did not necessarily predict doctrinal orthodoxy.

Hoge and Petrillo reported similar findings in a study of college students. Intellectual development and religious knowledge, or their absence, were unimportant for explaining which youth were religiously committed and which not. The important variables were whether or not they liked their religious training; had positive experiences; and enjoyed warm, personal relationships. Moreover, the more highly committed found these with their parents, peers, and church leaders. (1978:373-74.)

To summarize, the data suggest that there are a number of social factors that help explain one's continued affiliation with or one's disaffiliation from organized religion. Retaining ties had little to do with formal church structures; with fundamental beliefs; and with the norms of orthodox, conforming behavior. Rather, they had to do with socialization and social relationships that emphasized support and love rather than control and obedience.

Let us examine further the impact that modernization (rationalization of life processes) has had on Catholic family life.

Modernization and the Rationalization of Life Processes

The rise of bureaucratic organization, with its specific manifestations in large-scale corporations, government at all levels, labor unions, and the military, is very much a function of what Weber considers the movement away from traditional authority structures and toward what he calls legal-rational structures (Weber, 1921). Whether driven by a certain religious ethic or not, the fact is that these structures now dominate our lives. Gradually, they have given new meanings to a number of value orientations, and these value orientations in turn often develop a power to influence behavior in their own right. For purposes of understanding the dramatic changes that have taken place in Roman Catholicism, it is necessary to appreciate how circumstances of the past twenty-five years have encouraged Catholics to become more personally autonomous and less subject to traditional mechanisms of social control.

The creation of the special birth control commission during Vatican II, and the almost simultaneous invention of "the pill," stimulated independent thinking in the church among laity and clergy that was unknown in earlier eras. These events occurred during the same decade as the student movement, the civil rights movement, and the women's liberation movement.

In a society that places so much emphasis on the individual and her/his achievements, on freedom to do what you want when you want, and on equality of opportunity, it should not be surprising that eventually these values would begin to have their impact on family and religion. Remember, during the last twenty-five to thirty years, the majority of American Catholics were moving into the third, fourth, and fifth generation of life in the United States and were completing more and more years of formal education.

From the point of view of the individual Catholic, the confluence of structural opportunity, the invention of the pill, more formal education, the experience of Vatican II created a new situation, one for which the hierarchy was not prepared. Moreover, the family in its traditional Catholic structure and values was hard put to survive. The years since the encyclical *Humanae Vitae*

(1968) have led to a questioning of more and more traditional teachings, with the Vatican trying to find new ways to express them.

While the U.S. Conference of Bishops formally adheres to these teachings, they have given prime attention in recent years to major social issues like hunger, nuclear war, the war in Central America, underdevelopment, and the economy. Their major attention has been on matters of social morality.

One of the most dramatic actions in 1983, following the Peace Pastoral of 1982, was an effort by Joseph Cardinal Bernardin, Archbishop of Chicago and now probably the most influential American Catholic prelate, to join the personal and social elements of morality. In a speech at Fordham University on December 6, 1983, Bernardin used the metaphor of the "seamless garment" to propose that Catholics should see the sacredness of life and the struggle to protect life as sacred not only in an antiabortion stand but also, and at least as importantly, in their stand against poverty—in their commitment to insure that fetuses brought to term have a fair chance of a decent life—that poverty is an evil to be just as forcefully opposed, that Catholics have an obligation to share their wealth, that they should oppose capital punishment as another form of abortion or degradation of the sacred nature of life, and finally that they must oppose war as the ultimate form of degradation. In his own words, Bernardin states:

> The purpose of proposing a consistent ethic of life is to argue that success on any one of the issues threatening life requires a concern for the broader attitude in society about respect for human life. . . . Consistency means we cannot have it both ways: We cannot urge a compassionate society and vigorous public policy to protect the rights of the unborn and then argue that compassion and significant public programs on behalf of the needy undermine the moral fibre of the society or are beyond the proper scope of governmental responsibility. (Bernardin, 1983:6–7.)

I find this statement interesting for many reasons, including the way that it promises to affect Roman Catholics and perhaps others in this society. It has been criticized by the conservative Catholics who see abortion as a single issue not to be confounded by other issues. Bernardin's "seamless garment" of life becomes a divisive issue for them; it confounds their efforts and weakens their position. Conservative Catholics generally oppose abortion but support capital punishment and a strong military. Many also oppose large-scale welfare aid but support Reagan's military policies in Central America, which Bernardin and his supporters oppose. (O'Connor, 1984:19.)

At the same time, Bernardin's position attracts the attention of the liberal/progressive Catholics, who are found on all sides of the abortion issue (it should be noted that there is a formal organization of Catholics for a Free Choice; the organization was formed in 1975, publishes literature and makes a strong claim for legitimacy within the formal church structure [1981]). In the larger context of the "seamless garment," the value of the sacredness of life takes on a new meaning, and progressives may give it strong support. It seems a more rational approach to life than does the traditional antiabortion position. (Alegretti, 1984:14.)

Therefore, just as Cardinal Bernardin's effort suggests a new cleavage with the conservative, traditional Catholics, it provides a basis for a new consensus, at least a partial integration for the progressive Catholics who already have taken strong positions on peace and poverty. Thus, Bernardin's proposal also may provide a new basis for self-identity with the formal church organization. At the least, it provides a linkage.

To summarize this point, traditional teachings on marriage and family still are adhered to only by a *minority* of American Catholics. Clearly, however, the fact that an overwhelming percentage of Roman Catholics support birth control and the right of divorced Catholics to remarry shows that there is a selective "fit" between the Church's formal teachings and the practices of laity that crosses ideological lines. Conservatives are most loyal on abortion, woman's place in the home, premarital sexual abstinence, and homosexuality. Their integration with the Catholic bishops and with the Vatican is threatened not so much by teachings on personal morality but by those on social morality, such as the Peace Pastoral, *The Seamless Garment*, and the new document on the American economy.

For the progressives the positions are almost reversed. Thus, the conditions for an emerging polarization are becoming ever more apparent. For the conservatives God's laws are known and need only be applied; for the progressives life is a developmental and unfolding process, in which the individual and the society are inextricably intertwined in the creation of a history. The move toward polarization reflects in many ways the struggle going on in the larger society, as evidenced by the creationism versus evolution battle and the prayer in school and abortion law controversies. It appears that such variables as the degree of salience of issues and commitment to the organized church are likely to affect the struggle in the months and years ahead.

It is in this turbulent setting, then, that we briefly examine the final theme of the present paper: changing demographic patterns.

Religious Teachings and the Life Course: Possible New Directions Facing Catholics

Sullivan (1983) and Riley (1983), among others, have directed our attention to the demographic revolution that has taken place in the past fifty years, and its implications for the family. We are at a new and exciting period in family history. For the first time large numbers of young couples find themselves with two children of their own—while their parents and their grandparents are still alive. People now struggle to develop and/or maintain social networks across four generations. With increasing longevity, five generations are very probable for a considerable portion of the population. There are no records from history to provide guides for attitudes and behavior.

A host of research questions has been raised by Sullivan, Riley and others about the implications for people at all stages of the life course of the newly emerging extended-family networks, which also increasingly include ex-in-laws and children of several marriages. One logical extension of Cardinal Bernardin's "seamless garment" approach is for religious leaders and groups to help sponsor some of this research and to seek the evidence from research as a basis for policy planning. Whether this is the kind of issue that might draw both progressives and conservatives together is not at all clear at this time. What is clear, however, is that there are data from the 1980 census (McKenney et al., 1983) suggesting that some religious/ethnic groups may be more attentive to the needs of the elderly than the general American population. Are religion and ethnicity—or just ethnicity, or some combination of variables—responsible for the apparent continuing strength of the extended family through three and four generations in at least some sectors of the American population? More research is needed before we can begin to answer these questions—research that may have important policy implications for all those concerned with the changing nature of the family throughout the life course.

In contemplating the kinds of research questions that might be posed, the following formulations offered by Fee and colleagues (1980:239–40) may extend across generations as new ways to think about old relationships:

> First, we contend on the basis of the evidence that religious behavior is a "primary group" phenomenon, influenced most powerfully by one's intimate relationships in the family of origin, and family of procreation, as well as in the local

religious community. A papal encyclical on human sexuality or social justice has much less religious impact than does the quality of the Sunday sermon, the dedication of one's spouse, and the memories of one's childhood religious experiences that have been encoded in one's personal stories of God. For most people, the farther away a religious factor is from the place where they live (physically as well as psychologically), the less important it is likely to be.

Secondly, we also contend that the images, pictures, and stories which exist in the religious imagination provide much of the raw power of religion in people's lives. Furthermore, these facets of religious imagination are responsible for the tenacity with which many young people maintain their Catholic commitment despite inconsistencies in their propositional beliefs and their frustrations and dissatisfactions with the ecclesiastical institution. Theological systems, catechetical formulations, and creedal propositions are not unimportant. But, when it comes to how often a person prays, or how a person reacts to death, or how committed he or she is to the search for social justice, or how he or she relates to a marriage partner, religious images—stories of God—are far more important.

Modernization has made long life possible for most people; it has brought with it new emphasis on personal autonomy rather than obedience, and it also seems to have given rise to norms and patterns of social relationships that emphasize social support rather than social control. Of course, modernization also has made possible the great demographic transformation of American society. We must ask, however, about the impact these factors have across three, four, and even five generations of family. What kinds of new residential living arrangements may be forthcoming?

If love is a prime value of contemporary family life, how might research help us understand the conditions under which love is or is not fostered— within the nuclear family and across three, four, and five generations? Is there a relationship between nuclear family size and the kinds of social networks that can be developed and maintained across generations? Do church teachings foster, impede, or have little impact on love in the family?

How adequate are the current teachings of the church to meet the new situation? Is a hierarchical structure with norms that still are perceived to give primacy to law and control likely to offer effective options to families? Do these new teachings—for example, Bernardin's idea of a consistent life ethic expressed in the metaphor of the "seamless garment"—contain the seeds of the church's transformation to modernity, as some would aver, or of its destruction, as others fear?

Conclusion

In this paper we have examined the impact of modernization on the American Catholic family. The modernization process reached its culmination during the past twenty-five years; in convening Vatican II in 1960, Pope John XXIII said that it was time to open windows in the church, and open them he did. One of the most obvious consequences has been the degree to which personal autonomy has come to replace obedience as a prime value upon which to make decisions affecting matters of personal and social morality. Thus, while some ignore the Vatican's teachings on birth control, abortion, and divorce, others ignore it on poverty, capital punishment, war, and American capitalism. The gap is widening between the formal teachings as espoused by the popes in their encyclical letters and the actual attitudes and practices of Catholics as revealed in a succession of studies over the past twenty-five years.

While the gap is widening in general, it also is creating polarization between conservatives (laity and clergy), who profess to follow the traditional teachings, and progressives (laity and some clergy), who either focus on the spirit of the teachings or ignore them. On family matters the hierarchy itself has changed and altered its focus of attention. Having lost the battle over "the pill" and birth control, it has come to focus its attention on abortion. These public controversies, involving as they do most intimate aspects of human behavior, have led to growing challenge to papal authority and, by extension, to the authority of the bishops as teachers, as shown in the challenge to the Peace Pastoral and now to the pastoral on the American economy. What goes largely unsaid but not unnoticed is that, by issuing these pastorals as documents for discussion and revision by the laity, the bishops are acknowledging in effect the legitimacy of modern legal-rational thought over traditional authority.

One consequence is the gradual deinstitutionalization of Roman Catholic religiosity. Catholics young and old increasingly act like Protestants; they continue to identify themselves as Catholics while rejecting, or holding as doubtful and not binding, many, if not most, of the formal teachings and distancing themselves from the authority of the institution itself.

Thus, the shift is away from dogma and toward imagery; away from traditional authority emanating from Rome or the local bishop's seat and toward the *gemeinschaft*-like relations of local parish life; away from threats of excommunication and punitive control and toward pastoral support, love, and friendship. This shift is occurring even as we begin to glimpse the implications of the great demographic transformation that has taken place and that not only guarantees longer lives for people but challenges us all—including church leaders—to reexamine our beliefs and practices regarding family size and social networks across generations.

While religion still makes a difference among some Catholics in predicting attitudes, values, and behavior, that difference has grown smaller over time, so that now it is significant for only a small minority of the population. Also, only about 15 percent of Catholics are highly involved and committed to their religion. Like other Americans their major commitment is to making a living and living comfortably in what is essentially a secular setting. Perhaps this fact, more than any other, reduces the probability that the current polarization within the Catholic church over matters of personal and social morality touching the family will erupt into conflict causing schism.

Notes

1. For a detailed analysis of the modernization process and its relationship to religion and family life, see Hargrove, 1983. Weber, of course, was most concerned with the negative impact of modernization—especially bureaucratic organization—on the human condition (e.g., see Weber, 1921:212–54, 926–38). The focus of my concern is its impact on the traditional bureaucratic organization of the Vatican, and on the Catholic laity.

2. For an earlier elaboration on the movement toward greater commitment to personal autonomy among Roman Catholics, see D'Antonio, 1980.

3. The present paper was written and presented in March 1984, more than a year after the promulgation of the Bishops' Peace Pastoral and several months before the divisive public debate on abortion and "Religion and Politics," which itself was followed by the bishops' draft statement on the economy. This in turn was challenged by a counter-statement from a group of Catholic business and professional leaders. These events have helped to sharpen the lines of division and cohesion within and between the ranks of the laity and the hierarchy. Perhaps the most important fact about all this is that it could not have been imagined a generation ago.

4. Johnson and Weigert (1980) have provided an unusual insight into the way the themes of this paper have been reflected in the functioning of the confessional for both clergy and laity. Rather than finding a monolithic clergy defending traditional teachings on sex and procreation in the confessional, they were able to identify three types, with one defending tradition while, at the opposite end, a pastoral type emphasized individual conscience and love.

5. For example, see *The Birth Control Debate* (Hoyt, 1968), especially the third section, "Responses to *Humanae Vitae*." While not all responses were negative, the divisiveness of the encyclical was revealed by the range and sources of responses.

6. For a friendly critique of "Educational Guidance in Human Love," see Burtchaell, 1983; and see also the editorial, "Papal Shift in Sex Statement," 1983. The document is summarized in the *Washington Post*, December 2, 1983, pages A1 and A26.

7. See Hebblethwaite (1983) for a summary and critique of "Charter of the Rights of the Family."

8. For a review of the range and extent of the feminist movement within the Roman Catholic church, see "Women Doing Theology" (Beifus, 1984), a special feature in the *National Catholic Reporter* containing ten essays on feminism and religion.

9. For example, see *The Connecticut Mutual Life Report on American Values in the 80's: The Impact of Belief* (1981). The study was based on a national sample of Americans aged fourteen and older, via telephone interviews using random digit dialing. Indeed, it does show that religion makes a difference: people who are deeply committed religiously are more likely than the less religious to favor the traditional family, wife as homemaker, and to oppose abortion. Perhaps more telling, however, is the finding that the great majority of Americans do not have a high level of commitment to religion. A special Guttman scale of questions on religious commitment found that only 26 percent of the sample had a high level of commitment, with 50 percent having a low level and 24 percent having a moderate level. The researchers also found that only 15 percent of Roman Catholics—who constituted 28 percent of the sample—said they were highly committed to religion. Thus, these data lend further support to Fee and colleagues' (1980) findings that the majority of young Catholics lack commitment to the traditional institutional church.

Bibliography

Alegretti, J. 1984. "Critics of 'Consistent Life Ethic' Exhibit Disdain for U.S. Bishops." *National Catholic Reporter* (April 6):14–19.

Beifus, J. T. (Ed.) 1984. "Women Doing Theology" (special feature of 10 essays on feminism and religion). *National Catholic Reporter* (April 13).

Bellah, R. N. 1976. "The New Religious Consciousness and the Crisis in Modernity." In C. Y. Glock and R. N. Bellah (eds.), *The New Religious Consciousness*. Berkeley, CA: University of California Press.

Bellah, R. N. 1978. "Religion and Legitimation in the American Republic." *Society* 15 (May/June):16–23.

Bendix, R. 1960. *Max Weber, An Intellectual Portrait*. New York: Doubleday.

Bernardin, J. Cardinal. 1983. *The Seamless Garment*. Kansas City, MO: National Catholic Reporter Publishing Co. (This special publication contains two speeches by Joseph Cardinal Bernardin.)

"Bernardin Views Prolife Issues as 'Seamless Garment.' " 1983. *The Washington Post* (December 10):B6.

Burtchaell, J. T. 1983. "Vatican Sex Document 'on the Whole a Positive' Step." *National Catholic Reporter* (December 16):1, 24.

Catholics for a Free Choice. 1981. *Catholic Women and Abortion*. Washington, D.C. (2008 17th St., NW): Catholics for a Free Choice.

Cherlin, A. and F. F. Furstenberg, Jr. 1982. *The Shape of the American Family in the Year 2000*. Washington, D.C.: Trend Analysis Program, Social Research Services, American Council of Life Insurance.

Connecticut Mutual Life. 1981. *Report on American Values in the 80's: The Impact of Belief.* Hartford, CT (140 Garden St., 06511): Connecticut Mutual Life Insurance Co.

Cullen, P. 1984. (Column devoted to Catholic population growth.) *Our Sunday Visitor* (February 26):5.

D'Antonio, W. V. 1980. "The Family and Religion: Exploring a Changing Relationship." *Journal for the Scientific Study of Religion* 19(2):89–104.

D'Antonio, W. V. and J. Aldous (eds.) 1983. *Families and Religions: Conflict and Change in Modern Society.* Beverly Hills, CA: Sage.

D'Antonio, W. V. and M. Cavanaugh. 1983. "Roman Catholicism and the Family." In W. V. D'Antonio and J. Aldous (eds.), *Families and Religions: Conflict and Change in Modern Society.* Beverly Hills, CA: Sage.

deTocqueville, A. 1954. *Democracy in America* (2 vols). New York: Vintage Books.

Farrell, M. J. 1984. "Annulments: 15,000 % Increase in 15 Years." *National Catholic Reporter* (November 16):1, 9.

Fee, J., A. M. Greeley, W. C. McCready, and T. Sullivan. 1980. *Young Catholics.* New York: W. H. Sadlier.

Fitzpatrick, J. 1983. "Faith and Stability Among Hispanic Families: The Role of Religion in Cultural Transition." In W. V. D'Antonio and J. Aldous (eds.), *Families and Religions: Conflict and Change in Modern Society.* Beverly Hills, CA: Sage.

Gallup, G. 1984. *Religion in America.* Princeton, NJ: Princeton Religious Research Center.

Gerth, H. H. and C. W. Mills. 1958. *From Max Weber: Essays in Sociology.* New York: Oxford University Press.

Greeley, A. M. 1976. *Catholic Schools in a Declining Church.* Kansas City, MO: Sheed and Ward.

Hargrove, B. 1983. "The Church, the Family, and the Modernization Process." In W. V. D'Antonio and J. Aldous (eds.), *Families and Religions: Conflict and Change in Modern Society.* Beverly Hills, CA: Sage.

Hebblethwaite, P. 1983. "Vatican Family Rights Charter: 'No Surprises.' " *National Catholic Reporter* (December 16):8.

Heiss, J. 1977. "Social Traits and Family Attitudes in the United States." *International Journal of Sociology of the Family* 7 (July/December): 209–25.

Hoge, D. R. and G. H. Petrillo. 1978. "Determinants of Church Participation and Attitudes Among High School Youth." *Journal for the Scientific Study of Religion* 17(4):359–79.

Hoyt, R. G. (ed.). 1968. *The Birth Control Debate.* Kansas City, MO: National Catholic Reporter Publishing Co.

Johnson, C. L. and A. J. Weigert. 1980. "Frames in Confession: The Social Construction of Sexual Sin." *Journal for the Scientific Study of Religion* 19(4):368–81.

Lane, R. 1984. "Catholic Attitudes Toward Abortion: Are They Softening?" Paper delivered at the annual meeting of the Association for the Sociology of Religion, San Antonio, TX (August).

Lenski, G. 1963. *The Religious Factor.* Garden City, NY: Doubleday.

Lipset, S. M. and W. Schneider. 1983. *The Confidence Gap: Business, Labor and Government in the Public Mind.* New York: The Free Press.

McCarthy, J. 1979. "Religious Commitment, Affiliation and Marriage Dissolution." In R. Wuthnow (ed.), *The Religious Dimension.* New York: Academic Press.

McKenney, N., A. Tella, and M. Levin. 1983. "A Sociodemographic Profile of Italian Americans Based on the 1980 U.S. Census." Paper delivered at the conference, "The Italian Experience in the United States," at Columbia University, New York (October).

Mosher, W. D. and C. Goldscheider. 1984. "Contraceptive Patterns of Religious and Racial Groups in the United States, 1955-76: Covergence and Distinctiveness." *Studies in Family Planning* 15 (May/June):101-11.

O'Connor, R. J. 1984. "Nuke, Abortion Link Called 'Grotesque.' " *National Catholic Reporter* (April 6):19.

"Papal Shift in Sex Statement" (Editorial). 1983. *National Catholic Reporter* (December 16):12.

Pierson, E. and W. V. D'Antonio. 1974. *Female and Male: Dimensions of Human Sexuality*. Philadelphia: J. B. Lippincott.

Riley, M. 1983. "The Family in an Aging Society." *Journal of Family Issues* 4 (September): 439-54.

Roof, W. C. 1979. "Socioeconomic Differentials Among White Socioreligious Groups in the United States." *Social Forces* 58 (September):280-89.

Stark, R. and C. Y. Glock. 1970. *American Piety: The Nature of Religious Commitment*. Berkeley, CA: University of California Press (pages 22-39).

Sullivan. T. 1983. "Family Morality and Family Mortality: Speculations on the Demographic Transition." In W. V. D'Antonio and J. Aldous (eds.), *Families and Religions: Conflict and Change in Modern Society*. Beverly Hills, CA: Sage.

Sweetser, T. P. 1983. *Successful Parishes: How They Meet the Challenge of Change*. Minneapolis: Winston Press.

Thomas, D. L., V. Gecas, A. Weigert, and E. Rooney. 1974. *Family Socialization and the Adolescent*. Boston: Lexington.

Weber, M. 1921. *Economy and Society* (3 vols.) New York: Bedminster.

Westoff, C. 1979. "The Blending of Catholic Reproductive Behavior." In R. Wuthnow (ed.), *The Religious Dimension*. New York: Academic Press.

Westoff, C. and E. F. Jones. 1977. "The Secularization of U.S. Catholic Birth Control Practices." *Family Planning Perspectives* 9:203.

Williams, R. 1955. *American Society*. New York: Alfred Knopf.

" 'Yes' to Consistent Life Ethic." (Discussion of "seamless garment" talk of Joseph Cardinal Bernardin, given at Fordham University, December 6, 1983.) *National Catholic Reporter* (December 16):12.

6

Four C's of the Mormon Family: Chastity, Conjugality, Children, and Chauvinism

Tim B. Heaton

From its inception, Mormonism has been characterized by a blend of traditional American culture mixed with unique, sometimes even radical, elements. Such was the case with the nineteenth-century Mormon family system which combined aspects of Puritan family morality with a unique theology of family continuity in the hereafter and a radical form of marriage—polygamy. During the twentieth century, the Mormon family has been subjected to many of the same social forces that impact the nation. Parallels between Mormon and national trends might lead to the mistaken impression that the Mormon family is no longer distinctive. Perhaps it would appear that Mormons are running several years behind the rest of the country on a course that will eventually lead to convergence.

The thesis of this paper is that, despite being influenced by broader social forces, the Mormon family remains distinctive in many ways; that distinctive elements are integrated into a family system; and that this family system will continue to influence individual and organizational behavior in Mormondom

Tim B. Heaton is Associate Professor of Sociology and researcher with the Family and Demographic Research Institute, Brigham Young University. His research focuses on the demographics of the family life course. Dr. Heaton is author of numerous articles in professional journals. He received his Ph.D. from the University of Wisconsin. A former version of this chapter was published in *Dialogue*.

for years to come. The first section documents four areas of contemporary Mormon family distinctiveness. The second discusses the interrelatedness of these areas as they form the basis for a family system by considering the theological, demographic, and social bases for these aspects of the family system. The third section speculates about the future of this family system.

The Four C's

Chastity

Studies of adolescents and young adults demonstrate the conservative nature of Mormon premarital sexual behavior. In a comparison of Mormons at an intermountain university with several other college campuses, Christensen (1976) found that Mormon men and women have lower approval of and exposure to premarital coitus than other students with the exception of a Midwestern Mennonite college. These findings are corroborated in surveys of college students done by Smith (1974), who found low percentages of Mormons reporting nonmarital coitus when compared with Catholics, Protestants, or those with no religious preference. Similar conclusions apply to a small subset of adolescent Mormons in the 1971 National Survey of Young Women. Tabulations from this national sample (in possession of the author) indicate that 15 percent of Mormon teenagers had engaged in premarital intercourse compared to 26 percent for the entire sample. Obviously, not all Mormon youth conform to the Church's moral code, but evidence consistently indicates that premarital chastity is more common among Mormons than is generally the case.

These differentials in premarital sexual intercourse are confirmed in a more recent survey of high school students. Miller and associates (1985) surveyed students in several high schools in three Western states. Seventeen percent of the Mormon students reported premarital sexual experience, compared with 48 percent of Catholics, 51 percent of those with no religion, and 67 percent of Protestants. In a multiple regression analysis, religious affiliation was second only to church attendance in predicting sexual experience, with Mormons being significantly lower than other groups.

The high teenage birthrate in Utah appears to contradict claims that premarital sex is low among Mormons. When teenage abortions are taken into account to estimate teenage pregnancy, however, our conclusion is sustained

TABLE 1. PERCENTAGES WHO ARE PREMARITAL VIRGINS BY RELIGION
AND FREQUENCY OF CHURCH ATTENDANCE

Religion	Men Attendance			Women Attendance		
	Often	Never	Difference	Often	Never	Difference
Catholic	47	17	30	48	22	26
Protestant	63	27	36	55	37	18
Mormon	85	37	48	91	48	43

Source: Smith, 1974

(Chadwick, 1986; Smith, 1986). The low teenage pregnancy rate in Utah is consistent with survey reports of premarital chastity.

The religious influence on sexual behavior becomes even more evident when we compare active and inactive Mormons. In the above-mentioned 1971 National Survey of Young Women, only 3 percent of the active Mormons had experienced premarital intercourse, compared to 23 percent for the inactive group. Indeed, the inactive group was not appreciably different from the national average. Data collected by Smith (1974) yield a similar conclusion. Moreover, the differential in sexual experience between active and inactive Mormons is greater than that for Protestants or Catholics (see Table 1). The percentage point difference between most and least active is 30 for Catholic men, 36 for Protestant men, and 48 for Mormon men. Comparable figures for women are 26 for Catholics, 18 for Protestants and 43 for Mormons. Not only does membership in the Mormon church result in more conservative sexual behavior, but level of participation has a greater effect on sexual behavior than is generally the case.

To be sure, Mormons have been influenced by the sexual revolution of the '60s. Moreover, there is some evidence that Utahns are more conservative than those living elsewhere (Mauss, 1976). Nevertheless, the most active Mormons appear to have been more insulated from social trends. According to the surveys done by Smith (1974; 1976), between 1950 and 1972 premarital virginity changed little for Mormons who attended church regularly (from 95 to 98 percent for men, and from 96 to 98 percent for women); but there was a liberalizing tendency among those who did not attend church (from 63 to 52 percent for men, and from 85 to 62 percent for women). To say that Mormons simply follow national trends on a delayed basis does not accurately portray these differences between attending and nonattending Mormons.

Institutional control over sexual behavior establishes the church's influence over family life (Christensen, 1976). Sexual behavior is thus regulated by

TABLE 2. MARRIAGE PATTERNS OF MORMONS COMPARED WITH OTHER RELIGIOUS GROUPS

	Sex	Catholic	Protestant	Mormon	None
% over age 30 who	Male	88.6	94.9	97.5	81.0
have ever married	Female	91.2	95.9	97.2	86.7
% of ever married	Male	19.8	26.4	14.3	39.2
who have divorced	Female	23.1	30.9	18.8	44.7
% of ever divorced	Male	49.5	62.2	66.6	48.4
who are remarried	Female	35.2	53.0	53.0	37.3

Note: Nonwhites are excluded from the data.
Source: Heaton and Goodman (1985)

the moral codes of the church. Once legitimacy is conceded to the church to regulate sexual motivation, the stage is set for further religious influence on patterns of marriage, child-rearing, and sex role allocation. In short, there is convincing evidence that Mormons are less likely to engage in premarital sexual activity; and we argue that this willingness to submit to the moral authority of the church in nonmarital sexual behavior is a key component of the distinctive family life-style.

Conjugality

By conjugality, we refer to the tendency for Mormons to be married. In comparison with Catholics, Protestants, and persons with no religious preference, Mormons have a higher percentage of persons over age 30 who have ever married than any other religious group (see Table 2).

Data from the Canadian census also indicate that Mormons have an above average proclivity toward marriage: 74.2 percent have been married compared to a national figure of 72.2 percent. Since most people marry, differences in the percentage ever married may seem small. The relative likelihood of never marrying makes the comparison more dramatic. Catholics over 30 are more than three times more likely than Mormons to have never married. Protestants are about twice as likely, and those with no religion at least four times more likely to have never married than Mormons.

The marriage norm also shows up when we look at divorce rates (see Table 2). Mormons are less divorce prone than Catholics or Protestants, and are far below the unchurched in divorce. The low propensity to divorce has often gone unnoticed because Utah's divorce rate is above the national average. More recent analysis of census data points to possible explanations for the high state divorce rate (Goodman and Heaton, 1986). First, Utah has liberal divorce laws. Second, the married population of Utah is concentrated in the younger ages when the risk of divorce is greater. This accentuates the year-to-year divorce rate, even if the percentage who will ever get divorced is low. Finally, the high rate of remarriage in Utah creates a large group susceptible to multiple divorces which will increase the number of divorces, but not the percentage ever divorced.

Religious involvement is closely related to divorce. Data reported by Heaton and Goodman (1985) indicate that of Mormons who attend church regularly, 10.2 percent of men and 15.2 percent of women have experienced divorce compared to 21.6 percent of men and 26.3 percent of women who do not attend regularly. Of course, it is not clear from these percentages whether people who attend church don't get divorced or divorced people don't attend church. Temple marriage, however, gives some indication of the couples' religious commitment at the initiation of the marriage. Among ever married men, of those married in the temple only 5.4 percent have been divorced compared to 27.8 percent of the nontemple group. Among women, the comparable figures are 6.5 for temple marriages, and 32.7 for nontemple marriages. (Heaton and Goodman, 1985.) In other words, nontemple marriages run a six times higher risk of divorce than temple marriages.

Even when Mormons do get divorced, they are more likely to remarry than is generally the case (see Table 2). This high rate of remarriage attests to the high value placed on conjugality.

Contrary to popular opinion, the Mormon church does not contain an overabundance of single people. In fact, it may well be the strong emphasis placed on marriage that accentuates the plight of the singles. High rates of marriage, low divorce, and high remarriage after divorce clearly point to marriage as the normative status. Given the large group who conform to this norm, the unmarried form a minority group within the church.

Children

The most widely noted demographic characteristic of the Mormon family is its high fertility. Even in the early Utah period when the nation as a whole had a high birthrate, Mormon fertility was above the national average (Mineau et al., 1979). Above-average fertility has been maintained throughout the twentieth century, at least in Utah (Thornton, 1979). Although Utah fertility (often accepted as a barometer of Mormon fertility) has followed the national trend, the two lines do not run parallel. Indeed, the smallest difference between Utah and national birthrates in the recent past occurred in the mid-sixties. During the seventies the Utah rate increased while the national rate was declining, creating an even wider gap (Heaton and Calkins, 1983). Since 1980 the Utah rate has dropped substantially, but it still remains the highest state in the nation. In 1984, Utah's crude birthrate was 23.7, 50 percent higher than the national rate. Likewise, a national sample of Mormons shows their number of children ever born to be approximately 50 percent higher than other religious groups, even after excluding nonwhites. (Heaton and Goodman, 1985.) Thus, the pattern of high fertility has continued into the present. Fertility expectations of Utah's Mormon high school students also imply that differentials will persist into the future (Toney et al., 1985).

It is important to note that high Mormon fertility is not simply a result of reluctance to use birth control. In fact, information from a small sample of Mormons participating in a national study indicates that Mormons are just as likely as the national population to use modern methods of birth control at some point in their life (Heaton and Calkins, 1983). For Mormons, however, contraceptive use is often delayed until after child-rearing has begun, and frequency of use is lowered in order to obtain the larger desired family size. For lack of a better term, this tendency might be called positive pronatalism based on a desire for more children as contrasted with negative pronatalism based on ethical restrictions against the use of contraceptives.

Despite the clear documentation of a high fertility rate, surprisingly little empirical analysis has been done on the determinants of Mormon fertility. One recent analysis of a national sample of Mormons demonstrates two interesting aspects of their fertility (Heaton, 1986). First, no single variable is sufficient to explain why some Mormons have larger families. Marital commitment to a pronatalist ideology, association with a Mormon reference group, and socialization within a pronatalist context each share in the explanation. In combination, these factors can account for larger Mormon family size: Mormons who do not fit within these categories do not have fertility rates any higher than the national average. Second, the demographic determinants of fertility may affect Mormons in a different way than is generally the case. In national studies, higher socioeconomic status, as measured by income and education, often has a negative relationship with fertility rates. Among Mormons, however, family income and wife's education both have a positive relationship with fertility (Heaton, 1986; Thomas, 1979). Thus, Mormonism alters the socio-economic basis for fertility decision making.

As with premarital sexual experience, religious involvement has a stronger relationship with fertility among Mormons than is the case for other religious groups (Heaton and Goodman, 1985). Moreover, socioeconomic variables have a different effect on fertility of highly involved Mormons than is the case for less involved Mormons (Heaton, 1986). These differences add to the evidence that religiosity plays an important role in Mormon family size.

Qualitative analysis of Mormons with large families also points to the importance of religious belief (Bahr et al., 1982). In their interviews with women having at least seven children, Bahr and associates found a predominance of religious explanations for their behavior. Among the reasons given were: (1) each family has a predestined number of children; (2) having large families conforms to the counsel of church leaders; (3) interference in the reproductive process is wrong; and (4) spirits in heaven should have the opportunity of coming to good Mormon families. Although the reasons vary, they all reflect a religious orientation to fertility decisions.

In short, Mormons take seriously the biblical injunction to multiply and replenish the earth. The most religious and those with greater resources (that is, education and income) tend to have the largest families. Fertility is imbued with religious meaning. If any single demographic trait distinguishes Mormon families it is high fertility.

Chauvinism

Two elements of chauvinism have received some attention in empirical research, namely: the division of labor between husband and wife, and attribution of authority in the home. A division of labor is not necessarily chauvinistic; but in contemporary society it often turns out that way. Labor force participation provides control over economic resources, prestige and opportunities for advancement which are often lacking in the homemaking role.

Although earlier reviews of the literature on Mormon families do not find consistent evidence that Mormons are more chauvinistic than other groups (Thomas, 1983; Campbell and Campbell, 1977), more recent evidence shows greater consistency. Table 3 compares responses from Mormons selected from

TABLE 3. MORMON AND NATIONAL OPINIONS ON SEX ROLES (PERCENTAGE)

	Mormon	National
A preschool child is likely to suffer if his or her mother works.		
disagree	17.0	32.2
agree or not sure	83.0	67.8
It is more important for a wife to help her husband's career than to have one herself.		
disagree	26.3	41.4
agree or not sure	73.7	58.6

a random statewide survey of Utahns with a national sample in the General Social Survey (conducted by the National Opinion Research Center at the University of Chicago). In each case the Mormon sample is about twice as likely to take a more traditional position in favor of the motherhood role than is the national sample. According to Mormons, the mother should be the homemaker and the father should be the breadwinner.

In comparing role definitions (who should perform the task) and role enactment (who does perform the role), Mormons have different patterns than other religious groups (Bahr and Chadwick, 1984). Mormons have less egalitarian definitions of who should take the roles of provider, housekeeper, caring for children, socializing children and home repair then do other religious groups. When it comes to role enactment, Mormons are still less egalitarian in housekeeping, caring for children and socializing children; but the gap in role enactment is much smaller than is the case for role definition (Bahr, 1982).

Comparison of Mormon female employment rates challenges the ideology of a gender-based division of labor. Using Utah as a surrogate for Mormons, census data indicate that Utah women are much less distinctive in their employment patterns than they once were (Bahr, 1979). Closer inspection of these data, however, indicates that much of the convergence between Utah and national female employment rates is a result of greater increases in part-time employment on the part of Utah women. Even though the 1980 census indicates that female employment rates in Utah are virtually identical to the national rate, Utah's married women with children under age six are less likely to work than their national counterparts, and those who do work are more likely to work part-time (Heaton and Parkinson, 1985). A recent survey of Mormon women in the United States indicates a similar pattern of low employment when children are young, but high employment otherwise (Goodman and

Heaton, 1986). In short, Mormon women do work; but during the years when children are young, they devote less time to employment than do most women in the United States.

When the issue of chauvinism is stated more bluntly in terms of who has power to make the final decision on these roles, Mormon women have less power than women in other religious groups (Bahr and Bahr, 1977). In fact, Mormon men are reported to have more authority in decision making, even in the roles where women are expected to take more of the responsibility. In short, the traditional Mormon position on sex roles is more a matter of stated attitude, or perhaps even ideology, than one of actual behavior. Nevertheless, Mormons are more traditional when it comes to tasks such as taking care of the house and children; but men are attributed with more power in decision making when there is disagreement.

Consistent with the findings cited above, Mormons who attend church regularly are less inclined to have egalitarian views of the household division of labor than those who seldom attend church (Bahr and Chadwick, 1984). An average of 7 percent of the active Mormons give egalitarian definitions to the roles of provider, housekeeper, and caring for children, compared to 13 percent of the group who seldom attends church. Likewise, 9 percent of the actives and 14 percent of the inactives report egalitarian performance of these roles.

Information from a younger age group suggests that these trends may continue into the future. In a survey of college students from four universities, Mormons scored higher on a macho scale than Catholics, mainline Protestants, or persons with no religious preference; and the Mormon scores were comparable to fundamentalist Protestants (Brinkerhoff and Mackie, 1984). Using age as a surrogate for trends, there is no clear-cut trend toward egalitarian marital relationships (Albrecht et al., 1979). Thus, a traditional view of appropriate sex roles appears to be an inherent part of the Mormon family life-style.

The Mormon Family System

The four aspects of the Mormon family we have documented above are not isolated behavior patterns. Rather they are linked together by common theological underpinnings, by demographic interdependence, and by a social structure which integrates them into a particular life-style.

Theology

Mormon doctrine posits both a preexistence in which all persons live in spirit form before being born on earth, and a postmortal existence where all persons will continue to maintain an individual identity. The Mormon conception of heaven includes various levels or degrees of glory, the greatest of which is reserved for married couples who will continue their role as parents by creating spirit children. In temples, Mormons are married for time and eternity, thus initiating families which will persist in the hereafter. Families play a central role by (1) providing a mechanism for bringing premortal spirits to earth; (2) creating a training and proving ground for those who will acquire the role of parents in the postmortal existence; and (3) actually establishing eternal marriage bonds. Specific ethical injunctions regarding family life are often derived from this theological perspective (Smith, 1986; Christopherson, 1954). For example, McConkie (1966) discusses Mormon theology with many scriptural references, under such topics as preexistence, spirit children, heaven, celestial kingdom, sexual immorality, and celestial marriage. Talmage (1968) in his discussion of temples emphasizes the importance of the family both in this world and the world to come, especially his discussion in chapters 3 and 4.

Premarital and extramarital sexual relations are anathema because they threaten the integrity of the marital bond, and violate God's plan for bringing premortal spirits to earth (see McConkie, 1966, under *adultery*). Procreation, the theological term for reproduction, is viewed as a God-given responsibility which should occur within the family unit (Kimball, 1981). Indeed, exhortations to remain chaste became more prominent between 1951 and 1979 (Rytting and Rytting, 1982). Nonmarital sex is a serious sin, surpassed only by murder and denying a witness from the Holy Ghost. The Doctrine and Covenants instructs that unrepentant adulterers should be excommunicated (D&C 42:24–26). Although reasons for excommunication are confidential, common perception is that adultery is the single most common cause of excommunication. Bishops are instructed to interview the youth (ages 12–18) on a yearly basis and their conformity to the "law of chastity" is to be one of the topics discussed. In short, this aspect of theology is emphasized by organizational policy. Although Mormonism does not condemn all nonreproductive coitus, it is expected that those who engage in the pleasures of sex should be willing to accept the responsibilities of parenthood. Thus, marriage is the legitimate arena for sexual expression. Teenagers and adults are taught to abide by the church's moral code, and violations of this code can jeopardize one's membership in the church.

Obviously, marriage is essential to the entire plan. Indeed, only those who marry in a Mormon temple are eligible for the highest degree of celestial glory. The small minority who never have the chance to marry are consoled with the promise that they will have that opportunity in the postmortal existence, and are counseled to develop personal attributes that will help them perform well when the time arrives. Those who avoid opportunities to marry are advised that they are not in conformity with God's plan. Divorce is permitted, but not advised. Since ideal marriages are intended to survive the eternities, couples are encouraged to work out their problems rather than resort to divorce (Kimball, 1981).

Having and rearing children is a fundamental part of the process. In so doing, parents participate with God in furthering the development of premortal spirits, and gain experiences in preparation for their own role as eternal parents. The family is the divine organization designed for the purpose of reproduction and socialization of children. Any other institution is an inferior substitute, and couples who avoid having children are missing a key aspect of their own religious and spiritual development.

The importance of parenthood was reaffirmed in a recent talk by Ezra Taft Benson, the President of the LDS Church (1987). Husbands and wives are given the role of "co-creators" who "should eagerly and prayerfully invite children into their homes" (p. 3). They are instructed not to postpone childbearing or curtail family size for "personal or selfish reasons" (p. 5). Material goods or convenience cannot compare with "a righteous posterity" (p. 4). The greatest joys and blessings in life are derived from family roles.

The logical link between importance of the family and male authority is not well developed, but male authority is an integrated aspect of the theology. Men are designated to be the spiritual leaders and heads of Mormon households (Kimball, 1981). If deemed worthy, they are given the priesthood, which is defined as the authority to act in God's name. This priesthood can be used not only to direct the affairs of the church, but also to govern the household. Husbands are designated as the providers and wives as the homemakers. Of course, wives and mothers can seek spiritual guidance from God through prayer and can help with the provider role when necessary. Men are also encouraged to support their wives in homemaking tasks. Still, the ideal home has a father who is both spiritual leader and provider for the family. A mother's God-ordained role is "to conceive, to bear, to nourish, to love, and to train" (Benson, 1987:5). Women are taught that a primary expression of their faith is a willingness to acknowledge the role of priesthood authority in their lives (Relief Society Course of Study, 1986). In short, each of the aspects of the family we described in section one is embedded in a theology of the family.

One aspect of the theology which is not widely discussed is more egalitarian in its implications. When husband and wife are married in the temple, they jointly enter into an "order of the Priesthood" called the New and Everlasting Covenant of Marriage (McConkie, 1967). Identical blessings are promised to husband and wife, including thrones, kingdoms, principalities, powers, and dominions (D&C 132:19). Neither has access to these powers and privileges without the other, and neither is promised more than the other. Such a marriage suggests unity, interdependence, shared priesthood authority as parents, and cooperation, rather than hierarchy and male dominance. Greater emphasis on these aspects of the theology might fit more comfortably with current tendencies in many families.

Demographic Linkages

Restricting sexual activity within the marriage bonds has the dual effect of promoting near universal marriage and eliminating ambiguity regarding parentage. Sexual gratification can be a powerful motivational force. The requirement of marriage to legitimate such activity is a strong inducement to marry without undue delays, and to remain married. For those who do conform to the sexual moral code, parents and children know that they belong to each other and that there are no competitors for family membership outside the nuclear unit. Thus, the sexual code of conduct solidifies the notion of the family as an eternal unit.

Getting married and having children commits people to some form of family life. Conformity to the family norm creates a sense of fellowship with the church; and the church teachings and programs designed for families become directly relevant, thus linking individuals to the church as an institution. At the same time, reproduction and religious socialization of children provides a major source of growth in the organization. In this fashion, interdependence between the two institutions of church and family is established.

Rearing children also creates increased demands on the roles of provider and homemaker. As additional children are born, the economic demands grow, as do the necessary household and child care tasks. Children place an unremitting responsibility on parents. Specialization of roles becomes a common solution to the increased demand. At the same time, organization of the family unit becomes more difficult, and the need for authority and leadership increases. In many cases, the designation of a leader, a provider, and a homemaker facilitates management of the whole operation.

Social Structure

Conformity to the appropriate family behaviors is deeply ingrained into the social and normative structure. Those who violate the sexual code of conduct or who intentionally avoid marriage or having children are deviants. The wedding ring, station wagon, basement, and diaper pail (or Pampers box) are standard artifacts in Mormon culture.

The strong sense of community which develops in many Mormon congregations reinforces a family-centered life-style. Moreover, distinctive family traits help to reinforce the community bond. The demands introduced by marriage and children forms the basis for common interest, leisure activities, time schedules, and other similar elements of life-style. Children's friendships often form the basis for adult friendships, as does interchange of child care. Social networks have a large influence on involvement in church activities (Cornwall, 1985), and the shared exigencies of family life promote formation of social networks.

Programs of the church are designed to support this family-centered social structure. Family home evening and home teaching reinforce the ideal family which includes children and is headed by a man. The Primary, Young Men, and Young Women programs are designed to help in socializing children. The Relief Society is a women's organization that promotes the role of homemaker. Ironically, even though many congregations have recently changed the time of Relief Society meetings to accommodate working women, the lesson topics in these meetings have much more to do with maintaining a house and raising children than with jobs and working.

The development of the Correlation Program of the church in the 1960s and '70s created an even closer correspondence between families and the church as an organization. This program shifted more of the decision-making power to men and reduced the autonomy of the women's organization. (Cornwall, 1983.) It established a pipeline of authority from the president of the church down through the organizational hierarchy to the husband as head of the household. Children and wives were linked to the church through their fathers and husbands. Thus, the church programs, and the husband's role in these programs, further legitimizes his authority.

In sum, there are multiple bases of support for the particularistic aspects of the Mormon family. Theology, demographic requisites, and social structure mutually promote marriage and children. The church promotes family life, and the family reciprocates by socializing children to become active participants in the church. Thus, the interdependence between church and family is solidified.

Prospects for the Future

To this point, we have claimed the existence of distinctive traits of the Mormon family, and have discussed the theological, demographic, and social bases of support for these traits. The reader might get the false impression that the family is a very static institution. Clearly, the family is not impervious to change. A 50 percent decrease in fertility since the turn of the century, coupled with equally large increases in divorce and female labor force participation belie any static image of the Mormon family.

The ideology of the LDS church has been remarkably flexible in accommodating social change (Leone, 1979). The same central doctrine of eternal marriage was used to sanction polygamy in the nineteenth century as is currently used to promote family patterns described above. As the church has spread to more culturally diverse areas and as new social trends have been adopted by the LDS membership, policies and practices have modified accordingly. (Hansen, 1981.) Stress with the Mormon family system also provides impetus for social change (Christensen, 1972).

At the same time, any direct confrontation with the family ideology, at least since the dramatic exception of polygamy, have been ill-fated. The recent demise of the Equal Rights Amendment illustrates the point well. The church took opposition to the amendment, not because of opposition to economic equality for women, but because of the perceived threat the amendment poses to the family. Another case in point is President Hinckley's (1985) statement on the use of artificial insemination by single women. The procedure in question would allow more women to achieve one characteristic of the family, but other characteristics would be circumvented. Thus, the procedure is in contradiction to the family system and is unacceptable. In fact, the statements on reproductive medicine (Bush, 1985), homosexuality, and women holding the priesthood can all be seen as efforts by the church leaders to defend the family.

Recent changes in family size, divorce, and female labor force participation have not been a result of direct ideological confrontation. Rather, other considerations have come into play. Couples can now have three, four, or five children instead of eight, nine or ten and still feel they are multiplying and replenishing the earth. Justification for not having more is based on economic and emotional well-being of other family members, not on a rejection of the church's theology of the family. Likewise, women consider working as a means to supplement the income or to utilize talents, not as usurping the provider role of the husband. Divorce is a realization that not all marriages created on earth work out, not as a rejection of the eternal family ideal. In this fashion, behavior changes without directly confronting theological positions.

Other such changes may possibly occur in the future. Family size may decline even further without eliminating the Mormon fertility differential or destroying the notion that Mormons have a family-centered church. As medical technology advances, attitudes toward specific procedures affecting reproduction will possibly change without threatening fundamental doctrines of the church (Bush, 1985). Modification in the sanctions applied to violators of the sexual moral code may occur without changing the code itself. More allowance may be made to incorporate single adults into the programs of the church without denying the ultimate importance of marriage. Husbands and wives may be told to jointly arrive at important decisions without changing policies regarding the priesthood. Greater emphasis could be placed on the joint holding of priesthood responsibilities by husbands and wives with temple marriages. This theology could be used to encourage egalitarian rather than authoritarian marriage relationships.

Not only is change possible, it is very probable. The stresses and strains engendered by societal change in family structure must be dealt with. Working women, reconstituted families, and singles are each growing segments of the church membership who do not fit well within the existing structure. The reorientation toward appropriate sex roles will continue within the church. As they have done in the past, most Mormons will adjust to these changes while maintaining their sense of uniqueness. In fact, unwillingness to change may be more detrimental in the long run than open acceptance of change, as was the case with those who refused to accept the cessation of polygamy. At the same time, attempts to induce change through direct confrontation with the core ideology of the Mormon family will fall on deaf ears. Those who see change as a means to preserve the core values by alleviating existing stresses and strains will have more success. To observe, understand, and even participate in change in the Mormon family is the challenge before us.

Bibliography

Albrecht, S. L., H. M. Bahr, and B. A. Chadwick. 1979. "Changing Family and Sex Roles: An Assessment of Age Differences." *Journal of Marriage and the Family* 41 (1):41–50.

Bahr, H. M. 1982. "Religious Contrasts in Family Role Definitions and Performance: Utah Mormons, Catholics, Protestants, and Others." *Journal for the Scientific Study of Religion* 21 (3):200–217.

Bahr, H. M. 1979. "The Declining Distinctiveness of Utah's Working Women." *Brigham Young University Studies* 19 (4): 525–43.

Bahr, H. M. and B. A. Chadwick. 1984. "Religion and Family in Middle America and Mormondom: Secularization, Role Stereotypes, and Change." Paper presented at the annual conference of Family and Demographic Research Institute on Religion and the Family, March 1984, Brigham Young University.

Bahr, H. M., S. J. Condie, and K. L. Goodman. 1982. *Life in Large Families*. Washington, D.C.: University Press of America, Inc.

Bahr, S. J. and H. M. Bahr. 1977. "Religion and Family Roles: A Comparison of Catholic, Mormon, and Protestant Families." Pp. 45–61 in P. R. Kunz (ed.), *The Mormon Family*. Provo, UT: Brigham Young University Family Research Center.

Benson, E. T. 1987. "To the Mothers in Zion." Address given at a Fireside for Parents, 22 February, Salt Lake City, Utah.

Brinkerhoff, M. B. and M. M. MacKie. 1984. "Religious Denominations' Impact upon Gender Attitudes: Some Methodological Implications." *Review of Religious Research* 25 (4):365–78.

Bush, L. E. 1985. "Ethical Issues in Reproductive Medicine: A Mormon Perspective." *Dialogue* 18 (2):41–66.

Campbell, B. L. and E. E. Campbell. 1981. "The Mormon Family." Pp. 379–416 in C. H. Mindel and R. W. Habenstein (eds.), *Ethnic Families in America*. New York: Elsevier.

Chadwick, B. A. 1986. "Teenage Pregnancy and Out-of-wedlock Births." Pp. 23–26 in S. J. Bahr, T. B. Heaton, T. K. Martin (eds.), *Utah in Demographic Perspective*. Salt Lake City: Signature Books.

Christensen, H. T. 1972. "Stress Points in Mormon Family Culture." *Dialogue* 7 (4):20–34.

Christensen, H. T. 1976. "Mormon Sexuality in Cross-cultural Perspective." *Dialogue* 10 (2):62–75.

Christensen, V. A. 1954. "The Relationship Between Church Doctrine and the Family Among the Mormons." *International Review of History and Political Science* 11 (2):88–102.

Cornwall, M. 1983. "Women and the Church: An Organizational Analysis." Paper presented at the annual meetings of the Pacific Sociological Association, San Jose, California, April.

Cornwall, M. 1985. "Personal Communities: The Social and Normative Basis of Religion." Unpublished dissertation, Department of Sociology, University of Minnesota.

Goodman, K. L. and T. B. Heaton. 1986. "LDS Church Members in the U.S. and Canada." *AMCAP Journal* 12 (#1, 1986b):88–107.

Goodman, K. L. and T. B. Heaton. 1986. "Divorce." Pp. 121–44 in S. J. Bahr, T. B. Heaton, and T. K. Martin, (eds.), *Utah in Demographic Perspective*. Salt Lake City: Signature Books.

Hansen, K. J. 1981. *Mormonism and the American Experience*. Chicago: University of Chicago Press.

Heaton, T. B. 1986. "How Does Religion Influence Fertility?: The Case of Mormons." *Journal for the Scientific Study of Religion* 25 (2):248–58.

Heaton, T. B. and S. Calkins. 1983. "Family Size and Contraceptive Use Among Mormons: 1965-75." *Review of Religious Research* 25 (2):103–14.

Heaton, T. B. and K. L. Goodman. 1985. "Religions and Family Formation." *Review of Religious Research* 26 (4):343–59.

Heaton, T. B. and B. Parkinson. 1985. "Every Mom a Supermom: A Portrait of Utah's Amazing Mothers." Unpublished manuscript.

Hinckley, G. B. 1985. "Ten Gifts From the Lord." *Ensign* 15 (Nov.):86–89.

Kimball. S. W. 1981. *Marriage*. Salt Lake City: Deseret Book Company.

Leone, M. P. 1979. *Roots of Modern Mormonism*. Cambridge, MA: Harvard University Press.

Mauss, A. L. 1976. "Shall the Youth of Zion Falter? Mormon Youth and Sex, a Two-City Comparison." *Dialogue* 10 (2):82–84.

McConkie, B. R. 1966. *Mormon Doctrine*. Salt Lake City: Bookcraft.

McConkie, B. R. 1967. "The Eternal Family Concept." Devotional address given at the Second Annual Priesthood Genealogical Research Seminar, Brigham Young University, June 1967. Copy in author's possession.

Miller, B. C., J. K. McCoy, T. D. Olsen, and C. M. Wallace. 1985. "Background and Contextual Factors in Relation to Adolescent Sexual Attitudes and Behavior." Unpublished manuscript.

Mineau, G. P., L. L. Beau and M. Skolnick. 1979. "Mormon Demographic History II: The Family Life Cycle and Natural Fertility." *Population Studies* 33 (3):429–46.

Relief Society Course of Study. 1986. *Learn of Me*. Salt Lake City: The Church of Jesus Christ of Latter-day Saints.

Rytting, M. and A. Rytting. 1982. "Exhortations for Chastity: A Content Analysis of Church Literature." *Sunstone* 7 (2):15–21.

Smith, J. E. 1986. "A Familistic Religion in a Modern Society." Chapter 11 in K. Davis (ed.), *Comparative Studies of Marital Change*. New York: Russell Sage. (Forthcoming.)

Smith, W. E. 1974. *Social Disorganization and Deviant Behavior*. Provo, UT: Brigham Young University Press.

Smith, W. E. 1976. "Mormon Sex Standards on College Campuses, or Deal us Out of the Sexual Revolution!" *Dialogue* 10 (2):76–81.

Talmage, J. E. 1968. *The House of the Lord*. Salt Lake City: Deseret Book Company.

The Doctrine and Covenants. 1982. Section 132:19. Published by The Church of Jesus Christ of Latter-day Saints, Salt Lake City, Utah.

Thomas, D. L. 1979. "Correlates of Religious Commitment in Mormon Families: Some Preliminary Findings and a Challenge." Presented at the Fourteenth Annual Virginia F. Cutler Lecture, Brigham Young University.

Thomas, D. L. 1983. "Family in the Mormon Experience." Pp. 267–88 in W. V. D'Antonio and J. Aldous (eds.), *Families and Religions: Conflict and Change in Modern Society*. Beverly Hills, CA: Sage.

Thornton, A. 1979. "Religion and Fertility: The Case of Mormonism." *Journal of Marriage and the Family* 41:131–42.

Toney, M. B., B. Golesorkhi and W. F. Stinner. 1985. "Residence Exposure and Fertility Expectations of Young Mormon and Non-Mormon Women in Utah." *Journal of Marriage and the Family* 47 (2):459–65.

7

Contemporary Challenges for Religion and the Family from a Protestant Woman's Point of View

Letha Dawson Scanzoni

Introduction

If we're going to talk about challenges, we must first understand what we mean by the term. For some people, the first thing that comes to mind is the notion that both religion and family life are in grave danger today. Those concerned individuals are prone to react defensively to preserve a way of life that is being undermined by hostile forces. Those in far-right religious and political movements, for example, equate challenges with perceived assaults or attacks on the institution of the family. Thus, they issue battle calls against amorphous enemies who are given such labels as "secular humanism," "amoral feminism," or "godless liberalism," which they claim are bent on destroying the family and keeping God out of our schools.

Letha Dawson Scanzoni is a full-time professional writer with a special focus on the interface between religion and social issues. Her most recent book, *Sexuality*, was commissioned by Westminster Press for its "Choices: Guides for Today's Woman" series. Among her other books are *Sex Is a Parent Affair* (on sex education); *All We're Meant to Be: Biblical Feminism for Today* (with Nancy Hardesty); *Is the Homosexual My Neighbor? Another Christian View* (with Virginia Ramey Mollenkott); and a college textbook, *Men, Women, and Change: A Sociology of Marriage and Family* (with John Scanzoni). Her articles have appeared in a wide variety of publications, and she is a frequent lecturer for conferences, colleges, and theological seminaries.

Other persons think of challenges with a different set of meanings in mind. Rather than thinking in terms of assaults and battles, they think of challenges as opportunities to deal with questions, solve problems, and confront life's complexities creatively, wisely, and sensitively. A challenge viewed this way is a summons to a contest in which skills and endurance are put to the test. This meaning of the word *challenge* was demonstrated in a recent Winter Olympics as outstanding athletes raced down the snow-packed mountain slopes or performed with dazzling talent on ice skates.

I have this second meaning in mind in calling attention to some of the challenges relating to religious and family life today. I'm not thinking so much right now of such challenges as the nuclear war threat, or concerns about pollution, energy, and other environmental issues, or societal problems such as unemployment, the state of the economy, poverty, crime, and so on—all of which certainly do affect and challenge families and call for a religious response as well.

But here I want instead to focus on certain concepts, questions, ideas, and trends that are currently challenging both religious and familial presuppositions. In particular, let us look at five basic issues that need to be grappled with: *identity, gender roles, power, autonomy and attachment*, and *stability, order, and change*.

Identity

First, in considering the question of identity or definition, we find ourselves asking: "What is religion?" "What is a family?" Answers taken for granted will no longer do. As James Dittes has pointed out, scholars attempting to measure religiosity along a religious-secular dimension have debated "whether the dimension should be conceptualized as primarily a matter of *believing* or *belonging* or *behavior* or *beholding*" (1969:67). For many persons today, believing and beholding—in other words, a personal, individualistic, even mystical inner experience with God—may be considered more important than church affiliation or traditionally defined religious behaviors. J. Russell Hale's tenfold classification of nonchurchgoers showed that many who are outside organized, institutional religion have a privatized faith and may be what Hale calls "crypto-believers, secretly believing without belonging" (1980:8).

Similarly, many persons consider themselves to be members of a family—even though they do not fit the membership criteria of traditional definitions of the family as an institution. Recently I was asked to serve as consultant for a publisher of religious books, evaluating manuscripts on family-related topics. I noticed a major typo in one. The author wanted to say something about the nuclear family, and the letters *n* and *u* were inadvertently reversed in the typing, making it come out "the unclear family." I thought, "That's an interesting way to sum up the state of affairs today! Definitions of the family are anything but clear."

The 1980 White House Conference on Families, through changing its name from a conference on *the* family, recognized the diversity of families today. Of course, that recognition was surrounded by heated and bitter controversy. Conservatives were interested in promoting and preserving one specific form of family as the ideal—a family composed of a breadwinner father, a nonemployed homemaker/caretaker mother, and children. Even the Census Bureau's definition of a family as consisting of persons related by blood, marriage, or adoption and residing together wasn't wholly satisfactory to some conservatives. Why? Because such a definition still recognized single-parent households, persons remarried after divorce, blended families, voluntarily child-free marriages, dual-earner households requiring day care for children, and so on. And even more troubling to traditionalists has been the recognition that some persons who are *not* related by blood, marriage, or adoption nevertheless consider themselves to be in a *chosen and loving relationship with others whom they consider family* and with whom they share a sense of responsibility and commitment—for example, a gay male couple or a lesbian couple and any children brought into the relationship, or a cohabitating couple, including elderly widows and widowers who have chosen to live together and retain pensions or other benefits that would be lost by remarriage.

As theologian Rosemary Ruether points out, "conservative rhetoric about the 'biblical view of the family' lacks any sense of socioeconomic history of the family over the past three or four thousand years." For those voicing such rhetoric, Ruether writes, "It is as if the Bible endorses a version of the late Victorian, Anglo-Saxon patriarchal family as the model of family life proposed in the Scriptures." (1983:399.)

I agree with her assessment. Conservatives who are fearful of the deterioration of the family need to be reassured that the Bible portrays a much broader idea of the term *family* than they have assumed. Instead of speaking about families in the more narrow sense of the nuclear family unit, the scriptures speak of *households* consisting of all persons living together under one roof—whether spouses, parents, children, grandparents, children's spouses, other relatives, some unrelated persons, and servants, or some combination of these. The psalmist was thinking of such an arrangement when writing Psalm 68:6: "God sets the lonely in families" (New International Version) or "gives the lonely a home to live in" (Today's English Version).

In addition to family relationships "in nature" and "in law," to use anthropologist David Schneider's (1968) terms for biological and legal ties, the Bible recognizes *quasi-kin* relationships—relationships in which persons choose to be committed to one another in some way analogous to the caring, rights, and responsibilities of close kinship. One example is the story of Jonathan and David, each loving the other "as his own soul" and desirous of forming a bond together that went even beyond death and that included descendants, as the two men pledged. David's grief over Jonathan's death illustrates the pain of losing someone who is considered a chosen kin—a grief as deep as or deeper than that experienced at the death of an actual family member. Many years later, King David remembered his pledge to Jonathan and took into his palace the crippled son of Jonathan and *his* son, Jonathan's grandson (1 Samuel 18:1-5; 20:14-18, 41-42; 2 Samuel 1:25-26; 2 Samuel 9). Friends can be the functional equivalent of family (Lindsey, 1981).

Another biblical example of persons who pledged a family-like bond to one another is that of Ruth and Naomi. Both women had been widowed, and Ruth determined to go back with Naomi, her mother-in-law, rather than stay among her own people to find a husband. Her pledge of commitment to Naomi is now used in wedding ceremonies.

> "Do not urge me to go back and desert you," Ruth answered. "Where you go, I will go, and where you stay, I will stay. Your people shall be my people, and your God my God. Where you die, I will die, and there I will be buried. I swear a solemn oath before the Lord your God; nothing but death shall divide us." (Ruth 1:16-18, New English Bible.)

I mention these examples because we may be able to take as the bottom line the matter of *intentionality, commitment to bonding,* or *covenant* in trying to think through a theology of families that fits with the sociological realities of today's world.

The challenge of definition means taking into account real lives and loves of real human beings. We are being challenged to deal with *relationships*—not abstractions. And the questions may produce some cognitive dissonance if we prefer the simplicity of traditional answers. I think of the pastor who told me he had recently performed one of the most beautiful wedding ceremonies of his career. The bride and groom wrote their own vows—after having lived together for eleven years! Were they a family before that time or only after the ceremony? David and Vera Mace (1981) reported on a Quaker conference a few years ago in which the phenomenon of unmarried couples living together was discussed. A decision was made to avoid such terminology as "living in sin" and to consider using the term, "unregistered marriages" for such arrangements. Conference participants referred to similar arrangements years ago when Quaker couples were denied legal marriages; they also discussed what were termed "clandestine marriages," which were recognized as valid by the Roman Catholic church until the sixteenth-century Council of Trent.

But one could argue that people have the option of legal marriage today, that there must be boundaries in defining families—for reasons of property divisions and inheritance and for issues concerning the legitimacy of children, if nothing else—and that therefore cohabiting couples should enter legal marriage before society can recognize their union as valid. Such an argument still would not cover some situations, such as certain elderly widows and widowers who report that remarriage would mean the loss of pension or other benefits, a situation that was even more problematic before Social Security regulations on the remarriage of widowed persons were changed in 1979.

And there is another category of persons for whom legalized marriage is not an option at present—those homosexual men and women who wish to maintain an ongoing, monogamous same-sex relationship. Some in the cross-denominational gay Christian movement speak of their relationships as "covenantal unions" and have religious ceremonies as a public declaration of their love.

Again, might we not consider whether the *concept of covenant* could provide a way of meeting challenges in deciding what constitutes a family relationship today? Why should an expanded definition of family, which makes room for many more categories of persons who are longing for closeness, be considered threatening and harmful to family life? The biblical idea of covenant emphasizes a *relationship of continuity*—a shared history of memories, an ongoing relationship in the present, and an anticipation of a shared future. It emphasizes commitment, not capriciousness. The model is the covenant between God and the people of God and illustrates what the ideal ingredients of a marriage relationship might be. Notice those ideals in the following passage from scripture. As described by the prophet Hosea (2:19–20, Jerusalem Bible), God says,

> I will betroth you to myself forever,
> betroth you with integrity and justice,
> with tenderness and love;
> I will betroth you to myself with faithfulness,
> and you will come to know Yahweh.

Gender Roles

Moving now from the challenge of *defining* families, we need to look at a second challenge relating to religion and family life today: the challenge arising from the changing concepts of masculinity and femininity and the whole question of gender roles. Probably no other issue has had such a major impact in contemporary religious circles and families.

In recent years, we've been moving from fixed, assigned roles for women and men to a new freedom of individual choice based on interests and abilities without regard to a person's sex. Because of this, we're seeing an extreme polarization among Christians today—an ideological clash over the respective purpose and place of women and men.

Some Christians say that God created women and men for different roles from the very beginning and that even to question this assertion is to rebel against God. Other Christians say that both males and females were created in God's image and identically commissioned to be responsible for both family life and the world at large. In this view, roles are not God-designed or ordained. Rather, over the ages, *societies* assigned certain attributes and activities to persons with female bodies, and other activities and attributes to persons with male bodies. Thus, "femininity" and "masculinity" are *social constructs*, which many people find limiting. Mennonite biblical scholar Willard Swartley (1983) speaks of these two opposing interpretations of what the scriptures say as the "hierarchical" view and the "liberationist" view.

Swartley sums up the hierarchical view's main points in this way: "(1) Women are expected to be subordinate to men—in the home, church, and society. (2) Especially in the home, husbands are to exercise headship over wives, with roles prescribed in accord with this pattern. (3) Within the church, women are restricted from the preaching ministry and from teaching men.

Other forms of leadership are to be exercised under the authority and leadership of men." (Swartley, 1983:151.)

In contrast, let me read to you the liberationist view of the Evangelical
Women's Caucus:

> Evangelical Women's Caucus, International, is a nonprofit organization of
> evangelical Christians who believe that the Bible, when properly understood,
> supports the fundamental equality of the sexes. We find that the Scriptures ask
> both women and men to submit to one another out of reverence for Christ and
> enjoin all Christians, female and male, to exercise their gifts in response to God's
> call upon their lives.
>
> We see much injustice toward women in our society. The church especially
> has encouraged men to prideful domination and women to irresponsible passiv-
> ity. Our purpose, therefore, is to present God's teaching on female-male equality
> to the whole body of Christ's church and to "call both women and men to mutual
> submission and active discipleship." (From EWC brochure. Evangelical Women's
> Caucus, P.O. Box 209, Hadley, New York 12835.)

On the other side is the ultra-conservative organization founded by fundamentalist Beverly LaHaye, called Concerned Women for America, which, she
states, is devoted to saving the traditional American family from total destruction by preventing passage of the Equal Rights Amendment (as described in the
organization's 1984 mass mailing).

Some current religious teachings on gender roles have reached incredible
extremes—perhaps as part of a backlash against the gains made through the
women's movement. Another conservative writer, for example, suggests that
women were created to show men, by their submission to men, what it means
to submit to God. She writes:

> Each time a baby girl is born, a new incarnate picture of the human soul
> and of the human race is begun. She will visibly demonstrate the choices each
> soul, male or female, is permitted to make during a lifetime on this earth. She
> will grow either to become like the submitted and adorned Bride of Christ or like
> the harlot of Babylon. Without a beloved, incarnate model of submission and
> loyalty, the males of the world will not understand how to submit themselves to
> the mastery of God. (Miles, 1975:151.)

Other extreme teachings that have had widespread acceptance in Protestant circles, including theological seminaries, may be found in a massive, heavily
documented book called *Man and Woman in Christ*, by Stephen Clark (1980),
a Roman Catholic charismatic leader. Clark believes role differences are built

into the human race so that men are "more accomplishment-oriented" and women are more "helping-oriented," suited to a "care-service role" in contrast to the man's "governor-protector-provider role" (1980:440–41). At the same time, he warns men not to spend too much time in the company of women and discourages best-friend relationships between a husband and wife. Why? Because spending time with women will make a man "soft" and less manly, according to Clark. It will "feminize" the man. This reasoning surprised me, in view of Clark's insistence on innate differences between the sexes. Why would he then worry about men's "catching" femininity by exposure to women? Clark offers his own definition of a "feminized male." He is a man who behaves in ways "more appropriate to women," a man who "will place much higher emphasis and attention on how he feels and how other people feel. He will be much more gentle and handle situations in a 'soft' way." (Clark, 1980:636–49.) (When I reviewed Clark's book for the *Christian Century* [11 March, 1981:272], I commented, "In a world of competitiveness, muscle-flexing, violence, and threats of nuclear destruction, God give us more such men!") Not surprisingly, Clark calls for sex-segregated roles in the home, with men responsible for raising sons and women responsible for raising daughters.

Clark asserts that the Genesis statement that it was not good for the man to be alone did not mean that the man needed a woman for companionship. Rather, what was needed was human society, and that meant a woman was needed if the man was to be able to increase and multiply. "The man needed a wife with whom he could beget children," asserts Clark. He further comments on the Genesis creation story, saying that "one reason that animals will not do as a partner for man is their inadequacy for reproductive purposes. . . . Genesis does not describe woman as a companion to man but as a helper to him." He states that this phrase "is not a romantic evaluation of woman. Rather, it describes woman as 'useful' to man." (1980:21–22.)

Clark doesn't stop there. He goes on to claim that the male is the *ideal or representative human being*. "It is the man who is called 'Man' or 'Human' and not the woman," he writes. He says that what we meet at the end of the creation story is "Human and his wife." Clark's 753-page book is subtitled *An Examination of the Roles of Men and Women in Light of Scripture and the Social Sciences* and is taken very seriously in conservative circles as a sophisticated statement of gender-role rigidity, female subordination, and male dominance.

Within *mainline* Protestantism, gender-role debates have centered more around ordination and church leadership responsibilities, inclusive language in worship service, and discussions about the nature of God as *both* male and female and *neither* male nor female—with feminist theology raising new questions about the Motherhood as well as Fatherhood of God and calling for an end to exclusive usage of male pronouns when referring to the Deity.

I have concentrated primarily, however, on some of the teachings currently promoted within conservative Protestant circles because they have spilled over into mainline Protestant churches as well. The influence of such teachings has spread through the "electronic church" evangelists who zealously proclaim their messages to television audiences, through policy decisions promoted by conservative factions within denominations, and through books on family life by conservative authors that can now be found on book racks in drugstores, supermarkets, and department stores everywhere and that often appear to be the only family books conveniently available which claim to provide a Christian emphasis and biblical teachings on family life. Many mainline Protestant churches also show films produced by conservative Protestant groups and hold workshops such as Marabel Morgan's Total Woman seminars. Protestant Christians, like Catholic Christians, are eager for easily accessible materials that will help them in their marriages and child-rearing responsibilities. Conservative groups may be filling a vacuum that many mainline Protestant groups may have overlooked. Fundamentalists are zealously and aggressively spreading their particular outlooks on family life, based on restrictive interpretations of scripture, and are labeling them "God's order" or "God's plan" for marriage and family living.

At the same time, there are those Protestant Christians who integrate scripture, personal experience, and reasoning in such a way that a "theology of personhood" is called for—one that emphasizes the gifts, talents, dignity, and worth of each individual without regard to gender and that encourages both women and men to be all they can possibly be, developing both the instrumental or task-oriented side of life and the expressive or person-oriented side. Realizing that qualities once earmarked either masculine or feminine are really *human* qualities open to all persons, many deeply religious men and women want an egalitarian marriage relationship and are freely sharing child-rearing without insisting on adherence to inflexible gender roles either for themselves or their children. They see such behaviors as fully consistent with their Christian faith and their understanding of scripture, which they see as teaching justice, compassion, love, and freedom from all that would oppress.

Nevertheless, the loudest voices being heard in today's society are often those of the conservatives who insist on gender-role segregation and rigid, predetermined behavioral scripts for females and males. Innovation, negotiation, freedom to choose how one wants to pattern one's own marriage and family life are considered signs of moral decay. If we listen closely to the voices of many religious and political conservatives, we will see they are clamoring for the revival of an ancient idea—which brings us to the third in our list of contemporary challenges for religion and families: the issue of power.

Power

The ancient idea many conservatives would like to see implemented, especially in relationships between the sexes, is the notion that the universe has been arranged hierarchically and to act contrary to that arrangement is to violate nature's plan or the will of God. I have written about this elsewhere (Scanzoni, 1984) and can only briefly sum up some of these ideas here.

The idea originated not in the Bible but in some of the teachings of Plato and Aristotle and then spread through the Neoplatonists of the third century and their followers. It came to be known as the "scale of nature" or "the great chain of being" (Lovejoy, 1936). The image was that of a great chain stretching from heaven to earth, with everything ever created (from orders of angels to the tiniest particle of matter) having its proper place in the chain. This chain provided a picture of the cosmic order of things, the way the world was arranged. And society was expected to *reflect* that order.

During the Middle Ages and Renaissance periods, the "great chain of being" was incorporated into Christian thinking as a way of justifying the hierarchical ordering of both church and society. The word *hierarchy* derives from the Greek *hieros* (meaning "sacred") and *archos* (meaning "leader" or "ruler"). A *hierarch* was a keeper of sacred things, a sacred leader or ruler. Hierarchy as a societal order was considered a divinely sanctioned system of ranking groups and persons one above another on the basis of ascribed characteristics such as race, the social status into which one was born, and sex. Woman's place on the chain of being was considered lower than man's; thus subordination for women was considered natural.

If any creature tried to leave its place on the chain of being, it was considered to be acting "contrary to nature" and in violation of the order of the universe. The system depended upon "a place for everything and everything in its place." Each part had a natural superior to obey and a natural inferior over which to rule. If a rebellious angel tried to step up to a higher place, correction, punishment, or destruction was called for. The same was true of a husband who stepped down from ruling over his wife. For any part of the chain to leave its place in either direction was to make "the very nature of things its enemy." (Lewis, 1961:73–74.)

By the eighteenth century, the model of the great chain of being was being used to justify slavery. As Pulitzer Prize-winning author David Brion Davis points out in his book *The Problem of Slavery in Western Culture*, the idea of a natural or divinely ordained chain gave legitimation to slavery as illustrative of "a cosmic principle of authority and subordination" and should be considered to have "a necessary place in the ordered structure of being" (1966:68). The slave had a destiny to fulfill as a "link of nature's chain." An ideology of racial inferiority was promoted to defend the practice of enslaving black people, and some supporters of slavery suggested that to say black people were inferior was not degrading to blacks but rather confirmed God's wise omnipotence in creating such variety along the entire length of the Chain of Being!

Winthrop Jordan, in his book *White over Black* makes this statement in assessing what was happening during the eighteenth century. "It was no accident," he writes, "that the Chain of Being should have been most popular at a time when the hierarchical arrangement of society was coming to be challenged" (Jordan, 1968:228). I would suggest that the same thing is happening today during this time of rapid social change and the questioning of hierarchical patterns in the roles and relationships of men and women.

One example of the revival of the chain of being appears in a curriculum guide for young adults produced by a major Protestant publisher whose church school materials are used by both conservative and mainline Protestant churches. Commenting on gender roles, the widely read evangelical missionary author Elisabeth Elliot (1975) speaks of a design that includes "a hierarchy of beings under God" in which "every creature is assigned its proper position in this scale" and which "glorifies God by being what it is, by living up to God's original idea." In this scheme of things, she believes "that women, by creation, have been given a place within the human level that is ancillary to that of men." She says that women's "inferior place within the human locus" may be compared to the inferior place occupied by angels in relation to that of archangels and hastens to add that she is thinking of "inferior" in the sense of position, not worth. Such a qualifying statement does little to mitigate the effect of her message: women are subordinate to men, with all the repercussions this has for daily life.

The "chain of being" philosophy is closely linked to another kind of "chain" philosophy currently being propagated in certain Protestant circles. In one version it is called "the Chain of Command" and has been widely promoted by Bill Gothard, whose "Basic Youth Conflicts" seminars are held throughout the United States, often drawing many thousands who pay high fees to attend and obtain materials written by Gothard and unavailable to the general public. Borrowing from the military and from hierarchical models of the corporate world, Gothard believes marriage involves a chain of command in which the husband rules over the wife, who in turn cares for the children under her husband's leadership. One grotesque illustration in the Gothard materials illustrates the chain of command by depicting a hand (representing God) holding a hammer (representing the husband) which is hitting upon a chisel (representing the wife), which is carving out a diamond in the rough (representing the child).

Other materials speak of the chain of command using such terms as "the divine order" or the "headship principle." A line of command goes from Christ to the husband to the wife and then to the children, but it is to be understood that the husband is the head and the main authority over both the wife and children. Author Larry Christenson, whose book *The Christian Family* (1970) has been purchased by many hundreds of thousands of readers, emphasizes that a wife's authority over her children is *derived authority* that comes from her husband. "She exercises authority over the children on behalf of and in place of her husband," Christenson asserts, while at the same time the wife herself "lives under the authority of her husband, and is responsible to him for the way she orders the household and cares for the children." (1970:17–18.)

As Letty Cottin Pogrebin points out in her book *Family Politics* (1983), so much of the conservative rhetoric on families emphasizes control rather than caring. Male supremacy ideology fosters attitudes of *ownership* toward wives and children. Someone sent me a newspaper clipping a few years ago after I had spoken on male-female equality for a midwestern college lecture series open to the general public. The newspaper had printed a letter to the editor that said, "Letha Scanzoni claims groups like 'Moral Majority' could easily become interpreted as the idea of 'ownership of the wife by the husband.' I'm sure the husband purchased the marriage license so *should* be owner. I think very few women would deny they belong to their husbands, and most are pleased with it."

I'm also reminded of a book entitled *Me? Obey Him?* that is required reading for engaged couples in many fundamentalist churches. The author, Elizabeth Rice Handford, raises the question of a woman's responsibility in situations in which she feels that God is leading her directly opposite to a command of her husband. "Who should she obey?" asks Handford. Claiming that the Bible says the woman should ignore her own feelings about God's will and instead do as her husband says, Handford makes this astonishing declaration: "She is to obey her husband as if he were God Himself. She can be as certain of God's will, when her husband speaks, as if God has spoken audibly from Heaven!" (1972:34.)

Many groups that are emphasizing male headship require not only a married woman but also each *single* woman to have a "head," too. If she doesn't have a father or brother or other male relative to give her Christian guidance and protection, a church officer will be assigned to her. No matter how capable she is in her life and career, she is required by certain churches to consult with her male "head" about every decision and is expected to do as he says.

One of the most tragic outcomes of such teachings has been the way they have in some cases fostered and excused family violence. Counselors tell of battered wives who live in constant fear of their husbands' bullying ways and beatings. Yet, they are afraid to leave them because they have been told by pastors that leaving would be rebellion against God who has told wives to submit to their husbands in all things. Some religious leaders have told wives who have been raped by their husbands that a husband "has a right to do as he pleases with his wife's body."

A number of scholars have pointed out the part an ideology of male domination plays in incest (Herman, 1981; Fortune, 1983). Material available from the National Center on Child Abuse and Neglect indicates that some religious fathers have used scripture to justify their power in the household, even power used to obtain sexual favors from their children. In one case, a man actually had a throne set up in his house and forced his three daughters to perform sexual acts with him (Summit and Kryso, 1978:55). And I know of one religious leader who told parents not to worry if they hit their children so hard that the child was bruised black and blue because Proverbs 20:30 says, "The blueness of a wound cleanseth away evil."

The Swiss psychoanalyst Alice Miller has written a book entitled *For Your Own Good* (1983), in which she shows how certain authoritarian child-rearing methods that were used in Germany played a large part in the rise of Nazism and in the unquestioning obedience of the German commandants who headed up the concentration camps and carried out the Holocaust. Miller examined a study of child-rearing manuals published in Germany during the eighteenth and nineteenth centuries and was appalled by the use of fear and intimidation the manuals encouraged, along with an emphasis on "breaking the child's will," which required unquestioning obedience to all authority. Because of an obsessive concern about a child's "rebellious spirit" when permitted to think for himself or herself, the authors of these manuals advocated the invalidation of a child's own perceptions and experiences.

The child-rearing methods Miller discusses from the older manuals were often said to be based on Christian principles. Again, it was an authoritarian interpretation of Christianity. But what hit me was the emphasis on breaking a child's will. I had seen it in many contemporary conservative Christian child-rearing materials, and I remembered that Christenson's book, which I mentioned earlier in discussing "family order," drew heavily from an 1854 book for parents that had been published in Germany during the same period Miller examined. "Physical terror and pain" are emphasized as essential ingredients for Christian child-rearing. Both Miller and German theologian Dorothee Soelle (1982) have voiced great concern over the connection of fascism with these child-rearing methods. (Scanzoni, 1983.)

The widespread acceptance among many Protestant Christians of power, force, and domination/subordination ideology as suitable for Christian families is disturbing. Many Christians feels it is time to question the whole idea of a hierarchical ordering of religious and family life. Psychotherapist Anne Wilson Schaef (1981) has shown how male socialization, based on what she calls the "White Male System" or way of constructing reality, sees all relationships in terms of having one person up and the other down. Seeing another person as equal comes with difficulty in this way of thinking. Similarly, Matthew Fox (1979), a Roman Catholic priest and writer, has suggested that Christians move away from what he calls "Jacob's ladder" thinking, with its emphasis on climbing rungs and standing over others, and instead think of what he calls "Sarah's circle" thinking—the idea of persons standing in a circle as equals, holding hands, supporting one another—a circle growing ever wider to let more people in (chapter 2). A number of feminists have pointed out that the first example of domination in the history of humankind was that of man over woman. The Genesis account of sin's entrance into the world contains the prophecy that the woman's desire would be for her husband but he would "lord it over" her. These Christian feminists suggest that hierarchical relationships between the sexes provide a prototype of all sorts of oppression and abuses of power. Certainly the matter of power abuse is a very real challenge for all of us today and an appropriate topic in our consideration of religion and families.

Time won't permit a detailed discussion of our two remaining challenges: the autonomy/attachment issue and the matter of stability, order, and change— and Bill D'Antonio has already touched on the autonomy issue a bit, particularly with regard to religion. But I'll just say a few things about each because they do indeed present challenges for religion and family life.

Autonomy and Attachment

First I'll discuss the matter of autonomy and attachment. People today seem to be longing for intimacy at the same time that they fear it because they think it will cost them their freedom. We hear about a "fear of commitment" before marriage and feelings of "suffocation" and "entrapment" after marriage—particularly from many in the middle years. Some people want to have their cake and eat it too. A recent article in *Ms.* magazine quoted a man who described his ideal of a wife. "I want her to need me every minute," he said, "and I want her to leave me alone." (Lear, Dec. 1983:80.) The article was pointing out the emotional rations doled out to middle-aged women because of their marriage to men who have been socialized into traditional gender roles. Many wives are themselves starved for nurturance even though they are all the while freely offering nurturance to their husbands, who often simply take it for granted. At the same time, a wife's hunger for nurturance and need for assurance of attachment may be experienced by the husband as an unreasonable demand and encroachment on his freedom.

Sometimes, however, it is the wife who wants a greater sense of autonomy just when the husband is reaching a point of needing more attachment. All of us need to have both a sense of *being free* and of *belonging*, and keeping them in balance seems to be a problem in many marriages—particularly over the course of time. Sometimes one spouse values autonomy over attachment while the other values attachment over autonomy. What then? Sometimes the attachment side of life can deteriorate into self-abnegation, an engulfing possessiveness, and growth-stunting dependency. Sometimes the desire for autonomy deteriorates into an uncaring selfishness, an unempathic self-centeredness, a couldn't-care-less insensitivity. The ideal of *inter*dependence can be elusive if the balance between autonomy and attachment is thrown out of alignment because too much weight is put on either side.

Couples need religious guidance in thinking these matters through and working them out. Yet too often religious teachings on marriage have failed to grapple with such matters, presenting only simplistic guidelines for unimaginative gender-based role behaviors for husbands and wives ("A husband should do this because he's a husband, and a wife should do that because she's a wife.")

Both marital partners need to be shown the religious implications of *love*. The love described in the love poem of 1 Corinthians 13, Jesus' description of no greater love than that which lays down its life for one's friends, and the love of one's neighbor as oneself—all these biblical passages on love fit well with the description of love given by psychiatrist Harry Stack Sullivan:

> When the satisfaction or the security of another person becomes as significant to one as is one's own satisfaction or security, then the state of love exists. So far as I know, under no other circumstances is a state of love present, regardless of the popular usage of the word. (Sullivan, 1953:42–43.)

It is evidently such a definition that the writer of the epistle to the Ephesians had in mind in telling men to love their wives as their own flesh, with an emphasis on nourishing and care. Both spouses need to do this; love shrivels when it is only one-sided. If, as scripture says, God is love, then love needs to be viewed as a religious act and not simply a sentimental feeling. We all have much to learn about loving.

Stability, Order, and Change

Last, both religion and families are facing the challenges of rapid change as well as efforts to resist change for the sake of stability and order. Many of the fears being voiced today are anxieties about order. People want their world to make sense, to fit together, to have some sense of predictability and security. Too rapid changes can be frightening and disorienting, and so persons defensively hold on to the status quo. It feels good and right to them, and they are not about to let it go. People need to see that change needn't mean *disorder*; it can mean a *new* order worked out together by people who care and who want to find a way for all persons, male or female, to be all they can be and develop their full potential in learning, working, and loving.

What is the role of religion in the midst of so much change? Religion can function primarily in either of two ways. It can serve as a repressive force that legitimizes the status quo, stifles questioning, keeps categories of persons "in their place," and forces conformity to a family model that fails to deal with today's realities. *Or* religion can provide a stimulus and support for individuals and families (however defined), helping them face today's challenges head-on in a spirit of creative adventure, authenticity, confidence, justice, love, and bold faith unafraid to ask questions and seek new directions. Both religious approaches are at work in contemporary society.

Bibliography

Christenson, L. 1970. *The Christian Family*. Minneapolis: Bethany Fellowship.

Clark, S. B. 1980. *Man and Woman in Christ*. Ann Arbor, MI: Servant Books.

Davis, D. B. 1966. *The Problem of Slavery in Western Culture*. Ithaca, NY: Cornell University Press.

Dittes, J. 1969. "Secular Religion: Dilemma of Churches and Researchers." *Review of Religious Research* 10 (Winter):65–81.

Elliot, E. 1975. Commentary on the topic of gender roles in *I Am Somebody*, curriculum book for "Lifestyle Series," Sunday School course. Elgin, IL: David C. Cook Pub. Co.

Fortune, M. M. 1983. *Sexual Violence*. New York: Pilgrim Press.

Fox, M. 1979. *A Spirituality Named Compassion*. Minneapolis: Winston Press.

Hale, J. 1980. *The Unchurched*. San Francisco: Harper & Row.

Handford, E. R. 1972. *Me? Obey Him?* Murfreesboro, TN: Sword of the Lord Publishers.

Herman, J. L. 1981. *Father-Daughter Incest*. Cambridge, MA: Harvard University Press.

Jordan, W. D. 1968. *White over Black*. Chapel Hill, NC: University of North Carolina Press. Penguin Books paperback edition cited.

Lear, F. 1983. "Love Between Grown-Ups." *MS.* 12 (December):80–83.

Lewis, C. S. 1961. *A Preface to Paradise Lost*. New York: Oxford University Press.

Lindsey, K. 1981. *Friends as Family*. Boston: Beacon Press.

Lovejoy, A. O. 1936. *The Great Chain of Being*. Cambridge, MA: Harvard University Press.

Mace, D. and V. 1981. "What Is Marriage Beyond Living Together?: Some Quaker Reactions to Cohabitation." *Family Relations* 30:17–20.

Miles, J. M. 1975. *The Feminine Principle*. Minneapolis: Bethany Fellowship, Inc.

Miller, A. 1983. *For Your Own Good*. New York: Farrar, Straus, Giroux.

Pogrebin, L. C. 1983. *Family Politics*. New York: McGraw-Hill.

Ruether, R. 1983. "An Unrealized Revolution." *Christianity and Crisis* 43:399–404.

Scanzoni, L. D. 1981. "Human and Mrs. Human." (Review of Stephen Clark's *Man and Woman in Christ*), *The Christian Century* 98 (March 11):268–73.

Scanzoni, L. D. 1983. "Beware: Patriarchy is Hazardous to Children." *Daughters of Sarah* 9 (6) (November/December):4–8.

Scanzoni, L. D. 1984. "The Great Chain of Being and the Chain of Command." In J. Kalven and M. I. Buckley (eds.), *Women's Spirit Bonding*. New York: Pilgrim Press.

Schaef, A. W. 1981. *Women's Reality*. Minneapolis: Winston Press.

Schneider, D. 1968. *American Kinship: A Cultural Account*. Englewood Cliffs, NJ: Prentice-Hall.

Soelle, D. 1982. *Beyond Mere Obedience*. New York: Pilgrim Press.

Sullivan, H. S. 1953. *Conceptions of Modern Psychiatry*. New York: W. W. Norton & Co.

Summit, R. and J. Kryso. 1978. "Sexual Abuse of Children: A Clinical Spectrum." *American Journal of Orthopsychiatry* 48:237–51, as reprinted in *Sexual Abuse of Children: Selected Readings* (Washington, D.C.: National Center on Child Abuse and Neglect, U.S. Dept. of Health and Human Services, 1980:51–58).

Swartley, W. M. 1983. *Slavery, Sabbath, War, and Women*. Scottdale, PA: Herald Press.

8

Family Life: An Old Order Amish Manifesto

Marc A. Olshan

Introduction

The Old Order Amish[1] have rarely chosen to speak about themselves to the public at large. Instead, they have been willing to leave the task of explaining to the professional explainers and occasionally to enterprising neighbors whose only credential is their rural mailing address. Nor have the Amish generally proven to be willing collaborators with their would-be publicists. In fact, initial inquiries about the Amish way of life are likely to be answered with the Amishman's own question, well designed to stop the enthusiastic researcher dead in his tracks: "What good would it do for you to know?" The question reflects a genuine skepticism implying that, compared to doing, little good can come from merely talking or writing. In any case, the typical Amish response is not intended to encourage conversation.

Another standard reaction is a disavowal of any knowledge about the investigator's chosen topic: For example, "Oh, I wouldn't know anything about organic farming (or horses, or the history of the settlement)," or "Well, I'm

Marc A. Olshan is Associate Professor of Sociology at Bethany College in Bethany, West Virginia. He received his Ph.D. from Cornell University, where he wrote his dissertation on the Old Order Amish as a model for development. He has studied Hebrew and taught at Tel Aviv University in Israel.

not much of a farmer (or blacksmith or Amishman)." This expression of humility, if accepted at face value, relieves the now self-disqualified Amishman of the burden of further questions. Sometimes he might even elaborate on this strategy by helpfully suggesting that Enos (or Moses or Levi), who lives "down the road a way," is far more knowledgeable than he. The suggestion may bear fruit, but only in the form of an entertaining after-church conversation, for example, among members of the community about how they dealt with the stranger, and the degree of success they had in pawning him off on one another.

However, neither I nor, I suspect, many other researchers are fully deterred by this Maginot Line of disclaimers and counterquestions. We gather what information we can, and then proceed to turn out authoritative accounts of the Amish practices or beliefs in question. A few such accounts have found their way back to the Amish communities where they originated, and several have amused the people they claim to describe. In an article entitled "Who Are These People?" (Luthy, 1976:13–14), the Amish author relates the "findings" of several researchers who misinterpreted or erroneously described Amish life. Their misconceptions of the Old Order portray a people who supposedly use battery-powered televisions but who rely on oxen-pulled farmcarts and are prohibited from bathing, reading newspapers, eating ice cream, or attending school.

Social scientists born into Amish households and who subsequently left the church have certainly made valuable contributions to our understanding of the Amish. But their interpretations too are colored and perhaps limited in some respects by their personal histories. Therefore, to truly understand the Amish we must listen to what the Amish have to say about themselves.

Amish Publications

In light of Amish reluctance to ponder with strangers about Amish life, we might do well to look for other vehicles through which the Amish express themselves. One such source of self-interpretations and descriptions are Amish publications, of which a surprising number exist. For the social scientist they represent fertile and, for the most part, previously unworked soil.

Two nationally circulated newspapers, *The Budget*[2] and *Die Botschaft*,[3] consist almost entirely of letters submitted by "scribes" representing almost all of the Amish and Mennonite communities in North America. Most often the letters are dominated by references to the weather, lists of visitors from other

settlements, and descriptions of the mundane, seasonal tasks currently under-
way. Hostetler's content analysis of *The Budget* (1968:91) provides an excellent summary of daily activities but is not particularly revealing of the Amish
character. *The Diary*, a monthly published by an Old Order group in Lancaster
County, Pennsylvania, also prints news from Amish settlements but features
historical and genealogical articles as well.

The several hundred genealogies that have been privately published by
Amish families reflect a strong and pervasive interest in family history. Many
of these genealogies are printed by the Amish-operated Gordonville Print Shop
in Pennsylvania. This shop also publishes the minutes of the Old Order Amish
Steering Committee, some texts used in Amish schools, and Raber's *New American Almanac*, which lists Old Order church officials for each settlement.

All of these publications offer potential insights into who the Amish are. I
would argue, however, that the publications most expressive of Amish concerns and values are those produced by Pathway Publishers in Aylmer, Canada. The usefulness of these publications stems from their introspective character and from a format that encourages and draws heavily on readers'
contributions. All three Pathway periodicals feature several columns comprised
totally of letters from readers.

Blackboard Bulletin, another Amish publication, serves as a forum for
Amish teachers to share teaching techniques, philosophies, and opinions. In
the same magazine, letters from ex-teachers, parents, and pupils are published.
In addition, a regular feature solicits readers' opinions regarding a particular
issue or question (e.g., "Does a teacher have the right to forbid things at school
that he thinks are wrong, especially if these are not in the *ordnung* [rules of
the church]?") Then replies are printed two issues later. Inspirational articles
and poems, announcements of teachers' meetings, and some materials for class-
room use (such as stories to read aloud) are also included. The *Bulletin* is
published monthly except in June and July.

Young Companion is a magazine geared toward school-age or "young
people." It offers serialized stories, readers' comments on articles from previous months. It also includes a "Let's Talk It Over" section in which readers
give their opinions regarding a question posed two months earlier (for example,
"How should we react when tourists try to take our picture?"). Poems and
short nonfiction articles are also published.

Family Life is the most general of the three publications. Farming techniques, relations with non-Amish neighbors, the history of Amish settlements,

and the appropriate role of women are some representative subjects. Its editorials, new items, didactic stories, and how-to articles deal with any topic that might interest Amish fathers, mothers, and children. The mission of *Family Life* is explicit: "The promotion of Christian living with special emphasis on the appreciation of our heritage." David Wagler, one of the founding editors of Pathway Publishers, elaborated on that mission in the first issue of *Family Life*:

> The family is the heart of the community and the church. Even a nation is made up of families. If there is a strong family life, then the church, the community, and the nation will be likewise. If family life degenerates, then all will suffer.... This is the goal of *Family Life*—to be an instrument through which thoughts and ideas can be transmitted. (Wagler, 1968:3.)

Constraints of time and resources force the selection and analysis of a single feature in one of the Pathway Publications. *Family Life* is the logical choice because it has the largest circulation of the three and because of the more representative character of its readership. Further analysis reveals that the feature in *Family Life* generating the greatest volume of reader response that might reveal Amish values and concerns is a column called "What Do You Think?"[4]

The column first appeared in the October, 1970, issue of *Family Life* as a subheading of another column, "Across the Windowsill," which featured recipes and suggestions regarding household chores and raising children. "Across the Windowsill" itself dates back to the January, 1968, inaugural issue of *Family Life* and, from the beginning, solicited "contributions of original ideas [and] items of interest" from readers. Letters responding to this appeal were printed under the heading of "Some Mothers Write." Many of those letters expressed a desire to know if other mothers were having problems similar to those noted in the letters, or could offer opinions or solutions. The column's author, "Aunt Becky," encouraged such exchanges: "There are probably hundreds of other mothers who are struggling with the same problem. If you have a question, let the readers also answer it. Or if there is something you would like to bring up for discussion, do so." ("Across the Windowsill," 1970:37.) The enthusiastic response and the desire among readers to discuss a broad spectrum of family and community issues soon required the creation of a separate "What Do You Think?" column.

Beginning with the February, 1971, issue of *Family Life*, "What Do You Think?" printed readers' comments regarding a specific question or dilemma that had been offered for consideration two months previously. In addition to the responses, the column prints a new question submitted by a reader, which will generate letters to be published two months later, and so on.

Content Analysis of Amish Letters

A manifesto is usually defined as a public declaration or proclamation issued by a central political authority of some kind. Such a declaration would be anathema to the Amish not only on the grounds of its public nature, but also in its assumption of the existence of a central authority entitled to speak for the Amish as a group. Yet *Family Life* does provide, through its readers' letters, a public declaration, albeit one which was not intended as such. And, to the extent that those letters are representative of the Amish in general, they constitute a far more authoritative expression of Amish concerns and values than any outside observer could provide. The word *manifesto* has another meaning which is even more germane. It originally signified a proof or a piece of evidence. That is exactly what these letters represent, a heretofore unexamined piece of evidence that will shed additional light on the Amish character. Note, then, that the analysis presented here is both preliminary and limited in its objectives. It will only attempt to identify what values the readers' letters reflect and the frequency with which they are mentioned. A logical step beyond this descriptive level would be a comparison of these findings with data from similar non-Amish materials.

A second objective will be to test the proposition that the Amish exemplify in any significant way the characteristics of a folk society. I have argued elsewhere (Olshan, 1981) that the Amish worldview and Amish institutions are, in fact, essentially modern. My assertion is based on an acceptance of Peter Berger's definition of modernity: "Modernity means . . . that men take control over the world and over themselves. *What previously was experienced as fate now becomes an arena of choices*." (Berger, 1974:21, emphasis in the original.) The nature of the debate and dialogue that fill the pages of the various Pathway publications, particularly the reader response features, should illuminate this character. The mere existence of a "What Do You Think?" column would appear to be antithetical to the uncritical, unreflective, and tradition-oriented nature of a folk people.

An analysis of the column's content should allow us to more accurately assess the degree to which the Amish perceive themselves to be either as confronted with choices or as actors whose lines have already been written, living in a world where "the old is the best, and the new is of the devil."

The approach taken in examining this second dimension of readers' letters will also be rudimentary. I will attempt to tally explicitly positive references to the role of tradition or the need to adhere to the old ways, and other statements which clearly imply similar meanings. I will do the same with references that either advocate the need for change in traditional practices or which express a view of life involving choices in how to live.

Given even these limited objectives, several methodological problems present themselves. For example, some of the letters are written by non-Amish readers. About 50 percent of *Family Life*'s subscribers are not members of Old Order churches. I believe, however, that most such authors can be identified by the content of their letters. A mention of any practice or equipment that would be proscribed by Old Order communities (such as driving a car or using an electric stove) will remove the letter from consideration. Many non-Amish writers seem to feel obligated to identify themselves as such, thus reducing the problem still further.

Another problem, which is not so easily resolved, is the editing of letters. In some cases, the column's editors note that letters duplicating the reasoning in published letters either were not published or were published only in part. In other cases, responses that the editors deemed inappropriate were not printed. I am not aware of the exact extent of either of these practices. From a casual knowledge of the Pathway operation, however, I estimate they only have a moderate impact (at worst) on the frequency with which the various values appear.

Whether the letters are representative or typical of the entire Old Order population also depends on the degree of self-selection between writers and nonwriters. There is clearly some self-selection on the basis of sex; of the authors that can be positively identified, there are more females than males. But in many cases neither the content nor the manner in which the writer is identified in the column indicates sex. Most often letters are signed only with a set of initials or the name of a town or state. Self-selection may also take place along other diverse dimensions such as degree of conservatism, geography, income, or degree of literacy.

Pathway Publications subscribers in general cannot be treated as totally representative of the Old Order. Members of the most conservative Amish church districts would be less likely to subscribe. However, with a monthly circulation of over 14,000 (at least half of which represents Amish subscribers), *Family Life* probably reaches almost half of the approximately 15,000 Old Order households in North America. Moreover, because copies are shared within and between families, the above circulation figure should be treated as an extremely conservative estimate of readership. At the very least we can infer *Family Life* subscribers are not limited to a few atypical subgroups within the Old Order.

A further problem derives from the nature of the method itself rather than from the specific materials being examined here. One advantage of content analysis is that it allows the objective classification and quantification of data which might otherwise be left in the realm of the impressionistic. Inherent in that process, however, is the unavoidable step of interpretation that inevitably precedes the classification of any qualitative material. The problem of making erroneous inferences can be obviated to a large extent by attempting to analyze only statements that explicitly express or clearly imply personal values, or what the writer thinks ought to be valued. The same conservative approach will be taken in classifying statements as expressive of a traditional or modern stance. In other words, latent content or "the deeper layer of meaning" will be completely ignored and even that part of the manifesto content that does not self-evidently reflect a value position (or reveal a distinctly folk or modern worldview) will not be considered.

The array of methodological problems listed above is formidable. I am, however, treating this undertaking as supplementary to other research based on other methods. Even though the conclusions of this study must be severely qualified by the limitations of its method, the opportunity to even partially illuminate a facet of Amish life should not be ignored. So I will proceed.

The recording unit used is the theme or "the assertion of a value." The context unit selected, "the largest body of content that may be searched to characterize a recording unit" (Holsti, 1969:118), consists of the entire letter submitted by any individual. Letters vary considerably in length so that values (or worldviews) repeatedly espoused in a single letter by the more prolix writers might be disproportionately weighted. In practice, however, the longer letters tend to include descriptive and illustrative material, which usually does not qualify as a clear expression of a value (or folk vs. modern worldview) and therefore will not be coded.

Selection of Categories

The use of previously developed categories would be advantageous for at least two reasons. One, continuity of categories would facilitate comparison with other analyses measuring the same phenomena. And two, it would also relieve the researcher of the considerable task of delineating his own categories from scratch. Consequently, I examined several earlier attempts to identify and categorize values I hoped I would be able to build on. My search for an appropriate set of already existing categories was frustrated by what I believe is a systematic bias in the approach of social scientists to values.

Illustrating the character of this bias is Hadley Cantril's international survey of what he refers to as "human concerns."[5] Cantril claims to have avoided forcing respondents into making selections among arbitrary categories of concerns by asking the following open-ended question:

> All of us want certain things out of life. When you think about what really matters in your own life, what are your wishes and hopes for the future? In other words, if you imagine your future in the *best* possible light, what would your life look like then, if you are to be happy? (1965:23.)

Then, based on the responses received to a preliminary survey, categories of concerns were developed. Cantril's claim is that the individual is totally free to define for himself, in his own terms, what concerns him, and what he values. The bias derives, however, from the character of the question itself, which essentially directs the respondent to limit his consideration to worldly concerns. To the devout of various religions the question of what constitutes a happy life is downright irrelevant. Although the question might eventually be answered, as most questions in an interview are, for such individuals the responses will not be valid indicators of "what really matters." The wording of Cantril's question more or less precludes consideration of spiritual or transcendental concerns. It is no surprise, then, that of the dozens of categories resulting from a tabulation of responses, only two included even passing references to such concerns: "Miscellaneous aspirations having to do with public service or with religion or morality where the reference is not restricted to self or family" and "Resolution of one's own religious, spiritual, or ethical problems." (1965:Appendix A.)

Ralph White's "value analysis" categories (1947) contain no reference whatsoever to spiritual concerns. Holsti lists several other sets of value categories used in content analysis that mention spiritual concerns only tangentially

(Lasswell's category of rectitude and Cochran's mention of religion as a subheading under "general problems of society") (Holsti, 1969:108-11).

In one open-ended survey of the hopes of the American people, two types of explicitly religious responses turned up with sufficient frequency to merit their own categories: "Resolution of personal religious, spiritual, or ethical problems; gaining admittance to heaven"; and "Christian revival in general" (Watts and Free in Laszlo, 1977:25). Such broad classifications, however, would be of little use in differentiating the content of the Amish letters, almost all of which would qualify for inclusion in both categories.

Likewise, Robin Williams's discussion of fifteen major value orientations in America includes a "moral orientation" category (1970:452-500). While at least acknowledging the influence of moral and religious concerns, such a comprehensive designation does not provide any discriminatory power in classifying the materials at hand. The same can be said for Rokeach's Value Survey, which includes the single category "salvation" to account for all transcendental concerns (Feather, 1975:20). McCready and Greeley's (1976) typology of ultimate values deals almost entirely with transcendental concerns, but their categories represent attitudinal complexes and are not helpful in characterizing discrete expressions of values.

This relatively fruitless search of the literature required that I devise my own set of categories. I developed the categories after an informal preliminary reading of a large sample of letters. They are not only devoid of almost all values that most frequently appeared in similar analyses (such as a comfortable life, an exciting life, equality, security, freedom, happiness, pleasure, independence) but are, to a large extent, antithetical to such values. It was not my intent to exclude secular concerns; they simply did not appear very often.

TABLE 1
DESCRIPTION OF VALUE CATEGORIES

I. Discipline and Submission

    A. To God. Doing and being content with God's will, fearing and loving God. (E.g., "You are not the first one to be a victim of circumstances. But please do not forget to be content with the blessing which God has promised: namely, food, raiment, and shelter.")

    B. Of children to parents. Obedience and proper training. (E.g., "After the will has been conquered [and this should be done for the most part by the age of two], they will be ready to absorb your teachings from the Bible.")

C. To rules of the church. Honoring one's promise to live by the *ordnung*. (E.g., "How much easier it is for the Bishop and ministers if we all try to do our duty and stay under the church rules. We make a promise to live according to those rules when we join the church, and we all have to be true to that promise.)

II. Maintaining a Distance from the World

A. Guidance from God. Acting from pure or spiritual motives, as informed by prayer, rather than worldly motives. (E.g., "Ask the Lord for strength and guidance so you may not make the same mistakes.")

B. Guidance from the Bible. Acting in accordance with biblical precepts and standards. (E.g., "The Bible is still our best and most stable guide.")

C. Quietness and plainness/avoidance of worldly practices. Eschewing worldly standards and practices and emphasizing those that are uniquely Amish. (E.g., "I also think it is wrong to have images, knick-knacks, and photographs, and believe we should all work harder to keep our houses plain and simple and consistent with our dress.")

III. Valuing Others

A. Sympathy/understanding/patience/love/forgiveness. Striving for these qualities, regardless of the attributes of the other party. (E.g., "I believe that love and prayer are stronger tools than fault-finding and criticism.")

B. Respect/humility. Looking for the best in others and keeping in mind one's own limitations. (E.g., "Let us look on the good things our loved ones do instead of finding fault.")

C. Sharing/helping/offering hospitality. Freely and willingly engaging in these activities. (E.g., "God wants to use people to help to provide for each other's needs.")

IV. Family and Marriage

These institutions, especially through the opportunities they provide for working and praying together. (E.g., "Nothing is more pleasant than when married couples get along well.")

V. Community and Church

These institutions and the fellowship, unanimity, and support they represent. (E.g., "We go to church to grasp something, a bit of comfort, a bit of help, something to think on that will help us through the next week.")

VI. Salvation

The salvation of one's soul. (E.g., "My goal in life is not material possessions but eternal life for my husband, children and myself.")

VII. Privacy.

Being alone (either as a family or an individual) and away from the scrutiny of others. (E.g., "These are the times when I would like to live way back in the mountains where nobody sees or cares what I'm doing.")

Results

A ten-year period, from February of 1971 to January of 1981, was examined. All letters printed in the "What Do You Think?" column during this time were analyzed. The frequency with which each of the value categories was mentioned is reported in Table 2. The category "Privacy" does not appear in the final tally. In fact, it was mentioned only eight times. Other values mentioned more than once, but not frequently enough to justify including them in the list of value categories, were (numbers in parentheses indicate frequency) submissiveness of wife to husband (8),[6] frugality (6), honesty (6), the satisfaction of hard work (5), being content with one's lot (5), farm life (4), and serving as a light or example to the world (3).

Certainly the subject matter of any given question does, in part, determine the type of value most likely to be invoked. One can see, however, from the diversity of subjects covered (see Appendix), that there were ample opportunities to express whatever values were held.

The attempt to identify explicit expressions of a pro-tradition or anti-tradition attitude was unsuccessful. A rejection of grandfather's traditional practices, for example, might be based on a resurrection of even earlier traditions. One writer argued that "We should compare our traditions and standards handed down to us with the Perfect Pattern and prove all things thereby." The topic of immediate concern in this case was the practice of feeding children snacks in church to keep them quiet. Even though this is a traditional practice, the writer reasons it is wrong.

Similarly, with regard to the practices of "bed courtship" and the raising of tobacco, one reader states, "I am glad for those who are writing to work on the situation, instead of saying, 'Oh, we've always had it, so what can we do now?' "

Although explicit references to tradition are rare and, furthermore, difficult to classify as being either critical or supportive of tradition, the letters do shed some light on the role of tradition in Amish life. As seen in Table 2,

TABLE 2. FREQUENCIES OF REFERENCES TO VALUE CATEGORIES

DISCIPLINE & SUBMISSION			MAINTAINING DISTANCE FROM WORLD			VALUING OTHERS			FAMILY/ MARRIAGE	COMMUNITY/ CHURCH	SALVATION
To God	Of Children to Parents	To Rules of Church	Guidance from God	Guidance from Bible	Quiet/Plain Avoid Worldly Practices	Sympathy, Love Forgive- ness, etc.	Respect/ Humility	Sharing/ Helping			
101	76	19	50	80	92	83	56	55	51	13	23

readers often expressed the need to search for answers, either from the Bible or directly from God through prayer. This search was sometimes portrayed as an emotional and even tormenting experience. So, to the extent that the appropriateness of individual behavior and communal institutions is determined by reference to ultimate values as revealed in the Bible and through prayer (rather than by reference to the practices of past generations), the Amish are accurately characterized as wertrational (value-rational) rather than traditional.

Truly traditional behavior, in Weber's typology, is based on the habituation of long practice. It is often a matter of almost automatic reaction to habitual stimuli in a course that is repeatedly followed. Traditional or reactive behavior is based on an unself-conscious respect for the sanctity of the existing order. It "lies very close to the borderline of what can justifiably be called meaningfully oriented action, and indeed often on the other side." (Weber, 1964:116.) Whatever values might be invoked as evidence of a traditional orientation (such as submission to the rules of the church and emphasizing uniquely Amish practices), they are more than offset by the number of references to ultimate values or sources of guidance, which require individual interpretation rather than unthinking adherence to past practices.

Discussion

This analysis "rests on the assumption that cultural values which have been institutionalized in certain segments of the society are represented in the communications of individuals from those segments" (Riley and Stoll, 1968:373). Therefore, an evaluation of Amish-authored letters should yield a fuller understanding of what values are most important to the Amish. That evaluation reveals a set of values that in some respects varies significantly from the representations of those who have described Amish society. For example, in describing the Amish "charter" (the fundamental values and common ends recognized and accepted by the people), Hostetler includes the values of humility, stewardship, submission, marriage, family, children, a disciplined life, sharing, hospitality, separation from the world, and closeness to nature (Hostetler, 1980:76). In his much less comprehensive account, Kephart (1982:51–53) mentions simplicity, humility, conformity within the community, and separation from the world.

While these values are generally consistent with the findings presented here, the listings fail to indicate priorities and are too abstract to convey their significance for the Amish.

For example, Hostetler, Kephart, and other commentators all cite the value placed on being separate from the world. However, the unrelenting tension and struggle implied by adherence to that value have been, for the most part, overlooked. The wording of the category used here—"maintaining a distance from the world"—was deliberately selected to convey more accurately the significance for the Amish of being separate. All three components of this most frequently mentioned value represent a constant and purposeful rejection of the values and standards of "the world." In the words of one Amish writer, "The Christian life is a warfare."

The supposed placidness and passiveness of Amish life must be questioned. Separation from the world is not a static position that, once chosen, removes the newly baptized church member into a mythical Amishland, free from contact with the world and its problems. The truth of the matter is the Amish are not physically separated from the rest of the world. In fact, even the largest Amish settlements are located in counties where the Amish are a small minority.[7] Passing automobiles and airplanes, electric lines, junk mail, salespeople, customers, employers, doctors, bankers, and an array of inspectors and other government officials are all a daily part of Amish life. Because contact with the world is constant, separation from the world is achieved only through constant struggle.

Each Amish person decided as an adult to become Amish; this choice must be reaffirmed each day after the baptism following that decision. To waver, to stop actively struggling, is to stop being Amish. What evolves then, and is demonstrated in the *Family Life* letters as well as in face to face dealings with "worldly" people, is a communal confidence that falls just short of self-righteousness. This communal certainty is often balanced, however, by individual self-doubt regarding one's own ability to live up to Amish standards. The letters often reveal an agonized attempt to determine the correct, spiritual course of action. Prayer and biblical guidance were most often advocated as the best means to live, in the words of one writer, "a victorious Christian life."

The analysis of *Family Life* letters provides a fuller understanding of two other dimensions of the Amish character: (1) it shows an unexpected emphasis being placed on valuing other individuals, and (2) it demonstrates an equally unexpected paucity of references to the community and salvation. The value placed on sympathy, understanding, patience, love, and forgiveness may be another symptom of just how difficult it is to be Amish. A recognition of the need for these qualities is most likely born out of the inherent tension of being "in the world but not of it."

A preference for the less abstract "Sharing, helping, and hospitality" and "Submission to the Rules of the Church" categories may account in part for the relatively few References to "Community and church" (or Gemeinde). Similarly, the category "Family" is also closely related to the submission of children to parents. In the case of both sets of values, the distribution is significant to the extent that it reflects Amish perceptions rather than typologies that are derived primarily from alien worldviews.

A final insight into Amish life that can be gleaned from the "What Do You Think?" column is the role of *Family Life* itself. Its supportive function in the ongoing struggle of simply being Amish is evident from the comments of numerous readers. The following references to *Family Life* were embedded in answers to various questions submitted over the entire ten-year period examined:

"It lifts our spirits so and makes us feel we are not alone on this road."

"[The Pathway magazines] always make me feel happier and I want to try harder to be a better person after reading them."

"Reading *Family Life* shows us others also have these problems."

"Thanks for the many articles in *Family Life* about the wearing of the covering. To me this is like a cup of hot soup on a cold day."

The magazine's influence is not limited to the kind of psychological support indicated here. Readers also pointed out that *Family Life* might play a role in resolving interpersonal disputes, or in helping to set community standards:

"I believe if the parents in your community are at all concerned about teaching their children the right way, your letter in *Family Life* may have already accomplished much toward the solution."

"What would I do with neighbors who are continually misusing their borrowing privileges? I'd give them the October issue of *Family Life*."

The extent of *Family Life*'s influence is extremely problematic because, whatever its extent, that influence might be viewed by some as a threat to the community autonomy, which is one cornerstone of the Amish church.

This analysis was undertaken as a contribution toward deepening our understanding of the Amish by examining what some Amish had to say for themselves and about themselves. Their testimony helps reveal the dynamic and demanding character of Amish life. The Amish are not a people suspended in time, drifting in the past. They are a people actively attempting to govern their lives according to their own standards. Perhaps it is the larger society that can be more fairly described as drifting unthinkingly and uncritically toward ends that have not been agreed on or even fully considered.

APPENDIX. Sample Questions to Which Readers Responded (1980)

DATE OF QUESTION	PARAPHRASE OF QUESTION
January	Shouldn't the family have a daily Bible reading in the home?
February	To what extent should we limit our farming or business activities on Sunday?
March	Isn't it wrong for small groups of women to gather before or after church and whisper and laugh while glancing at others around the room?
April	Does the church have the right to restrict families from moving into a settlement?
May	Does the biblical teaching against women speaking in church apply to the teaching or preaching of the word only, or does it also include giving a voice in church matters?
June	Isn't it wrong for ministers to chew gum before and during church services?
July	Is it wrong to charge interest on a loan to younger members of the church struggling to make ends meet when I don't really need the money to get by?
August-September	After moving to a new settlement where we have no relatives we often feel homesick. Are we too closely attached to our relatives?
October	We have some farm equipment that needs changing to meet church standards. We want to do it, but it seems so expensive. Are there hidden blessings we are cheating ourselves out of by waiting too long?
November	Our handicapped child is gaped at and picked on by other children. The child sometimes shows off or fights back. Should we punish our child? How can we deal with the other children?
December	Should a woman go ahead and assume responsibilities that are usually the man's if he doesn't fulfill them? Should she initiate the Bible reading or outside work or would she be going outside of her calling?

Notes

1. There is no single, formally organized group known as the Old Order Amish. The term encompasses many relatively diverse and autonomous churches.

2. For additional background information see "A History of the Budget" (Luthy, 1978).

3. *Die Botschaft* is an English-language weekly started in 1975 in response to the increasing number of letters from liberal, non-Amish contributors. *The Budget* printed such letters, along with some of the commercial advertising which was thought to have a harmful effect on the Old Order communities. Letters in *Die Botschaft* come from Old Order Amish and Old Order Mennonite communities only.

4. The column was discontinued with the April 1983 issue of *Family Life*.

5. While "concerns" are not synonomous with "values," Cantril's explication of his own work indicates that he is treating them as such. The scale he developed "was utilized in this study as a means of discovering the spectrum of values a person is preoccupied or concerned with and by means of which he evaluates his own life." (Cantril, 1965:22.)

6. The issue of the wife's submissiveness to the husband was mentioned far more often than eight times. However, the value was most often presented as conditional on the husband's own submission to God. Those references were not interpreted as establishing that the wife's submissiveness was itself valued.

7. The largest concentration of Amish is in the five-county area centered in Holmes County, Ohio. The roughly 23,000 Amish living in that area comprise about 4 percent of the total population of Holmes, Wayne, Coshocton, Tuscarawas, and Stark counties. In the second largest settlement, located in Lancaster County, Pennsylvania, the Amish also make up about 4 percent of the county's population. Both estimates are based on an average of 199 people per church district (Hostetler, 1980:99), and a total of 114 districts in the Holmes County area and 77 districts in Lancaster County (*New American Almanac*, 1984).

Bibliography

"Across the Windowsill." 1970. *Family Life* (October):37.

Berger, P. L. *Pyramids of Sacrifice*. New York: Basic Books, Inc.

Cantril, H. 1965. *The Pattern of Human Concerns*. New Brunswick, NJ: Rutgers University Press.

Family Life. Aylmer, Ontario, Canada: Pathway Publishers.

Feather, N. T. 1975. *Values in Education and Society*. New York: The Free Press.

Holsti, O. R. 1969. *Content Analysis for the Social Sciences and Humanities*. Reading, MA: Addison-Wesley Publishing Company.

Hostetler, J. A. 1968. *Amish Society*. Baltimore: Johns Hopkins.

Hostetler, J. A. 1980. *Amish Society*. Baltimore: Johns Hopkins.

Kephart, W. M. 1982. *Extraordinary Groups*. New York: St. Martin's Press.

Laszlo, E. et al. 1977. *Goals for Mankind*. New York: E. P. Dutton.

Luthy, D. 1976. "Who Are These People?" *Family Life* (November):13–14.

Luthy, D. 1978. "A History of the Budget." *Family Life* (June):19–22 and (July):15–18.

McCready, W. and A. M. Greeley. 1976. *The Ultimate Values of the American Population*. Beverly Hills, CA: Sage Publications.

New American Almanac. 1984. Baltic, Ohio.

Olshan, M. A. 1981. "Modernity, the Folk Society, and the Old Order Amish: An Alternative Interpretation." *Rural Sociology* 46: 297–309.

Riley, M. W. and C. S. Stoll. 1968. "Content Analysis" in *International Encyclopedia of the Social Sciences*. D. L. Sills, ed. The Macmillan Company and the Free Press. Vol. 3:371–77.

Wagler, D. 1968. "What Is Family Life?" *Family Life* (January):3.

Weber, M. 1964. *The Theory of Social and Economic Organization*. New York: The Free Press.

White, R. K. 1947. "Black Boy: A Value-Analysis." *Journal of Abnormal Social Psychology* 42:440–61.

Williams, R. 1970. *American Society*. New York: Knopf.

Family and Religious Change in a Peripheral Capitalist Society: Mid-Nineteenth-Century Ireland

Eugene Hynes

W hen we look at nineteenth-century Ireland we cannot avoid the catastrophic Great Hunger of 1845–49. Out of eight and a quarter million, the famine killed up to a million and a half people and drove another million into exile. (For the most recent estimate of fatalities, see Mokyr, 1983:chapter 9.) To understand that tragedy we must understand the society that suffered through it. Both the family system and the religious beliefs and practices of the majority of rural Ireland's people changed dramatically in the decades before and after the famine. In this paper I will describe these changes in the family and religion, and show how they were related to each other. It will be necessary first to sketch the economic and class structure of the society.

Pre-famine Irish society was overwhelmingly rural. Although its social structure was complex, general contours are evident. Landlords were at the apex of the class system; they owned but rarely worked the land. Beneath them were farmers who rented. The farmers' tenure was secure as long as

Eugene Hynes teaches sociology in the Humanities and Social Science Divison of GMI Engineering and Management Institute, Flint, Michigan. Besides world-systems analyses of religion and family, he has research interests in various aspects of nineteenth-century Ireland, in the work of Melvin Kohn, and in the role of engineers in the labor process. He received his Ph.D. from Southern Illinois University.

they paid the rent. These farmers produced grain, dairy products, or beef for the market and potatoes for their own use. But not everyone could be a farmer; land supply was limited, and rising population intensified competition for land, driving rents upward. However, a growing export trade in foodstuffs (a result of the growing British market and improvements in transportation) enabled the farmers to pay their rents.

Lower than the farmers were the landless, conventionally divided into two groups: laborers and cottiers. Both groups worked for farmers. The laborers were hired when the workload on the farms demanded extra hands. Cottiers, on the other hand, held one-season leases on small patches of the farmers' land. On these patches they built their cabins and grew potatoes. They paid their rent by laboring for the farmer. Both cottiers and laborers relied on the potato—a food with a high return per acre—as their staple. However, as their living conditions worsened through the pre-famine decades, they were forced to adopt varieties of potatoes that were more prolific but were also more prone to disease. From east to west within the country, the size of farm-holdings declined so that in western areas, and especially along the seaboard, the distinction between farmers and cottiers/laborers began to blur. Small farmers, or members of their families, were simultaneously laborers, or rented land by the season like cottiers. In these small-holding areas the sharp distinction between the farmers and the landless began to disappear.[1]

As evidenced by better diet, clothing and housing and wider use of consumer goods, in the decades before the famine the farmer class improved their living standard (see Cullen, 1980:202). With the change they also adopted a new set of values. Historians have characterized them variously as "peasant capitalists," a "rural middle class," a "bourgeois" class that was espousing new standards of propriety and respectability (see Hynes, 1978:141, for references; Smyth, 1983:27-28; and Connolly, 1983:276). Though a minority before the famine, the farmers, partly because the famine killed mainly the landless and small farmers, became the numerically dominant, and socially most powerful, stratum of rural society (Hynes, 1978:144-45).[2] To understand their values regarding religion and family life and how they changed, we must understand this farmer class.

The Devotional Revolution

In the 1830s only about a third of rural Irish Catholics regularly attended mass. By the 1870s well over 90 percent attended and have done so until recently. (Larkin, 1972; Miller, 1975; Hynes, 1978; Connolly, 1982.) This "devotional revolution" involved more than an increase in regular attendance at mass. For example, within the Catholic church, bishops increased their authority and cooperated more fully with each other to promote ecclesiastical discipline. The ratio of priests to lay people was one in 2,676 in 1800 and one in 2,996 in 1840, but it increased to one in 1,560 in 1871 (Connolly, 1983:33). Also, the poor, unadorned church buildings of pre-famine days and the virtual lack of ceremonial ritual such as singing and the use of incense at church services, now gave way to displays of elaborate ceremony in ostentatious buildings. Another contributing factor to the devotional revolution was the institution of confraternities, organizations, and devotional practices, all controlled by the clergy. Hence, the parish church became central to religious life. (Whelan, 1983.) Meanwhile, another set of religious practices declined—those that the clergy labeled "superstitions." Those include beliefs in a non-Christian supernatural realm and their associated "magical" practices. Such practices included communal gatherings at holy wells and other sites, and festivals at turning points in the cycle of the agricultural year. The "customary and communal" was now being superseded by the "canonical." (Miller 1975.)

The upsurge in piety also included the spread of such individual devotional aids as medals, prayer books and scapulars. Pre-famine clerical authority had been based on external control: priests sought "public reparation for public offence," which shows they thought in terms of a community. After the famine, however, the church was much more successful in instituting "internal control" so that guilt rather than shame kept the faithful from straying. (Connolly, 1983:131–32; 272–76.) Traditional satire of the clergy and of the central beliefs of Christianity almost vanished in the post-famine years (Connolly 1983:272–73). The Catholicism that the farmer class adopted was authoritarian and puritanical. Because the farmer class became the dominant class, this became the dominant religious orientation of the whole society.[3]

The Stem Family Economy

In the mid-nineteenth century the Catholic church was successful in getting virtually all its nominal members to "practice" their religion, that is, to attend mass every Sunday and to meet other canonical requirements. The success was due not just to internal reforms in the church, such as the strengthening of the power of the bishops, but also to the fact that the people were receptive to the church's teaching. The farmers' situation in society explains their receptivity. Elsewhere, I have argued that the farmers' situations made control of land increasingly crucial and that efforts to attain such control required each family to discipline its individual members (Hynes, 1978:147).

The "stem family system" that resulted has been widely described and investigated. This system is perhaps best known to those social scientists who are not Irish specialists, through the ethnographic reports of Arensberg and Kimball, based on fieldwork in the early 1930s. (Arensberg, 1937; Arensberg and Kimball, 1940, 1968.)[4] The essence of the system was that one heir, typically a son, inherited the farm. This son's marriage was arranged with the daughter of some similarly placed farmer family. This matchmaking occasioned intense bargaining between the families, with the man's inheritance balanced by the woman's dowry. In other words, the greater the value of the land the bigger the dowry. (Connell, 1968; Jackson, 1984.) Normally the dowry of the wife was used to marry the groom's sister or to provide in some way for other siblings. Men couldn't marry without land; women couldn't marry without dowries. These marriages typically took place at late ages and many never married. (Kennedy, 1973; Carney, 1980.) Those without prospects of marriage either emigrated or remained lifelong celibates. Marital fertility was high but there was little premarital or extramarital sexual activity.

The stem family system was a response of the farmer class to the economic situation. In turn, it explains its receptivity to the official Catholic teachings that resulted in the devotional revolution. Wallerstein, et al., have argued that households as income-pooling units "are not primordial entities which exist and somehow participate in a larger economic system" but instead are "created by the operations of the capitalist world economy" (1982:438; see also *Review*, 1983). With this perspective, we notice that the growing market for food in Britain made the export of Irish foodstuffs more profitable for those who had land. After the Napoleonic Wars ended in 1815, demand for grain to feed the army dropped sharply. As a result, it became more profitable to use land to graze livestock rather than for tillage. This meant, however, that a family needed more acres to make a living and required fewer people to work those acres. Those who could do so held onto the land they controlled. The stem family was adopted therefore as a strategy to keep enough land in the family's hands. When possible, families increased their holdings, often at the expense of their neighbors. (Smyth, 1983:27–28.) Under the system the farm was inherited by one heir and kept intact rather than being subdivided in each generation. This way men controlled the land, and fathers could usually post-pone retirement until very late in life. Thus, farmers' sons married late, if at all. The high proportion of people who never married acted as a control on the number of mouths that could become dependent on a given farm. This stem family system was already widespread among the farmer class before the fam-ine (see Hynes, 1978:143 for references) and after the famine became more rigid and more widespread. (Connolly, 1983:276; Jackson, 1984; Fitzpatrick, 1982:62–67; 1983:369.)

Family and Religion

To understand the connection between the stem family and the Catholi-cism that resulted from the devotional revolution, let's consider some patterns of social life inside and outside the family. The late ages at which most mar-ried and the high proportions of never-marrieds meant that usually a large number of single adults lived in the community. Because of this, one might expect rampant illicit sexual activity, but the evidence we have shows very low levels of pre- or extramarital sex (Jackson, 1984:1013). I suggest that one rea-son for this was that the people themselves were fully aware of the threat to the entire family should illegitimate mouths have to share the available resources (see Connolly, 1983:215). As a result, the Irish were receptive to the puritani-cal, anti-sex elements that the official Catholic church propagated. The Cathol-icism that grew to dominance was, in fact, an extremely puritanical version (among many writers see Whyte, 1971; Messenger, 1969; Lee, 1979). For example, an increasing separation of the sexes occurred in all areas of life. The pre-famine clergy also launched "all-out attacks" on only a few traditional observances such as wakes and patterns, "both of which . . . were opposed partly as examples of popular magic, but primarily as threats to popular morals." (Connolly, 192:115.) "Morals," in the language of Irish Catholics, meant sex-ual purity. As a result, "prudery seeped through Irish society and came close to being equated with morality itself." (Lee, 1979:40.)

The increasing separation of the sexes implied a rigid sex-role division stressing sex roles in labor and socialization patterns. Within the farmer fam-ily, the spouses each had their own sphere. The woman was responsible for raising the children and managing the house; the man was responsible for managing and working the farm to support the whole family.

Women's status dropped compared to men's in the society (Lee, 1979; Jackson, 1984). Perhaps the most important causes were related to the operation of the stem family system. First, since all the single women in a community (but only the *inheriting* single males) were in the marriage market, the law of supply and demand reduced the value of any particular woman. Plus, she needed a dowry, for which she had to rely on her father or brother. Second, she had to "keep her reputation." This further increased her receptivity to the puritanical elements in Catholicism already discussed. Third, even when married, the woman was still subordinate to the man because he controlled the land. The widening gulf between males and females would foster receptivity to beliefs stressing male authority and the different and subordinate position of women in the society. (Hynes, 1978:149.) Post-famine Catholicism was indeed male chauvinist, but whether it was more so than Catholicism in other places is difficult to decide. My impressions are that it was. (See, e.g., Rose, 1975.) Certainly it was more sexist than earlier in Ireland (Lee, 1979; Jackson, 1984).

The problem the farmer family faced was one of personnel management—how to mobilize the labor of all its members while subordinating their interests to the long-term ability of the farm to support them all. To mitigate the problem it was necessary that all family members accept the authority of the father and acknowledge the unity of the family. The farmer class absorbed Catholic teachings which emphasized the sanctity of the family and also the necessity of unquestioning obedience to those in authority. In schools that the Catholic church controlled, increasing numbers of dutiful teachers stressed docility and acceptance of the existing patriarchal system. (Lee, 1979:41–42.)

Smyth describes the development of a "specific historical consciousness which stressed the centrality of the family farm" (1983:28) in Irish society and shows how people competed for land as families rather than by aggressive individualism. Similarly, Knott (1984) has described the immense social and cultural significance of a family's ties to a particular piece of land. It might be said that the family and its particular farm came to be united symbolically and that this identification was the reason why in arranging marriages for heirs it was vitally important to "keep the family name on the land."

Among the most important, pervasive, and visible elements woven into the Catholicism that we have examined are the puritanical thread, the patriarchal authoritarian strand, and familism. We can see how each of them was particularly acceptable to those who adopted the stem family system. If we could examine the psychosocial interior of those families, we would find ways in which the family and religion systems both reinforced and undermined each other. For example, Connor (1976) has argued that where there is a strong familial bond, together with emotional closeness between children and their mother, there is likely to be general suppression of sexuality. And Slater has further suggested that where women are considered inferior, they treat their sons in ways that tend to perpetuate sexism and promote a "need to dominate and control women and to flee from their emotionality" (1977:88). From a psychoanalytical perspective, Russell (1984) has argued that the constellation of factors found in the rural Irish family—problematic family unity, close mother-son ties, an aloof father, and the suppression of sexuality— motivates religious beliefs that stress the Holy Family, Jesus as an obedient son, and the asexual nature of Mary and de-emphasize God the Father. Using the theories of Foucault and Elias, Inglis has argued that mothers' overwhelming responsibility for child-rearing, a result of the separation of spouses' roles, together with their lack of public economic power, led them to emphasize their moral qualities and that, in alliance with the church, mothers were thus the principal agents of reproducing successive generations of obedient Catholics (Inglis, 1984).

In the small-holding regions of the west, the "family economy" of the farmers made them receptive to authoritarian and puritanical Catholicism. As already noted, even though Irish farms there were smaller and poorer than elsewhere in Ireland and there were few farmers pure and simple, a "family economy" showed itself in several ways that we could predict from our analysis of the wider picture. Two points about western Ireland are worth noting. First, illegitimacy rates, though low throughout the country, were lowest there. I suspect these low rates were due to the importance (for nearly the entire population in those areas) of the family economy. Almost everyone who lived and worked on a small family farm, to help make ends meet also engaged in other economic activity such as illicit distilling, domestic spinning and weaving, etc. (See references in Hynes, 1978:153, note 10.) It is noteworthy that these lowest illegitimacy rates were found precisely in those areas of the country, the poor west, where the devotional revolution was latest in arriving (Connolly, 1983:215). The family economy preceded its religious legitimation. The highest illegitimacy rates were found in areas where the farmer class was stronger, commercial agriculture more developed, and the "devotional revolution" came earlier. It is plausible to suggest that the illegitimate children were produced not by the farmer class but by laborers/cottiers where they formed a separate landless stratum.

The second notable point about the western small-farm areas relates to the practice of seasonal migration to do harvest work elsewhere in Ireland or in Britain. O'Gráda (1973, 1980) has examined this issue and concludes that temporary migration or emigration was not used to escape poverty but as a "means of consolidating peasant property, at least temporarily" (1980:189). In other words, migration (and emigration) was a practice designed to maintain a family farm even when it was too small and poor to support a family. Smyth's (1983:33) evidence also supports this interpretation.

That this family-centered belief system was strongly entrenched is seen also in the behavior of Irish women who emigrated. Women responded to their falling power and status by leaving in greater numbers than men. (Ireland was the only country in which this was the case.) Jackson (1984:1018) sees this as women's refusal to accept their servile role in a patriarchal society. While their actions may seem to indicate autonomy, Diner, who has studied these women in the U.S., concludes that they do not. Their leaving Ireland and their work in America "stemmed from family loyalties," enabling them to better support and succor parents and siblings than if they had stayed in Ireland. (Diner, 1983:xiv.) Even in America these women postponed marriage because children would reduce their capacity to send money to their family in Ireland.

This stress on family loyalty should not be interpreted to mean that intra-family conflict was unknown. What were the rights, for example, of brothers whose father died without clearly designating an heir, of emigrant children who returned home, or of young widows? Given the central importance of land in the society and the frequent confusing kinship claims to particular farms, much of the agrarian violence throughout nineteenth-century Ireland involved clashes between various sets of relatives over who rightfully should occupy a farm. (Fitzpatrick 1982.)

The stem family system and its associated authoritarian and puritanical Catholicism were not perfectly compatible and mutually supportive. But it is important to realize that the needs of the family system took priority. And where Catholicism offered supportive teaching, the people accepted it. But Catholic teaching that ran counter to behavior involved in the family system was ignored. For example, clergymen fulminated against the abuse of alcohol, but did so in vain; drinking was one of the major activities of the large numbers of the unmarried men who were the product of the stem family system. The church preachings fall on deaf ears in other areas too: favoring of early marriage, hostility towards emigration, condemnation of certain social movements (especially those in the later part of the nineteenth century, when farmers organized against landlords to get a "firmer grip on their farms"). (See Hynes, 1978:147-48 for supporting references.)

Discussion

The world-systems perspective reduces the danger of provincialism in analyses of social phenomena but it carries with it the danger of economic reductionism. (For a world-systems treatment of religion in core societies, see Smith, 1986.) In the case examined in this paper it is clear that we cannot understand the changes that occurred in the family system and in religion without being conscious of local realities and the constraints these imposed on the options people would choose. It was the interaction between local circumstances and trans-national economic change that shaped the more immediate context within which people lived their lives.[5] The people selectively adopted official Catholic teachings and by looking at their circumstances we can plausibly explain why they accepted some teachings and rejected or ignored others. If economic considerations were of crucial importance to nineteenth-century Irish farmers, which is understandable in a society where quite literally "land was life," it does not follow that economic factors would in other places and at other times carry such overwhelming weight. In the Irish case, however, the claim that circumstances were more important than religious beliefs in shaping behavior is strongly supported by Eversley's (1981) findings that Irish Quakers' demographic behavior was much more similar to that of the Irish Catholics, among whom they lived as a small minority, than to that of their English co-religionists whom they "resembled closely in socioeconomic composition and life-style" (1981:86).

The Irish case illuminates the connection between the spread of a commercially oriented agriculture where the farms were controlled by those who worked them and a distinctive family system, which included the agricultural class adopting a particularly authoritarian and puritanical version of Catholicism. Examining this case, however, does more than enable us to better understand one society—albeit fascinating—at one point in time. By placing it in the context of a worldwide economic system, we can notice unseen connections, discover instructive parallel developments elsewhere, and understand the genesis of the drama's structure within which people acted their roles. For example, rather than just asking how sons fit into the stem family system (see Park, 1963:442), we can understand the development of the system. Most of the "new social history of the family," written from the "modernization" perspective, has concerned itself with case studies of countries or communities as they "modernized" (see Cherlin, 1983), and focused on internal processes rather than on external connections. As a result, we lack a sense of understanding of the interconnections between diverse phenomena around the world. In fact, in the numerous detailed studies of specific communities or issues that have been published, we lack a framework in which all of the various bits of the puzzle might fit. So the world-systems theory is here used because it promises to provide such a framework. Against its standard we can evaluate the significance and importance of any individual piece of research.

Irish family and religious patterns, in light of the country's peripheral position in the world market, suggest that there may be parallels in other peripheral countries undergoing commercialization of agriculture. Our perspective helps us to realize that the 1845–48 famine, which historians conventionally call "the last great European subsistence crisis" (Mokyr, 1983:262, 275), is also quite possibly the first great "modern" famine (see Gibbon, 1975; Perleman, 1977; Franke and Chasin, 1980:Part 1).

But comparisons do not have to be limited to such a general level of analysis. Let's take one example: Brazil. Examining this country provides a wealth of instructive parallels, and differences, with the Irish situation. There, too, the spread of agrarian capitalism involved class conflict. As in Ireland, the winners adopted a variety of Catholic principles that stressed the spirit of obedience, submission to authority figures, and love of the family. (Ribeiro de Olivera, 1979a:321–22.) And in both cases we find similar a "religious" response among those classes who were to lose the war: "messianism." (Ribeiro de Olivera, 1979a:316; Connolly, 1983:13, 109; O'Farrell, 1976; Donnelly, 1983.) Also, as had happened in Ireland, the clergy in Brazil opposed "popular superstitions" and traditional religious leaders and practices and attempted to substitute new devotional practices, feasts and associations they would control. As a result of this conflict "official Catholicism" was shaped and molded by those who adopted and adapted it to their own life circumstances. Because local circumstances differed between the two countries, so did the resultant

Catholicism. Where Irish Catholicism emphasized the Holy Family, for example, in Brazil nobles maintained control of slaves partly through ties of godfatherhood to children that created a "spiritual family" (Ribeiro de Olivera, 1979a:314; 1979b); godparenthood, an aspect of Catholicism virtually ignored in Ireland, thus came to be stressed in Brazil.

Notes

1. Most of the claims made in this paper about Irish society are not controversial among Irish historians; fuller documentation for many of them is found in Hynes (1978). Debate over the prevalence of the stem family system is reviewed later.

2. For a very useful study of one locality over time, see Smyth (1983). Fitzpatrick (1980) documents the virtual disappearance of farm laborers in the decades after the famine.

3. Major changes also occurred in denominations other than Catholicism but space precludes dealing with these here. Connolly (1985) reviews the relevant studies.

4. Gibbon and Curtin (Gibbon, 1973; Gibbon and Curtin, 1978; 1983a; 1983b) have questioned the widespread assumption that the stem family became predominant in rural Ireland in the nineteenth century and have also questioned the accuracy of Arensberg and Kimball's ethnography. It is well known that because of family life-cycle changes, even if stem family practices were universal in a society, only a minority of households would have three generations present at any one census date. Gibbon and Curtin (1978) found that between 12 and 13 percent of households were three generational in a sample of 1911 census returns. They accept Laslett's suggestion that 25 percent of households would be three generational in a pure stem system and thus argue that their data point to about half the population following stem practices.

Assuming, however, as I do for this paper, that the key feature of the stem family was impartible inheritance by one heir, a large number of variables influence the proportion of three-generational households at any given time. If the marriage of the heir took place after his parents' death, or if the older parent(s) moved to a separate residence on the succession of the heir or his marriage, there would be no three-generation phase. I cite these two cases not as hypothetical possibilities but as actual patterns described by historians and ethnographers of rural Ireland. (See Varley, 1983:387 for references.) Without a full understanding of the precise patterning of the events comprising the replacement of one family head by another (inheritance, marriage, residential arrangements, deaths, births, etc.) it is impossible to specify what percentage of households we would expect to be three generational in structure on a given census date. A figure of 12 to 13 percent is meaningless until interpreted. Fitzpatrick (1983) interprets very similar findings to support his claim that stem practices were very widespread. He also reconstructs household histories to show that in the first decade of this century succession to household head was by stem family practices in 74 percent of the known cases in two western areas studied. (1983:Table 9.) Hannan (1982) also disagrees with Gibbon and Curtin. Arguing that a system can be said to be viable if it reproduces itself Hannan used aggregate census data to examine succession rates, that is, the ratio between married farmers and farmers' sons, and how these rates changed over time. His data show stability in the system up to the end of World War II followed by a precipitous decline afterward.

For a quick though slightly dated guide to the literature on Irish family life in the last century, including conflicting interpretations by K. H. Connell (1968) and Kennedy (1973) on the impact of Catholicism, see Clarkson (1981).

5. International economic changes that crucially impacted rural Ireland included not only the changing market for food in Britain but, very important, the growing markets for labor in core societies that facilitated emigration and the development of British textile factories which undermined Irish cottage-based spinning and weaving, thereby removing an important source of income and power for rural Irish women (Hynes, 1978).

Bibliography

Arensberg, C. M. 1937. *The Irish Countryman*. New York: MacMillan.

Arensberg, C. M. and S. T. Kimball. 1940. *Family and Community in Ireland*. Cambridge, MA: Harvard University Press. (Expanded 2nd Edition 1968.)

Carney, Francis J. 1980. "Household Size and Structure in Two Areas of Ireland, 1821 and 1911" Pp. 149–65 in L. M. Cullen and F. Furet, eds. *Ireland and France, 17th to 20th Centuries: Toward a Comparative Study of Rural History*. Paris: Editions de l'Ecole des Hautes Etudes en Sciences Sociales.

Cherlin, A. 1983. "Changing Family and Household—Contemporary Lessons from Historical Research." *Annual Review of Sociology* 9:51-66.

Clarkson, L. A. 1981. "Marriage and Fertility in Nineteenth-Century Ireland." Pp. 237–55 in R. B. Outhwaite, ed. *Marriage and Society: Studies in the Social History of Marriage*. New York: St. Martins Press.

Connell, K. H. 1968. *Irish Peasant Society: Four Historical Essays*. Oxford: Clarendon Press.

Connolly, S. 1982. *Priests and People in Pre-famine Ireland*. Dublin: Gill and MacMillan.

Connolly, S. 1985. *Religion and Society in Nineteenth-Century Ireland. Studies in Irish Economic and Social History 3*. Dundalk: Dundalgan Press.

Connor, J. W. 1976. "Family Bonds, Maternal Closeness and the Suppression of Sexuality in Three Generations of Japanese Americans." *Ethos* 4:189-221.

Cullen, L. M. 1980. "The Social and Cultural Modernization of Rural Ireland, 1600-1900." Pp. 195–212 in L. M. Cullen and F. Furet, eds. *Ireland and France, 17th to 20th Centuries: Toward a Comparative Study of Rural History*. Paris: Editions de l'Ecole des Hautes Etudes en Sciences Sociales.

Diner, H. R. 1983. *Erin's Daughters in America: Irish Immigrant Women in the Nineteenth Century*. Baltimore: Johns Hopkins University Press.

Donnelly, J. S. 1983. "Pastorini and Captain Rock: Millenarianism and Sectarianism in the Rockite Movement of 1821-4." Pp. 102–39 in S. Clark and J. S. Donnelly, Jr., eds. *Irish Peasants: Violence and Political Unrest 1780-1914*. Madison, WI: University of Wisconsin Press.

Eversley, D. E. C. 1981. "The Demography of the Irish Quakers, 1650-1850." Pp. 57–88 in J. M. Goldstrom and L. A. Clarkson, eds. *Irish Population, Economy and Society: Essays in Honour of the Late K. H. Connell*. Oxford: Clarendon Press.

Fitzpatrick, D. 1980. "The Disappearance of the Irish Agricultural Labourer, 1841-1912." *Irish Economic and Social History* 7:66-92.

Fitzpatrick, D. 1982. "Class, Family and Rural Unrest in Nineteenth-Century Ireland," Pp. 37-75 in P. J. Drudy, ed. *Ireland: Land, Politics and People*. New York: Cambridge University Press.

Fitzpatrick, D. 1983. "Irish Farming Families Before the First World War." *Comparative Studies in Society and History* 25:339-74.

Franke, R. and B. Chasin. 1980. *Seeds of Famine: Ecological Destruction and the Development Dilemma in the West African Sahel*. Montclair, NJ: Allenheld, Osmun and Co.

Gibbon, P. 1973. "Arensberg and Kimball Revisited." *Economy and Society* 2:479-98.

Gibbon, P. 1975. "Colonialism and the Great Starvation in Ireland 1845-9." *Race and Class* 17:131-39.

Gibbon, P. and C. Curtin. 1983a. "Irish Farm Families: Fact and Fantasy." *Comparative Studies in Society and History* 25:429-53.

Gibbon, P. and C. Curtin. 1983b. "Some Observations on 'The Stem Family in Ireland Reconsidered.'" *Comparative Studies in Society and History* 20:393-95.

Gibbon, P. and C. Curtin. 1978. "The Stem Family in Ireland." *Comparative Studies in Society and History* 20:429-53.

Hannan, D. F. 1982. "Peasant Models and the Understanding of Social and Cultural Change in Rural Ireland." Pp. 141-65 in P. J. Drudy, ed. *Ireland: Land, Politics and People*. New York: Cambridge University Press.

Hynes, E. 1978. "The Great Hunger and Irish Catholicism." *Societas: A Review of Social History* 8:137-56.

Inglis, T. F. 1984. *Social and Cultural Reproduction: Catholicism and the Family in Modern Ireland*." Ph.D. thesis. Carbondale, IL: Southern Illinois University.

Jackson, P. 1984. "Women in 19th Century Irish Emigration." *International Migration Review* 18:1004-20.

Kennedy, R. E., Jr. 1973. *The Irish: Emigration, Marriage and Fertility*. Berkeley, CA: University of California Press.

Knott, J. W. 1984. "Land, Kinship and Identity: The Cultural Roots of Agrarian Agitation in Eighteenth- and Nineteenth-Century Ireland." *Journal of Peasant Studies* 12:93-108.

Larkin, E. 1972. "The Devotional Revolution in Ireland, 1850-75." *The American Historical Review* 77:625-52.

Lee, J. 1979. "Women and the Church Since the Famine." Pp. 37-45 in M. MacCurtain and D. O'Corrain, eds. *Women in Irish Society: The Historical Dimension*. Westport, CT: Greenwood Press.

Messenger, J. C. 1969. *Inis Beag: Isle of Ireland*. New York: Holt, Rinehart and Winston.

Miller, D. W. 1975. "Irish Catholicism and the Great Famine." *Journal of Social History* 9:81-98.

Mokyr, J. 1983. *Why Ireland Starved: A Quantitative and Analytical History of the Irish Economy, 1800-1850*. London: Allen and Unwin.

O'Farrell, P. 1976. "Millennialism, Messianism and Utopianism in Irish History." *Anglo-Irish Studies* 2:45-68.

O'Gráda, C. 1973. "Seasonal Migration and Post-Famine Adjustment in the West of Ireland." *Studia Hibernica* 13:48-76.

O'Gráda, C. 1980. "Demographic Adjustment and Seasonal Migration in Nineteenth-Century Ireland." Pp. 181–93 in L. M. Cullen and F. Furet, eds. *Ireland and France, 17th to 20th Centuries: Toward a Comparative Study of Rural History*, Paris: Editions de l'Ecole des Hautes Etudes en Sciences Sociales.

Park, G. 1963. "Sons and Lovers: Characterological Requisites of the Roles in a Peasant Society." *Ethnology* 1:412–24.

Perleman, M. 1977. *Farming for Profit in a Hungry World: Capital and the Crisis in Agriculture*. Montclair, NJ: Allenheld, Osmun and Co.

Review. 1982. Special Issue, Volume 7, Number 2. *The Household and the Large-Scale Agriculture Unit*.

Ribeiro de Olivero, P. A. 1979a. "The 'Romanization' of Catholicism and Agrarian Capitalism in Brazil." *Social Compass* 26:309–29.

Ribeiro de Olivero, P. 1979b. "Popular Catholicism and Hegemony in Brazil." *Archives des sciences sociales des religions* 47:53–79.

Rose, C. 1975. *The Female Experiment: The Story of the Women Movement in Ireland*. Galway: Arlen House.

Russell, J. C. 1984. "Family Experience and Folk Catholicism in Rural Ireland." *The Journal of Psychoanalytic Anthropology* 7:141–70.

Slater, P. 1977. *Footholds: Understanding the Shifting Family and Sexual Tensions in our Culture*. New York: E. P. Dutton.

Smith, P. 1986. "Anglo-American Religion and Hegemonic Change in the World System, c. 1870-1970." *The British Journal of Sociology* 37:88–105.

Smyth, W. J. 1983. "Landholding Changes, Kinship Networks and Class Transformation in Rural Ireland: A Case Study from County Tipperary." *Irish Geography* 16:16–35.

Varley, A. 1983. "The Stem Family in Ireland Reconsidered." *Comparative Studies in Society and History* 25:381–92.

Wallerstein, I., W. G. Martin and T. Dickinson. 1982. "Household Structures and Production Processes: Preliminary Thesis and Findings." *Review* 5:437–58.

Whelan, K. 1983. "The Catholic Parish, the Catholic Chapel, and Village Development in Ireland." *Irish Geography* 16:1–15.

Whyte, J. H. 1972. *Church and State in Modern Ireland*. Dublin: Gill.

10

The Effect of Domestic/Religious Individualism on Suicide

Steven Stack

Introduction

One method for relating the institutions of marriage/family and religion is through their shared emphasis on collectivistic values (Aldous and D'Antonio, 1983:9). Family life and religion can be linked together to the extent that they share values such as self-sacrifice for a broader social purpose; and a sense of duty, obligation, and caring for their members (Aldous and D'Antonio, 1983:15). In contrast to these collectivistic values, individualistic values are stressed by the larger society, including the economic institution (D'Antonio, 1983:82–85). Outside of the marriage/family-religion institutional complex, values such as individual achievement, competition, and efficiency predominate on the social scene. Furthermore, in terms of cultural change, many writers have argued that the strength of collectivistic values in the family/religion complex has declined over the last few centuries, given the emphasis on the values of individualism in the other institutional areas of life (Hargrove, 1983; Durkheim,

---

Steven Stack is Associate Professor of Sociology, Auburn University, Alabama. Professor Stack's research has focused on suicide as it is influenced by social integration. His numerous publications have established him as one of the leading experts in the study of suicide from a Durkheimian perspective. His latest concerns have been an attempt to address family and religious integration's effect on suicide rates. He received his Ph.D. from the University of Connecticut.

1966). Many observers of recent social trends maintain that the decline in collectivistic values in the domestic/religious complex has been further accentuated in the last twenty or so years (Bellah, 1976, 1978; Yankelovich, 1981; D'Antonio, 1980:96). Bellah has argued that the American emphasis on self-interest is no longer adequately restrained by religion. Yankelovich (1981:10) contends that American culture is now overwhelmingly marked by values such as "duty to myself" and self-fulfillment. The increased intensity of individualism over collectivism has been associated with various trends such as female labor-force participation, which decreases the probability of subordination to and love within the family (Aldous and D'Antonio, 1983:15; Degler, 1980).

The present paper's purpose is to gauge the effect of the fall in collectivistic values in the domestic/religious complex on suicide in the United States. The time frame is the period of considerable change in the nature of both religion and the family: 1954–1978. This period was marked by a substantial increase, for example, in both divorce and maternal labor-force participation within the institutional network of the family, and by considerable decline in some key indicators of religiosity, such as church attendance among the young. The present paper first outlines the theoretical reasons for predicting a higher suicide rate given a decline in the strength of the institutions of marriage/family and religion. Second, this study tests the assumption that changes in marriage/family variables are associated with changes in religious variables. Then, the paper presents an index of family/religion individualism and tests a series of hypotheses regarding the relationship between this individualism index and various suicide rates, including the suicide rate of the age cohort thought to be most affected by the increase in individualism—the youth cohort.

Religion and Suicide

The relationship between religion and suicide has been approached through at least two theoretical perspectives. First, there is the position that links the rise of individualistic culture to the decay in the general social fabric including religion, and such decay to problems of suicidal behavior (Durkheim, 1966; Halbwachs, 1978; Morselli, 1882; Masaryk, 1970). Second, there is the perspective that links specific qualities of religion to a lower propensity towards suicide (Stack, 1983b; Stark et al., 1983). In the former school a decline in religion is viewed as a consequence of a more general rise in self-interest, a force that makes life less meaningful and thereby promotes suicide. In the second school religion is taken out of this greater macrosociological perspective and is dealt with cross-sectionally without much reference to historical trends.

Probably most of the sociological work on the effect of religion on suicide has drawn on Durkheim's (1966:152–70) concept of religious integration (Stack, 1982:55–56). Durkheim asserted that integration depends on the subordination of an individual's interests to those of a group. An integrated society is one in which the culture of collectivism predominates over that of individualism. (Durkheim, 1966:209–16.) Durkheim maintained that personal well-being and happiness were a function of the individual's subordination to collective life. Such subordination is viewed in positive terms, as giving the individual a sense of purpose and making people think more about the trouble of others as opposed to dwelling on their own personal woes. (Durkheim, 1966:209–10.) Durkheim contended that a religion would decrease suicide in proportion to the sheer number of shared beliefs and practices in the religion. For this reason he argued that Catholics had a lower suicide rate than Protestants.

Other writers link religion to suicide through particular beliefs, practices, and other characteristics of religion. While Durkheim argued that the content of religious belief and practices was unimportant relative to the quantity of such, other writers focus on the content of a few life-saving aspects of religion. Certainly some beliefs (such as the virgin birth) would not have as much of a life-saving quality as others. For example, Stark and Bainbridge (1980) contend that a common life-saving feature of American religions is the belief in an afterlife. Given the promise of a happy afterlife, worldly, life-threatening crises such as the death of loved ones, unemployment, poor health, and divorce can be endured more readily. In addition, such earthly adversity also might be considered by a religious person as being relatively short-lived compared with eternal life. Such a perspective on time can help one to cope with hard times.

Stack (1983b:364–65) outlines additional ways in which specific aspects of religion may decrease the likelihood of suicide in the face of traumatic life events. First, religious books such as the Bible often describe role models such as Job who endured enormous suffering—greater than that of most everyday people—but who did not commit suicide. Those who are religious and compare their own sufferings with that of these idealistic role models may be more apt than the irreligious to take their own problems in stride. Second, the religious can read meaning into suffering and so can cope with it. Suffering can be viewed, for example, as God's plan or as penance for one's sins. Third, as Gouldner (1975) points out, religion provides an alternative stratification based on morality, not materialism. Those who fail to get ahead in secular society may derive considerable self-esteem from their rank in the religious order of morality. A quest for spiritual success may replace the quest for material success. Fourth, religion sometimes glorifes the state of poverty—"it is easier for a camel to go through the eye of a needle than for a rich man to enter the kingdom of God." Given that the poor have the highest rate of suicide (Stack, 1982), a religion that associates poverty with heavenly reward will help them to cope with their impoverishment and, hence, lower both their own rate and the national rate of suicide. Finally, the religious war against Satan may raise the passions of the religious, uniting them against a common enemy, and so may reduce suicide in a manner similar to a political event such as war.[1]

Research on the relationship between religion and suicide has been marked by conflicting results. While Durkheim's pioneering work on the subject found a relationship between religious affiliation and suicide, Pope's (1976:63–72) reanalysis of Durkheim's data casts serious doubt on whether there ever was a relationship between religious affiliation and suicide. A review of the research indicates that, for studies coming after Durkheim, there is usually no relationship between religious affiliation and suicide (Stack, 1982:55–56). However, this does not mean that religion is irrelevant to the prediction of suicide. Instead, studies using measures other than affiliation usually have found significant and sometimes substantial relationships between religiosity and suicide (Stark et al., 1983; Breault and Barkey, 1982; Stack, 1983a, 1983b). For example, Stack's (1983a) study of church attendance found that it was the leading predictor of suicide rates among the younger age cohorts. In comparative or cross-national research, religious book production rates have been associated with suicide rates (Stack, 1983b; Breault and Barkey, 1982). Finally, Stark, Doyle and Rushing (1983:128) report a negative correlation of -.36 between church membership rates and suicide rates in large American SMSAs. In summary, there is considerable evidence in support of a relationship between religion and suicide if one uses a measure of religion other than affiliation. Actually, both of the perspectives on religion and suicide may be viewed as correct if we measure the concept of subordination in terms of religiosity, as opposed to Durkheim's concept of integration based on the sheer number of shared religious beliefs and practices. The present study tests the following hypothesis:

H_1: The lower the religiosity in society, the greater the suicide rate.

A key problem with the existing work on religion and suicide is that a control for the state of the family is often absent (Stark et al., 1983; Stack, 1983a, 1983b; Pope and Danigelis, 1981). This is especially true in the work employing measures other than religious affiliation. In addition, essentially all but one of the works dealing with time-series analysis of trend data omit the religious factor altogether (Stack, 1983a). More work is needed to see if the religious variable exerts an effect on suicide that is independent of the effect of family variables over time. That is, is the effect of religion tied to a more general third variable—individualism? The present paper addresses this issue.

Domestic Life and Suicide

The present study focuses on two related dimensions of marriage and the family in its formulation of hypotheses regarding domestic life and suicide: divorce and mother's labor-force participation. Theoretical interpretations of the relationship between domestic variables and suicide rates range from the classic Durkheimian formulation of integration to current work relating role conflict and mother's labor-force participation to suicide potential (Durkheim, 1966; Stack, 1978). Both themes can be taken as measures of the degree of individualism in society.

As with the case of religion, the institutions of marriage and the family can act to reduce suicide potential through the subordination of the individual to the collectivity. For example, parents sacrifice some of their own interests and desires in order to meet those of their children. Financially, a new bicycle may be bought instead of a new business suit; a spouse ordinarily subordinates many of his/her needs to those of the partner; a mother may give up her career if she perceives that it may be detrimental to her parental role. Such subordination or collectivism involves putting the needs of others above or at the same level as one's own needs. This sense of mutual obligations constitutes the essence in life's meaning in Durkheim (1966:208-11) and, more generally, a haven in a "heartless world" in the marriage/family literature (for example, Lasch, 1977).

The importance of domestic institutions has been noted in the research on suicide (Maris, 1969:109-14; 1981; Stack, 1980, 1981a, 1981b; Heer and MacKinnon, 1974; see Stack, 1982, for a review). These writers draw associations between suicide and divorce from a variety of standpoints including structural conditions, role transformations, and psychological states common to the divorced population. For example, there is social isolation for the noncustodial parent—still typically the male. For both parents there is some loss of companionship. Sexual tensions are common. On an economic plane there is the structural problem of trying to maintain two households on about the same income, a condition that easily can feed anxiety, depression, and other negative psychological states conducive to suicide as the divorced couple experiences financial strain. Studies on the psychological states of the separated and divorced tend to corroborate the allegations of the structuralists. For example, Weiss (1975) reports a relatively high incidence of depression, prolonged introspection regarding the causes of the divorce, low self-esteem, guilt over the perceived self-produced loss of one's spouse, and a general deep sense of disorientation and loss. The negative consequences of divorce on well-being are not surprising, given the high priority that Americans give to a happy marriage. This is usually valued as number 1 or 2 in the annual Gallup poll (U.S. Bureau of the Census, 1976b:XLIII). Some observers of the relationship between divorce and suicide note that some divorcees who blamed their spouses for all their unhappiness become profoundly disillusioned and suicidal when they find themselves just as unhappy after they have rid themselves of their alleged problem (Lester and Lester, 1971:66). In any event the micro-oriented literature on the psychological states common among the divorced finds many patterns—depression, low self-esteem, and so on—that are common among the suicidal population (Lester and Lester, 1971:41–51; Lester, 1983:134–47). Thus, the second hypothesis tested here is as follows:

H_2: The greater the rate of divorce, the greater the suicide rate.

Caution must be exercised, however, in relating the micro-oriented research on the consequences of divorce to the present study, which is based on strictly ecological data. The reader should note that one cannot determine from these data how many suicides involve divorced persons. The paper can only demonstrate an association between the divorce rate on the one hand and the suicide rate on the other hand. Given the ecological nature of the data, it is entirely possible that the association between these two factors may be picking up divorce-related variables (such as the greater phenomenon of marital instability) which, in turn, are related to suicide.

A second aspect of domestic collectivism is mother's labor-force participation (MPLF). The present study asserts that MPLF constitutes a key consideration for the analysis of domestic collectivism from the standpoint of structuralist explanations of suicide. It assumes that MPLF reduces the amount of mother-child interaction. The degree of mother-to-child subordination should be somewhat reduced by the mother's participation in the labor force. However, this argument needs some tempering. For example, the mothers involved may be subordinating their self-interests in the economic institution. Work also can provide a source of integration. However, it seems reasonable to assume that the degree of potential family-based collectivism will probably decline in response to increased levels of MPLF. Finally, it is anticipated that the subculture surrounding work—a subculture largely based on individualistic values—will probably not be an effective substitute for collectivistic, family-centered values.

The research evidence on MPLF and suicide has been marked by some mixed results. Cross-national research (Miley and Micklin, 1972; Stack, 1978) and an investigation of Chicago (Newman et al., 1973) found support for the general thesis that female labor-force participation is associated with higher suicide rates. However, the association is sometimes found to be negative, not positive (Cumming et al., 1975). Cumming, Lazer and Chisholm (1975) found that suicide rates were lower for working women than for nonworking women in a British Columbian sample. This result can be interpreted in a number of preliminary ways which stress the benefits of MPLF. For example, the British Columbian women may have experienced high levels of collectivism at the work place which offset low levels at home. In addition, financial gains for the family that are achieved through female employment (and which should reduce economic anomie) may offset the collectivistic and psychological costs. For whatever reason, more research is needed to resolve the controversy over this variable's relation to suicide. The present study contributes by employing a time-series analysis, something not found in past, basically cross-sectional work.

The MPLF-suicide connection also can be interpreted from the standpoint of a role-conflict explanation of suicide. According to Gibbs and Martin (1964), suicide should vary inversely with the degree to which persons occupy incompatible statuses. For working mothers, MPLF can exemplify such status incompatibility. To the extent that women experience incompatibility between their duties as homemakers and as workers, it would be anticipated that the resulting role conflict and overload would increase the probability of suicide. In addition, to the extent that mates take offense at their wives working for such reasons as feeling like failures in the traditional provider role, MPLF could increase the male role conflict and suicide. A theoretical shortcoming of this perspective is that it neglects a consideration of the benefits of MPLF. Instead, it tends to focus on the costs involved. Finally, this perspective needs to address the issue of whether or not we might anticipate a change in the relationship, given a change in sex-role orientation stemming from the women's movement or as a response to substantial increases in MPLF itself. That is, with more cultural support for MPLF in our period of great gender-role change, the impact of MPLF on suicide might decline. It is beyond the scope of this paper to address these issues. Rather, it tests the more conservative position in the following hypothesis:

H_3: The greater the mother's labor-force participation, the greater the rate of suicide.

Methodology

The present investigation analyzes suicide rates from the U.S. as a whole for the period 1954–1978. The data on suicide are taken from Diggory (1976) for the 1954–1968 period. The remaining data were obtained through the cooperation of the U.S. National Center for Health Statistics. The rates refer to the number of suicides per 100,000 population. This period was chosen because it is the only period for which yearly data were available for the study's index of religiosity, church attendance. The analysis stops at 1978 because this was the most recent year for which final data on suicide were available from the U.S. National Center for Health Statistics at the time data were being collected.

Suicide rates were computed for four groups. First, a rate was computed for the general population (suicides/100,000 general population). Second, suicide rates are utilized for a subpopulation known to be disproportionately affected by trends in domestic and religious individualism: young adults, ages 15–29. For example, this age cohort was by far the most affected by religious individualism in the last twenty-five years. Its church attendance rate fell from a high of 48 percent in 1958 to a low of 28 percent in 1973. (Carroll et al., 1979:21; Gallup, 1982.)[2]

Since the present study uses official data on suicide, some caution should be exercised in interpreting its results. Critics of the official data have contended that suicide is often underreported for such reasons as the protection of family reputations (Douglas, 1967). While there undoubtedly is a downward bias in the reporting of suicide in some localities, the real issue is whether any alleged bias is systematic with regard to the unit of analysis. However, research by such writers as Sainsbury and Barraclough (1968), Mendelsohn and Pescosolido (1979), Shepherd and Barraclough (1978), Barraclough and White (1978), and Sainsbury (1973) indicate that any systematic bias in suicide reporting is minimal. In addition, the unit of analysis in the present study involves variation in the yearly suicide rate. There is no evidence of a time-related systematic bias in the underreporting of suicide (Marshall, 1978:764).

Religious Individualism

The present investigation uses average church/synagogue attendance as its measure of religiosity. Specifically, the measure is calculated on the basis of a number of national surveys given each year by the Gallup Poll. Each year the surveys took an average of the percentage of the American adult population responding "yes" to the question:

Did you yourself happen to attend church or synagogue in the last seven days?

Taken from Gallup (1982:32), data on national church attendance are available back to 1939. However, data before 1954 are available for only 1939 (February), 1940 (November), 1947 (May), and 1950 (April). A problem with the data before 1954 is that they are based on a single observation per year. Since church attendance varies somewhat according to the month of the year, peaking in April and October, the data before 1954 are viewed as unreliable. (Gallup, 1976, 1981:31–32.) The present investigation uses the data on national church attendance in Gallup (1982:32) for the period 1955–1978. In addition, it adds the data for 1954 from Erskine (1964:671) which is an average of church attendance estimates for five different weeks in 1954. These data are most suitable for assessing the influence of religiosity on the suicide rate of the national, adult (over 18) population.

Data were also collected on the church attendance rate of the 18- to 29-year-old cohort. These were taken from the same surveys mentioned above and follow the same methodologies. (Gallup, 1981; Erksine, 1964.)[3]

Church attendance is one of the few measures of religious collectivism for which yearly data are available. An alternative measure, church membership, was not used since it does not represent as much religious collectivism as attendance at rituals.[4] A strength of the church attendance measure is that available evidence indicates that it is related to other dimensions of religiosity. Johnstone's (1975:83–85) analysis of national data indicates that church attendance was correlated with measures of belief and knowledge. Church attendance was related to important religious beliefs such as belief in Satan and numerous measures of religious knowledge. Also, other research has noted the linkage between church attendance and adherence to orthodox religious beliefs (Hoge and Carroll, 1978; Martin and Nichols, 1962; Hynson, 1975; Hoge and Petrillo, 1978). Finally, church attendance has been linked to participation in still other rituals (Gallup, 1976:25). In short, the present study follows Demerath (1968:367–68) in arguing that the trend in the percentage of adults reporting church attendance is one of the more reliable indicators of overall religious change. In order to make the measure of domestic/religious individualism unidimensional, the church attendance scores were subtracted from 100 to form church absence rates.

Domestic Individualism

Domestic individualism is measured along two dimensions: the rate of mother's participation in the labor force and the divorce rate. The rate of mother's participation in the labor force (MPLF) is measured as the percentage of married women with husbands present and with children under six years of age, who are in the labor force. It is anticipated that the group of married women who might experience the greatest role conflict would be those with preschool-aged children. Older children are normally enrolled in school. Mothers of older children can more readily avoid role conflict, given their lower involvement in child care. In addition, there is less reason to believe that MPLF would constitute mother's lack of subordination to the family when the home is empty when the children are at school. The data are from the U.S. Bureau of the Census (1976a, 1971–1980). A limitation of this index is that it does not distinguish between full-time and part-time women workers. The former might experience more role conflict and overload as well as a lower level of domestic collectivism. However, usually at least two-thirds of working women are full-time workers, so this is not a major limitation. (Harris and Henderson, 1981:216.) In any event data were unavailable to construct a more refined measure based on full-time workers. The measure used here is an improvement over the past research based on the proportion of women in the labor force. Such an index counts women such as single females, who are unlikely to experience role conflict between work and household duties.

The rate of divorce is measured as the number of divorces per 1,000 married females. The data are from the U.S. Bureau of the Census (1976a:64; 1971–1980). A crude divorce rate was not used, due to sensitivity to changes in the age structure of the population (Kenkel, 1977:328).

In addition to the domestic and religious variables, the present inquiry also includes variables from three other perspectives on suicide. The purpose in including these variables is mainly to weight the explanatory power of domestic/religious individualism against some alternative condition thought to promote suicide. The three additional variables are economic anomie, presidential elections, and suggestion/imitation.

Economic Anomie

The measure of economic anomie used in the present study is the number of unemployed workers as a percentage of the civilian labor force. The age-specific unemployment rate is used in order to match the data on age-specific church attendance and suicide rates. The data were taken from U.S. Bureau of Labor Statistics (1982:478–501). The data on unemployment and church attendance did not match perfectly because of age cutoffs in the unemployment source; however, they were matched as closely as possible. The unemployment rate for 16–24-year-olds was matched with the suicide rate for 15–29-year-olds. This was done since the data source on unemployment provided only data for ten-year age cohorts. The relevant hypothesis is as follows:

H_4: The greater the unemployment rate, the greater the rate of suicide.

Presidential Elections

Boor (1981, 1982) has presented evidence of a presidential death dip whereby suicides tend to drop in the period before a presidential election. This can be interpreted from the standpoint of a Durkheimian theory of political integration and suicide. The present paper models the effect of presidential elections as a dummy variable, where 1 = a presidential election year and 0 = other years. The following hypothesis is tested:

H_5: The suicide rate will be lower in presidential election years compared with other years.

Suggestion/Imitation

The literature also contains studies that confirm a suggestion/imitation theory of suicide (Phillips, 1974; Bollen and Phillips, 1982). In this view suicide stories published in the media will promote additional suicides through the processes of suggestion and imitation. No one to date, however, has modeled this theory using the year as the unit of analysis. A key issue is whether or not suicide stories simply determine *when* and not so much *why* people kill themselves. It is possible that a suicide story may simply move up the date of suicides among people who would have committed suicide anyway within a few months. If this is the case, the number of suicide stories in the media per year would not be related to the national suicide rate. The present article measures media stories on suicide in the same fashion as the literature on the monthly suicide rate: the number of front-page stories on suicide in the *New York Times*. (Phillips, 1974; Wasserman, 1983, 1984.) The data source is the *New York Times* Index. The hypothesis to be tested here is:

H_6: The greater the media coverage of suicides, the greater the suicide rate.

Time-Series Issues

Since some readers may not be familiar with econometric methods of time-series analysis (a 1982 review by Miller et al. of methods in studying marriages and families failed to deal significantly with these techniques), the present paper discusses some of the relevant details.

Three somewhat related issues face the researcher in time-series analysis. These are autocorrelation, trending, and finding the appropriate lag structure. These issues are important since, if certain assumptions are not met regarding them, the results of a time-series analysis will be erroneous. That is, for example, if autocorrelation exists in the error terms from a regression analysis of time-series data, one of the fundamental assumptions of regression analysis has been violated. The results of such an analysis probably would not be valid.

Autocorrelation is said to be present when the error terms from an analysis are not independent; that is, e_t and e_{t-1} are significantly correlated. Expressed another way, autocorrelation exists when two variables are correlated: the error term and the lag of the error term.[5]

Tests for autocorrelation include the Durbin-Watson d and b statistics, the Geary test based on the number of sign changes in the residual plot, and the Von Neuman ratio (Habibagahi and Pratschke, 1972; Parker, 1980). The present study employs the Durbin-Watson d statistic in its test for autocorrelation for the following reasons. Durbin's b statistic is appropriate only for models with lagged dependent variables, and there are none in the present analysis. Both the Geary test and the Von Neuman ratio require more cases than those found in the present data set (Johnston, 1972:250).[6]

A second problem in time-series analysis is the problem of trending; that is, the dependent and/or independent variables tend to increase or decrease over time (Wonnacott and Wonnacott, 1979:200–201). This is often the case in sociological analyses such as those of female crime rates (Austin, 1982), educational enrollments (Ralph and Rubinson, 1980; Rubinson and Ralph, 1984; Walters, 1984), economic output (Walters and Rubinson, 1983), income ratios (Devine, 1983), and crime trends (Cohen and Felson, 1979; Cohen et al., 1980). When two variables vary together over time, the trending can produce high R^2 values. For example, Cohen reports R^2 statistics of 99 (Cohen et al., 1980; Cohen and Felson, 1979).

The problem of trending is related to the problem of autocorrelation since autocorrelation means that successive observations are dependent on each other, such as in positive autocorrelation where the second observation tends to resemble the first observation and so on (Wonnacott and Wonnacott, 1979:2112).[7]

One possible solution to the problem of trending is to transform all the variables into change values by the first difference technique.[8] The first difference method, however, is based on the assumption that p = 1. Kmenta (1971:290–92) illustrates that this should be used only if we know that p = 1. Econometricians agree that, unless one knows that p = 1, one should use a technique to estimate it before transforming the data into change values (Wonnacott and Wonnacott, 1979:218; Stewart and Wallis, 1981:232; Ostrom, 1978:38–40). Since the present study uses data wherein the p value is unknown (which is almost always the case in the social sciences), it will adopt what is known as an iterative first differences method for transforming the data into change values with less of trend to them, or with the trend removed.[9]

The present study adopts the Cochrane-Orcutt iterative first difference technique. This is the differencing technique used most widely in sociological time-series analysis. (Rubinson and Ralph, 1984; Wasserman, 1983, 1984; Stack, 1981a, 1982; Stack and Haas, 1984; Box and Hale, 1984:482; Walters, 1984; Walters and Rubinson, 1983.)[10]

Note that data analyzed under the Cochrane-Orcutt iterative first difference technique refer to change scores and not the original data points. The data are transformed from straight levels or rates to changes in levels or rates.

The desired effect of this transformation of data is to detrend the series and purge it of the associated problem of autocorrelation.

The reader should be cautioned about high R^2 values in analyses using iterative first difference techniques. These techniques tend to minimize the sum of the squared errors so that one can obtain an underestimate of the true variance and a high degree of variance explained. See Buse (1973) for a discussion. While literally all analyses of time-series data in sociology report high R^2 statistics, few mention this bias. For example, R^2 statistics are reported as follows: up to 98 (Devine, 1983), up to 88 (Wasserman, 1983), between 82 and 93 (Wasserman, 1983), up to 99 (Walters, 1984), and up to 89 (Box and Hale, 1984). The present investigation, it is anticipated, also will report high R^2 values, but these are common in time-series analysis, especially that based on iterative procedures.[11]

To help clarify the issues of trending and autocorrelation, the paper now turns to an assessment of two plots of one of its independent variables, the divorce rate. Figure 1 illustrates the upward, somewhat parabolic trend in the divorce rate over time. Analysis of these data together with data on the suicide trend (also marked by a general upswing) was marked by the problem of autocorrelation. The present analysis begins by taking the first difference of each variable in order to detrend the series of each. Figure 2 illustrates the plot of the first difference of the divorce rate. This simple transformation (which assumes that p = 1) greatly reduces the upswing in the curve. The Cochrane-Orcutt procedure searches for a value of p < 1 which should reduce the degree of autocorrelation further than that for the data in Figure 2.

Figure 1. Divorce Rate

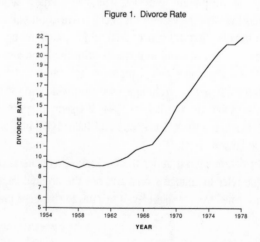

188

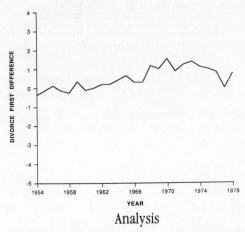

Figure 2. Divorce Rate First Difference

Analysis

The matrix of zero-order correlation coefficients is given in Table 1. Both indicators of domestic individualism (divorce and mother's participation in the labor force) are highly related to the total suicide rate. Religious individualism—measured as church absence—is also highly related to suicide ($r = .82$). The presidential election and media dummy variables are not significantly related to suicide. Finally, as anticipated, the unemployment rate bears a significant positive relationship to suicide. However, it should be pointed out that time (year) is also correlated both with the suicide rate and with trends in the independent variables from the domestic/religious complex. These high correlations indicate trending in the data and the likelihood that the disturbance terms are autocorrelated. Figure 3 provides the plot of the suicide rate against time.

There are some problems of multicollinearity among the independent variables. The indicators of domestic individualism are highly correlated ($r = .96$). In addition, the religious individualism factor is highly correlated with each of these domestic variables ($r = .86$, $r = .88$). Charts plotting these three variables indicate that generally they all increased together over the period under analysis (see Figures 1, 4, and 5).

These correlations are all marked by the problem of trending among the three religious/domestic variables. It is not clear, therefore, whether or not changes in the variables are associated with one another. To test for the associations among the three core independent variables, the present study transformed the original data points by the iterative first difference technique of Cochrane-Orcutt. The results of the regressions applied to these data are given

TABLE 1. PEARSON CORRELATION MATRIX, MEANS, STANDARD DEVIATIONS

Variables	1	2	3	4	5	6	7	8	9
1. Church absence	—	.88*	.85*	-.04	.01	.22	.90*	.82*	.91*
2. Mother's labor-force participation		—	.96*	-.02	-.03	.43*	.99*	.95*	.99*
3. Divorce rate			—	-.06	-.01	.53*	.98*	.93*	.93*
4. *New York Times* suicide stories				—	-.14	.16	-.03	.05	-.02
5. Presidential election year					—	-.02	-.02	-.06	.00
6. Unemployment rate						—	.44*	.62*	.38
7. Domestic/Religious Individualism Index							—	.95*	.98*
8. Total suicide rate								—	.93*
9. Year									
Mean	56.1	25.8	13.2	1.44	.24	5.33	0	11.2	1966
SD	3.00	7.95	4.63	1.16	.44	1.25	9.51	.93	7.35

*$p < .05$.

in Table 2. In all cases changes in one variable are indeed associated with changes in another variable. Hence, even with detrended data, free of the problem of autocorrelation, these independent variables are closely associated.

The results of the plots of the independent variables, bivariate zero-order corrrelation, and the iterative first difference equations in Table 3 all point in the same direction. That is, the indicators of domestic and religious individualism are relatively inseparable. They form a common variable or factor measuring the greater phenomenon of individualism.

To test for the problem of autocorrelation and trending with respect to the suicide variable, a regression analysis using untransformed data and ordinary least squares (OLS) techniques was performed for each independent variable on the total suicide rate. Four of the six regressions had Durbin Watson *d* statistics that indicated the presence of positive autocorrelation. A seventh regression which regressed time on suicide, also was marked by autocorrelation. Given these problems of autocorrelation, the analysis now turns to the Cochrane-Orcutt estimates based on transformed data. These data refer to changes in the variables, the original data points having been transformed using the technique of iterative first difference.[12]

Table 3 provides the results of the Cochrane-Orcutt iterative first difference procedures with each of the variables entered into the analysis by itself.

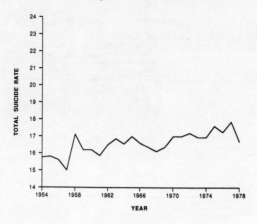

Figure 3. Total Suicide Rate

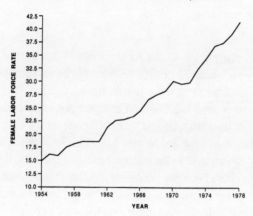

Figure 4. Mother's Labor - Force Participation Rate

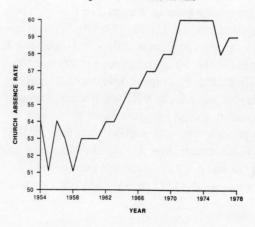

Figure 5. Church Absence Rate

TABLE 2. COCHRANE-ORCUTT ITERATIVE FIRST DIFFERENCE ESTIMATES OF THE BIVARIATE RELATIONSHIPS BETWEEN DOMESTIC AND RELIGIOUS INDIVIDUALISM, 1954-1978

Independent Variables	Dependent Variables		
	Church Absence	MPLF	Church Absence
Divorce rate	.495[a]	1.66	
	.129[b]	.185	—
	3.81*	8.99*[c]	
MPLF			.274
	—	—	.063
			4.37*
Durbin-Watson *d*	2.38	1.47	2.24
Autocorrelation	None	None	None
R^2	93	63	91

[a]Regression coefficient.
[b]Standard error.
[c] *t* ratio.
* *t* statistic significant at .05 level.

Columns 1 and 3 provide the results for the religious and marital individualism variables. In each case 70 percent or more of the variance is explained. Given the close association in these trends, however, when two or three of these variables are entered together into analyses not reported here, one or two become totally insignificant. The beta coefficient for the significant individualism variable often exploded to over 1.00. This indicates that, given the multicollinearity among the individualism variables, the betas for some are biased upwards and the betas for the others are biased downward.

The present paper contends that these intercorrelations and trends indicate that the three variables are all measuring the same underlying weakening of social collectivism. For this reason, in the multivariate analysis the three are combined into a single index of individualism through a principal components analysis (Kleinbaum and Kupper, 1978:389-92). The first of the three factors from the principal components analysis was used, since this is the one that loads most heavily on the individual components. The resulting principal component is referred to as the Domestic/Religious Individualism Index. It measures church absence, divorce, and MPLF which are all conceptualized as measures of individualism. Its plot appears in Figure 6.

A separate principle components analysis was done for the variables representing the youth cohort, ages 15-29. The cumulative percentages of eigenvalues for the first principal component were 97 and 96 respectively for the components representing the total and youth populations.

TABLE 3. COCHRANE-ORCUTT ITERATIVE FIRST DIFFERENCE ESTIMATES OF THE EFFECTS OF THE INDEPENDENT VARIABLES ON THE TOTAL SUICIDE RATE, 1954–1978

Variables	Equation					
	1	2	3	4	5	6
Divorce rate	.186*[a] .073[b] 10.74[c]	—	—	—	—	—
MPLF	—	.108* .010 11.19	—	—	—	—
Church absence rate	—	—	.017 .063 .027	—	—	—
New York Times suicide stories	—	—	—	.075 .049 1.55	—	—
Presidential election year	—	—	—	—	- .125 .117 -1.06	—
Unemployment rate	—	—	—	—	—	.213* .070 3.04
Durbin-Watson *d* statistic	1.93	1.89	2.18	2.27	2.21	2.38
Autocorrelation	none	none	none	none	none	none
R^2	82	84	70	70	70	78

[a]Regression coefficient.
[b]Standard error.
[c]*t* ratio.
**t* statistic significant at .05 level.

Figure 6. Domestic/Religious Individualism Index

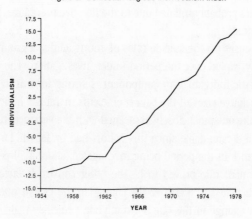

193

TABLE 4. COCHRANE-ORCUTT ITERATIVE FIRST DIFFERENCE ESTIMATES OF THE DOMESTIC/RELI-GIOUS INDIVIDUALISM INDEX AND UNEMPLOYMENT ON THE TOTAL SUICIDE RATE, 1954–1978

Variables	Total Suicide Rate	Male Suicide Rate	Female Suicide Rate
Domestic/Religious Individualism Index	.751**	.468**	.384**
New York Times stories	.030	.028	.041
Presidential election year	.021	-.055	-.130
Unemployment	.207**	.381**	.267*
R^2	96	86	34
Durbin-Watson *d* statistic	1.92	1.88	1.99
Autocorrelation at .05 level	None	None	None

*Associated *t* statistic significant at the .10 level.
**Associated *t* statistic significant at .05 level.

Table 4 presents the results of the three regressions employing the domestic/religious individualism principal component in an analysis of the total, male, and female suicide rates. Column 1 suggests that the principal component influences suicide in the anticipated direction. The greater the change in the religious/domestic individualism, the greater the change in the total suicide rate. In contrast, neither national election years nor media stories influence the overall suicide rate. As in Marshall's (1981) investigation, the greater the change in the unemployment rate, the greater the change in the suicide rate.

With respect to the sex-specific rates, the religious/domestic component is significantly related to both, as is the rate of unemployment. In all three regressions, the presidential election year variable is insignificant. None of the regressions is marked by autocorrelation. The equations have R^2s between 34 and 96, but these are probably inflated due to the iterative procedure (Buse, 1973), as discussed earlier.

Table 5 focuses on the suicide rates of young adults, a group whose suicide rate nearly tripled over the period under investigation. The effect of the religious/domestic individualism component is strong for this age cohort. In addition, the relative sizes of the beta coefficients in Table 5 indicate that this component is the one most closely associated with the variance in suicide over time. This is understandable since this cohort had by far the largest drop in church attendance in the period being investigated (about a 50 percent drop). The unemployment rate proved to be the other consistent factor predicting suicide. As anticipated, the greater the change in the rate of unemployment, the greater the change in the rate of young adult suicide. Again, presidential

TABLE 5. COCHRANE-ORCUTT ITERATIVE FIRST DIFFERENCE ESTIMATES OF THE EFFECT OF THE DOMESTIC/RELIGIOUS INDIVIDUALISM INDEX AND OTHER VARIABLES ON YOUTH SUICIDE RATES, 1954–1978

Variables	Total 15–29 Suicide Rate	Suicide Rate: Males, 15–29	Suicide Rate: Females, 15–29
Domestic/Religious Individualism Index	.902**	.965**	.880**
New York Times suicide stories	.013	.020	.172*
Presidential election year	-.016	-.031	-.101
Unemployment rate (16–24)	.127**	.139**	.235**
R^2	98	96	67
Durbin-Watson *d* statistic	2.10	1.98	1.89
Autocorrelation at .05 level	None	None	None

*Associated *t* statistic significant at the .10 level.
**Associated *t* statistic significant at .05 level.

election years bear no significant impact on suicide, independent of the other variables in the equation. The media-stories variable significantly increases the rate of female suicide, using $p < .10$. This is the only evidence found in the present study in support of the suggestion theory of suicide.

Conclusion

The present investigation has tested a model of suicide that combines trends in the marital/family and religious institutions into a common component. It offers strong support for the notion that families and religions change together over time. It supports the notion of such writers as Aldous and D'Antonio (1983) that the two institutions may represent the same set of collectivistic values. As these values decline, so will the relative importance of both institutions. As the importance of the domestic/religious institutional complex declines, the study finds a rise in the rate of suicide both for the general population and for the age cohort at the center of the decline, the youth cohort. Past research on suicide based on just a single variable in the religious/domestic complex is bound to exaggerate the effect of that one variable, taken out of the context of greater cultural change (for example, Stack, 1983a).

One unanticipated finding should stimulate further work. Both for the general population and for the youth cohort, the model works better for males than for females. While it is beyond the scope of the present paper to systematically explain this differential, two lines of explanation might be tested in future work. First, it very well may be that males suffer more from MPLF than do their wives. That is, they may experience, for example, more role conflict than their wives from their wives' employment. This explanation was suggested for some similar findings in a cross-national study. (Stack, 1978.) Second, the increase in suicide potential from MPLF may be tempered for the mothers involved, given the benefits of employment such as adult companionship, career mobility, and extra income; so while this trend is associated with increased suicide for females, the increase is not as great as it might be, since the benefits of employment for the mothers offset some of the costs. In contrast, for the males the principle benefit may only be additional income.

The economic anomie theory received strong support. In five or six regressions, the unemployment rate was significant (at the .05 level). This finding is consistent with previous work. However, the associations between unemployment and suicide are sometimes stronger for males than for females. This is often interpreted from the standpoint of gender-role theory: in this view the male is still under much greater pressure to be employed, and to be the principal breadwinner, than the female. Hence, unemployment should promote more anomie for the male than for the female as long as sex roles regarding employment expectations are different between the sexes.

Some caution should be exercised in generalizing the results of the present study since it is based on the U.S., a nation marked by relatively high levels of economic individualism. The results may not replicate for other nations with high levels of economic collectivism and integration. For example, it might be that in such nations as Japan or Sweden the trends in domestic and religious individualism may be tempered or even offset by economic collectivism. That is, in a context of economic collectivism, the relationship between domestic/religious individualism and suicide might disappear or be reduced. One indicator of economic collectivism is the percentage of the labor force belonging to unions. The U.S. and Sweden represent opposite poles among industrial nations on this index: approximately 20 percent and 80 percent unionized, respectively Possibly a future study might replicate this investigation for the Swedish case.

Notes

1. Tittle and Welch (1983) interpret the association between low religiosity and deviance from several theoretical perspectives. While their article does not deal with suicide per se, the broad theoretical arguments reviewed have some relevance to the present discussion. First, from the perspective of functionalism, religion fosters moral commitments and controls deviance by

linking supernatural sanctions to moral precepts. For the present purpose, it is assumed that the greater the religiosity, the greater the moral revulsion or potential feelings of guilt towards suicide, and the lower the propensity to suicide. Second, from the perspective of differential association theory—given that most religious people tend to be conventional (e.g., opposed to suicide)—the greater the associations with religious people (e.g., attendance at religious services), the less the likelihood of deviance (e.g., suicide). Third, various psychological and social-psychological perspectives suggest a negative association between religiosity and suicide. For example, Gorsuch (1976) contends that religious involvement fosters behavioral ideals whereby the contemplation of rule-breaking behavior sets in motion strong feelings of cognitive dissonance, which effectively lowers the incidence of deviant behavior. Fourth, from a standpoint of deterrence theory also, we would suspect a negative association between religiosity and suicidal behavior. The main idea here is that the greater the potential costs of deviance, the lower its incidence. Given that those who ponder deviating from religious norms against suicide could anticipate informal negative sanctions from the religious community, they should be less likely to attempt suicide. Finally, conflict theory also might predict a negative association between religiosity and suicide. Given that the frustrations associated with perceived failure promote suicidal behavior, religion can reduce suicide potential by diverting individual aspirations to the afterlife. This is similar to Gouldner's notion of the positive function of religion as an alternative stratification system. In a Marxist perspective, religion functions in this fashion as an opium of the people. Using Merton's (1938) theory of anomie, religion can take the edge off of the anomie felt by the lower class. To the extent that religion detracts people from exploitative social arrangements, subordinate status, and other problems associated with deviant behavior, it should reduce suicide potential.

2. In contrast, church attendance rates remained relatively constant for those over fifty years old and declined only somewhat for the middle-aged group (thirty to forty-nine). As we might expect, moreover, suicide rates did not increase substantially for the older age cohorts; in fact, the suicide rate for the elderly actually decreased in this period. In contrast, the youth suicide rate increased by nearly 300 percent. A second reason why the present study focuses on the youth suicide rate is that this group also experienced the greatest upswing in domestic individualism. For example, it has the highest divorce rate, since most divorces occur in the first seven years of marriage and since people generally marry in their early twenties. (Eshleman, 1981.) In analyses not reported here, the effect of domestic/religious individualism was usually not significant in the prediction of the suicide rates of the older cohorts, who were relatively insulated from domestic and religious change. It is beyond the scope of this paper to search for explanations for the changes in the suicide rates of the older cohorts. Instead, the reader is referred to two studies. The work of Marshall (1978) indicates that the decline in the elderly suicide rate is largely attributable to the improvement of Social Security benefits. Ahlburg and Shapiro (1984) attribute the low middle-aged suicide rate to the improved labor-market position of this group relative to the increasingly poor labor-market position for the younger cohort.

3. For several years some age-specific church attendance rates were not available. For these years linear point interval estimates were made to fill in the missing values.

4. Another possibility for a measure of religiosity would be religious book production (Breault and Barkey, 1982). However, annual data on the number of books produced are not available for most years for the U.S. Instead, annual data on religious books refer to the number

of new titles and new editions (U.S. Bureau of the Census, 1976a:803, 808). Since the number of titles says nothing about the actual numbers of each respective title produced, these data were not used.

5. There are two broad categories of autocorrelation. In positive autocorrelation a positive error tends to be followed by another positive error, and negative errors tend to be followed by additional negative errors. Here, the greater the value of the variable e_t, the greater the value of e_{t-1}. A plot of residuals from such an analysis would resemble an S or sine curve. In contrast, in negative autocorrelation a negative error term tends to be followed by a positive error term, and vice versa. Here, the greater the value of e_t the less the value of e_{t-1}. A plot of residual values here would show a line zigzagging back and forth from positive to negative error terms. The first-order autoregressive function can be expressed as $e_t = p\, e_{t-1} = V_t$, where p is a regression coefficient and V is a random variable. (Ostrom, 1978:16.) Each disturbance term is equal to a proportion (p) of the preceding disturbance term plus a random variable (V). P values range between -1 and $+1$. Perfect positive autocorrelation occurs if $p = 1$; perfect negative autocorrelation occurs if $p = -1$; and a value of $p = 0$ always means the total absence of autocorrelation.

6. As Kelejian and Oates (1974) point out, the Durbin-Watson d statistic can be calculated as follows: $d = 2(1-p)$. Given that the coefficient varies between -1 and $+1$, the range of d is from 0 to $+4$. Hence, $p = 0$ implies $d = 2$ and no autocorrelation; $p = -1$ implies $d = 4$, perfect negative autocorrelation; $p = +1$ implies perfect positive autocorrelation. In the social sciences positive autocorrelation is far more common than is negative autocorrelation (Ostrom, 1978). Durbin and Watson (1950, 1951) established upper and lower limits for d in testing for the presence of autocorrelation in analyses of different sample sizes and different numbers of predictor variables. An expanded version of their table for small samples and greater numbers of predictor variables is available in Johnston (1984:554-57). As Johnston (1984:315-16) points out, if $d < d_L$, then positive autocorrelation is present; if $d_u < d < 4-d_u$, autocorrelation is absent; if $d_L \leq d \leq d_u$, the test is inconclusive. In the present study with a sample of 25 and one independent variable, the appropriate d values for testing for positive autocorrelation would be d-lower $= 1.29$, and d-upper $= 1.45$ (Johnston, 1984:556-57). A d value of less than 1.29 would mean that the error terms were marked by positive autocorrelation; a value in between and including 1.29 and 1.45 would be in a gray or inconclusive area; a value between 1.46 and 2.54 would mean an absence of positive autocorrelation; values above 2.54 would indicate either negative autocorrelation (>2.72) or inconclusiveness in another gray region (2.54-2.71).

7. In one study that reported Durbin-Watson statistics and failed to transform the original data, only 4 of 24 OLS regressions were free of autocorrelation (Ralph and Rubinson, 1980).

8. Here one transforms all the original data points into first differences: $Y_t - Y_{t-1}$ and $X_t - X_{t-1}$; then one estimates the equation as follows: $Y_t - Y_{t-1} = a + b(X_t - X_{t-1}) + (e_t - e_{t-1})$.

9. A second technique that has been used to address trending and/or autocorrelation has been the autoregressive model, a model where a lagged dependent variable is introduced as an independent variable (e.g., Cohen and Felson, 1979; Devine, 1983): $Y_t = b\, Y_{t-1} + e_t$. This technique, however, may not be appropriate because, theoretically, one must have some reason to expect the previous values of the dependent variable will affect the present values. While this may be true in studies of macroeconomic indicators such as inflation, numerous sociological

dependent variables, such as suicide, are thought to be affected mainly by independent variables and not by previous values of the dependent variable. If this technique is chosen, OLS is probably not an appropriate technique to apply to the data since the estimates will probably overestimate b, underestimate p, and Durbin-Watson's *d* will be biased toward 2.00 (Ostrom, 1978:51; Hibbs, 1974:292; Kelejian and Oates, 1974:261). Hence, econometricians advocate use of generalized least squares (GLS) rather than OLS techniques. These techniques include the application of IV-Pseudo GLS techniques to results based on instrumental variables (Ostrom, 1978:53–55) and several maximum likelihood search techniques. Nevertheless, authors generally have uncritically applied OLS techniques to autoregressive equations (Cohen and Felson, 1979; Devine, 1983).

Since the present study does not assume that suicide in year t−1 somehow causes suicide in the year t, it does not use an autoregressive time model for precisely this theoretical reason.

10. The Cochrane-Orcutt method first uses OLS to obtain estimates of the error terms. These residuals then are used to obtain first-round estimates of the value of p, where $p = \Sigma\, e_t e_{t-1}/\Sigma e_{t-1}^2$ and $t = 2, 3, \ldots$ T. Then the value of p is used to transform the original data points (Johnston, 1984:323–24): $Y' = Y_t - pY_{t-1}$ and $X' = X_t - pX_{t-1}$. The transformed data then are entered into another analysis to obtain a second-round estimate of p. The data are transformed again using this value, and the procedure continues through enough iterations or rounds until the estimates converge. The final form of the equation uses the best estimate of the value p and, again, is based on transformed data where the equation relates *changes in* Y to *changes in* the X variables.

The present study uses an econometric software package called Shazam to perform the Cochrane-Orcutt analyses (Johnston, 1984:326; White, 1978).

11. Finally there is the issue of lag structures in time-series problems. That is, does a variable have an immediate effect on the dependent variable during the year both are measured, or does the influence of the independent variable occur at some later point in time? For example, is the effect of unemployment on suicide more or less immediate, or does it affect suicide at some future point in time? To address this question several lagged variables were constructed from each original independent variable. These were lagged up to three years in time to test for stalled effects. In all cases the nonlagged variable was the one most closely associated with the variance in suicide. Hence, the analysis reported here does not include any lagged variables. The findings on the unemployment rates are consistent with past research by Brenner (1976, 1984) who also reported immediate effects of unemployment on suicide.

12. In a series of OLS runs not reported here, the total suicide rate was regressed on each independent variable and year. Controlling for year (time), MPLF and the divorce rate were still significantly related to suicide. Church absence was not significantly related to suicide once the effect of year was controlled. In the equation with year and unemployment as exogenous variables, both year and unemployment were significantly related to suicide. Neither the media nor the presidential election variables were significantly related to suicide with year controlled. These equations either were free of autocorrelation or had *d* statistics in the gray area. However, all of the religion/domestic-oriented equations were marked by severe multicollinearity between year and the religion or domestic variable. In fact, the beta coefficients all exploded to values far greater than 1.00, another sign of multicollinearity. The effect of year loaded on the religion or domestic or vice versa. These equations, then, are thought to be marked by bias.

Bibliography

Ahlburg, D. and M. Shapiro. 1984. "Socioeconomic Ramifications of Changing Cohort Size." *Demography* 21:97–108.

Aldous, J. and W. D'Antonio. 1983. "Families and Religions Beset by Friends and Foes." Pp. 9–16 in W. D'Antonio and J. Aldous (eds.), *Families and Religions.* Beverly Hills, CA: Sage Publications.

Austin, R. 1982. "Women's Liberation and Increases in Minor, Major, and Occupational Offenses." *Criminology* 20(November):407–30.

Barraclough, B. M. and S. White. 1978. "Monthly Variation in Suicidal, Accidental, and Undetermined Poisoning Deaths." *British Journal of Psychiatory* 132:279–82.

Beach, C. M. and J. G. MacKinnon. 1978. "A Maximum Likelihood Procedure for Regression with Autocorrelated Errors." *Econometrica* 46 (January):51–58.

Bellah, R. N. 1976. "The New Religious Consciousness and the Crisis in Modernity." IN C. Y. Glock and R. N. Bellah (eds.), *The New Religious Consciousness.* Berkeley, CA: University of California Press.

Bellah, R. N. 1978. "Religion and Legitimation in the American Republic." *Society* 15:16–23.

Bollen, K. and D. Phillips. 1982. "Imitative Suicides." *American Sociological Review* 47:802–9.

Boor, M. 1981. "Presidential Elections and Suicide." *American Sociological Review* 46:616–18.

Boor, M. 1982. "Reduction in Deaths by Suicide, Accidents, and Homicides Prior to United States Presidential Elections." *Journal of Social Psychology* 118:135–36.

Box, S. and C. Hale. 1984. "Liberation/Emancipation, Economic Marginalization, or Less Chivalry: The Relevance of Three Theoretical Arguments to Female Crime Patterns in England and Wales, 1951–1980." *Criminology* 22(November):473–98.

Breault, K. D. and K. Barkey. 1982. "A Comparative Analysis of Durkheim's Theory of Egoistic Suicide." *Sociological Quarterly* 23:321–32.

Brenner, H. 1976. *Estimating the Social Costs of National Economic Policy.* Washington, D.C.: U.S. Government Printing Office.

Brenner, H. 1984. *Estimating the Effects of Economic Change on National Health and Social Well Being.* A study prepared for the Joint Economic Committee of the U.S. Congress. Washington, D.C.: U.S. Government Printing Office.

Buse, A. 1973. "Goodness of Fit in Generalized Least Squares Estimation." *American Statistician* 27:106–9.

Carroll, J., D. W. Johnson, and M. Marty. 1979. *Religion in America, 1950 to the Present.* San Francisco: Harper and Row.

Cohen, L. and M. Felson. 1979. "Social Change and Crime Rate Trends." *American Sociological Review* 44(August):588–607.

Cohen, L., M. Felson, and K. Land. 1980. "Property Crime Rates in the U.S." *American Journal of Sociology* 86(July):90–116.

Cumming, E., C. Lazer, and L. Chisholm. 1975. "Suicide as an Index of Role Strain Among Employed and Not Employed Married Women in British Columbia." *Canadian Review of Sociology and Anthropology* 24:462–70.

Danigelis, N. and W. Pope. 1979. "Durkheim's Theory of Suicide as Applied to the Family." *Social Forces* 57:1081–1106.

D'Antonio, W. 1980. "The Family and Religion: Exploring a Changing Relationship." *Journal for the Scientific Study of Religion* 19:89–104.

D'Antonio, W. 1983. "Family Life, Religion, and Societal Values." Pp. 81–108 in W. D'Antonio and J. Aldous (eds.), *Families and Religions*. Beverly Hills, CA: Sage Publications.

D'Antonio, W. and J. Aldous (eds.) 1983. *Families and Religions: Conflict and Change in Modern Society*. Beverly Hills, CA: Sage Publications.

Degler, C. N. 1980. *At Odds: Women and the Family in America from the Revolution to the Present*. New York: Oxford University Press.

Demerath, N. J. 1968. "Trends and Anti-trends in Religious Change." Pp. 349–448 in E. B. Sheldon and W. E. Moore (eds.), *Indicators of Social Change*. New York: Russell Sage.

Devine, J. 1983. "Fiscal Policy and Class Income Inequality: The Distributional Consequences of Government Revenues and Expenditures in the U.S., 1949–1976." *American Sociological Review* 48(October):606–22.

Diggory, J. 1976. "United States Suicide Rates, 1933–1968: An Analysis of Some Trends." Pp. 30–65 in E. Shneidman, *Suicidology: Contemporary Developments*. New York: Grosse and Straton.

Douglas, J. 1967. *The Social Meaning of Suicide*. Princeton, NJ: Princeton University Press.

Durbin, J. and G. S. Watson. 1950. "Testing for Serial Correlation in Least Squares Regression, Part I." *Biometrica* 37:409–28.

Durbin, J. and G. S. Watson. 1951. "Testing for Serial Correlation in Least Squares Regression, Part II." *Biometrica* 38:159–78.

Durkheim, E. 1966. *Suicide*. New York: The Free Press.

Erskine, H. 1964. "The Polls: Church Attendance." *Public Opinion Quarterly* 28:669–79.

Erskine, H. 1965. "The Polls: Personal Religion." *Public Opinion Quarterly* 29:145–57.

Eshleman, J. R. 1981. *The Family*. Boston: Allyn and Bacon.

Gallup, G. 1972. *The Gallup Poll: Public Opinion, 1935–1971*. New York: Random House.

Gallup, G. 1976. "Religion in America, 1976." *The Gallup Opinion Index*, Report No. 130. Princeton, NJ: Gallup International.

Gallup, G. 1981. "Religion in America." *The Gallup Opinion Index*, Report No. 184. Princeton, NJ: Gallup International.

Gallup, G. 1982. "Religion in America." *The Gallup Opinion Index*, Report No. 201–2. Princeton, NJ: Gallup International.

Gibbs, J. 1982. "Testing the Theory of Status Integration and Suicide Rates." *American Sociological Review* 47:277–37.

Gibbs, J. and W. T. Martin. 1964. *Status Integration and Suicide*. Eugene, OR: University of Oregon Press.

Gorsuch, R. L. 1976. "Religion as a Significant Predictor of Important Human Behavior." In W. Donaldson, *Research in Mental Health and Religious Behavior*. Atlanta: Psychological Studies Institute.

Gouldner, A. 1975. *The Coming Crisis of Western Sociology*. New York: Avon.

Habibagahi, H. and J. L. Pratschke. 1972. "A Comparison of the Power of the Von Neuman Ratio, Durbin Watson and Geary Tests." *Review of Economics and Statistics* 54(May):179–85.

Halbwachs, M. 1978. *The Causes of Suicide*. New York: Free Press.

Hargrove, B. 1983. "The Church, the Family and the Modernization Process." Pp. 21-48 in W. D'Antonio and J. Aldous (eds.), *Families and Religions*. Beverly Hills, CA: Sage Publications.

Harris, R. and J. J. Henderson. 1981. "Effects of Wife's Income on Family Income Inequality." *Sociological Methods and Research* 10:211-32.

Heer, D. and D. MacKinnon. 1974. "Suicide and Marital Status: A Rejoinder to Rico-Velasco and Mynki." *Journal of Marriage and the Family* 36(February):6-10.

Henry, A. F. and J. F. Short, Jr. 1954. *Suicide and Homicide*. New York: Free Press.

Hibbs, D. 1974. "Problems of Statistical Estimation and Causal Inference in Dynamic Time Series Models." Pp. 252-308 in H. Costner (ed.), *Sociological Methodology*. San Francisco: Jossey-Bass.

Hoge, D. and J. Carroll. 1978. "Determinants of Commitment and Participation in Protestant Churches." *Journal for the Scientific Study of Religion* 17:107-27.

Hoge, D. and G. Petrillo. 1978. "Determinants of Church Participation and Attitudes Among High School Youth." *Journal for the Scientific Study of Religion* 17:359-79.

Hynson, L. 1975. "Religion, Attendance and Belief in an Afterlife." *Journal for the Scientific Study of Religion* 14:285-87.

Johnston, J. 1972. *Econometric Methods* (2nd ed.). New York: McGraw-Hill.

Johnston, J. 1984. *Econometric Methods* (3rd ed.). New York: McGraw-Hill.

Johnstone, R. 1975. *Religion and Society*. Englewood Cliffs, NJ: Prentice Hall.

Kelejian, H. H. and W. E. Oates. 1974. *Introduction to Econometrics*. New York: Harper and Row.

Kenkel, W. 1977. *The Family in Perspective* (4th ed.). Santa Monica, CA: Goodyear Publishing.

Kleinbaum, D. and L. Kupper. 1978. *Applied Regression Analysis and Other Multivariate Techniques*. North Scituate, MA: Duxbury Press.

Kmenta, J. 1971. *Elements of Econometrics*. New York: Macmillan.

Lasch, C. 1977. *Haven in a Heartless World: The Family Besieged*. New York: Basic Books.

Lester, D. 1983. *Why People Kill Themselves* (2nd ed.). Springfield, IL: Charles C. Thomas.

Lester, D. and G. Lester. 1971. *Suicide: The Gamble with Death*. Englewood Cliffs, NJ: Prentice Hall.

Maris, R. W. 1969. *Social Forces in Urban Suicide*. Homewood, IL: Dorsey Press.

Maris, R. W. 1981. *Pathways to Suicide*. Baltimore: Johns Hopkins University Press.

Marshall, J. 1978. "Changes in Aged White Male Suicide: 1948-1972." *Journal of Gerontology* 33:763-68.

Marshall, J. 1981. "Political Integration and the Effect of War on Suicide: United States, 1933-1976." *Social Forces* 59:771-85.

Martin, C. and R. C. Nichols. 1962. "Personality and Religious Belief." *Journal of Social Psychology* 56:3-8.

Masaryk, T. 1970. *Suicide and the Meaning of Civilization*. Chicago: University of Chicago Press (originally published, 1882).

Mendelsohn, R. and B. Pescosolido. 1979. "The Self as Victim: Rethinking Sociological Theories of Suicide." Paper presented at the annual meetings of the American Public Health Association.

Merton, R. 1938. "Social Structure and Anomie." *American Sociological Review* 3:672-82.

Miley, J. and M. Micklin. 1972. "Structural Change and the Durkheimian Legacy: A Macrosociological Analysis of Suicide Rates." *American Journal of Sociology* 78:657-73.

Miller, B., B. C. Rollins, and D. Thomas. 1982. "On Methods of Studying Marriages and Families." *Journal of Marriage and the Family* 44 (November):851-73.

Morselli, E. A. 1882. *Suicide: An Essay on Comparative Moral Statistics*. New York: Appleton-Century.

Newman, J., K. R. Whittemore and H. G. Newman. 1973. "Women in the Labor Force and Suicide." *Social Problems* 21:220-80.

Ostrom, C. 1978. *Time Series Analysis*. Beverly Hills, CA: Sage Publications.

Parker, R. 1980. "Correlation in Time Series Regression: the Geary Test." *Sociological Methods and Research* 9:99-114.

Phillips, D. 1974. "The Influence of Suggestion on Suicide." *American Sociological Review* 39 (June):340-54.

Phillips D. 1983. "The Impact of Mass Media Violence on U.S. Homicides, 1973-1978." *American Sociological Review* 48(August): 560-68.

Pope, W. 1976. *Durkheim's Suicide: A Classic Reanalyzed*. Chicago: University of Chicago Press.

Pope, W. and N. Danigelis. 1981. "Sociology's One Law." *Social Forces* 60:495-516.

Ralph, J. and R. Rubinson. 1980. "Immigration and the Expansion of Schooling in the U.S., 1890-1970." *American Sociological Review* 45 (December):943-54.

Rubinson, R. and J. Ralph. 1984. "Technical Change and the Expansion of Schooling in the United States, 1890-1970." *Sociology of Education* 57 (July):134-51.

Sainsbury, P. 1973. "Suicide: Opinions and Facts." *Proceedings of the Royal Society of Medicine* 66:579-87.

Sainsbury, P. and B. Barraclough. 1968. "Differences Between Suicide Rates." *Nature* 220(4):1252.

Shepherd, D. and B. M. Barraclough. 1978. "Suicide Reporting: Information or Entertainment?" *British Journal of Psychiatry* 132:283-87.

Stack, S. 1978. "Suicide: A Comparative Analysis." *Social Forces* 57(December):644-53.

Stack, S. 1980. "The Effects of Marital Dissolution on Suicide." *Journal of Marriage and the Family* 42(February):83-92.

Stack, S. 1981a. "Divorce and Suicide: A Time Series Analysis, 1933-1970." *Journal of Family Issues* 2(March):77-90.

Stack, S. 1981b. "Suicide and Religion: A Comparative Analysis." *Sociological Focus* 14(August):207-20.

Stack, S. 1982. "Suicide: A Decade Review of the Sociological Literature." *Deviant Behavior* 4:41-66.

Stack, S. 1983a. "The Effect of the Decline in Institutionalized Religion on Suicide: 1954-1978." *Journal for the Scientific Study of Religion* 22(September):239-52.

Stack, S. 1983b. "The Effect of Religious Commitment on Suicide: A Cross-national Analysis." *Journal of Health and Social Behavior* 24 (December):362-74.

Stack, S. and N. Danigelis. 1985. "Modernization and Gender Suicide Rates, 1919-1972." In R. Tomasson (ed.), *Comparative Social Research* (Vol. 8). Greenwich, CT: JAI Press (forthcoming).

Stack, S. and A. Haas. 1984. "The Effect of Unemployment Duration on National Suicide Rates: A Time Series Analysis, 1948–1982." *Sociological Focus* 17 (January):17–30.

Stark, R. and W. S. Bainbridge. 1980. "Towards a Theory of Religion: Religious Commitment." *Journal for the Scientific Study of Religion* 19:114–28.

Stark, R., D. Doyle and J. Rushing. 1983. "Beyond Durkheim: Religion and Suicide." *Journal for the Scientific Study of Religion* 22:120–31.

Stewart, M. and K. Wallis. 1981. *Introductory Econometrics* (2nd ed.). New York: Halstead Press.

Tittle, C. and M. Welch. 1983. "Religiosity and Deviance." *Social Forces* 61(March):653–82.

Treas, J. 1983. "Trickle Down or Transfers? Postwar Determinants of Family Income Inequality." *American Sociological Review* 48 (August):546–59.

U.S. Bureau of Labor Statistics. 1982. *Labor Force Statistics Derived from the Current Population Survey: A Databook* (Vol. 1). Washington, D.C.: U.S. Government Printing Office.

U.S. Bureau of the Census. 1976a. *Historical Statistics of the United States: Colonial Times to 1970*, Part 1. Washington, D.C.: U.S. Government Printing Office.

U.S. Bureau of the Census. 1976b. *Social Indicators*. Washington, D.C.: U.S. Government Printing Office.

U.S. Bureau of the Census. 1971–1980. *U.S. Statistical Abstract*. Washington, D.C.: U.S. Government Printing Office.

Walters, P. B. 1984. "Occupational and Labor Market Effects on Secondary and Postsecondary Educational Expansion in the U.S., 1922–1979." *American Sociological Review* 49(October):659–71.

Walters, P. B. and R. Rubinson. 1983. "Educational Expansion and Economic Output in the U.S., 1890–1969." *American Sociological Review* 48(August):480–93.

Wasserman, I. 1983. "Political Business Cycles, Presidential Elections, and Suicide Mortality Patterns." *American Sociological Review* 48:711–20.

Wasserman, I. 1984. "Imitation and Suicide: A Re-examination of the Werther Effect." *American Sociological Review* 49(April):427–36.

Weiss, R. 1975. *Marital Separation*. New York: Basic Books.

White, K. 1978. "A General Computer Program for Economic Methods—Shazam." *Econometrica* 46(January):239–40.

Wonnacott, R. and T. Wonnacott. 1979. *Econometrics* (2nd ed.). New York: John Wiley and Sons.

Yankelovich, D. 1981. *New Rules: Searching for Self-Fulfillment in a World Turned Upside Down*. New York: Random House.

III. Socialization: Growing Up Religious

11

The Influence of Three Agents of Religious Socialization: Family, Church, and Peers

Marie Cornwall

Introduction

How is it that people come to believe, feel, and behave religiously? Social scientists have addressed this question in a number of ways, but the most fruitful research focuses on religious socialization. Of particular interest is not only why people are religious, but why they are religious in the way they are. Sociologists have predicted the decline of religion for the past one hundred years, but it is now clear that religion has not lost its importance in modern society. A new focus in the research, therefore, is to understand how society maintains religion and how religion is transferred to the next generation. Religious institutions no longer operate as monopolies. The modern pluralistic world offers a multitude of religious perspectives from which individuals may choose. What are the processes by which people come to adopt a particular religious identity?

Marie Cornwall is Assistant Professor of Sociology, Brigham Young University. For several years she was the project director for the Religious Activity Project sponsored by The Church of Jesus Christ of Latter-day Saints. Her published research has focused on how to measure religiosity, the processes of religious disaffiliation, and the role of personal communities in maintaining religious commitment. She is currently conducting cross-cultural research on religiosity in Mexico, Great Britain, and the United States. She received her Ph.D. from the University of Minnesota.

This paper studies the impact of religious socialization on the religiosity of adults. Three agents of religious socialization are examined: parents, the church, and peers. After reviewing the research which demonstrates the importance of these three agents, elements of the socialization process are outlined and a model to test the interrelatedness of these elements is presented. The paper concludes with a discussion of three processes of religious socialization.

Much of the literature examining the influence of religious socialization has been based on data collected from adolescent respondents (Johnson, 1973; Thomas et al., 1974; Albrecht et al., 1977; Aacock and Bengston, 1978; Hoge and Petrillo, 1978). These studies, and other research which has examined the antecedents of adult religiosity (Himmelfarb, 1977, 1979; Greeley and Rossi, 1966; Greeley, 1976), suggest the importance of three agents of religious socialization: (1) parental religiosity and family religious observances, (2) the religiosity of one's peers—particularly the religiosity of one's spouse in studies utilizing adult samples, and (3) exposure to church socialization, most notably religious education.

One limitation in much of this research has been a focus on the relative influence of parents, the church, and peers in the socialization process. Greeley, for example, looked at the impact of a parochial school education on the religiosity of Catholics. He and Rossi (Greeley and Rossi, 1966) concluded that religious training in the home had a greater influence on the religious development of children than did a parochial school education. Other research among Jews (Himmelfarb, 1977) and Lutherans (Johnstone, 1966) supported these findings. Having underscored the relative importance of the family, and the relative unimportance of church and peer socialization, researchers have neglected to ask the next question. How are family, church, and peer socialization processes interrelated? For example, how do family processes influence friendship choices and church attendance? While Greeley originally concluded a parochial school education by itself did not have a substantial influence on adult religiosity, in more recent research he has found a parochial education does have an important influence on adult religiosity by helping integrate the individual into the Catholic community (Fee, Greeley, McCready, and Sullivan, 1981). An understanding of the influence of family, church, and peer socialization requires a more careful examination of how these factors influence one another as well as how they influence adult religiosity. Himmelfarb (1979) has made a significant step towards this kind of understanding in his study of religious socialization based on data collected from a random sample of Jews in Chicago. He suggests that "parents socialize their children by channelling them into other groups or experiences (such as schools and marriage) which will reinforce (have an additive influence on) what was learned at home and will channel them further into similar adult activities" (Himmelfarb, 1979:478).

In a test of his theory, he found that while parental religiosity was not the best predictor of any of the types of adult religious involvement used in the model, its indirect effect through other agents of religious socialization was very substantial. There was a direct positive influence of parents' observance of ritual on (1) hours of Jewish schooling, (2) Jewish organizational participation, and (3) spouse's ritual observance at marriage. Each of these variables had a strong positive effect on adult religious involvement. Himmelfarb concluded parents are influential because they channel their children into experiences and environments which support the socialization received at home.

Theoretical perspectives on the importance of religious socialization generally have focused on the importance of "social learning" and the construction of a religious worldview. For example, Yinger has noted that religiosity, particularly church participation, is a learned behavior. "One learns his religion from those around him. . . . Fundamentalist parents tend to bring up children who share the fundamentalist tradition; liberal religious views are found most often among those who have been trained to such views." (1970:131.)

A sociology of knowledge perspective suggests the importance of socialization processes in the development of a religious worldview. Individuals come to adopt a particular worldview through early childhood religious socialization or as an adult by switching worlds through re-socialization. The world is built up in the consciousness of the individual by conversation with significant others: parents, peers, and teachers. The subjective reality of the world is maintained by this same conversation. "If such conversation is disrupted (the spouse dies, the friends disappear, or one comes to leave one's original social milieu), the world begins to totter, to lose its subjective plausibility. . . . The subjective reality of the world hangs on the thin thread of conversation." (Berger, 1967:17.)

Berger also introduces the concept of "plausibility structures" such as the nuclear and extended family, friendship networks, or churches and other voluntary organizations which socialize individuals into a particular worldview and help them maintain their subjective reality. While Berger suggests that the nuclear family is a tenuous plausibility structure, Lenski (1963) suggests that the family is the core of vital subcommunities which sustain religious commitment in the modern world. Lenski, in fact, argues that religious institutions are highly dependent upon subcommunities of individuals who effectively socialize and indoctrinate group members.

An adequate study of the processes of religious socialization should incorporate each of the elements discussed above. This requires careful attention to:

1. The impact of family, church, and peer socialization on adult religiosity as well as the interrelatedness of these three agents.

2. Channelling processes by which parents and other family members encourage participation in experiences and environments which support the socialization received at home.

3. The role of the family in providing a religious worldview.

4. The role of the family in modelling religious behaviors.

Methodology

Sample

Respondents were randomly selected from complete membership lists from twenty-seven different Mormon wards (congregations) from all parts of the United States. These twenty-seven wards had previously been chosen from a larger sample of Mormon stakes (typically made up of from six to twelve wards) which had been selected randomly from the different administrative areas of the church in the United States.

A membership roster was obtained from each of the ward units used in the sample and a list of households was randomly selected from each roster. Using this procedure, a total of thirty-two active and forty-eight inactive families was obtained within each of the twenty-seven units. Level of religious participation was previously obtained from the local bishop. Inactive households were oversampled because pretest data indicated they would be less likely to respond to the study than would active families. One adult member in each household was designated for inclusion in the sample by a toss of a die. Adult children over the age of eighteen were included in the sampling universe. When only one adult lived in the household or when there was only one adult who was a member of the LDS church, that person was included in the sample. The final sample consisted of 1,874 members over the age of eighteen.

A thirty-two-page questionnaire with appropriate cover letters requesting participation in what was described as one of the most important studies of Mormon religiosity ever undertaken was mailed to all adults in the sample. Follow-up postcards and additional copies of the questionnaire were mailed to nonrespondents over the next eight-week period. Adjusting for the 576 questionnaires that were undeliverable, the response rate was 74 percent from active members and 48 percent from less active members. The overall response rate was 64 percent. Despite the efforts taken to get accurate membership rosters, church records for those who are not currently attending religious services were found to be seriously inaccurate. Consequently, the majority of the undeliverable questionnaires were returned from less active members. The sample is representative of Mormons who could be located using information available from current church records. Respondents, therefore, probably have more positive feelings towards the LDS church and may be more religious than the general population.

Only the respondents baptized before age nineteen are included in this analysis. About one-third of the respondents are adult converts and the amount of family religious socialization reported by them is much lower than that reported by lifelong members. These adult converts were not socialized in their youth by family, peers, and the religious institution but acquired their belief and commitment through socialization experienced in the conversion process.

While the majority of lifelong members are baptized at age eight, about 10 percent of the lifelong members in the sample were baptized in their teenage years. Because they were exposed to some degree of church and peer socialization during their teenage years, we felt it appropriate to include them in the analysis. A total of 570 respondents in the sample had been baptized before age nineteen. Table 1 presents a description of the sample according to age, education, marital status and gender. In the sample 43 percent of the respondents were weekly attenders; 39 percent reported they seldom or never attend.

Measurement

Family socialization. The amount of religious socialization in the family was measured by three variables. Respondents were asked to indicate the religious preference of their parents when the respondents were age twelve to eighteen. FAMILY is a dummy variable coded one if both parents were present in the home and both were members of the LDS church and zero if one or both

TABLE 1
Demographic profile of respondents
(Respondents baptized before age 19 only)

	Number	Percent
Age		
Less than 19	28	5
20 to 24	78	14
25 to 34	219	38
35 to 44	103	18
45 to 54	46	8
55 to 64	44	8
65 and over	52	9
	570	100
Education		
Less than 12 years	58	12
High School	182	32
Some college	210	37
College graduate	56	10
Post graduate	54	9
	570	100
Marital status		
Married	410	71
Never married	117	21
Divorced/separated	27	5
Widowed	14	3
	568	100
Gender		
Female	314	55
Male	256	45
	570	100

parents were not LDS or if one parent was not present in the home. FAMILY is an indicator of whether or not respondents came from a complete LDS family.

Respondents also reported the frequency of their parents' church attendance. PCHURCH is the average frequency of church attendance for both parents when the respondent was age twelve to eighteen. If only one parent was present in the home, PCHURCH is the frequency of that parent's church attendance.

YHRO is a measure of the amount of religious observance respondents experienced in the home during their teenage years. The scale is composed of four items measuring frequency of family prayer, family religious discussions, family Bible or scripture reading, and family discussions of right and wrong. Home religious observance is stressed by LDS church leaders, and, furthermore, parents are strongly encouraged to take an active role in the religious development of their children.

Church socialization. The amount of socialization received through church participation was measured by two variables: YATTEND, a measure of the frequency of attendance at religious services during the teenage years, and SEMINARY. Seminary is a program of religious study offered to LDS students in the ninth through twelfth grades. In most areas of the United States students attend early-morning seminary prior to attending regular school. In Utah students are allowed "released time" from their regular studies to take a seminary course during the day. Response categories were (1) never attended (2) attended occasionally, (3) completed one to two years, and (4) completed three to four years. Because seminary has not always been available in all parts of the country, we expected, and found, a moderate age effect for attendance at seminary (correlation of −.30). Younger respondents were more likely to report having attended. Because of this age effect, the analysis is based on a covariance matrix of residuals after controlling for age.

Peer socialization. Two measures of peer socialization were used: FRIENDS and DECLINE. Respondents were asked to indicate how many of their friends were active members of the LDS church during their teenage and young adult years. Response categories included (1) none of them (2) a few of them (3) about half of them (4) most of them and (5) all of them. FRIENDS is a measure of the proportion of one's friends who were active LDS during the teenage years, and DECLINE is a measure of the amount of decline in proportion of active LDS friends between the teenage and young adult years. DECLINE was computed by subtracting the proportion of active friends who were LDS during the young adult years (nineteen to twenty-five) from the proportion of active friends who were LDS during the teenage years.

Dimensions of religiosity. Four measures of religious belief and commitment are used in the analysis: two scales measuring a more personal mode of religiosity and two scales measuring the institutional mode of religiosity (for a full discussion of the dimensions of religiosity, see Cornwall, et al., 1986).

1. Traditional orthodoxy is defined as belief in traditional Christian doctrines such as the existence of God, the divinity of Christ, life after death, Satan, and the Bible. These are beliefs that are not unique to Mormonism.

Acceptance or rejection of such beliefs is largely independent of affiliation with a particular religious group or institution. Traditional orthodoxy was measured with a five-item scale (see Table 2).

2. Spiritual commitment was measured using a five-item scale which focuses on degree of commitment to God. Items tap feelings such as loving God with all one's heart, willingness to do whatever the Lord wants, and the importance of one's relationship with God.

3. Particularistic orthodoxy refers to the acceptance or rejection of beliefs peculiar to a particular religious organization. Particularistic orthodoxy includes acceptance of such doctrines as the prophetic calling of Joseph Smith and the current church president, the authenticity of the Book of Mormon, and adherence to the belief that The Church of Jesus Christ of Latter-day Saints is the only true church on earth. Four items were used to measure particularistic orthodoxy.

4. Church commitment is the affective orientation of the individual towards the religious organization or community. It measures the attachment, identification, and loyalty of the individual towards the church organization or religious community. Five items were used to measure church commitment.

Table 2 presents the results of a factor analysis of the several items which were combined into four separate religiosity scales. A factor analysis of these items produced three factors. All the spiritual commitment items load on the first factor with two items from the traditional orthodoxy scale. The particularistic orthodoxy items and the church commitment items load on the second factor. The particularistic orthodoxy items and the traditional belief items load on the third factor. When only the traditional orthodoxy items and the particularistic orthodoxy items are entered into a factor analysis, two distinct factors emerge. The traditional items load on one factor and the particularistic items load on the other. In addition, when other religiosity measures are included in the factor analysis (such as church attendance, frequency of personal prayer, and frequency of home religious observance), the overlap between church commitment and particularistic orthodoxy factors disappears. For this reason, four separate religiosity scales will be used as measures of religiosity.

Findings

Two levels of statistical analysis are reported in this paper. First, zero-order correlations among the several variables are examined, and then, in

TABLE 2. VARIMAX FACTOR PATTERN OF RELIGIOSITY ITEMS

	I	II	III	Mean	Std. Dev.	# of Cases
Spiritual Commitment						
My relationship with the Lord is an important part of my life.	.83	.21	.19	4.34	.94	907
I love God with all my heart.	.79	.08	.17	4.53	.82	903
The Holy Ghost is an important influence in my life.	.74	.30	.24	4.04	1.19	902
I am willing to do whatever the Lord wants me to do.	.73	.27	.09	4.15	1.04	893
Without religious faith, the rest of my life would not have much meaning.	.73	.28	.21	4.08	1.26	906
Traditional Orthodoxy						
I believe in the divinity of Jesus Christ.	.68	.16	.36	4.64	.75	899
I have no doubts that God lives and is real.	.55	-.05	.30	4.61	.97	902
Satan actually exists.	.27	.12	.71	4.56	.79	906
There is life after death.	.32	.09	.67	4.62	.72	909
The Bible is the word of God.	.32	.13	.59	4.51	.72	904
Particularistic Orthodoxy						
Joseph Smith actually saw God the Father and Jesus Christ.	.21	.51	.69	4.37	.86	908
The president of the LDS church is a prophet of God.	.15	.54	.67	4.44	.90	906
The Book of Mormon is the word of God.	.18	.54	.65	4.42	.88	905
The Church of Jesus Christ of Latter-day Saints is the only true church on earth.	.14	.63	.57	4.21	1.11	905
Church Commitment						
I do not accept some standards of the LDS church.	.11	.78	.09	3.92	1.40	884
Some doctrines of the LDS church are hard for me to accept.	.15	.68	.17	3.40	1.49	901
I don't really care about the LDS church.	.12	.65	.10	4.32	1.23	853
The LDS church puts too many restrictions on its members.	.26	.64	.57	3.91	1.12	902
Church programs and activities are an important part of my life.	.49	.57	.19	3.28	1.46	900

Factor	Eigenvalue	Pct. of Var.	Cum. Plt.
1	8.55	45.0	45.0
2	2.05	10.8	55.8
3	1.20	6.3	62.1

order to examine the complex interrelationships among variables, a path model is developed and tested. It is always useful to examine the zero-order correlations[1] between two variables to get an initial estimate of the amount of association between them. However, measures of association are not always indicators of a causal relationship. For example, the amount of association between two variables may actually be due to their correlation with a third variable. Or sometimes the amount of association between two variables is masked by the effects of another variable. The primary question to be addressed in the following statistical analysis is the interrelatedness of the family, peer and church socialization variables as well as their impact on adult religiosity.

Table 3 presents a correlation matrix of the religious socialization variables with the four measures of religious belief and commitment. The correlations between the family socialization variables (FAMILY, PCHURCH, and YHRO) and the four religious belief and commitment scales are not very large, ranging from a high of .19 (SPIRIT and YHRO) to a low of .04 (SPIRIT and FAMILY). Compared with other family variables, correlations between YHRO and the four adult religiosity measures are relatively strong, ranging between .14 and .17, although all three family socialization variables have an impact on particularistic belief. The correlation matrix also reveals LDS family completeness and parental church activity have a greater influence on institutional religiosity (PARTIC and CHURCH) than on personal religiosity (TRAD and SPIRIT).

Church socialization variables and measures of adult religiosity are also moderately correlated. SEMINARY is correlated .22 and .15 with church commitment and particularistic orthodoxy and .05 and .09 with spiritual commitment and traditional orthodoxy. The same pattern holds for the correlation between YATTEND and religious belief and commitment, although the differences are not as great. The greater the amount of church socialization, the greater the level of *institutional* belief and commitment. Church socialization does not have as great an impact on *personal* belief and commitment.

A similar pattern is found when we examine the relationship between the proportion of active LDS friends (FRIENDS) and religiosity: low, nonsignificant correlations with personal religiosity (.06 and .03), and moderate correlations with institutional religiosity (.21 and .15).

Family socialization variables are highly correlated with both the peer socialization and the church socialization variables. The correlation between FAMILY and SEMINARY is .40 and the correlation between FAMILY and FRIENDS

TABLE 3. CORRELATION MATRIX OF RELIGIOUS SOCIALIZATION VARIABLES AND RELIGIOUS BELIEF AND COMMITMENT, LIFELONG MEMBERS ONLY, CONTROLLING FOR AGE

		Family socialization			Church socialization		Peer socialization	
	GENDER	FAMILY	PCHURCH	YHRO	YATTEND	SEMINARY	FRIENDS	DECLINE
GENDER	1.00							
FAMILY	-.03*	1.00						
PCHURCH	.03*	.47	1.00					
YHRO	-.09	.33	.60	1.00				
YATTEND	-.16	.30	.63	.39	1.00			
SEMINARY	-.07*	.40	.37	.32	.41	1.00		
FRIENDS	-.11	.45	.34	.32	.43	.60	1.00	
DECLINE	.08	.19	.16	.11	.20	.17	.50	1.00
TRAD	-.18	.06*	.08	.17	.12	.09	.07*	-.24
SPIRIT	-.21	-.00*	.03*	.19	.07*	.05*	.03*	-.33
PARTIC	-.18	.18	.15	.16	.15	.22	.21	-.26
CHURCH	-.19	.10	.11	.14	.19	.15	.15	-.37

GENDER (0 = female; 1 = male)
FAMILY, family complete LDS (0 = single parent or one parent not LDS; 1 = both parents present and both LDS)
PCHURCH, frequency of parents' church attendance
YHRO, frequency of home religious observance: frequency of family prayer, family religious discussions, scripture reading, and family discussions about right and wrong
YATTEND, church attendance of respondents when age 12–18
SEMINARY, years attendance at seminary
FRIENDS, proportion of friends who were active LDS when respondent was age 12–18
DECLINE, decline in proportion of friends active LDS between teenage years and the young adult years
TRAD, traditional orthodoxy
SPIRIT, spiritual commitment
PARTIC, particularistic orthodoxy
CHURCH, church commitment
* p > .05

is .45. The size of the correlations between PCHURCH and YHRO and both FRIENDS and SEMINARY is also moderately strong.

The size of correlations between the four measures of belief and commitment and the amount of decline in proportion of active LDS friends is larger than any other coefficients in the table. The religiosity measures are more highly correlated with DECLINE than any other variable in the model, suggesting that peer socialization during the young adult years has a significant impact on both personal and institutional modes of religiosity.

An effect for sex is also apparent in Table 3. (The negative coefficient indicates that men report lower levels). Women report higher levels of home religious observance, greater frequency of attendance at religious services, a greater proportion of active LDS friends during the teenage years, and more decline in active LDS friends from the teenage years to young adulthood. Furthermore, they also report higher levels of adult religious belief and commitment. While the effect of gender on frequency of attendance at religious services, active LDS friends, and adult religiosity is not surprising, one might question the theoretical link between gender and the amount of home religious observance reported in the teenage years. Two explanations for this are possible. First, response bias may account for the slight correlation. Women report higher levels of religiosity and recall greater religious activity in their homes during the teenage years. However, another explanation is just as compelling. It may mean that women experience more home religious observance in their youth than men. Much of the responsibility for initiating home religious observance may fall upon women, and perhaps the young women themselves act as an important catalyst for encouraging parents and siblings to have family prayer, scripture reading, and the like.

At this point, the analysis suggests family socialization variables have less impact than church and peer socialization variables. However, because the family, church, and peer socialization variables are highly correlated, further analysis must be done to isolate the impact of each of the variables and to examine their interrelatedness.

LISREL (Joreskog and Sorbom, 1984) is a computer program which facilitates path modelling while controlling for measurement error. LISREL estimates the unknown coefficients in a set of linear structural equations. The advantages of LISREL over other analysis programs are (1) it provides a chi square measure of fit, (2) it requires specificity of assumptions about measurement error, and (3) it handles reciprocal causation or interdependence among the variables in the model. It also allows for the introduction of latent, unobservable variables.

LISREL was used for this analysis because it enables us to control for the effect of uncorrelated errors. Recall data is often suspect, and the introduction of measurement error is particularly likely with respect to data about frequency of parental church attendance and frequency of religious observance in the home. We are able to take into consideration the correlation of error terms between PCHURCH and YHRO by requesting the calculation of the error term.

LISREL also allowed us to specify and account for the interdependence of the YATTEND, FRIENDS, and SEMINARY variables. Interdependence is a problem because it is difficult to know whether attending church during the teenage years influences friendship patterns or whether friendship patterns influence attendance at church. The same is true, of course, for the relationship between FRIENDS and SEMINARY. These relationships are reciprocal. For path modelling purposes, the relationship between FRIENDS and SEMINARY and between YATTEND and FRIENDS is assumed to be reciprocal. However, we assumed the relationship between YATTEND and SEMINARY is monocausal. Those teenagers who attend church on a regular basis are more likely to attend seminary, but attendance at seminary is not as likely to influence attendance at religious services.

The findings presented here are the result of an iterative process. Early model specification was based on both empirical results (correlation matrix and regression analysis) and theoretical insights. In some cases, the T-value (less than 2.05) suggested the path should be dropped from the model. In other cases, the modification index indicated a path should be included. Once the model was fit, both theoretically and empirically, the same model was used to predict the four measures of belief and commitment.

Final model specification assumed a direct effect of six variables on adult religiosity: home religious observance, seminary attendance, proportion of friends who were active LDS during the teenage years, amount of decline in proportion of active LDS friends between the young adult years and the teenage years, frequency of respondent's church attendance as a youth, and gender.

Each of the three family variables operate differently in the socialization process. Model specification assumed the FAMILY variable would influence parental church activity, proportion of active LDS friends, and seminary attendance. While the correlation matrix also suggested a moderate association between

FAMILY and YATTEND, DECLINE, and the religiosity measures, early efforts to fit the model produced nonsignificant t-values for these paths. Theoretically, we would expect LDS family completeness would have the strongest direct effect on frequency of parental church attendance. When both parents are present and both belong to the same church, their level of religious activity is likely to be higher than if parents are of different religions, or only one parent is present. Friendship choices and seminary attendance are also directly affected because of the lack of support in the family for in-group association and church participation.

PCHURCH is correlated with YHRO, YATTEND, SEMINARY, and FRIENDS, but early efforts to fit the model suggested a direct effect of PCHURCH on YHRO and YATTEND only. The influence of family religious socialization on seminary attendance and friendship patterns is felt directly through FAMILY and YHRO, rather than PCHURCH. However, as might be expected, parental religious activity is strongly correlated with amount of religious observance in the home, and with frequency of attendance at church during the teenage years. Teenagers are more likely to attend church if their parents attend with them.

Final model specification is presented in Figure 1. The results of the LISREL analyses are displayed in Figures 2 through 5. The chi-squares for all models ranged between 10 and 16 with 14 degrees of freedom, indicating no significant difference between the model and the data (probability levels between .20 and .73).

The standardized path coefficients[2] presented in Figures 2 through 5 demonstrate the direct and indirect effects of the several variables in the model. Each figure contains essentially the same structural equation model but a different measure of adult religiosity is examined.

Because each model is essentially the same except for the dependent variable, the relationships among the family socialization variables (FAMILY, PCHURCH, and YHRO), the peer socialization variables (FRIENDS, and DECLINE), and the church socialization variables (YATTEND and SEMINARY) are the same across all models. Understanding the processes of religious socialization requires careful examination of the relationships among these variables alone. In the following discussion, the size of relevant path coefficients will be noted within parentheses.

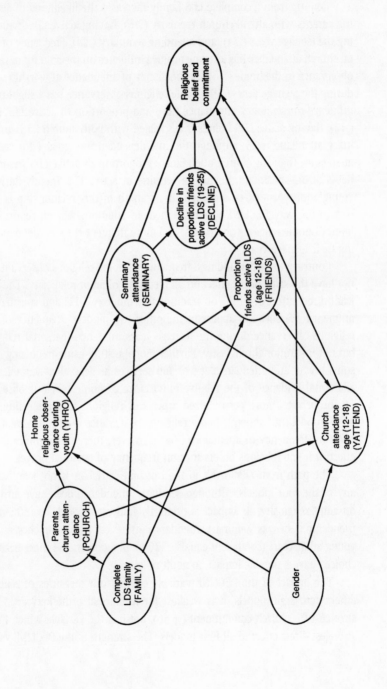

Figure 1. Model of Religious Socialization

Coming from a complete LDS family increases the likelihood of also having parents who attend church regularly (.46), having active LDS friends during the teenage years (.24), and attending seminary (.24). Frequency of parental church attendance has a strong positive influence on the amount of religious observance in the home (.76) and frequency of attendance at worship services during the teenage years (.59). Home religious observance has a slight positive influence on seminary attendance (.09) and proportion of active LDS friends (.12). Having active LDS friends is associated with both church (.13) and seminary attendance (.23) although the interdependence is greater for seminary attendance than for church attendance. Proportion of active LDS friends also has a strong positive influence on decline in active LDS friends during the young adult years (.64), although the strength of this relationship is due in part to the way DECLINE was calculated. In addition, women report higher levels of home religious observance and more frequent church attendance during their teenage years.

Contrary to earlier findings, frequency of home religious observance does not have the same direct effect on all measures of adult religiosity. The significant direct effect of YHRO on traditional orthodoxy (.11) and spiritual commitment (.17) does not appear in the other two models. Frequency of home religious observance during the teenage years influences personal religiosity, but not institutional religiosity. Further model testing using frequency of personal prayer and attendance at worship services as dependent variables gives additional evidence of the relative importance of home religious observance on the private, more personalized aspects of religion. In the meeting attendance model (not shown), home religious observance does not have a direct effect on frequency of attendance (.04). However, there is a significant direct effect of home religious observance on frequency of personal prayer.

The path from SEMINARY to the outcome variables is not significant in any of the four models. Although seminary attendance does have an impact on adult religiosity, its impact is primarily indirect through its influence on friendship networks. Seminary attendance influences friendship choices in the young adult years (coefficient equals −.20 in all models), and these friendship choices have a notable impact on adult religiosity.

The impact of the DECLINE variable on the four measures of religiosity differs across all models. It is weakest for traditional orthodoxy (−.32) and strongest for church commitment (−.56), but it is the variable which has the strongest direct effect in all four models. The strength of the DECLINE variable

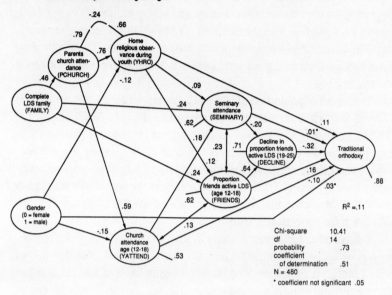

Figure 2. LISREL Model of Religious Socialization for Traditional Orthodoxy, Lifelong
Members Only, Controlling for Age.

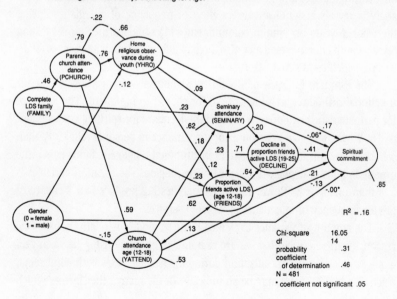

Figure 3. LISREL Model of Religious Socialization for the Spiritual Commitment,
Lifelong Members Only, Controlling for Age.

in predicting adult religiosity can in part be understood in light of recent research suggesting the importance of the teenage and young adult years in the development of a religious identity (Albrecht, Cornwall, Cunningham, forthcoming). Religious change frequently occurs during these years. Those who drop out or disengage from religious participation do so during the teenage or young adult years.

The impact of proportion of active LDS friends during the teenage years is different for each dimension of adult religiosity. The path coefficient for the FRIENDS variable is almost twice as large for the institutional measures (.38 and .40) as for the personal measures (.16 and .21), suggesting peer relationships have a greater impact on institutional religiosity than on personal religiosity. The significance of such patterns emphasizes the importance of in-group association for institutional religiosity and the relative less importance of such association for personal religiosity.

A direct effect for gender is found in the two personal religiosity models, but gender has no direct influence on institutional religiosity once the effect of other variables is controlled. Women report higher levels of traditional orthodoxy ($-.10$) and spiritual commitment ($-.13$), but the coefficients for gender are nonsignificant in the institutional religiosity models.

Attendance at meetings during the teenage years has a stronger influence on institutional commitment than on personal religious commitment. Data analysis reveals a significant direct effect of frequency of attendance during the teenage years on church commitment (.11) only. Further model testing reveals youth church attendance also directly influenced adult attendance (standardized coefficient equals .08).

The R-square for each model differs significantly from a low of .11 for traditional orthodoxy to a high of .26 for church commitment. The R-square for particularistic orthodoxy is .20 and the R-square for spiritual commitment is .16. We are less able to account for the variance in personal religiosity than we are to account for the variance in institutional religiosity, but even so, the overall amount of explained variance using religious socialization variables is less than one-fourth. However, other model testing produced an R-square of .29 for frequency of attendance at worship services.

The amount of variance explained in these models is relatively low. One reason for this may be that we are examining the relationship between religious experiences and socialization during the teenage years with adult religiosity. The low R-square may be an indicator of the many other factors which

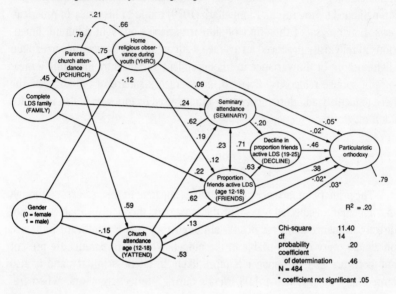

Figure 4. LISREL Model of Religious Socialization for Particularistic Orthodoxy, Lifelong Members Only, Controlling for Age.

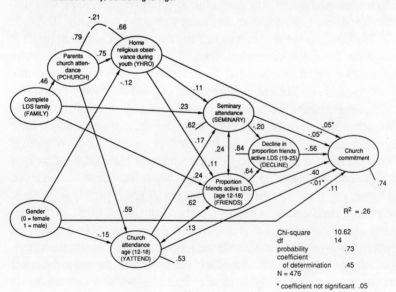

Figure 5. LISREL Model of Religious Socialization for Church Commitment, Lifelong Members Only, Controlling for Age.

influence religiosity as the individual becomes an adult. This interpretation is strengthened by the results Himmelfarb (1979) found in his study of American Jews. His analysis of the effect of similar variables on eight different dimensions of religiosity produced an average R-square of .30. He was able to explain slightly more of the variance in his dependent variables by including a measure of spouse religiosity. Even so, an average R-square of .30 suggests the need to identify additional, currently unmeasured factors which also influence adult religiosity.

Conclusions

The primary importance of the family is apparent in this research, although in somewhat unexpected ways. For the most part, the family variables did not directly influence adult religiosity, although they had a significant influence on almost every other variable in the model. When both parents are present and both are LDS, a teenager is more likely to attend seminary and is also more likely to have active LDS friends during the teenage years. When frequency of parental church attendance is high, the teenager attends church more frequently. And when home religious observance is high, teenagers are also more likely to associate with LDS friends. Family religious socialization affects adult religiosity to the extent that it influences intervening variables: church and seminary attendance, and integration into a network of LDS peers.

The family, however, has a particularly important influence on personal religiosity. There was a consistent direct effect of home religious observance for models examining the personal mode of adult religiosity (traditional orthodoxy, spiritual commitment, and frequency of personal prayer), but not for the models examining the institutional mode of religiosity (particularistic orthodoxy, church commitment, and frequency of church attendance). Why is there no direct effect of family socialization variables on institutional religiosity? One explanation is participation in and commitment to the religious group is more heavily dependent upon the degree to which individuals are integrated into that group and has established a pattern of group participation. Thus, peer group associaton has a greater impact on institutional religiosity than on personal religiosity, and family socialization has a greater direct impact on personal religiosity than on institutional religiosity. Family socialization therefore influences the institutional modes of religiosity in adulthood to the extent that it contributes to the development of friendship ties with people who are active participators in the same religious group. On the other hand, family socialization influences personal religiosity by providing the foundation for a religious worldview, as well as by channelling people into networks of associations which foster the maintenance of that worldview.

Church and peer socialization have a significant impact on adult religiosity as well. Consistent with Himmelfarb's conclusions, these data suggest parents channel their children into religious activities and religious networks which reinforce what is learned at home and encourage continued participation in adult activities which sustain belief and commitment. However, church and peer socialization also channel individuals. Seminary attendance acts as an important mechanism for increased integration within an LDS network and sustains integration through the young adult years and into adulthood.

The Processes of Religious Development

Extrapolating from these findings, we can begin to identify the processes by which individuals acquire a religious identity. Parents influence the development of a religious identity by supplying their children with a symbolic reference for understanding and interpreting a religious life, by modelling religious behavior on both the personal and institutional levels, and by encouraging the integration of their children into networks of relationships with others who share the same beliefs and the same group identity.

Symbolic references and the construction of religious meaning. Every person must develop a worldview or meaning system by which he or she can understand and interpret life experiences. Sociologists refer to this process as the social construction of reality because reality construction is highly dependent upon the symbolic references provided by others: parents, siblings, friends, and associates (Geertz, 1966). For the most part, these symbolic references take the form of "stories" (Greeley, 1982; Fowler, 1984) or "conversations" (Berger, 1967). Within these stories are images which represent, resonate, and articulate religious experience. The child, according to Greeley, "more explicitly and more self-consciously than the rest of us wants a story that will clarify reality for him" (1982:57). Fairy tales and folktales, Bible stories and family stories are all equally true within the mind of the young child seeking to understand the world and how it works. Within the family, the individual begins to create his own religious worldview. The foundations upon which this worldview rests are created out of the family environment and the more religiously oriented the family, the more central religion will be within the child's personal construction of reality.

Modelling religious behavior. Along with the construction of a religious worldview, the individual must also learn the norms and expectations of the religious group. The exact parameters of these expectations (for example, daily prayers, tithe paying, daily scripture reading) are defined by the particular religious group to which he or she belongs and become a part of the religious worldview during the socialization process. A young child learns what these expectations are by listening to stories and conversations told to them by their peers and by adults. In addition, however, children also learn about the norms and expectations of the religious group from parents and others whose own religious behavior provides the child with additional information about the practical application of religious norms and the contexts in which they are most appropriate. The extent to which these norms and expectations become an integral part of the beliefs and behaviors of a group member is therefore dependent upon both the development of a worldview that incorporates a belief in the norms and expectations of the group and the extent to which he or she has had opportunities to observe the practical application of those expectations.

Channelling. As with any type of social group, religious groups are particularly concerned with encouraging commitment on the part of its members. The vitality of the group is highly dependent upon the degree to which members are committed to the survival of the organization itself, to other members of the group, and to the norms and expectations of the group (Kanter, 1972). It is generally agreed that commitment is very much a product of the extent to which individuals are integrated into the religious community (Roof, 1978; McGaw, 1980; Cornwall, 1985; 1987). For example, the role of friendship ties and social networks in the conversion process has been demonstrated in the literature (Lofland and Stark, 1965; Lofland, 1977), and social scientists are beginning to assert that affective commitment develops prior to full acceptance of the belief system.

This, and other research on the channelling effect of parents (Himmelfarb, 1979), and the church (Fee et al., 1981) not only confirms the importance of social ties in religious development, but also begins to identify how the family and the church influence friendship choices. People are channelled into networks of association at fairly young ages and this channelling continues to be a vital force during the teenage and young adult years.

Implications

Having identified these three salient processes of religious development (symbolic references, modelling, and channelling), we know families have a strong influence on the religious development of individuals and we have a better understanding of why. While more research is needed to understand these processes and how they interact with one another, religious educators and church leaders can begin now to emulate what families have been able to do so well for so many years. We must therefore begin to ask in what ways youth leaders can enhance religious development in children and youth by sharing religious experiences and personal stories, by modelling religious behavior, and by encouraging integration into networks of people who share the same religious faith.

The research reported here is helpful in other ways, as well. The data strongly suggest interfaith marriages and single parent families place the religious development of children at risk. Family completeness affects parental religious activity. It also influences seminary attendance and proportion of active LDS friends during the teenage years, even after controlling for the effect of parental religious activity and home religious observance. It may be that parents in interfaith marriages or single parent families are less integrated into a religious network themselves and are therefore less able to help integrate their children. It may also be that these parents (either intentionally or unintentionally) channel their children into experiences which do not foster identity with one particular religious group. Presented with the option to choose between two groups, they opt for neither one. There is insufficient data available about the effects of interfaith marriages on the religious development of children. But given the increasing numbers of such marriages (Caplow et al., 1983), more research is needed in that area.

Finally, these findings again point to two critical periods of religious development: adolescence and young adulthood. In addition to the physical, social and cognitive changes experienced during the teenage and young adult years, individuals are much more likely to be confronted with alternative worldviews and their attendant life-styles, as well as new friendship choices. It is likely the strength of attachments, the plausibility of parental worldviews, and the practicalities of modelled behaviors play a central role in maintaining a religious identity during this critical period. All of which suggests the need for further examination of the processes of faith development during these critical years.

Notes

1. Zero-order correlations measure the amount and direction of association between two variables. The larger the correlation, the greater the amount of association. Correlations vary from −1.00 to + 1.00. However, in social science research of this type a correlation greater than .40 is considered a relatively strong association.

2. Path coefficients are measures of the amount of association between two variables controlling for the effect of all other variables in the model. The coefficient represents the amount of change in the independent variable which is associated with one standardized unit of change in the dependent variable.

Bibliography

Aacock, A. and V. Bengston. 1978. "On the Relative Influence of Mothers and Fathers: A Covariance Analysis of Political and Religious Socialization." *Journal of Marriage and the Family* 40:519–30.

Albrecht, S. L., B. Chadwick, and D. Alcorn. 1977. "Religiosity and Deviance: Application of an Attitude-Behavior Consistency Model." *Journal for the Scientific Study of Religion* 16:263–74.

Albrecht, S. L., M. Cornwall, and P. Cunningham. 1988. "Religious Leave-taking: Disengagement and Disaffiliation Among Mormons," in D. G. Bromley (ed.) *Falling from the Faith: The Causes, Course, and Consequences of Religious Apostasy*, forthcoming.

Berger, P. L. 1967. *The Sacred Canopy: Elements of a Sociological Theory of Religion*. Garden City, NY: Doubleday.

Caplow, T., H. M. Bahr, and B. A. Chadwick. 1983. *All Faithful People: Change and Continuity in Middletown's Religion*. Minneapolis, MN: University of Minnesota Press.

Cornwall, M. 1985. "The Normative Bases of Religion: A Study of Factors Influencing Religious Behavior." Paper presented at the annual meetings of the Association for the Sociology of Religion, Washington, D.C.

Cornwall, M. 1987. "The Social Bases of Religion: A Study of Factors Influencing Religious Belief and Commitment," *Review of Religious Research* 29:44–56.

Cornwall, M., S. L. Albrecht, P. H. Cunningham, and B. L. Pitcher. 1986. "The Dimensions of Religiosity: A Conceptual Model with an Empirical Test." *Review of Religious Research* 27:226–44.

Fee, J. L., A. M. Greeley, W. C. McCready, and T. Sullivan. 1981. *Young Catholics in the United States and Canada*. New York: Sadlier.

Fowler, J. W. 1984. *Becoming Adult, Becoming Christian: Adult Development and Christian Faith*. San Francisco: Harper and Row.

Geertz, C. 1966. "Religion as a Cultural System," in M. Banton (ed.), *Anthropological Approaches to the Study of Religion*. London: Tavistock Publications.

Greeley, A. M. and P. Rossi. 1966. *The Education of Catholic Americans*. Chicago: Aldine.

Greeley, A. M., W. C. McCready, and K. McCourt. 1976. *Catholic Schools in a Declining Church*. Kansas City, MO: Sheed and Ward.

Greeley, A. M. 1982. *Religion: A Secular Theory*. New York: Free Press.

Himmelfarb, H. S. 1977. "The Interaction Affects of Parents, Spouse, and Schooling: Comparing the Impact of Jewish and Catholic Schools." *Sociological Quarterly* 18:464-71.

Himmelfarb, H. S. 1979. "Agents of Religious Socialization Among American Jews." *Sociological Quarterly* 20:447-94.

Hoge, D. and G. Petrillo. 1978. "Determinants of Church Participation and Attitudes Among High School Youth." *Journal for the Scientific Study of Religion* 17:359-79.

Johnson, M. 1973. "Family Life and Religious Commitment." *Review of Religious Research* 14:144-50.

Johnstone, R. L. 1966. *The Effectiveness of Lutheran Elementary and Secondary Schools as Agencies of Christian Education*. St. Louis: Concordia Seminary.

Kanter, R. M. 1972. *Commitment and Community*. Cambridge, MA: Harvard University Press.

Lenski, G. 1963. *The Religious Factor*. Garden City: Doubleday.

Lofland, J. and R. Stark. 1965. "Becoming a World-Saver: A Theory of Religious Conversion." *American Sociological Review* 30:862-74.

Lofland, J. 1977. *Doomsday Cult*. New York: Irvington Publishers.

McGaw, D. B. 1980. "Meaning and Belonging in a Charismatic Congregation: An Investigation into Sources of Neo-Pentecostal Success." *Review of Religious Research* (Summer):284-301.

Roof, W. C. 1978. *Community and Commitment: Religious Plausibility in a Liberal Protestant Church*. New York: Elsevier.

Thomas, D., V. Gecas, A. Weigert and E. Rooney. 1974. *Family Socialization and the Adolescent*. Lexington, MA: D. C. Heath.

Yinger, M. J. 1970. *The Scientific Study of Religion*. New York: Macmillan.

12

Religious Sources
of Gender Traditionalism

Merlin B. Brinkerhoff, Marlene MacKie

Over the past decade, interest in the causes, consequences, and correlates of sexism has increased manifold. Where racial prejudice and discrimination were topics of concern to sociologists of religion during the 1960s and 1970s, gender has similarly emerged in the 1980s as worthy of our attention. Wilson (1978) claims that "religion is probably the single most important shaper of sex roles." Nevertheless, empirical documentation linking the two variables is scarce. Although comprehensive in scope, much of what has been written remains descriptive, somewhat polemical, and impressionistic (see, for example, Lampe, 1981; Ruether, 1975, 1981; Roberts, 1984). Much of the empirical work that does exist merely touches on the interrelationships between

Merlin B. Brinkerhoff is Professor of Sociology and Associate Vice-President (Research) at University of Calgary. He received his Ph.D. from University of Washington, Seattle. His sociological interests encompass gender and family, Latin America, work and organizations, and religion. His work examines the subjects of apostasy, religion's impact on gender attitudes, religion and the quality of life, religious social distance, rewards and costs of religious involvement, conservative church growth in Latin America, and Mormons and conservative Christians. His two most recent books are *Family and Work* and *Work Organizations and Society*. He serves on editorial boards of *Review of Religious Research, Canadian Journal of Sociology*, and *Social Inquiry*.

Marlene MacKie is Professor of Sociology at University of Calgary, Calgary, Alberta, Canada. She is a specialist in gender relations in Canada, one of her publications being *Contemporary Women and Men: A Gender Socialization*. She received her Ph.D. from the University of Alberta, Canada.

religion and gender by conceptualizing religion minimally as either a simple correlate or as one of many variables in a multivariate model (see, for example, Mason and Bumpass, 1975; Lipman-Blumen, 1972; Dempewolff, 1974; and Henley and Pincus, 1978). Other investigations have given the religious variable short shrift by measuring it with a single indicator such as attendance or affiliation (see, for example, the study by Brinkerhoff and MacKie, 1984, which was constrained by secondary data analysis). In short, the current state of empirical research on the relationship between religion and gender is quite unsophisticated. The purpose of this paper is to investigate this matter somewhat more thoroughly.

But why posit a relationship between religion and gender? A traditional perspective on gender relations and the status of women appears to be deeply rooted in Western religious thought. Although our religious heritage does contain material supportive of female-male equality, "there can be little doubt that the parables, stories, teachings, and gospels of the Judeo-Christian tradition that our culture has chosen to emphasize are those that perpetuate gender-stereotyping" (Richardson, 1981:100, emphasis in original deleted). Among the religious sources of gender traditionalism are the following:

1. Although English translations of scripture are sometimes more sexist than the original Hebrew, Greek, and Aramaic versions, elsewhere it is obvious that the scripture was written exclusively for men (Roberts, 1984:350). Examples are the Ten Commandments ("Thou shalt not covet thy neighbor's wife...") and the covenant made by the Israelites with God during the Exodus, which made circumcision a requirement (Walum, 1977:130).

2. Relatedly, although Old Testament attitudes towards women are inconsistent (the book of Proverbs depicts women as sources of great wisdom), the "overall effect is clearly that women have a subordinate position" (Roberts, 1984:351).

3. The New Testament conveys ambivalent messages concerning gender. The Gospels depict an attitude toward women that was unusually egalitarian for the time and culture. Jesus "violated Judaic law by touching menstruating women, by speaking alone with a woman not his wife, by allowing women to witness and testify to his resurrection" (Walum, 1977:129). However, the Epistles foster the doctrine of female inferiority. "Wives, submit yourselves unto your own husbands, as unto the Lord. For the husband is head of the wife, even as Christ is the head of the church." (Ephesians 5:22–23.)

4. Although the Protestant reformers abolished the requirement of clergy celibacy, traditional gender imagery occurs in the writings of Luther, Calvin, and Knox (Roberts, 1984:355). For example, ambivalence is seen in the teaching of Martin Luther in that men and women are equally called to life in Christ but that "the 'natural' order of the universe decrees women's lesser status and obedience to her husband" (Langdon, 1980:38).

5. Religious imagery appears to buttress male supremacy. God is father, judge, shepherd, king. Jesus and the twelve apostles are all male. The Christian tradition has two divergent views of the nature of womanhood: Eve, the first "sinner" responsible for humankind's expulsion from paradise; and Mary, immaculately conceived virgin and mother of God. However, no matter how revered the Virgin Mary is, she remains human and, as such, subordinate to the masculine Trinity. Theologian Mary Daly (1975:156) concludes: "If God in 'his' heaven is a father ruling 'his' people, then it is in the 'nature' of things and according to divine plan and the order of the universe that society be male-dominated."

6. Finally, church organization has traditionally assigned different roles to women and to men. The hierarchy of church structure is consistent with both religious teaching and the fact that most of the major prophets and leaders of Western religions have been men. With few exceptions men are the authority figures—deacons, priests, clergymen, bishops, cardinals, popes. While many of the large Protestant denominations have agreed recently, after much deliberation, to ordain women, so far the numbers involved are small and many women clergy have been diverted into marginal roles (Roberts, 1984:362). According to Bullough (1973, quoted in Roberts, 1984:360), "regardless of what a religion teaches about the status of women, or what its attitudes toward sex might be, if women are excluded from the institutions and positions which influence society, a general misogynism seems to result."

How is contemporary religion related to gender attitudes? Religion is broadly defined as a combination of beliefs, values, and behaviors which provides an overall worldview (see McGuire, 1981). It is well documented that in preindustrial societies, religion permeated all aspects of social life. With increasing industrialization and secularization, religion became more privatized. It has, for the most part, withdrawn from the public sphere, becoming closely linked with the family. There is an intrinsic relationship between religion and family values. The family, the primary agent of gender socialization, derives many of its ideas about gender from religion. Ruether (1974:9) claims (perhaps extravagantly) that religion is "undoubtedly the single most important shaper and enforcer of the image and role of women." Moreover, the family determines the child's exposure to subsequent socialization agents, including the church, and interprets the meaning of these secondary influences (see D'Antonio, 1980; Lampe, 1981). McMurry (1978:83), who regards religion and family as reactive institutions which exert conservative influences, concludes that "women who are exposed to more of this influence through greater involvement should be more traditional." During the socialization process, certain attributes such as compassion, self-sacrifice, obedience, and humility may be internalized as both feminine and religiously appropriate (see Lampe, 1981:29). Based on these observations, it is hypothesized that *the more religiously involved will portray more traditional gender attitudes*.

It may well be that formal involvement is not a necessary condition to produce traditional gender attitudes. That is, people may possess a worldview or belief system that is highly religious in orientation but be quite independent of any official religion or denomination. (Bibby, 1983; Geertz, 1966; McGuire, 1981:75–104.) After all, religiosity may have multiple dimensions, with the ideological aspect being independent from the ritualistic one (Glock and Stark, 1965). For this reason one might hypothesize that the *stronger the religious belief system, the more traditional the gender-role attitude independent of ritualistic involvement*.

However, many people do belong to specific religious denominations which are characterized by coherent bodies of values, beliefs, and practices derived from prescribed doctrines and organizations. Such denominations can serve as socialization agents, teaching gender attitudes reflecting particularistic doctrine, beliefs, and rituals. For example, a denomination's position on women in the clergy, or its opposition to the Equal Rights Amendment (Chalfant et al., 1981:345; Johnson, 1983; Tedlin, 1978) may very well influence members' gender attitudes. Moreover, denominations vary considerably in the extent and nature of women's participation in their formal organizational structures (Driver, 1976). Such structures convey attitudes about gender—impressionable children see important church roles as a male prerogative and experience only males making ceremonial contact with the Deity. Based on this premise, it is hypothesized that *gender attitudes are related to denominational affiliation*. Some denominations are more conservative than others because they cling more tenaciously to the past as they adhere to a more literal interpretation of scripture. Therefore, one can posit that members from those *denominations that are more fundamentalistic will be more conservative on gender matters.* (See Brinkerhoff and MacKie, 1984; Hesselbart, 1976; Thornton and Freedman, 1979; Thornton et al., 1983.) The term *fundamentalist* refers to such doctrinal beliefs as Bible literalness, divinity of Christ, salvation through Christ, and separation from the world (Ammerman, 1982; Hunter, 1981).

Since religious and gender socialization may both take place within the context of the official religion, one must distinguish between the affiliation one is born into and that with which one may later identify. These, of course, may differ. (Lazerwitz and Harrison, 1980.) Since a great deal of the socialization takes place when one is a child, one might expect the childhood denomination to have the major impact; however, Brinkerhoff and MacKie (1984) and Lipman-Blumen (1972) report one's current religious identification to be more important. This may result from people associating and identifying with groups who have similar values and beliefs to theirs. If their ideas about gender and other important matters have changed over time, they may switch group identifications, including religions, to bring consistency. Hence, current identity may be more important than childhood affiliation. Also, for a specific denomination to have an impact upon gender attitudes, *identification may be more important than actual belonging*, which is at times only nominal at best. Finally, caution must be exercised in the discussion of denominational influence because greater variation exists within denominations than between them. This is especially true when denominations are categorized broadly into Catholics, Protestants, Jews and "Nones." (See Bouma, 1973; Brinkerhoff, 1978; Means, 1966; Rhodes and Nam, 1970.) Extensive "within variation" is not unique to Protestant groups but also holds for Catholics (Greeley, 1964, 1972). High "within groups variation," therefore, may render denomination a rather weak correlate of attitudes and behavior. To illustrate, D'Antonio and Stack (1980:406) report that upon investigating specific denominations, "the attitudes of Baptists more closely approach those of Catholics in all abortion situations than they do those of other Protestants."

Recently, considerable attention has been given to the Moral Majority and its impact upon society. Although it purports to be "an organization established to restore moral values to society" (Roberts, 1984:128), theologians do not concur that all the values and attitudes stressed by the Moral Majority are basic to Christianity, e.g., their support of war spending. "What we see in the

Moral Majority is a powerful folk religion which has blended Christianity and Americanism" (Roberts, 1984:129). Following this reasoning it is predicted that those people who *adhere to the tenets of this unofficial, folk religion, the Moral Majority, will also tend to be traditional in terms of gender attitudes.*

In summary, it is hypothesized that religious belief, religious behavior, denominational identification, and agreement with the principles of the Moral Majority all will be correlated with gender attitudes. However, the limited, existing empirical research reports contradictory findings regarding these relationships. On the one hand, Martin et al. (1980) found religious affiliation to be the best predictor of gender conservativism, and McMurry (1978) reported religious activity to be more highly correlated with it than are the standard demographic factors. On the other hand, Barrish and Welch (1980), on the basis of a multi-university sample, found support for none of the above relationships and concluded that background factors are more important. Why this disparity in findings? Barrish and Welch (1980:72) suggest that McMurry's data are old (a 1964 sample) and that social attitudes have changed and "derive more from current political concerns and imagery than from conventional religious belief systems." Although employing different measures, our own recent work from a random, urban sample (Brinkerhoff and MacKie, 1984) supports the linkages between religion and gender attitudes.

Since the Brinkerhoff-MacKie (1984) study was based on secondary data, selected measures were deemed inadequate (for example, church attendance served as the single indicator for all of religiosity); consequently, more complete measures are required. Furthermore, some interesting findings invited further and more sophisticated investigation. The Mormons were by far the most traditional denomination on the gender attitude scale. They were even more conservative than Catholics with regard to the specific attitude toward abortion. However, the Mormon subsample was small. Overall, our Catholics were more liberal vis-à-vis gender than other studies have reported (Campbell, 1966; McMurry, 1978; Meir, 1972; Porter and Albert, 1977; and Seaman et al., 1971).

As far as the Mormons are concerned, the literature provides little guidance on their gender attitudes. Indeed, Thomas (1983:280) recently stated that *"research evidence is virtually nonexistent* that compares the extent to which children reared in Mormon families either accept or reject traditional sex roles" (emphasis added). Nevertheless, Thomas concludes "that acceptance of traditional sex roles would be relatively high for active Mormon families." Both the

Mormon organizational structure and its ideological system would lead to such a conclusion. Women are not allowed to hold the Mormon priesthood. Where women may be leaders in some women's organizations, the men by virtue of possessing the priesthood virtually control the exercise of power. During many socialization experiences in their youth organizations, boys and girls are segregated, presumably to be treated differently. These organizational characteristics may contribute to Mormons' ideas about gender. With regard to beliefs, women are taught that their power is derived through their husbands within the organization. Mormon theology emphasizes women's role in the home (Thomas, 1983) in this highly patriarchal system (O'Dea, 1957). This is not to imply that Mormon women are denigrated, for it is one of very few religions that posit a "Mother-in-Heaven" (Heeren et al., 1984; Roberts, 1984:372; Thomas, 1983; Vernon, 1980:279). According to Mormon beliefs, women, along with their husbands, can share in exaltation—they also can become Gods. With only this cursory excursion into the historical and modern Mormon social system, one might hypothesize that *Mormons would tend to be traditional on matters of gender*.

Finally, because of both the paucity and the conflicting findings in this area, the Barrish and Welch (1980:72) admonition seems appropriate: "Until further studies on the religiosity-sexism linkage are conducted, it seems wise to view the relationship as highly tentative, and to follow Wuthnow's (1973:128) sage advice about maintaining a healthy skepticism toward simplistic depictions of religiosity as a force in the service of social conservativism."

Methodology

The Sample

The data for this paper are derived from a 1983 questionnaire study of 938 students which was carried out at the University of Calgary ($n = 355$), an Alberta Bible college ($n = 71$), Brigham Young University ($n = 236$), and the University of Nebraska ($n = 276$). Comparisons between Canadian and American students and between state school and denominational school students should prove enlightening. The fact that these data were obtained from introductory social science students does, of course, restrict their generalizability. On the one hand, youth's views may inform us of the shape of the future. Wuthnow argues that "youth, being generally better educated and apparently more aware of current trends than many older people, are more likely to be exposed to such trends" and, further, that "young people may also be more receptive to cultural innovations than their elders since they are still in the process of forming basic values" (1976:856). (See also Ryder, 1965:848.) However, a number of studies show that gender attitudes vary with age, with younger respondents holding more egalitarian attitudes than older ones (Boyd, 1984; Thornton et al., 1983).

Measurement

The definition of religiosity, as well as its measurement, has been the focus of considerable attention. The number and composition of dimensions running through the concept have been explored. (For example, see Faulkner and DeJong, 1966; King and Hunt, 1975; Nudelman, 1971; Stark and Glock, 1968.) Although not without limitations, one can argue that measuring denominational identification is important because of differences in specific doctrines, values, beliefs, practices, and organizational structures which may influence gender attitudes. When focusing on denomination, two important distinctions must be made. First, the religious affiliations in which respondents were raised must be differentiated from those with which they currently identify. Furthermore, "identification" is more important than "belonging," since nominal membership may have little or no actual impact. Second, denomination can be categorized broadly (Catholic, Protestant, Jew, and Nones) or specifically (such as Greek Catholic, Baptist). Brinkerhoff and MacKie (1984) reported "current identification," specifically categorized, to be the strongest denominational predictor of gender attitudes. In the study reported here, identification with Current Denomination was tapped by asking "Do you presently *feel a part* of some religious group?" Responses then were classified somewhat broadly into "Nones," "Catholics," "Mainline Protestants," "Conservative Christians" or "Fundamentalists," and "Mormons." (Mormons are maintained as analytically distinct because of their claim to be non-Protestant, the objective of building on a past study, and their "well-known" position vis-à-vis family/gender matters.)

Several measures in this study were created in a similar fashion and may be summarized briefly here. Batteries of items, or questions, to tap both behaviors and attitudes were answered on Likert-type formats. These items then

were subjected to exploratory factor analysis, using principal factoring iterations (see Kim, 1975; Rummel, 1967; and Zeller and Carmines, 1980). Based
on the magnitudes of the loadings and their rotational patterns, items that did
not appear to contribute to the underlying variable in question were eliminated. Because the common variance explained was sufficiently high on first
factors for all cases, and because the remaining factors had low eigenvalues
and low loadings, only the first factors are employed here. Those items of a
given battery meeting the criterion of a factor loading of .40 or greater (this
may be seen as somewhat conservative, since Kerlinger [1979:189] accepts the
common criterion of .30) then were summed into the scales presented in Table
1. This approach to scale construction *"has been a most popular and effective technique in social research"* (emphasis in original, Lin, 1976:192; see
also Smith, 1974). Finally, Cronbach's alpha (1967) is presented as a measure
of reliability. The ranges of the summed scales, their means and standard deviations also are found in Table 1.

The Macho scale, which is the major dependent variable in this analysis,
illustrates the operations summarized in Table 1. Villemez and Touhey (1977)
built a scale of twenty-eight items which (with slight variations to make them
applicable to both Canadian and American respondents) were administered
using five-point, Likert-type response categories. As shown, eighteen of these
items clustered together to account for 85 percent of the variance, had factor
loadings greater than .40, and had a reliability coefficient of .89. When the
eighteen items are summed into a scale, it has a range from 18 to 85, a mean
of 52.1, and a standard deviation of 12.1.[1]

Two broad dimensions of religiosity commonly found in the literature
include religious ideology (or belief) and ritualism (or behavior). Employing
items derived, in part, and modified from many of these studies, five scales
were developed which are used as variables to explore this study's hypotheses.
Religious Belief is derived from a set of twelve items having four response categories. Fundamentalism is a subset of four of these items and is based on
Ammerman's (1982) differentiation between fundamentalism and evangelicalism—the former, but not necessarily the latter, possessing the four qualities
of biblical literalness, personal salvation through Jesus Christ, divinity of Jesus
Christ, and separation from the world. Religious Behavior, or ritualism, includes
twenty items of a personal nature (such as praying, reading the Bible) and of a
congregational nature (such as attending meetings, contributing money to a
church), presented on a five-point scale. Four of these items form a subset

TABLE 1. MEASURING GENDER ATTITUDES AND RELIGION: A SUMMARY TABLE OF THE PARAMETERS IN SCALE CONSTRUCTION FOR FOUR UNIVERSITY SAMPLES

| Scale Name | Number of Items | Factor Analysis:[a] First Factors | | | | Summed Scale Values[b] | | | Number of Respondents[c] |
		Range of Loadings	Percentage of Variance	Eigenvalue	Stand-ardized Alpha	Range	Mean	Standard Deviation	
Macho	18	.40-75	84.8	5.72	.89	18-85	52.1	12.1	921
Religious Belief	12	.59-.85	100.0	6.66	.94	13-48	37.7	8.3	899
Fundamentalism	4	.61-.84	100.0	2.29	.84	4-16	12.0	3.1	888
Religious Behavior	20	.40-.85	93.0	10.89	.96	20-97	57.2	19.1	907
Church Participation	4	.81-.88	100.0	2.77	.90	4-20	11.8	4.8	909
Overall Religiosity	31	.48-.84	89.1	16.58	.97	37-143	95.0	26.7	897
Moral Majority	11	.40-.87	100.0	3.65	.83	11-44	28.3	6.2	883

[a]Using principle factoring with iterations (Kim, 1975).

[b]The higher the score, the higher the "machismo," the higher the religiosity scores.

[c]Sample sizes vary due to nonresponses. In any scale where a respondent failed to answer 25 percent or more of the items, he/she was eliminated; for the occasional nonresponse, the mean of the items answered was employed for the missing response.

termed the Church Participation scale to illustrate formal, congregational involvement. Finally, although many argue the case for multidimensionality, the items in the Belief and Behavior scales are combined to form the Overall Religiosity scale. (In short, at least for these data, as reflected in Table 1, a common dimension seems to underlie these religiosity items.) A series of statements consistent with the views of the Moral Majority (for example, "prayer should be allowed in our schools") were posed with a four-point response ranging from "strongly disagree" to "strongly agree." Eleven of these clustered to form the Moral Majority scale.

Some (including Roof and Perkins, 1975) have suggested the importance of the variable "religious salience" in studies of religiosity. Respondents were presented with several aspects of the self and requested to rank the importance of each. Religious Salience was an evaluation of the importance of "myself as a religious person" on a four-point scale. Similarly, Gender Salience was measured by their ratings of "myself as a male or female person."

It has been argued that religion breeds social conservativism and that the more "fundamental" denominations would be more conservative in their attitudes. Based on these assumptions, the denominations are grouped into five categories according to their mean scores on the four-item Fundamentalism scale. The Alliance, Baptist, Church of Christ, Evangelical, and Pentecostal denominations form the "fundamentalist" or Conservative Christian group, with means ranging from 14.75 to 15.5 (out of a possible score of 16.0); the other Protestants become the Mainline Protestants; while the Catholics (a mean of 11.8), Mormons (13.8), and Nones (8.9) were kept distinct. Both the seven non-Christians and the respondents from denominations with only one member were excluded since the latter may indicate individual rather than group fundamentalism.

Because attitudes and values are at least partially shaped during youth, selected measures of religious background may prove important to ideas about gender. For example, a question was posed to assess whether respondents still held to the beliefs taught in church while growing up (Persistent Believer). Finally, the parents' religious affiliations also were tapped.

A series of demographic and background questions, measured by single indicators, were asked in order to serve as explanatory or control variables. These include age, sex, year in school, type of university, major, self-reported grades, marital status, community size, political orientation, ethnicity, socioeconomic status (based on father's occupation using the Treiman [1977] international scale), and parents' educational levels. Some of these demographic and self-evaluative measures are explored in the analysis for their impact on the relationships between religion and gender.

Data Analysis

Statistical analysis is largely descriptive and mainly exploratory. Initially, the hypotheses adumbrated earlier are cursorily examined using simple zero-order correlation coefficients. Where the independent variables are categorical in nature (for example, Denomination), dummy variable analysis is entertained. The commonly supported position of Labovitz (1970) is followed, treating ordinal data as if they were interval.

Finally, because no causal claims are made, four models are explored by nonhierarchical stepwise regression. This multivariate procedure allows several variables to enter into the predictive equation in the order of the magnitude of variance explained in the dependent variable, i.e., Macho in this case. By altering the predictor variables in various models, hints of the relative impact of different factors, interaction effects, evidence of spuriousness, and so on are suggested. This procedure should lead to the development of a more sophisticated model in this important field of endeavor.

Because the sample is composed of university students and must be considered nonrandom and nonrepresentative, tests of statistical significance are not presented. That is, inference is not the question in this exploratory analysis. With sample sizes of the magnitudes presented in this study, most correlation coefficients (R^2s) are statistically significant.

Some Exploratory Findings

Simple Relationships

Initially, in order to explore the linkages between religion and gender, the various scales and dimensions of religiosity are correlated with three "indicators" of gender attitude conservativism: the dependent variable—the Macho scale—and two indicators dealing directly with attitudes about abortion. This approach both offers evidence of validity and fits the findings to a body of literature on abortion. Table 2 contains the correlations which suggest several tentative conclusions. First, it is rather obvious that the data support McMurry (1978) and

Martin et al. (1980), rather than Barrish and Welch (1980). That is, the religious factors seem much more strongly related to all three gender attitude measures than do the demographic/background variables. (The measures are very similar to those used by Barrish and Welch; consequently, differences cannot be accounted for solely by different items.) Some might suggest that the relatively large number of Mormon students, who tend to be both *religiously involved and traditional* on gender attitudes, may have biased the results somewhat. The counter argument, of course, is that the large number of "Religious Nones" at the University of Calgary may bias the results in the opposite direction; that is, the two samples are "offsetting in their effects on religiosity measures. Comparative sociologists argue for the selection of research sites that allow for maximum variation in the independent variable(s); the strategy in the present study meets this requirement. We cannot focus on the Mormons as an important group without a similar sampling procedure. Finally, an earlier paper (Brinkerhoff and MacKie, 1984) using somewhat different measures on a *random sample* of an older, urban population *corroborates* the findings presented here.

To interpret the table further, note that the Overall Religiosity scale accounts for 22.3 percent of the variance in gender attitude as reflected by the Macho scale, while respondent's sex accounts for only 7.8 percent of the variance. Sex is the best predictor of the Macho scale among the demographic variables, unless the religious affiliation of the parents is considered to be a background factor. (Sex is less powerful as a predictor of the abortion attitude, however.) Although at first glance these coefficients appear somewhat weak, in comparison with other studies, the *R*s are quite respectable. Furthermore, when comparing the religious variables as predictors of gender attitudes with the demographic variables (for example, SES), one can only conclude that they are substantial.

Second, the pattern is consistent across the Macho scale and the two single indicators of gender. The higher the religiosity, the more conservative one is on matters of gender. Interestingly, and in agreement with Martin et al. (1980), one's current religious identification appears to be the strongest religious predictor of Macho. In all three cases it is a stronger correlate than is childhood affiliation. Bear in mind that for this analysis Religious Affiliation and Identification have been classified into five groupings: Religious Nones, Catholics, Mainline Protestants, Conservative Christians (or Fundamentalists), and Mormons are treated as dummy variables. Based on previous research (Brinkerhoff

TABLE 2. RELIGIOUS AND DEMOGRAPHIC FACTORS' IMPACT ON GENDER ATTITUDES: SOME EXPLORATORY ZERO-ORDER CORRELATIONS

| | Gender Attitudes | | | | | | | | |
| | Macho Scale | | | Abortion is Sin | | | Abortion by Choice | | |
Independent Variables	R	R^2	n	R	R^2	n	R	R^2	n
Religiosity Scales:[a]									
Belief	.424	.180	887	.689	.475	863	.463	.214	890
Fundamentalism	.428	.183	876	.618	.381	854	.405	.164	879
Behavior	.472	.223	892	.674	.455	869	.477	.228	895
Church participation	.450	.203	895	.641	.411	870	.473	.223	898
Overall	.472	.223	884	.702	.493	862	.494	.244	887
Attendance	.388	.151	902	.620	.384	877	.469	.220	905
Moral Majority	.642	.413	880	.766	.587	865	.550	.303	880
Denominational:									
Childhood[b]	.483	.233	859	.535	.286	834	.359	.129	862
Current identity[b]	.506	.256	888	.654	.427	863	.448	.200	891
The Self:									
As religious	.429	.184	912	.635	.403	886	.447	.200	915
As gender	.088	.008	917	.070	.005	891	.002	.000	920
Persistent believer	.323	.104	806	.406	.165	789	.288	.083	808
Political View	.302	.091	895	.284	.081	869	.248	.062	898
Demographic Background:									
Sex[b]	.280	.078	917	.000	.000	892	.046	.002	920
Marital status[b]	.173	.030	911	.172	.030	886	.143	.021	914
Year in university	.092	.008	913	.094	.009	888	.074	.006	916
Grades	-.055	.003	907	-.031	.001	885	.020	.000	910
Community size	-.148	.022	909	-.133	.018	883	.091	.008	912
SES	.052	.003	872	.011	.000	848	.017	.000	874
Father's education	.083	.007	891	.055	.003	868	.023	.001	894
Mother's education	.044	.002	891	.017	.000	867	.004	.000	894
Father's religion[b]	.401	.161	869	.417	.174	845	.269	.072	871
Mother's religion[b]	.412	.170	879	.450	.203	854	.289	.084	882
University[b]	.520	.270	921	.568	.322	895	.408	.167	924

[a]A positive sign means the greater the religiosity, the higher the Macho score (or more traditional in gender attitude).
[b]Categorical variables requiring dummy variable analysis.

and MacKie, 1984), even stronger relationships would be expected to result if more specific classifications were employed, such as Presbyterians, Pentecostals, Methodists, etc.

Third, selected variables must be considered correlates and not causal in nature. As a variable the Moral Majority scale seems to be strongly related to Macho and to both abortion items. Caution must be exercised in considering this finding in any causal sense; rather, it is probably another measure of conservativism which bears a distinctive religious connotation and, therefore, correlates highly with Macho. Indeed, this would lead to the prediction that Moral Majority also should correlate highly with current religious identification, just as Macho does (although the data are not presented here, the R^2 is .426). Similarly, the self-report of political views, although not as highly related, also must be considered another general measure of conservativism.

Finally, the University affiliation is one "apparent" nonreligious variable that is strongly correlated with gender attitudes. However, is it really a nonreligious variable? Both the Bible college and BYU were selected for the study because they, in fact, are religious institutions. BYU is made up mainly of Mormon youth who are among those of this age group most strongly committed to the church, and undoubtedly the Bible college also is attended by strongly committed Conservative Christians; that is, the most committed youth may be in attendance at these schools rather than at alternative schools. The religious factors undoubtedly interact with the University variable to influence the relationship with gender attitudes. These interaction effects are examined later in the analysis to discover if it is the religious factor, or conversely the University factor, that correlates with conservative gender attitudes. It probably can be assumed that religion, in a time-ordering perspective, occurred *prior* to University attendance. In any event both religious identification and university are strongly related. (Treating the variables at the nominal level, the Lambda coefficient is .50, relatively high.) Time and space do not permit the discussion of other correlates in any depth, but it should be noted that self-perception as a religious person is much more strongly correlated with gender attitudes than is perception of self as gender, that is, as a male or female person.

Categorical Predictors

The data in Table 2 provide some information about the direction of the relationships for selected variables; that is, overall, the greater the religiosity, the more traditional the gender attitudes. However, the categorical variables such as denomination, sex, marital status, and university do not disclose equivalent information regarding direction; that is, the coefficients do not indicate which classes are more conservative (for example, are males or females more conservative?). Therefore, the data in Table 3 go beyond the size of the coefficients for some of those nominal variables for which dummy variable analysis was employed earlier. Rather than present findings for all categorical factors in

Table 2, the data pertinent to the dependent variables have been confined to the Macho scale and the item "Abortion Is Sin," along with four of the independent variables.

Table 3 illustrates that Current Religious Identification is strongly related to gender attitudes. In this table "Constant," the reference category, refers to Mormons with a mean value of 60.512. These data indicate that the Mormons are only slightly more conservative on gender attitudes than are the Fundamentalists, followed by the Mainline Protestants and then the Catholics. The "Religious Nones" are the most egalitarian according to these data; of course, this finding is in agreement with others (see, for example, Dempewolff, 1974; Lipman-Blumen, 1972; McMurry, 1978), who all report the nonaffiliated to be less traditional. Catholics appear to be less traditional than either group of Protestants or than the Mormons; this result is contrary to those of Meir (1972), Campbell (1966), and McMurry (1978:84) who reports "Catholics to be less favorable towards female equality." On the other hand, it corroborates the findings of Brinkerhoff and MacKie (1984) when they used a different measure of gender egalitarianism on a random sample. Even on the "Abortion Is Sin" item on which Catholics have explicit doctrine, the Catholics are more liberal than the Mormons and Fundamentalists. Although the data are not reported here, other aspects of denomination (childhood affiliation, parents' religious affiliation) follow the same basic pattern; that is, on the Macho scale, the least conservative are the Religious Nones, followed by the Catholics, with Mormons being the most traditional. On matters regarding abortion, the Mormons and Fundamentalists are always more conservative than the Catholics.

Interpreting the relationships between denomination and gender attitudes must be done with considerable caution due to the nature of the sample. Over 95 percent of the Mormons were sampled from BYU, while approximately 65 percent of the Conservative Christians came from the Bible college. Both groups may attract the most traditional or conservative of Mormon and fundamentalist youth. Cannon and Christensen's (1978) research, for example, illustrates that Mormon youth at BYU are highly traditional and have become more so over time. Mainline Protestants and Catholics, if sampled from religiously sponsored institutions, may be relatively more conservative than those examined here from the Universities of Calgary and Nebraska. A "within groups" analysis (for example, comparing Conservatives at the Bible college with those from the public universities) might clarify this; however, there are too few non-BYU Mormons to entertain such analyses with these data. The earlier Brinkerhoff

TABLE 3. CURRENT RELIGIOUS IDENTIFICATION AND SELECTED DEMOGRAPHIC VARIABLES BY THE MACHO SCALE AND "ABORTION IS SIN" ITEM

Independent Variables and Categories	Gender Attitudes					
	Macho Scale			"Abortion Is Sin"		
	b	Standard Error of b	beta	b	Standard Error of b	beta
Current religious identification:						
Nones	-14.852	.947	-.560	-1.813	.077	-.376
Catholic	-11.777	1.062	-.381	-.594	.086	-.749
Mainline Protestant	-9.775	1.036	-.327	-1.030	.084	-.211
Fundamentalist	-.670	1.458	-.015	-.126	.116	-.031
Constant[a]	60.512			3.732		
	$R = .506; R^2 = .256; N = 888$			$R = .654; R^2 = .427; N = 863$		
Sex:						
Female	-6.927	.785	-.280	-.797	.075	-.000
Constant[b]	56.262			2.894		
	$R = .280; R^2 = .078; N = 917$			$R = .000; R^2 = .000; N = 892$		
Marital status:						
Divorced	-3.528	3.519	-.035	-.824	.319	-.091
Single	3.661	1.326	-.106	.123	.123	.039
Cohabitation	-6.261	2.642	-.087	-.784	.244	-.119
Constant[c]	49.184			2.824		
	$R = .173; R^2 = .030; N = 911$			$R = .172; R^2 = .030; N = 886$		
University:						
BYU	10.113	1.036	.365	.966	.081	.389
Bible	11.382	1.410	.245	1.055	.122	.257
Calgary	-4.276	.836	-.172	-.459	.074	-.205
Constant[d]	50.328			2.739		
	$R = .520; R^2 = .270; N = 921$			$R = .568; R^2 = .322; N = 895$		

[a]The constant is the predicted value for the omitted category, Mormon.
[b]Predicted value for males.
[c]Predicted value for married.
[d]Predicted value for University of Nebraska.

and MacKie (1984) study with a random sample of older adults corroborate the findings presented here. Mormons and Conservative Christians are more traditional on gender attitudes. The additional caveat that must be included involves the age of the respondents. The sample is highly educated, relatively young in age, and probably more "liberal" than the average adherent to their denominations.

With regard to other categorical variables, as expected females are more egalitarian than males. Respondents who are single, followed by those who are married, tend to be most conservative. Finally, on the University variable, those who attend the Bible college are slightly more conservative than BYU students (which might be expected, given the denominational characteristics of the schools), while those from the University of Calgary are the most egalitarian.

Some Exploratory Models

Up to this point, scales have been constructed, and selected simple bivariate and regression coefficients have been examined. These results suggest that the grouping of religious factors are more strongly associated with gender attitudes than are the background or demographic variables. Since these factors (such as denomination and sex) may interact to influence gender attitude (for example, Macho), multivariate techniques must be brought to bear on these relationships. This will enable an overall assessment of the impact of different variables on the gender attitude measures. Table 4 presents a summary of the proportion of variance in both Macho and the "Abortion Is Sin" indicator, as explained by four sets of independent variables considered jointly. This multiple regression analysis is divided into four models based both on technical concerns and on the theoretical and empirical import of the variables employed for prediction. Multiple regression requires the use of dummy variables for nominal level, or categorical, variables such as Denomination or University. Because more than two sets of dummy variables used simultaneously in an equation render interpretation somewhat difficult, this analysis is limited to a single dummy variable, Current Denomination Identification. (Sex and marital status may be considered noncategorical when conceptualized as the "degree of femaleness" and the "degree of 'marriedness.'" In doing so, the usual caveat is required.) In a stepwise multiple regression approach, the option of deciding when a variable enters into the explanatory schema (equation) exists; however, unless the dummy variables are entered in at the beginning, the interpretation may become problematic.

How are the variables to be placed in the predictive model chosen? Of course, the primary considerations are theoretical. Second, the findings in Tables 2 and 3 should provide direction. Therefore, based on theory, findings, and the above-mentioned technical restrictions, four models are presented in Table 4. In Model 1, Current Denomination was entered into the equation first, by design, where the Moral Majority scale, Sex, Marital Status, and the Overall

Religiosity scale appear in the order of the magnitude of the remaining variance explained in the dependent (or predicted) variables, the Macho scale and Abortion Attitude. In Table 4, a summary table, Model 1 illustrates that the coefficient R^2 is .263—or 26.3 percent of the variance in Macho is accounted for by Current Denomination. Of the remaining unexplained variance, Moral Majority enters first to explain an additional 17.1 percent, followed by Sex which accounts for 6.8 percent; Marital Status adds just .6 percent, followed by Overall Religiosity (.3 percent). The total variance explained in the Macho scale by these five variables is 51.1 percent; however, fully 50.1 percent was accounted for by only the first three variables. It is interesting to observe that when the Abortion Attitude is predicted, Current Denomination explains 43.9 percent of the variance, Moral Majority adds another 20 percent, and Overall Religiosity adds an additional .6 percent, while Marital Status and Sex contribute nothing. Note that for the other variables free to enter into the equation after Denomination, Moral Majority is the strongest predictor, with the remaining variables altering their order for the two dependent variables.

It may not be surprising, but the findings thus far would suggest that Denomination, Moral Majority, and Overall Religiosity may share some of the explanatory power. Removing Denomination from the equation and adding the "Self as Religious"—which is fairly strongly correlated with the gender items as reflected in Table 2—lends some confirmation to this notion, as shown in Model 2. When the "Self as Religious" variable is entered into Model 2, little is added to the prediction of the Abortion Attitude (.4 percent), and almost nothing to the explanation of Macho. It should be noted that the total variance explained is only slightly reduced for both gender attitude measures when Denomination is eliminated. As suspected, this would suggest that the religious variables (including assessing Self as Religious) appear to be interacting to influence gender.

Focusing on Model 3, with Moral Majority removed, the proportion of total variance explained decreases somewhat (about 5 percent for Abortion Attitude and 10 percent for Macho) from Model 2. This confirms that the independent variables, Denomination and Moral Majority, jointly influence gender attitudes, with Moral Majority being slightly stronger. When both are eliminated from the equation, as shown in Model 4, Religiosity emerges as the strongest predictor. In this four-variable model, Sex adds 9.2 percent in explaining Macho, but the other variables account for almost nothing. For the Abortion Attitude, Model 4 has only Religiosity making any real difference. It appears,

TABLE 4. PROPORTION OF VARIANCE EXPLAINED FOR SELECTED FACTORS AFFECTING THE MACHO SCALE AND ABORTION ATTITUDE IN ALTERNATIVE MULTIPLE REGRESSION MODELS

Model and Dependent Variable	Factors[a] (Independent Variables) in Order of Entry					Total Variance Explained—R^2
Model 1						
Macho Scale:	Denomination[b] .263	+ Moral (1.71)[c] .433	+ Sex (.068) .501	+ Marital Status (.006) .507	+ Religiosity (.003) .511	= .511
Abortion Attitude:	Denomination[b] .439	+ Moral (.200) .639	+ Religiosity (.006) .646	+ Marital Status (.000) .646	+ Sex (.000) .646	= .646
Model 2						
Macho Scale:	Moral .406	+ Sex (.066) .472	+ Marital Status (.005) .478	+ Religiosity (.001) .478	+ Self (.001) .479	= .479
Abortion Attitude:	Moral .586	+ Religiosity (.020) .606	+ Self (.004) .610	+ Marital Status (.000) .610	+ Sex (.000) .610	= .610
Model 3						
Macho Scale:	Denomination[b] .257	+ Sex (.078) .335	+ Religiosity (.029) .364	+ Marital Status (.011) .375	+ Self (.002) .377	= .377
Abortion Attitude:	Denomination[b] .443	+ Religiosity (.105) .548	+ Self (.002) .549	+ Marital Status (.001) .550	+ Sex (.001) .551	= .551
Model 4						
Macho Scale:	Religiosity .213	+ Sex (.092) .305	+ Marital Status (.011) .316	+ Self (.005) .321		= .321
Abortion Attitude:	Religiosity .491	+ Self (.010) .501	+ Marital Status (.001) .502	+ Sex (.001) .503		= .503

[a]Abbreviated factors are: Denomination = Current Denominational Identification; Moral = Moral Majority Scale; Sex = Sex; Religiosity = Overall Religiosity, combining Belief and Behavior Scales; Self = Self as Religious Person.

[b]Dummy variable entered first in the equation.

[c]Coefficients in parentheses refer to the amount of variance explained by that variable from the portion of variance left unexplained by those factors that occurred prior to the equation. Those without parentheses refer to the total cumulative variance explained by all variables entered into the equation to that point; they are R^2's.

then, that Religiosity is joining Denomination and Moral Majority in sharing much, but not all, of the variation explained. Model 1 remains the most powerful predictive model. Of course, other models have been examined for which the data cannot be presented here.

Some general findings might be usefully summarized. When Overall Religiosity is broken into its two components, the Belief and the Behavior scales, little difference in the amount of explained variance occurs; that is, they do no better separately than when combined, as presented in the four models. However, it is interesting that Belief always enters into the equation before Behavior when attempting to predict Abortion and does so about half the time with Macho. Recall that University is a strong predictor of gender attitudes at the bivariate level. Earlier it was suggested that this may be due, in part, to interaction with Denomination. If University is exchanged for Denomination as the dummy variable in Model 1, the findings are similar, with the amount of variance explained decreasing slightly (to 49.9 percent for Macho, and 61.6 percent for Abortion). Adding Self as Religious to the equations has only slight effect on the Abortion Attitude but almost no impact on the Macho scale. Probably much of the predictive power of the "Self as Religious" is shared by the other religious predictors. Among the demographic factors, Sex is of some modest influence on Macho but adds almost nothing to Abortion Attitude. Sex remains weak even when entered into the equation first, a model examined but not reported here. In fact, one can conclude that the religious factors have far greater influence in all multiple regression models when compared with any of the background factors. This finding concurs with McMurry (1978) and questions Barrish and Welch (1980).

Some Conclusions

This paper argues that religion has an impact on the traditionalism surrounding gender attitudes. Demographic variables have little import. The findings appear to be related to denominational identification, as well as independent belief systems and behaviors. The overall best predictor of gender attitudes is position on the Moral Majority scale; however, this should not be interpreted in a causal sense. Probably both degree of modernism on gender attitudes and position on the Moral Majority scale are linked to some other causal variable(s). Both are ideological systems which relate to another ideological system—one dealing with ideas about religion (for example, the nature of human beings, the ultimate meaning of life, etc.). Furthermore, it appears that gender attitudes are not strongly related—at least for this University sample—to the usual background factors, for example, sex, SES, etc. However, they do relate to denomination. This suggests that specific religious groups do have some degree of consistency or homogeneity in their beliefs and values about religion, the Moral Majority, and gender attitudes, providing a common worldview for their committed adherents.

As shown, the Mormons tend to be the most traditional denomination with regard to gender attitudes. Although data have not been thoroughly examined, one suspects that Mormons would score high on the Moral Majority scale, be highly committed on the Belief and Behavior scales, and so on. The Mormons' position on women's roles is entirely consistent with Brinkerhoff's (1978:215) finding in a study of the impact of gender on high school youth's educational and occupational orientations. He concluded: "Substantively, those Mormons who are highly involved or committed to the belief system and organization structure, aspire to goals consistent with the belief that woman's major role is that of mother and homemaker." In another study Brinkerhoff and MacKie (1984) reported that married Mormon adults are highly traditional on gender attitudes *but* are highly egalitarian with regard to reported behaviors—division of household labor and familial decision making. How might this discrepancy between attitudes and behavior be explained? Is it a function of the small sample, the measurement? Perhaps O'Dea's (1957:255) conclusion that Mormons have a conflict between "social idealism born of Mormon beliefs and political conservatism" may provide a hint. He notes (1957:249) that early Mormons "came close to accepting the equality of women with men" while "accepting patriarchal ideals of family organization." In short, man is the head of the family, but woman is considered his equal in many ways; for example, both are eternal intelligences (O'Dea, 1957:250). The Macho scale used in this study probably captures the Mormon patriarchal ideology, while selected behaviors illustrate the social idealism of egalitarianism.

In any event, for this study, it is fairly conclusive that Mormons possess a highly conservative gender ideology. One must remember that the findings involving denomination may be questioned because the respondents from BYU could be more committed and more traditional than average Mormon youth. On the other hand, since university students are usually somewhat more modern and closer to the forefront of societal change than are the rank and file, one might expect a random sample of highly religious Mormons to be even more traditional. Vernon (1980:287) argues that women and men within the Mormons experience different churches, and he concludes that "the societal changes in the roles of women have already changed both churches, or the experience of both males and females within the church and promises to introduce even further changes." With the high gender conservativism found among the Mormon students—the highly committed, intelligent, presumably future leaders—one can only speculate whether these changes will eventually alter the patriarchal belief system.

Notes

1. These means and standard deviations of the Macho scale are different from those of Villemez and Touhey (1977) and others using this scale (e.g., Barrish and Welch, 1980) because the items were scored from 1 to 5 rather than from 0 to 4, and because only eighteen of the items met the rigorous criteria to be employed in the scale, rather than the full twenty-eight used by the others. All items for the various scales are available from the authors upon request.

Bibliography

Ammerman, N. T. 1982. "Comment: Operationalizing Evangelicalism: An Amendment." *Sociological Analysis* 43:170–72.

Barrish, G. and M. R. Welch. 1980. "Student Religiosity and Discriminatory Attitudes Towards Women." *Sociological Analysis* 41 (Spring):66–73.

Bibby, R. W. 1983. "Searching for Invisible Thread: Meaning Systems in Contemporary Canada." *Journal for the Scientific Study of Religion* 22(2):101–19.

Bouma, G. D. 1973. "Beyond Lenski: A Critical Review of Recent 'Protestant Ethic' Research." *Journal for the Scientific Study of Religion* 12:141–55.

Boyd, M. 1984. *Canadian Attitudes Toward Women: Thirty Years of Change*. Ottawa: Women's Bureau, Labour Canada.

Brinkerhoff, M. B. 1978. "Religion and Goal Orientations: Does Denomination Make a Difference?" *Sociological Analysis* 39 (3):203–18.

Brinkerhoff, M. B. and M. M. MacKie. 1984. "Religious Denominations' Impact upon Gender Attitudes: Some Methodological Implications." *Review of Religious Research* 25 (4):365–78.

Bullough, V. L. 1973. *The Subordinate Sex: A History of Attitudes Toward Women*. Urbana, IL: University of Illnois Press.

Campbell, D. F. 1966. "Religion and Values Among Nova Scotian Students." *Sociological Analysis* 27(Summer):80–93.

Cannon, K. L. and H. T. Christensen. 1978. "The Fundamentalist Emphasis at Brigham Young University: 1935-1973." *Journal for the Scientific Study of Religion* 17:53–57.

Chalfant, H. P., R. E. Beckley, and C. E. Palmer. 1981. *Religion in Contemporary Society*. Sherman Oaks, CA: Alfred Publishing.

Cronbach, L. J. 1967. "Coefficient Alpha and the Internal Structure of Tests." Pp. 132-67 in W. A. Mehrens and R. L. Ebel (eds.), *Principles of Educational and Psychological Measurement*. Chicago: Rand McNally & Company. (See also the 1951 original in *Psychometrika* 16:297-334.)

Daly, M. 1975. "God Is a Verb." Pp. 153-70 in U. West (ed.), *Women in a Changing World*. New York: McGraw-Hill.

D'Antonio, W. V. 1980. "The Family and Religion: Exploring a Changing Relationship." *Journal for the Scientific Study of Religion* 19 (2):89-104.

D'Antonio W. F. and S. Stack. 1980. "Religion, Ideal Family Size, and Abortion: Extending Renzi's Hypothesis." *Journal for the Scientific Study of Religion* 19(4):397-408.

DeJong, G. F., J. E. Faulkner, and R. H. Warland. 1976. "Dimensions of Religiosity Reconsidered: Evidence from a Cross-Cultural Study." *Social Forces* 54(June):866-90.

Dempewolff, J. A. 1974. "Some Correlates of Feminism." *Psychological Reports* 34(April):671-76.

Driver, A. B. 1976. "Review Essay: Religion." *Signs* 2 (Winter):434-42.

Faulkner, J. E. and G. DeJong. 1966. "Religiosity in 5-D: An Empirical Analysis." *Social Forces* 45:246-54.

Geertz, C. 1966. "Religion as a Cultural System." Pp. 1-46 in M. Banton (ed.), *Anthropological Approaches to the Study of Religion*. London: Tavistock Publications.

Glock, C. Y. and R. Stark. 1965. *Religion and Society in Tension*. Chicago: Rand McNally.

Greeley, A. M. 1964. "The Protestant Ethic: A Time for a Moratorium." *Sociological Analysis* 25(2):20-30.

Greeley, A. M. 1972. *The Denominational Society*. Glenview, IL: Scott, Foresman.

Heeren, J., D. Lindsey, and M. Mason. 1984. "The Mormon Concept of Mother in Heaven: A Sociological Account of Its Origins and Development." *Journal for the Scientific Study of Religion* 23(4):396-411.

Henley, N. M. and F. Pincus. 1978. "Interrelationship of Sexist, Racist and Homosexual Attitudes." *Psychological Reports* 42 (February)83-90.

Hesselbart, S. 1976. "A Comparison of Attitudes Toward Women and Attitudes Toward Blacks in a Southern City." *Sociological Symposium* 17 (Fall):45-68.

Hunter, J. D. 1981. "Operationalizing Evangelicalism: A Review Critique and Proposal." *Sociological Analysis* 42(4):363-72.

Johnson, S. 1983. *From Housewife to Heretic*. New York: Anchor Press/Doubleday.

Kerlinger, F. 1979. *Behavioral Research: A Conceptual Approach*. New York: Holt, Rinehart and Winston.

Kim, J. O. 1975. "Factor Analysis." Pp. 468-514 in N. H. Nie, C. Hull, J. Jenkins, K. Steinbrenner, and D. Bent (eds.), *Statistical Package for the Social Sciences*. New York: McGraw Hill.

King, M. B. and R. A. Hunt. 1975. "Measuring the Religious Variable: National Replication." *Journal for the Scientific Study of Religion* 14:13-22.

Labovitz, S. 1970. "The Assignment of Numbers to Rank Order Categories." *American Sociological Review* 35:515-25.

Lampe, P. E. 1981. "Androgyny and Religiosity." *International Journal of Women's Studies* 4(1):27-34.

Langdon, M. E. 1980. "Images and Ideals of Victorian Women, 1820–1850." Unpublished master's thesis, Department of History, University of Calgary.

Lazerwitz, B. and M. Harrison. 1980. "A Comparison of Denominational Identification and Membership." *Journal for the Scientific Study of Religion* 19(4):361–67.

Lin, N. 1976. *Foundations of Social Research.* New York: McGraw-Hill.

Lipman-Blumen, J. 1972. "How Ideology Shapes Women's Lives." *Scientific American* 266(January)33–42.

Martin, P. Y., M. W. Osmond, S. Hesselbart and M. Wood. 1980. "The Significance of Gender as a Social and Demographic Correlate of Sex Role Attitudes." *Sociological Focus* 13(October):383–96.

Mason, K. and L. L. Bumpass. 1975. "U.S. Women's Sex Role Ideology, 1970." *American Journal of Sociology* 80(March):1212–19.

McGuire, M. B. 1981. *Religion: The Social Context.* Belmont, CA: Wadsworth.

McMurry, M. 1978. "Religion and Women's Sex Role Traditionalism." *Sociological Focus* 11(2):81–95.

Means, R. L. 1966. "Protestantism and American Sociology: Problems of Analysis." *Sociological Analysis* 27:128–37.

Meir, H. C. 1972. "Mother-centeredness and College Youths' Attitudes Towards Social Equality for Women: Some Empirical Findings." *Journal of Marriage and the Family* 34(February):115–21.

Nudelman, A. E. 1971. "Dimensions of Religiosity: A Factor-analytic View of Protestants, Catholics, and Christian Scientists." *Review of Religious Research* 13:42–56.

O'Dea, T. F. 1957. *The Mormons.* Chicago: University of Chicago Press.

Porter, J. R. and A. A. Albert. 1977. "Subculture or Assimilation? A Cross-cultural Analysis of Religion and Women's Role." *Journal for the Scientific Study of Religion* 16(4):345–59.

Rhodes, A. L. and C. B. Nam. 1970. "The Religious Context of Educational Expectations." *American Sociological Review* 35:253–67.

Richardson, L. W. 1981. *The Dynamics of Sex and Gender* (2nd ed.). Boston: Houghton Mifflin.

Roberts, K. A. 1984. *Religion in Sociological Perspective.* Homewood, IL: Dorsey Press.

Roof, W. C. and R. B. Perkins. 1975. "On Conceptualizing Salience in Religious Commitment." *Journal for the Scientific Study of Religion* 14:111–28.

Ruether, R. R. 1974. *Religion and Sexism.* New York: Simon & Schuster.

Ruether, R. R. 1975. *New Woman, New Earth.* New York: Seabury Press.

Ruether, R. R. 1981. "The Feminist Critique in Religious Studies." Pp. 52–66 in E. Langland and W. Gove (eds.), *A Feminist Perspective in the Academy.* Chicago: University of Chicago Press.

Rummel, R. J. 1967. "Understanding Factor Analysis." *Journal of Conflict Resolution* 11(4):440–80.

Ryder, N. B. 1965. The Cohort as Concept in the Study of Social Change." *American Sociological Review* 30:843–61.

Seaman, J. M., J. B. Michel and R. C. Dillehay. 1971. "Membership in Orthodox Christian Groups, Adjustment and Dogmatism." *Sociological Quarterly* 12(Spring):252–59.

Smith, K. W. 1974. "On Estimating the Reliability of Composite Indexes Through Factor Analysis." *Sociological Methods and Research* 2(4):484–510.

Stark, R. and C. Y. Glock. 1968. *American Piety: The Nature of Religious Commitment*. Berkeley, CA: University of California Press.

Tedlin, K. 1978. "Religious Preference and Pro/Anti Activism on the Equal Rights Amendment Issue." *Pacific Sociological Review* 21 (January):55–66.

Thomas, D. L. 1983. "Family in the Mormon Experience." Pp. 267–88 in W. V. D'Antonio and J. Aldous (eds.), *Families and Religions: Conflict and Change in Modern Society*. Beverly Hills, CA: Sage Publications.

Thornton, A., D. F. Alwin and D. Camburn. 1983. "Causes and Consequences of Sex-Role Attitudes and Attitude Change." *American Sociological Review* 48:211–27.

Thornton, A. and D. Freedman. 1979. "Changes in the Sex Role Attitudes of Women, 1962–1977: Evidence from a Panel Study." *American Sociological Review* 44 (October):831–42.

Treiman, D. 1977. *Occupational Prestige in Comparative Perspective*. New York: Academic Press.

Vernon, G. M. 1980. "Mormon Women." Pp. 279–87 in G. M. Vernon, *Mormonism: A Sociological Perspective*. Salt Lake City, UT: University of Utah Press.

Villemez, W. J. and J. C. Touhey. 1977. "A Measure of Individual Differences in Sex Stereotyping and Sex Discrimination: The 'Macho' Scale." *Psychological Reports* 41:411–15.

Walum, L. R. 1977. *The Dynamics of Sex and Gender*. Chicago: Rand McNally.

Wilson, J. 1978. *Religion in American Society*. Englewood Cliffs, NJ: Prentice Hall.

Wuthnow, R. 1973. "Religious Commitment and Conservatism: In Search of an Elusive Relationship." In C. Glock (ed.), *Religion in Sociological Perspective*. Belmont, CA: Wadsworth.

Wuthnow, R. 1976. "Recent Pattern of Secularization: A Problem of Generations?" *American Sociological Review* 41(October):850–67.

Zeller, R. and E. G. Carmines. 1980. *Measurement in the Social Sciences: The Link Between Theory and Data*. Cambridge, England: Cambridge University Press.

13

Familial Influence on Religious Involvement

Gerald N. Stott

Folk wisdom informs us that "As the twig is bent so grows the tree" and that "The child is the father of the man." Biblical verse (Proverbs 22:6) declares, "Train up a child in the way he should go: and when he is old, he will not depart from it." The family is considered a primary force in shaping the values and attitudes of its members, especially its young members.

Children are typically socialized (or indoctrinated) by the religious beliefs and practices of their parents. In fact, many parents feel morally bound to instruct their children in religious matters. Just how effective is this indoctrination? Does the "tree" really grow as the "twig" is bent? If so, a strong positive correlation should exist between the religious involvement of parents and their offspring. Moreover, this correlation should occur not only when the offspring are young and under the supervision of their parents, but also after children become adults and leave their parents' supervision.

Gerald N. Stott is Associate Professor of Sociology, Southeast Missouri State University, Cape Girardeau, Missouri. His current research interests focus on the interplay between religion and the other primary institutions, especially economics, family, and education. He received his Ph.D. from Southern Illinois University.

Past Findings

Extant research typically supports the belief that parents do indeed influence the belief and practices of their offspring, but disagreement exists as to the strength of the influence. See, for example, reviews of research on the topic by Hyman (1959), Kalish and Johnson (1972), and Hoge et al. (1982). In his review of previous research, Hyman (1959) found generally *"moderate"* correlations between the values of parents and their offspring (the median Pearson's r for the numerous studies cited was approximately .5). Bengtson (1975:369) in a three-generation study reported weak to moderate value transmission and concluded that "generalizations concerning family influences on the development of values should be made with caution: similarities between parents and youth reflect their commonality of social location rather than direct transmission." Necombe and Svehla (1937) found *"high"* correlations between parent and child attitudes for their heterogeneous religious sample but much weaker correlations in their subsamples of strongly religious people in specific denominations. They also noted declining correlations with increasing age of the offspring. A study of alcohol and drug usage among college students by Perkins (1985) found parental attitudes to have little direct effect on their offspring's alcohol and other drug usage. Commitment to Judeo-Christian traditions was, however, found to be a significant moderating influence.

Focusing specifically on religious involvement, Hoge, Petrillo, and Smith (1982) report generally *"weak"* parent/child correlations. Furthermore, they found denomination to be a better prediction of adolescent religious involvement than parental religiosity. Kalish and Johnson (1972) found daughter/mother correlations on a religious value scale to be noticeably stronger than mother/grandmother correlations. They concluded that value similarities between generations are strongest between the adjacent generations who have most recently lived together. A recent study by Potvin and Sloane (1985) reports that adolescents whose parents are regular church attenders are five times more likely to score high on religious practice than adolescents whose parents are infrequent or nonchurch attenders. Furthermore, Hunsberger (1980) reports noticeably negative relationships between parental religious instruction and religious apostasy of the child. Dudley and Dudley (1986), however, report only moderate relationships between the religious values and attitudes of parents and those of their adolescent offspring.

Variances in the strength of the parent/child relationships cited can, in part, be explained by (1) the fact that parent/child *behavior* correlations are typically stronger than parent/child *value* correlations; (2) the subjective nature of such terms as *weak, moderate,* or *strong* (e.g. Bengtson, [1975], reports "weak to moderate" intra-family value transmission with an r of .53 on one of his two scales, while Hoge and Petrillo [1978], report r's of .48 and .60 as evidence of "very strong" parental influence); and (3) the age of the child— parental influences typically decline as the child becomes older and more independent.

Purpose of Study

This paper specifically investigates the short- and long-range influence of familial religious socialization among Southern Baptists and Mormons (members of The Church of Jesus Christ of Latter-day Saints). Both of these denominations have high retention rates among their members (Roof and Hadaway, 1979) and emphasize childhood religious indoctrination.

Mormon doctrine, for example, declares: "And again, inasmuch as parents have children in Zion, or in any of her stakes which are organized, that teach them not to understand the doctrine of repentance, faith in Christ the Son of the living God, and of baptism and the gift of the Holy Ghost by the laying on of the hands, when eight years old, the sin be upon the heads of the parents" (Doctrine and Covenants 68:25).

My data are derived from a systematic sample of Southern Baptists and Mormons in the St. Louis metropolitan area. Five hundred Mormons and five hundred Southern Baptists were mailed questionnaires; 238 Southern Baptists and 261 Mormons returned completed surveys. A list of the variables used in this study and how they are operationalized is provided in the appendix.

Analysis

As was already mentioned, children are typically socialized into the beliefs and practices of the parents. Hence, measures of parental religious involvement should provide useful indicators of religious socialization. Two such indicators in my data are the father's and the mother's church attendance during their child's last year of high school. If these measures are viable indicators of familial religious socialization, we should expect a high correlation between the child's church attendance during his or her last year of high school and his or her parents' church attendance for the same period. The correlations are presented in Table 1 and, as expected, they are rather strong. The father/child church attendance correlation is .58 for the Mormons and .53 for the Baptists. The corresponding mother/child correlations are .66 and .59. Thus, parental church attendance is an excellent predictor of their child's church attendance. Note also that the mother's church attendance is a better predictor of the child's church attendance than is the father's church attendance.

Another indicator in my data of childhood religious socialization is the respondent's self-reported religiosity during his last year of high school. Childhood religiosity correlates with the father's church attendance at .37 for the Mormons and at .32 for the Baptists; correlations with the mother's church attendance are .44 and .35 respectively. Notice also that the two measures of childhood religious involvement—church attendance and religiosity—correlate strongly together at .68 for the Mormons and .62 for the Baptists.

These findings clearly support the belief that parents play a dominant role in the religious socialization of their offspring. The child's religious involvement definitely tends to mirror his or her parents' religious involvement. But what is the temporal efficacy of this childhood socialization? Are patterns of religious involvement acquired as a child maintained as an adult?

An analysis of the respondents' adult religious involvement with both their childhood religious involvement and their parents' church attendance should provide a tentative answer to this question.

Notice in Table 1 that parental church attendance correlates only weakly with respondents' adult church attendance: the father/adult respondent correlations are .05 for the Mormons and .22 for the Baptists, and the mother/adult respondent correlations are .13 and .10 respectively. Also weak and typically nonsignificant are the correlations of parental church attendance with the other measures of their adult offspring's religious involvement (that is, testimony, prayer, tithing, and self-reported religiosity). It appears that the impact of parental religious socialization is rather transitory, waning considerably after the child becomes an adult.

The relatively temporal effect of parental religious socialization is further supported by the fact that only mild correlations exist between the respondents' childhood and adult attendance (Mormon .16, Baptist .12) and between childhood and adult religiosity (.29 and .18 respectively). In addition, these two

TABLE 1. CORRELATIONS* BETWEEN PAST AND PRESENT MEASURES OF RELIGIOUS INVOLVEMENT FOR MORMONS AND SOUTHERN BAPTISTS

	Adult Church Attendance		Adult Religiosity		Adult Testimony		Adult Tithing		Adult Prayer		Childhood Religiosity		Childhood Church Attendance	
	LDS	SBC	LDS	SBC	LDS	SBC	LDS	SBC	LDS	SBC	LDS	SBC	LDS	SBC
Childhood Religiosity	.12[a]	.01	.29[c]	.18[b]	.15[b]	.05	.13[a]	-.02	.19[c]	.00			.68[c]	.62[c]
Childhood Church Attendance	.16[b]	.12[a]	.18[b]	.18[b]	.19[b]	.07	.14[a]	.16[a]	.16[b]	.11	.68[c]	.62[c]		
Father's Church Attendance	.05	.22[c]	.03	.11	.07	.11	.14[a]	.24[c]	.07	.16[a]	.37[c]	.32[c]	.58[c]	.53[c]
Mother's Church Attendance	.13[a]	.10	.06	.12	.09	.05	.22[c]	.13	.05	.08	.44[c]	.35[c]	.66[c]	.59[c]
Best Friends' Religion	.56[c]	.44[c]	.55[c]	.49[c]	.46[c]	.30[c]	.61[c]	.47[c]	.42[c]	.34[c]	.22[c]	.14[a]	.25[c]	.05
Spouse's Religiosity	.51[c]	.37[c]	.54[c]	.46[c]	.50[c]	.30[c]	.58[c]	.46[c]	.43[c]	.25[c]	.12[a]	.05	.19[b]	-.01

*Pearson's r is the measure of correlation used. For justification of its use with ordinal data see Labovitz (1970).

a = P < .05   b = P < .01   c = P < .001

LDS = Mormons   SBC = Southern Baptists

measures of childhood religiosity correlate only weakly with three other measures of adult religious involvement: testimony, tithing, and prayer.

To this point this analysis has focused on the family of orientation, and specifically, parental influence. Let us now look briefly at the family of procreation and specifically at the husband/wife religious involvement relationship. Regretfully, only one variable in my data set—spouse's religiosity—measures the spouse's religious involvement. Additional measures would be desirable, but this measure does provide tentative information about the relationship. Among the Mormons, four of the five measures of adult religiosity correlate with spouses' religiosity at .50 or higher, while correlations between spouses' religiosity and the two measures for the respondents' childhood religious involvement are in the teens. The Baptist correlations, though not as strong, reflect the same pattern. Typically the couples in the analysis are religiously quite similar. While it is possible that marital selection accounts for this similarity (measures of religious involvement at the time of engagement are lacking), the weak correlations between the respondents' past religious involvement and spouses' present religious involvement suggest that marital socialization is the more likely cause.

The final variable in Table 1 which remains to be examined is the number of best friends who are of the same faith as the respondents. Correlations between "friends" and the respondents' five adult religious measures range from .42 to .61 for the Mormons and from .30 to .49 for the Baptists, and are all significant at the .001 level.

The correlations between "friends" and the respondents' childhood religious involvement measures are, however, noticeably weak. In short, childhood religious involvement is a poor predictor of the faith of the adult respondents' best friends. Yet the number of present best friends who are of the same faith as the respondent is an excellent predictor of the respondent's present religious involvement. These several findings make eminent sense if we view parents, spouse, and friends as comprising primary groups for the respondents. Primary groups, because of their intimate, face-to-face, wholistic nature, strongly influence the beliefs and practices (whether sacred or secular) of their members. In fact, this is why they are called primary groups, because they play a *primary* role in shaping the beliefs and values of their members.

When an individual leaves one primary group and joins another, the influence of the former group on the individual wanes while the influence of the new group increases. Hence, the parent/child, spouse/spouse, and friends/adult respondent correlations are all substantial.

While the parent/adult child, spouse/child respondent, "friends"/child respondent, and adult/child correlations are typically weak, the substantial correlations reflect primary group relations for the respondents. The weak correlations reflect relationships in which the respondent/other were not a primary group at the time of measurement.

It is possible that my analyses are inadequate. Intervening variables could be masking the true relationships. Such a variable could be convert status. It is well-known that both Baptists and Mormons are quite active in proselyting. In my sample, 56 percent of the Mormons and 53 percent of the Baptists are converts. If the converts were raised, by and large, in homes in which there was little religious involvement but after conversion as adults became religiously active, a strong correlation would exist between parent and child religious involvement, but a weak or possibly negative correlation would exist between parent and adult-child religious involvement. If the parent/child and the parent/adult-child correlations are both strong for the lifelong members, the negative or weak parent/adult-child convert association would mask over the strong association for the lifelong members.

In order to test for this possible masking effect, converts and lifelong members were analyzed separately (see Tables 2 and 3). As expected, childhood church attendance correlates strongly with parents' church attendance for both converts and lifelong members. Of greater interest, however, is that the parent/adult-child associations are still typically weak for both the converts and the lifelong members. Thus, even for those individuals who were reared in their present faith, parental religious involvement is a poor predictor of adult religious involvement.

Controlling for convert status, however, does make a difference in the child/adult correlations, particularly for the Mormons. In Table 1 the correlations of childhood church attendance with the five measures of adult religious involvement range from .14 to .19 for the Mormons and from .07 to .18 for the Baptists. When converts and lifelong members are differentiated (Tables 2 and 3), the Mormon correlations range from .36 to .44 for the lifelong members but from only .03 to .08 for the converts; corresponding correlations for the Baptists range from .14 to .36 and from −.02 and .16 respectively. Childhood religiosity correlations follow the same pattern. Thus, for the converts of both denominations childhood religious involvement shows little relationship

TABLE 2. CORRELATIONS* FOR LIFELONG AND CONVERT MORMONS

	Adult Church Attendance		Adult Religiosity		Adult Testimony		Adult Tithing		Adult Prayer		Childhood Religiosity		Childhood Church Attendance	
	LLM	CON	LLM	CON	LLM	CON	LLM	CON	LLM	CON	LLM	CON	LLM	CON
Childhood Religiosity	.35[c]	.00	.53[c]	.15[a]	.43[c]	.00	.33[c]	-.07	.44[c]	.08			.65[c]	.65[c]
Childhood Church Attendance	.40[c]	.06	.44[c]	.04	.40[c]	.09	.40[c]	-.03	.36[c]	.08	.65[c]	.65[c]		
Father's Church Attendance	.14	.06	.09	.07	.11	.10	.15	.12	.18[a]	.04	.26[b]	.24[b]	.46[c]	.56[c]
Mother's Church Attendance	.17[a]	.20[b]	.15	.11	.13	.14	.24[b]	.23[b]	.18[a]	.01	.32[c]	.30[c]	.55[c]	.64[c]
Best Friends' Religion	.73[c]	.43[c]	.67[c]	.44[c]	.62[c]	.32[c]	.72[c]	.49[c]	.53[c]	.35[c]	.36[c]	.01	.45[c]	.05
Spouse's Religiosity	.60[c]	.41[c]	.58[c]	.50[c]	.52[c]	.47[c]	.68[c]	.49[c]	.49[c]	.38[c]	.23[c]	-.01	.36[c]	.07

*Pearson's r is the measure of correlation used. For justification of its use with ordinal data see Labovitz (1970).

a = P < .05   b = P < .01   c = P < .001

LLM = Lifelong member   CON = Convert

TABLE 3. CORRELATIONS* FOR LIFELONG AND CONVERT SOUTHERN BAPTIST

	Adult Church Attendance		Adult Religiosity		Adult Testimony		Adult Tithing		Adult Prayer		Childhood Religiosity		Childhood Church Attendance	
	LLM	CON	LLM	CON	LLM	CON	LLM	CON	LLM	CON	LLM	CON	LLM	CON
Childhood Religiosity	.22[b]	-.12	.33[c]	.09	.18[a]	-.04	.17[a]	-.08	.14	-.04			.64[c]	.59[c]
Childhood Church Attendance	.26[b]	.04	.36[c]	.06	.18[a]	-.02	.28[b]	.12	.14	.16	.64[c]	.59[c]		
Father's Church Attendance	.29[b]	.21[a]	.07	.15	.19[a]	.05	.30[b]	.27[b]	.08	.29[b]	.34[c]	.25[b]	.55[c]	.50[c]
Mother's Church Attendance	.11	.14	.18[a]	.09	.10	.01	.11	.22[b]	-.05	.29[b]	.29[b]	.33[c]	.57[c]	.59[c]
Best Friends' Religion	.57[c]	.32[c]	.56[c]	.44[c]	.39[c]	.23[b]	.61[c]	.38[c]	.37[c]	.33[c]	.35[c]	.00	.25[b]	-.07
Spouse's Religiosity	.43[c]	.25[b]	.51[c]	.40[c]	.37[c]	.16	.65[c]	.23[b]	.33[c]	.09	.19[a]	-.02	.14	-.12

*Pearson's r is the measure of correlation used. For justification of its use with ordinal data see Labovitz (1970).

a = P < .05   b = P < .01   c = P < .001

LLM = Lifelong member   CON = Convert

to adult religious involvement; but among the lifelong members the childhood/adult religiosity measures are substantial for the Mormons and typically moderate for the Baptists.

Interestingly, lifelong member correlations between measures of childhood religious involvement and best friend's religion or spouse's religiosity are, in general, moderately strong. Contrary to my earlier conclusions, this suggests that for lifelong members the selection of spouse and friends (as well as socialization after selection) influences the high respondent/spouse and respondent/friends correlations.

Summary and Conclusions

Measures of the respondents' childhood religiousness correlated moderately to highly with measures of their parents' religious involvement. Neither childhood nor parents' religious involvement, however, associated even moderately with the respondents' adult religious involvement. Adult religious involvement did, on the other hand, correlate highly with spouse religiosity and with the number of best friends who were of the same faith as the respondent. Taken together, these findings suggest that the primary groups which individuals participate in strongly influence their religious involvement. The family of orientation, the family of procreation, and closest friends are classical examples of primary groups. Religious measures for each of these groups correlate strongly with measures of the respondents' religious involvement during the time the respondents were participating members of these groups. But these correlations decline substantially when the respondents are not part of the group.

Due to possible differences in childhood socialization, lifelong members and converts were analyzed separately. Controlling for convert status had no noticeable effect upon the parent/adult-child correlations, but it did significantly alter the child/adult correlations. Among the lifelong members, child/adult correlations were moderately strong for the Mormons and mildly strong for the Baptists, but for the converts of both groups the correlations were negligible.

Assuming causality between the variables, my data suggest the following relationship: (1) parents' religious involvement strongly influences the childhood religious involvement of their offspring; (2) childhood religious involvement negligibly influences adult religious involvement of both Mormons and Baptist converts: (3) the influence of childhood religious involvement on the adult religious involvement of lifelong members is moderate for Mormons and mild for Baptists; (4) parents' religious involvement only weakly influences their child's adult religious involvement; (5) a strong positive reciprocal relationship exists between the respondents' adult religious involvement and (a) their spouses' religiosity and (b) the faith of their best friends; and (6) childhood religious involvement of lifelong members weakly to moderately influences religiosity of spouse and faith of best friends (probably through both selection and socialization).

These findings support the vast majority of research on socialization. My emphasis on the critical role of temporal primary groups helps us to understand why parent/offspring correlation on values and behavior vary so much in strength from study to study. As the child ages, the primacy of the family of orientation wanes. It becomes less and less a primary group for the child, while other groups (friends, spouse, etc.) become more primary. Thus parent/child correlation tends to vary from strong for children to weak for adult offspring.

While a tree may grow as "the twig is bent," humans are more supple than old wood. Present "bending" more than past "bending" directly shapes present religious involvement. Present influences, however, are naturally shaped by past influences.

As Bengtson (1972:369) points out: "The family serves as an important mediating link in selecting or orienting the child to the multiple reference groups to which he or she can turn for value development in a pluralistic society." Parental religious indoctrination, hence, has an indirect, if not a direct, influence on the religious involvement of adult offspring.

APPENDIX
ITEMS USED TO MEASURE THE VARIABLES

Childhood Religiosity

Which category best described you during your last year of high school (or when you were 17 years old)?

(5) very religious
(4) fairly religious
(3) mildly religious
(2) not very religious
(1) not at all religious

Adult Testimony

Have you received spiritual confirmation of the truthfulness of the gospel?

(3) I'm certain I have
(2) uncertain
(1) I have not

Best Friend's Religion

Of your five closest friends, how many are members of your denomination?

(1) none
(2) one
(3) two or three
(4) four
(5) five

Adult Tithing

Last year what percentage of your income did you contribute to religion?

(1) zero or almost nothing
(2) 1 percent to 3 percent
(3) 4 percent to 9 percent
(4) 10 percent
(5) 11 percent or more

Adult Prayer

How often do you pray privately?

(1) I never pray
(2) I pray only on special occasions
(3) I pray once in a while but not regularly
(4) I pray several times a week
(5) I pray once a day or more

Adult Church Attendance

How often do you attend Sunday worship services?

(5) every week or just about
(4) two or three times a month
(3) several times a year
(2) once or twice a year
(1) I don't go to church

Childhood Church Attendance
Father's Church Attendance
Mother's Church Attendance

How frequently did *you, your father,* and *your mother* attend church during your last year of high school (or when you were 17 years old)?

	You	Mother	Father
(5) nearly every week	_____	_____	_____
(4) two or three times a month	_____	_____	_____
(3) several times	_____	_____	_____
(2) once or twice	_____	_____	_____
(1) didn't attend at all	_____	_____	_____

Adult Religiosity
Spouse Relgiosity

Which category best describes you (your spouse)?

	You	Spouse
(5) very religious	_____	_____
(4) fairly religious	_____	_____
(3) mildly religious	_____	_____
(2) not very religious	_____	_____
(1) not at all religious	_____	_____

Bibliography

Bengtson, V. L. 1975. "Generation and Family Effects in Value Socialization." *American Sociological Review* 40:358-71.

Doctrine and Covenants. 1981. Doctrine and Covenants of The Church of Jesus Christ of Latter-day Saints. Salt Lake City: The Church of Jesus Christ of Latter-day Saints.

Dudley, R. L. and M. G. Dudley. 1986. "Transmission of Religious Values from Parents to Adolescents." *Review of Religious Research* 28:3-15.

Hoge, D. R. and G. H. Petrillo. 1978. "Determinants of Church Participation and Attitudes Among High School Youth." *Journal for the Scientific Study of Religion* 17:359-79.

Hoge, D. R., G. H. Petrillo and E. I. Smith. 1982. "Transmission of Religious and Social Values from Parents to Teenage Children." *Journal of Marriage and the Family* 44:569-80.

Hunsaker, B. 1985. "Parent-University Student Agreement on Religious and Nonreligious Issues." *Journal for the Scientific Study of Religion* 24:314-20.

Hunsberger, B. 1980. "A Reexamination of the Antecedents of Apostasy." *Review of Religious Research* 21:158-70.

Hunsberger, B. and L. B. Brown. 1984. "Religious Socialization, Apostasy and the Impact of Family Background." *Journal for the Scientific Study of Religion* 23:239-51.

Hyman, H. H. 1959. *Political Socialization: A Study in the Psychology of Political Behavior.* Glencoe, IL: The Free Press.

Kalish, R. A. and A. I. Johnson. 1972. "Value Similarities and Differences in Three Generations of Women." *Journal of Marriage and the Family* 34:49-54.

Labovitz, S. 1970. "The Assignment of Numbers to Rank Order Categories." *American Sociological Review* 35:515-24.

Newcomb, T. and G. Svehla. 1937. "Intra-Family Relationships in Attitude." *Sociometry* 1:180-205.

Perkins, H. W. 1985. "Religious Traditions, Parents and Peers as Determinants of Alcohol and Drug Use Among College Students." *Review of Religious Research* 27:15-31.

Potvin, R. H. and D. M. Sloane. 1985. "Parental Control, Age, and Religious Practice." *Review of Religious Research* 27:3-14.

Roof, W. C. and C. K. Hadaway. 1979. "Denominational Switching in the Seventies: Going Beyond Stark and Glock." *Journal for the Scientific Study of Religion* 18:363-77.

Troll, L. E., B. L. Neugarten, and R. I. Kraines. 1969. "Similarities in Values and Other Personality Characteristics in College Students and Their Parents." *Merrill-Palmer Quarterly of Behavior and Development* 15:323-36.

14

The Impact of Parental Views of the Nature of Humankind upon Child-Rearing Attitudes

Lawrence O. Clayton

In the past, child development theorists and researchers have indicated that the preschool years are of tremendous significance to personality development. Allport (1961) concluded that the young child's sense of self is simply a product of the way in which his parents perceive him. Dreikurs reported similar findings when he said of the child, "He absorbs the family values, mores and conventions, and tries to fit within the pattern" (or the standards set by the parents) (1964:19). Agreeing, Stone and Church said, "Perhaps the most important single principle of human development is the self-fulfilling prophecy which says simply that our children become what we expect them to become" (1973:205). White stated that "the child's character is shaped by his identification with his parents during his earliest years, and through such identification, he accepts and assimilates their values, beliefs and patterns of behavior" (1975:31).

Lawrence O. Clayton is an ordained United Methodist minister. His major professional positions have been pastor, Central Texas Conference of the United Methodist Church; Director, Johnson County Mental Health Clinic in Cleburne, Texas; and Director, United Methodist Counseling Services in Oklahoma. He has presented over two hundred professional workshops, serves on the boards of six agencies, is a consultant to five hospitals, is an adjunct professor in the Department of Family Relations and Child Development, Oklahoma State University, and is an approved supervisor for the American Association for Marriage and Family Therapy. He received his Ph.D. from Texas Woman's University.

Others have stated that views of humankind have an impact on mental-health and child-rearing issues. For example, Gordon stated, "Much of cultural identity is closely tied to religious identity. Each group has its own cultural goals and traditions, from which its patterns of child-rearing flow." (1980:2.) This study was developed to test the following assumptions: persons who view others as basically bad are relatively authoritarian in their child-rearing attitudes; persons who consider others as basically good are relatively permissive in their child-rearing attitudes; and, finally, persons who view others as neither good nor bad are relatively moderate in their child-rearing attitudes.

Research Hypotheses

The following null hypotheses were tested at the .05 level of significance. When parents are grouped according to their view of the nature of humankind as moral, immoral, or amoral, there is no significant difference between their scores in each of the following variables: Child-Rearing Attitudes, Encouraging Verbalization, Fostering Dependency, Seclusion of the Parent, Breaking the Will, Martyrdom, Fear of Harming the Child, Marital Conflict, Strictness, Irritability, Excluding Outside Influence, Deification, Suppression of Aggression, Rejection of Homemaking Role, Equalitarianism, Approval of Activity, Avoidance of Communication, Inconsiderateness of Spouse, Suppression of Sex, Ascendance of the Parent, Intrusiveness, Comradeship and Sharing, Acceleration of Development, Dependency of Parent.

This study is limited to the following: a randomly selected sample of parents of preschool children residing in Cleburne, Texas. Also taken into account are the limitations of pencil and paper questionnaires (specifically, Wrightsman's Philosophy of Human Nature Instrument [WPHNI] and the Parent Attitude Research Instrument [PARI]) as well as the limited accuracy reflecting behavior indicated by the attitudes and perceptions of the parent surveyed.

Definitions

According to Thomas (1979), the moral view of the nature of humankind is that people are born essentially good. The immoral view of the nature of humankind is that people are born essentially bad. And, finally, the amoral view of the nature of humankind is that people are born neither good nor bad, but that goodness or badness is the product of learning and experience.

Review of Literature

The central issue of this study is whether human beings come into the world essentially immoral, moral, or amoral. Support for each of these views is best represented by the thoughts of Calvin, Pelagius, and Arminius, respectively.

John Calvin believed that, because of Adam's disobedience in the Garden of Eden, the entire human race became essentially bad or immoral (Dillenberger, 1975:159). And because of this immoral character, Calvin continued, humans were incapable of doing any good of their own design. A contrasting view was developed by an Irish monk by the name of Pelagius who settled in Rome hundreds of years before the birth of John Calvin. Greatly upset over the moral state of the Romans about the year A.D. 400, Pelagius began to preach that people were essentially good or moral. (Latourette, 1954:185.) Synthesizing the beliefs of both Calvin and Pelagius, Jacob Arminius claimed that man was neither totally good nor bad and, therefore, was capable of both moral and immoral behavior (Harrison, 1974).

These variant views of humankind were translated into educational philosophies by the Puritans, as well as Jean Jacques Rousseau and John Locke. The leading proponents of the Calvinistic view of the nature of mankind were people who wanted to purify the Church of England. Their religious belief that humans were essentially immoral had an impact upon their child-rearing practices and upon their educational philosophies. For example, because they believed children to be innately vile, they "did not hesitate to nourish them with threats, moralizing and the whip" (Thomas, 1979:55).

Rousseau became the disciple, in an educational sense, of the ancient monk Pelagius. Rousseau taught, "All things are as good as they came from the hands of their creator" (1955:1). He also believed that children, left to their own devices, were naturally curious, not evil. They would, therefore, make some bad choices. But, similar to Pelagius's view of what happened to Adam and Eve in the Garden of Eden, bad choices would not make children evil, just human (Thomas, 1979).

John Locke, British philosopher and supporter of the amoral philosophy of man, believed that children are born into the world with characters that resembled blank tablets, or *tabula rasa*, upon which experience inscribes its indelible lessons (Stone and Church, 1973).

Methodology

The sample consisted of 330 of the total population of 2,205 parents residing within the city limits of Cleburne, Texas, who currently had at least one preschool child living in their homes. The sampling technique was stratified random sampling of race and sex of parent within each census tract in the city. Subjects chosen were given three instruments: Wrightsman's Philosophy of Human Nature Instrument (WPHNI), Parent Attitude Research Instrument (PARI), and Background Information Form (BIF).

The first instrument, developed by Wrightsman (1965), assesses the parent's philosophy of human nature. It consists of 84 items, 14 for each of the six subscales: (1) trustworthiness, (b) altruism, (c) independence, (d) strength of will, (e) complexity, and (f) variability. The scores on the first four subscales, as Wrightsman has shown, can be combined to give an overall indication of the parent's positive or negative view of human nature. Therefore, in this study the last two subscales were not used.

Robinson and Shaver (1973), using inter-subscale correlations, reported split-half and test-retest reliabilities for the WPHNI. Wrightsman (1974) also established long-term reliability of the WPHNI, reporting that "a number of predictions about hypothesized differences in favorableness about human nature were confirmed." Further, along with Nottingham and Gorsuch, Wrightsman (1970) did a factoral replication of the theoretically derived subscales and reported that the first four subscales were, in fact, well replicated in the factor structure.

The second instrument, developed by Schaefer and Bell (1958), also assesses parental child-rearing attitudes. It consists of 115 items, five for each of the 23 subscales. Each item is presented in a standard A - a - d - D form. It is, therefore, a forced choice instrument. Total scores can vary from 20 to 5 on each of the 23 subscales or from a total score of 460 to 115.

The third instrument contains questions designed to determine the subject's sex, race, educational level, marital status and income level.

Procedure

The author's research assistants were given the pieces of paper with race and sex of the participants in each census tract. Randomization was insured by numbering the houses in each census tract starting at the upper left side, and then selecting the houses to be approached by using a table of random numbers. Research assistants approached each house and asked the occupants who had preschool children to fill out the WPHNI, PARI and BIF. The survey continued until reaching the appropriate percentages of both sexes and of each ethnic group.

By a random discard of the necessary number of research packets, any category of respondents exceeding the numbers represented in the appropriate sample was brought to the correct level. Incomplete questionnaires were also discarded.

Parents, according to their view of the nature of humankind as revealed by their scores on WPHNI, were placed in three groups:

Group 1 consisted of those parents who scored + 10 or more (moral); Group 2 was made up of parents who scored −10 or less (immoral); and Group 3 contained the parents who scored between + 9 and −9 (amoral).

Findings

A multivariate analysis of covariance performed among the groups measured the 23 child-rearing attitude subscales of PARI, with race, sex, marital status serving as dichotomous dummy variables in the case of most multilevel nominal variables. Hotelling's T^2 calculated results of $T^2 = .47047$, $F = 3.00692$, $P = < .0001$. These figures indicate that, when parents are grouped according to their views of the nature of humankind as moral, immoral, and amoral, an overall significant difference exists among parents' child-rearing attitudes. Also showing attitude differences are the results of the Univariate F-tests performed on each of the 23 parents' subscales of PARI (see Table 1). Finally, Tukey pair-wise comparisons (at the .05 level of significance) computed specific group differences (see Table 2).

Discussion

Interestingly, the first major finding of this study is that there are no significant differences among parent groups based on variables of Strictness, Equalitarianism, and Dependency of Parent. The variable of Strictness may be explained by Rokeach (1960), who theorizes that there may be two types of authoritarianism—one negatively oriented and the other positively oriented. It may well be that parents who view humankind as moral or amoral hold

TABLE 1. UNIVARIATE ANALYSIS OF COVARIANCE OF THE MORAL, IMMORAL, AND AMORAL GROUPS IN THE PARI SUBSCALES

Variable	Group 1	Group 2	Group 3	F^a	P
Encouraging Verbalization	16.11	15.30	15.29	5.35590	.005
Fostering Dependency	10.54	12.04	10.75	9.35521	.000
Seclusion of the Parent	10.94	12.99	13.13	21.97811	.000
Breaking of the Will	11.05	12.61	12.01	9.04198	.000
Martyrdom	10.91	12.99	12.39	15.39572	.000
Fear of Harming the Child	13.30	14.11	14.60	6.17171	.002
Marital Conflict	15.19	14.41	15.00	2.99440	.050
Strictness	14.03	14.25	14.77	1.72964	.179
Irritability	13.74	14.53	14.42	3.02511	.050
Excluding Outside Influences	11.44	12.77	11.99	7.19547	.001
Deification	12.59	13.60	12.98	4.76644	.009
Suppression of Aggression	12.10	12.97	12.46	3.80708	.023
Rejection of Homemaking Role	12.45	13.50	12.34	6.41248	.002
Equalitarianism	15.03	14.84	15.01	.24788	.174
Approval of Activity	12.51	13.54	13.19	4.48861	.012
Avoidance of Communication	10.58	12.41	11.26	10.20917	.000
Inconsiderateness of Spouse	13.12	13.94	13.97	4.80191	.009
Suppression of Sex	10.09	12.02	10.81	11.32485	.000
Ascendance of the Parent	13.11	13.88	13.83	3.49599	.031
Intrusiveness	11.05	12.26	11.95	5.92514	.007
Comradeship and Sharing	16.48	15.69	16.69	5.11654	.007
Acceleration of Development	10.93	13.35	11.12	20.36249	.000
Dependency of Parent	13.37	13.49	13.63	.23595	.790

^{a}Degrees of Freedom = (2,327).

TABLE 2. TUKEY PAIR-WISE COMPARISONS OF GROUP 2 (IMMORAL) AND GROUP 3 (AMORAL) ON THE PARI SUBSCALES

Variable	Group 1		Group 2		Group 3
Encouraging Verbalization	16.11	>	15.30	=	15.29
Fostering Dependency	10.54	<	12.04	>	10.75
Seclusion of the Parent	10.94	<	12.99	>	13.13
Breaking of the Will	11.05	<	12.61	>	12.01
Martyrdom	10.91	<	12.99	>	12.39
Fear of Harming the Child	13.30	<	14.11	=	14.60
Marital Conflict	15.19	>	14.41	<	15.00
Strictness	14.03	=	14.25	=	14.77
Irritability	13.74	<	14.53	=	14.42
Excluding Outside Influences	11.44	<	12.77	>	11.99
Deification	12.59	<	13.60	>	12.98
Suppression of Aggression	12.10	<	12.97	>	12.46
Rejection of Homemaking Role	12.45	<	13.50	>	12.34
Equalitarianism	15.03	=	14.84	=	15.01
Approval of Activity	12.51	<	13.54	>	13.19
Avoidance of Communication	10.58	<	12.41	>	11.26
Inconsiderateness of Spouse	13.12	<	13.94	=	13.97
Suppression of Sex	10.09	<	12.02	>	10.81
Ascendance of the Parent	13.11	<	13.88	=	13.83
Intrusiveness	11.05	<	12.26	>	11.95
Comradeship and Sharing	16.48	>	15.69	<	16.69
Acceleration of Development	10.93	<	13.35	>	11.12
Dependency of Parent	13.37	=	13.49	=	13.63

[a]Degrees of Freedom = (2,327).

those views just as strictly as do those who view others as essentially immoral (range 14.03-14.77).

In contrast, a rather different dynamic seems to have been operating on the variable of Equalitarianism. Apparently, parents in every group very strongly believe children are equal to adults (range 14.84-15.03). This result is quite inconsistent with parent group scores on other variables that measure parent authoritarianism: Breaking the Will, Excluding Outside Influences, Suppression of Aggression, Suppression of Sex, and Acceleration of Development. On each of these variables, Group 1 parents (moral) scored lowest, Group 2 parents (immoral) scored highest, and Group 3 parents (amoral) scored between the two extremes. So parents, according to these results, are most likely affected by the social desirability of equality. Still the variable of Dependency of Parents seems to have been affected by another dynamic. Evidently none of the parents tested tend to be dependent upon their children. This clearly supported the relatively low scores of all the parent groups (range 13.37–13.63).

A second major result of this study is that parents viewing others as moral scored highest on the variables of Encouraging Verbalization, Marital Conflict, and Comradeship and Sharing. On the other hand, they scored lowest on the following sixteen variables: Fostering Dependency, Seclusion of the Parent, Breaking the Will, Martyrdom, Fear of Harming the Child, Irritability, Excluding Outside Influence, Deification, Suppression of Aggression, Rejection of Homemaking Role, Approval of Activity, Avoidance of Communication, Ascendance of the Parent, Intrusiveness, Acceleration of Development, and Suppression of Sex. These findings, in other words, are generally consistent with the original assumption: parents who see human nature as basically moral are comparatively permissive in their child-rearing attitudes. These parents tend to be persons who typically allow children to be themselves. Generally, the only pressure they place on their children is for them to express themselves. Though not as surprising as it first appears, these parents experience more marital conflict than do parents in other groups. According to the test scores, the conflict may result directly from their willingness to allow others to be themselves, because these are the same parents who scored low on both the variables of Suppression of Aggression and Inconsiderateness of Spouse. This practice is somewhat consistent with the advice of many authorities in the social sciences (Dreikurs, 1964; Kelly, 1962; Maslow, 1962).

A third major finding of this study is that parents who view others as basically immoral are relatively authoritarian in their child-rearing attitudes. These parents scored highest on the variables of Fostering Dependency, Breaking the Will, Martyrdom, Fear of Harming the Child, Irritability, Excluding Outside Influence, Deification, and Suppression of Aggression, as well as on Approval of Activity, Avoidance of Communication, Inconsiderateness of the Spouse, Suppression of Sex, Ascendance of the Parent, Intrusiveness, and Acceleration of Development. This group scored lowest, however, on Encouraging Verbalization, Rejection of Homemaking Role, Marital Conflict, and Comradeship and Sharing. Generally, these parents do not allow their children to be themselves. The impact of this group's negative views of the nature of humankind upon child-rearing attitudes is consistent with the original assumption and is perhaps most strikingly conveyed by the parents' exclusion of outside influence. As Kelly suggests (1962), the people who feel others are no good desire to force what they consider acceptable behavior on others.

Agreeing with Kelley, Brody (1964) shows that highly authoritarian persons tend to restrict outside influences. As added support, it is helpful to note that this group of parents scored highest on Avoidance of Communication, while scoring lowest on the variables of Encouraging Verbalization and Comradeship and Sharing, and moderately low on Seclusion of the Parent. This means, in other words, that these parents are close neither to their children nor to others. This lack of closeness may stem from their fear that allowing their children or others to be close will cause them to be perceived as they perceive themselves—as no good. It may also explain why this group scored lowest in Marital Conflict while scoring highest on the variable of Inconsiderateness of Spouse.

Another dynamic evidenced by this group of parents is the high score of Martyrdom, Irritability, and Deification. Perhaps Feldman best explains these high scores by the concept of projective identification, or the splitting of the intropsychic self into good and bad representations. "In conflicted marriages, projection is mobilized as a defense which involves projecting these 'all-bad' self-representations upon the spouse. The 'all-good' other representation is retained, leading to an experience of self as the victim. The 'all-good' other representation is projected upon a lover or a child." (1982:419.)

The fourth and final major finding of this study is that parents seeing others as basically amoral tend to score much differently from both the other parenting groups, but lower than those who saw others as basically moral and higher than those who saw others as essentially immoral. There is, therefore, a direct relationship between the degree of parents' belief in the nature of humankind issues and their parenting scores on these variables. Because this group of parents tended to have moderate scores on both WPHNI and PARI, they may have a rather moderate orientation toward life in general.

Based upon the findings of this study, the following conclusions are drawn: parents who believe the nature of humankind to be moral tend to be relatively permissive in their child-rearing attitudes; parents who view the nature of humankind as immoral tend to be relatively authoritarian in their child-rearing attitudes; and, finally, parents who believe the nature of humankind is amoral tend to be relatively moderate in their child-rearing attitudes. There appears to be a number of implications of this research both for those studying the family empirically and those treating it clinically.

Researchers typically consider child-rearing attitudes as the point of departure in their theories; that is, as independent variables in the prediction of various child outcomes. The present research suggests the existence of antecedent conditions that modify child-rearing attitudes; namely, that these attitudes are an outgrowth of parents' views of the basic nature of humankind.

From a clinical perspective, the therapeutic goal, as Minuchin (1981:215) has pointed out, is often to impose a reality on the client in order to "convert" the client from a dysfunctional to a functional worldview; that is, one that does not need the symptom and allows for greater diversity of attitude and behavior. Minuchin (1981) utilized the technique of appealing to universal symbols, family truths, and expert advice to alter these worldviews. The question that needs to be addressed, however, is whether the therapist is aware of the client's overall worldview. (Indeed, the therapist may not even be aware of his or her own worldview.) Thus, the present research suggests that an understanding of the client's view of the nature of humankind is critical in an evaluation of client behavior. Rather than initially focusing on client behavior per se, the therapist may more profitably begin by addressing the underlying worldview that provides the genesis for the dysfunctional and otherwise irrational behavior presented.

Clearly, much work remains to be done. For example, it may be helpful to examine other parental worldviews to see if they impact child-rearing attitudes in a similar manner to the views evaluated in this study. Similarly, clinicians require assessment studies to adequately evaluate the various therapeutic approaches to modifying a client's underlying worldview. It is the hope of this author that the present study may sow the seeds for such ongoing professional activities.

Bibliography

Alport, G. 1961. *Nature of Personality*. New York: Holt, Rinehart and Winston.

Brody, G. 1964. "Relationship Between Maternal Attitudes and Behavior." *Journal of Personality and Social Sciences*, 317–23.

Dillenburger, J. 1975. *Calvin: Selected Writings*. Missoula, MT: Scholars' Press.

Dinkmeyer, D., and R. Dreikurs. 1963. *Encouraging Children to Learn: The Encouraging Process*. Englewood Cliffs, NJ: Prentice-Hall.

Dreikurs, R. 1964. *Children: The Challenge*. New York: Hawthorne.

Feldman, L. 1982. "Dysfunctional Marital Conflict: An Integrative, Interpersonal-intrapsychic Model." *Journal of Marriage and Family Therapy*, 8, 417–28.

Gordon, I. 1980. "Significant Cultural Factors in Effective Parenting." In M. Fentini and R. Cardenas (eds.), *Parenting in a Multicultural Society*. New York: Longman.

Harrison, E. 1974. *History of Theology*. Grand Rapids, MI: Baker.

Kelly, E. 1962. "The Fully Functioning Self." In A. Combs (chair.), *Perceiving, Behaving, Becoming: A New Focus for Education*. New York: American Society of Child Development.

Latourette, B. 1953. *History of Christianity*. New York: Harper and Row.

Maslow, A. 1962. "Some Basic Propositions of a Growth and Self-actualization Psychology." In A. Combs (chair.), *Perceiving, Behaving, Becoming*. New York: American Society of Child Development.

Minuchin, S., and H. Fishman. 1981. *Family Therapy Techniques*. Cambridge, MA: Harvard University Press.

Mower, O. 1957. "Religion, Science, and Mental Health." *Proceedings of the First Academy Symposium on Inter-discipline Responsibility for Mental Health*. New York: New York University.

Nottingham, Jr., R. Gorsuch, and L. Wrightsman. 1970. "Factoral Replication of the Theoretically Derived Subscales of the Philosophy of Human Nature Instrument. *Journal of Social Psychology*. 129–30.

Robinson, J., and P. Shaver. 1973. *Measures of Social Psychological Attitudes*. Ann Arbor, MI: Institute of Social Research.

Rogers, C. 1939. *Clinical Treatment of the Problem Child*. Boston: Houghton Mifflin.

Rokeach, M. 1960. *The Open and Closed Mind*. New York: Basic Books.

Rousseau, J. 1955. *Emile* (B. Foxley, trans.). New York: Everyman's, 1955.

Schaefer, E. and R. Bell. 1958. "Development of a Parental Attitude Research Instrument." *Child Development*. 29, 339–61.

Stone, J., and J. Church. 1973. *Childhood and Adolescence*. New York: Random House.

Thomas, R. 1979. *Comparing Theories of Child Development*. Belmont: Wadsworth.

White, B. 1975. *The First Three Years of Life*. Englewood Cliffs, NJ: Prentice-Hall.

Wrightsman, L. 1965. "Personality and Attitudinal Correlates of Trusting and Untrustworthy Behaviors in a Two-person Game." *Journal of Personality and Social Psychology*. 4, 328–32.

IV. Worldviews, Families, and Religions

15

The New Christian Right's View of the Family and Its Social Science Critics: A Study in Differing Presuppositions

Patrick H. McNamara

Introduction

The problems of the nature of social order and its relationship to individual action are recurring central issues in the social sciences (Alexander, 1982). These order and action issues, couched in the form of structures and roles, plus individual freedom and activities, are familiar themes in the writings of contemporary family researcher/theorists. The social order vs. individual freedom dilemma is explored by John Scanzoni in *Shaping Tomorrow's Family* (1983). Taking into account feminist critiques of female subordination in what Scanzoni calls the "conventional family" and aware of the rapid growth of single-parent families, dual wage-earner households, and the dramatic shrinkage in number of father-working/ mother-staying-at-home-with-children families, Scanzoni contrasts two models of the family. "Conservatives," viewing society as an organic whole, see the family threatened with dissolution as ascendant individualism and insistence upon "freedom" and "rights" (action)

Patrick H. McNamara is Associate Professor of Sociology at the University of New Mexico. He received his Ph.D. at UCLA, where he was a research associate with the Ford Foundation–sponsored Mexican American Study Project. His interests are in religion and ethnic groups. He is the editor of *Religion North American Style*. He was the 1984 president of the Association for the Sociology of Religion.

erode authoritative hierarchical norms (order) once governing family relation-ships. Since family and society "constitute one organic whole," modern cries for individual freedom and self-fulfillment must be resisted and authority and discipline restored if society as we know it is to endure. (Scanzoni, 1983:56.)

Scanzoni explicitly embraces his second model, which he terms the "progressive" view of the family. This viewpoint holds that equal-partner rela-tionships and a negotiatory model of husband-wife and parent-child relation-ships constitute the basis of a family form compatible with the basic dynamic of Western societies—participatory democracy. The conservative model, with its patriarchy-based hierarchical relationships requiring subordination of some human beings to others, is simply "out of phase" with Western democratic trends (1983:93); a "morphostatic" script of fixed roles and behavioral pre-scriptions ill prepares children to take their places in a dynamically changing society insistent upon individual self-fulfillment and freedom to choose one's roles and to modify them as one desires. Scanzoni is well aware of the chal-lenge to "progressives" to integrate the individual's ideals of action along the lines of freedom and personal growth with those ideals pointing toward the social order's required commitment, trust, and responsible caring for children; but he is convinced a more flexible conception of family structure and roles can effect this reconciliation (1983:193–94).

The New Christian Right's (hereafter NCR) view of the family is one ex-ample of the "conservative" model and recently has drawn the critical atten-tion of social scientists, notably authors represented in the D'Antonio and Al-dous volume, *Families and Religions* (1983). Barbara Hargrove sees the rise of the so-called Moral Majority as "a demand for the reassertion of the authority of the church over the family, and of the family over the individual, more in the pattern of earlier stages of modernization" (1983a:45). While some evangeli-cals, according to Hargrove, acknowledge that the family is changing "even among their own members" and advocate counseling and other forms of sup-port to deal with the changes, "the more militant evangelicals" refuse to com-promise with changing sex roles or with premarital sexuality or abortion. "All these changes are viewed as a Satanic attack on the very foundations of Chris-tian morality, to be resisted at all costs." (Hargrove, 1983b:136.) External reg-ulation of a world in which "civilization is defined as control" is a hallmark of conservative Protestant views on the family, says Hargrove (1983b:137). Sex-ual repression is far from unhealthy; it is God-ordained and promotes respect for the other person. A wife submissive to her husband expresses the will of

God as revealed in scripture. While an "accent on individualism and its necessary correlate, freedom of choice," has influenced the stances of *mainline*
Protestant churches more adaptive to modern culture (1983b:121), Hargrove
points out that *conservative* Protestants see an issue framed by their oppo-
nents as "freedom" (abortion is a good example) "simply as one of expressing
willingness or unwillingness to obey the will of God, whose power is evident
in the fact of conception" (1983a:39).

Further pursuing conservative/mainline contrasts, D'Antonio points to three
major religious values affecting the family, but susceptible to varying interpretations as they are applied. Conservative Protestants concretize these values in
specific normative terms: (a) sacredness of life is defined vis-à-vis divorce and
abortion; (b) patriarchy is expressed in obedience of wife to husband and children to parents, together with the prohibition of women at the altar; (c) concern for others remains focused on a person-to-person level and does not
include an obligation to change oppressive institutional structures. By contrast, mainline Protestant as well as Catholic theologians "have been struggling to develop an ethic of developmental sexuality and personality growth
that changes the focus away from the negative control mechanisms (sex as
sinful, immoral behavior) and toward greater concern for the integrity of
individuals" (1983:103). D'Antonio's principal contention in this essay, however, is that conservative Christians, in supporting the free enterprise system
and individual entrepreneurship—which have given rise to and, in turn, been
supported by values of equality, freedom, and the right to self-fulfillment—
will ultimately be unable to restore their cherished mechanisms of social control. They fail to recognize how closely the legitimacy of the very norms and
values they fear (individual freedom, etc.) "is tied to dominant economic and
political structures" which they support (1983:105). D'Antonio's comment is
succinct and pointed:

> The struggle of the Moral Majority to restore the mechanisms seems doomed
> because, in fact, less than one-third of the adult population supports them. The
> irony is that the Moral Majority supports the social structures and the ideology of
> the larger society that make improbable coexistence of traditional family struc-
> tures and values. (1983:105-6.)

A direct focus of New Christian Right Moral Majority views of threats to
the family characterizes Jeffrey Hadden's essay in the above-cited volume. Hadden
is explicitly critical of such views and points out that (a) little space or time is

given to elaborating *positive functions* of the family in NCR's critique of modern culture. What is wrong with American families is stressed at the expense of "roles of nurture, love and support" (1983:254). Adultery, abortion, premarital sex, divorce, and remarriage receive more elaboration than finding new and creative ways of showing and maintaining parent-child love and husband-wife affection in the face of such pressures as dual wage-earner families, etc. Instead, (b) "the overwhelming message that comes across in their printed and audiovisual messages" is that the family as an institution is principally charged with control over the "base impulses of human beings" (1983:254). Family members are all human beings weakened by original sin who can too easily go astray without obedience to biblical injunctions concerning discipline of children; submissiveness of wives to husbands; and husbands' avoidance of temptations to anger, lust, and drunkenness. (c) No clear cause-and-effect analysis appears for the alleged evils attacking the family (divorce, abortion, etc.). These are sometimes cited as actively destroying the family; at other times, the breakdown of Christian values is what permits them to flourish (1983). (d) A theology of love is too little evident. NCR fails to spell out "how love could overcome the tensions and contradictions of modern life" (1983:265). These approaches are pictured as reducing NCR's potential for gaining a broader following among Americans concerned with tensions between family and society, yet who are unable to agree with fundamentalist catalogues of evils ("too much permissiveness," etc.) and remedies (firmer discipline, wives remaining at home, etc.).

Purpose

Both approaches to the conservative family model sketched above—the explicitly critical review by Scanzoni and the more implicit critiques of NCR ideology by Hargrove (1983a), D'Antonio (1983), and Hadden (1983)—are based on presuppositions that deserve clarification in a broader context of alternative models of scientific theory and methodological procedure. Much of the above social scientific analysis of NCR families is informed by presuppositions that result in a tendency to describe NCR views of the family as unprogressive and, therefore, out of phase with modern values. By emphasizing the social control dimensions, the NCR view of the family fails to address pressing contemporary needs, and freedom. These presuppositions act as blinders preventing social scientists from seeing dimensions of the NCR position that emphasize agency and personal autonomy. This failure by social scientists to perceive relevant dimensions of the family discussed by NCR "insiders" results in a blockage of what Max Weber (1978) called the act of *verstehen*, whereby the *meanings* social actors bring to their beliefs and activities are grasped (or attempt is made to do so). The purposes of this treatise, then, are to (a) place the discussion of the NCR family within the larger issue of the role of presuppositions in differing models of scientific theory and methodological procedures; (b) articulate the presuppositions and resultant blind spots inherent in the worldview portrayed by social scientists' critiques of NCR families; (c) develop, from sources not utilized by social scientist "critics," an "insider's" view of NCR family worldviews, with the attendant presuppositions; and (d) draw conclusions pointing to ways in which NCR family ideology can be understood better as a result of making clear the relevant presuppositions. It is hoped that these purposes will contribute in a small way toward better understanding and to ways of realizing how religion and family values combine to meet individual and group needs.

Presuppositions and Postpositivist Thought

Brown (1977) and Suppe (1977) have reviewed the process by which philosophers of science in the twentieth century—such as Polanyi, Popper, Hanson, and Kuhn, to cite but a few—have moved away from the long-established terrain of positivism or logical empiricism, with its sharp separation of data or facts on the one hand and theory on the other. For the positivist, empirical facts are knowable and known antecedently to the interpretive overlay of the mind with its theoretical conceptions. In fact, objectivity is assured only if "the facts" are available for anyone to see; understanding is provided by the human mind bringing to bear theoretical formulations that "make sense" out of that which is evident to any observer. Progress occurs as theoretical frameworks are refined to effect a more comprehensive and parsimonious explanation of the data, or when a new paradigm (Kuhn, 1970) arises to displace a previous one and better account for the data at hand. In any case, the world of sensory data and the world of theoretical formulations remain two separate worlds and must be so if science is to be "objective" and "verifiable."

The postpositivist view holds that empirical data are never simply "seen" atheoretically. Theoretical presuppositions are at work in the very act of looking at the world around us; an act of observing is already theory-laden. Every scientist and layperson brings presuppositions to the most basic activities of observing, thinking about, and attempting to make sense out of the data he or she confronts. These presuppositions are essential to understand what Brown refers to as "the new image of science":

> Science consists of a sequence of research projects structured by accepted presuppositions which determine what observations are to be made, how they are to be interpreted, what phenomena are problematic, and how these problems are to be dealt with. When the presuppositions of a scientific discipline change, . . . the scientist's picture of reality [is] changed. (1977:166.)

Sociological theorists also have used the critique of positivism as a point of departure. Jeffrey Alexander begins his search for a "theoretical logic" for sociology by reviewing the antipositivist critique and subsequently focuses on "the postpositivist persuasion" which entails, in part, clarifying those "problematic presuppositional decisions that fragment generalized sociological debate" (1982:69). In summary, Alexander's work demonstrates the importance of examining and clarifying one's presuppositions.

Family theorists Thomas and Edmondson have explored the significance of postpositivist thinking for theoretical work focusing on the family. They argue that family theory of the postpositivist variety generates knowledge that is "increasingly seen as constructed knowledge rather than discovered knowledge in the positivistic sense" (1986:61). They ask to what extent "truth claims emanating from family theory" will be "based on a foundation of consensus of the scientific community," rather than upon a positivist "correspondence" theory of data with scientist's knowledge (1986:62). Furthermore, they ask if the "consensus criteria of knowledge" will serve the interest of theorists "who believe they have an emancipatory responsibility when it comes to the study of the family," a question relevant both to theorists and to family practitioners and therapists (1986:63). At stake here are knowledge claims about the family and the basis of such claims. If the postpositivist family theory calls attention to the constructed nature of scientific knowledge relying on the consensus view of "truth claims," and if it also assumes that "agency and intentionality" of family actors is part of the reality of family life, then the necessity of making explicit the underlying presuppositions is apparent.

The hitherto common portraits of NCR-conservative families and family ideals as unprogressive and out of phase with modern society are themselves based upon taken-for-granted presuppositions. The "new image of science" is helpful, for, in bringing out the inevitability of the observer's prior theoretical convictions or notions, it strongly suggests the ethical desirability of acknowledging and examining one's presuppositions. Of no less importance, it underlines the centrality of actors' own beliefs, viewpoints, intentions, and behaviors. These must be grasped if a genuine understanding of a group is to be achieved and the researchers' presuppositions made explicit.

Presuppositions in Sociological Critiques of NCR Family Ideals

Warner's work (1979) is one of the few efforts to identify presuppositional biases of social scientists who examine various religious groups. He observes that evangelical Christianity is often "overlooked, or discounted, stereotyped, and patronized" by sociologists. Sociologists tend to see concern for personal challenge—that is, to get one's own moral life in order—as somehow secondary to social challenge or the effort to identify and criticize those socioeconomic structures that inhibit individuals and groups from attaining a fuller human existence. Second, sociologists inherit an evolutionary bias which sees the Western world as increasingly disenchanted (the Weberian legacy). Through this bias theological liberalism is seen as an advance in sensible adaptation and compromise, while contemporary evangelicalism is "a temporary and retrogressive, albeit disruptive, phenomenon, a symptom of the growing pains of society" (1979:7). Its belief system is a kind of anachronism. Finally, social scientists, in Warner's view, too easily fall prey to a "we versus they" mentality in which "we" are more privileged and enlightened, while "they" are backward and unenlightened.

To the degree that social analysts adopt such a view, they are unable to analyze the degree to which popular evangelicalism meets cognitive, emotional, and interpersonal needs often unmet in the larger culture or in alternative systems of faith (Warner, 1979:8). In these typical social science analyses, the demands of the inner life are neglected, and personal agency and autonomy exercised in the choice to examine one's own life and put it in order according to an internalized ethic of repentance and freedom from sin is not acknowledged. In addition to the general presuppositional biases discussed above, Warner's analysis introduces some specific presuppositions more or less latent in the critiques of Scanzoni (1983), Hargrove (1983a), and D'Antonio (1983).

First, *the socioeconomic structures of the larger society constitute formidable pressures that must be adapted to if intolerable strain and contradic-*

tions are not to invade family relationships. For Scanzoni, Western participatory democracy is an overriding dynamic whose impact families cannot and *should not* try to counter. This dynamic has set in motion irresistible trends toward husband-wife equality and toward negotiatory rather than strictly authoritative disciplining of children. Tension is bound to characterize any family role, relationship, or policy that reasserts or reflects hierarchical relationships. For D'Antonio, the demands of a bureaucratized work world, an inflationary economy, a consumer society "selling" a higher material standard of living to all comers are forces whose impact is not just underrecognized by NCR advocates; NCR actively supports the structures and ideologies (free enterprise) of advanced Western capitalist structures and ideologies deeply affecting family life today.

Second, *loving relationships cannot easily develop nor be fully expressed in "fixed-role structures," which are simply incompatible with the dynamics of change characterizing Western societies*. Scanzoni reviews at some length Swidler's four dimensions along which the meaning of love is changing in today's world. (a) "Choice vs. commitment": love as commitment involves "fixed unswerving loyalty—'my partner right or wrong no matter what the cost' "; such a notion cannot coexist with demands for continual growth and change. (b) "Rebellion vs. attachment": here "rebellion" indicates a modern "restlessness" in search of meaning wholly out of "sync" with the modern drive for honesty and equality in relationships. The latter cluster of virtues demands constant "negotiation and negotiation of personal relationships." (c) "Self-realization vs. self-sacrifice": in traditional relationships spouses feel obligated to sacrifice for one another. In the newer mode, self-development is the norm. Each partner has a right to pursue what will fulfill him or her, though not without some mutual yielding to "maximize joint profit." (d) "Libidinal expression vs. restraint": the former phrase is more in accord with the modern drive for enhancing individual growth and allowing for new experiences including freedom in emotional expressivity. (Scanzoni, 1983:74–81, quoting Swidler, 1980.) These characterizations reinforce Scanzoni's conviction that "morphostatic" relationships of traditional marriages, celebrated by conservative spokespersons, engender tensions between husbands and wives and parents and children; "we are entering an era in which negotiation processes are becoming a *way of life* permeating family as well as all other institutions" (Scanzoni, 1983:153; emphasis in original).

Third, as Hadden and other critics who focus on NCR worldviews assume (as distinguished from those of conservative families), *there is very little of a "positive" theology of love, nurture, and support and considerable emphasis on the need for social control*. The "Christian admonitions" seem rooted in negatives and in warnings to avoid and oppose current trends—divorce, adultery, ERA, women working full-time outside the home, etc. The family is a locus where control mechanisms must be employed. The emphasis, thus, is on disciplining children rather than on ways of showing love and affection; wives' subordination to husbands takes precedence over shared love and mutual growth and equal-partner decision making.

In summary, in the very "act of observing" NCR families and/or family ideals, the social scientists cited previously bring with them fundamental assumptions that are rooted in values widely shared and disseminated within the social science community and within the ranks of those having received a "secular" higher educational experience and, finally, shared also by "mainline" church theologians. Elaborated above, these assumptions reflect a bedrock conviction not always articulated: each human being, born with practically unlimited potential for growth and development, must be allowed within the family, as well as in other social institutions, maximum freedom for self-development and the fullest self-expression. Subordinate roles are inconsistent with this ideal and must be changed toward partnership roles. This conviction constitutes a "truth claim" whose consequences, as Warner has indicated, are a tendency to relegate NCR family ideals to the categories of backward and unenlightened, and a blindness to the personal and group needs that these ideals, norms, and practices may serve within the NCR community of families. It is to these needs, ideals, and presuppositions that we now turn.

Presuppositions of the Christian Family Viewed Through Pastoral Literature

The presuppositions discussed above make it difficult for researchers "carrying" them to utilize Weber's *verstehen* approach to understanding social actors. If, as Thomas and Edmondson indicate, the postpositivist view of family theory requires attention to *"agency* and *reasons* for behavior" or "intentionality" (1984:65; emphasis in the original), it is indeed crucial methodologically to grasp in as much detail as possible how NCR believers themselves view the family.

Marsden (1983) provides a helpful starting point. He points out that contemporary fundamentalism has several dimensions which include a polemical side and private or faith-nurturing side. NCR critics rely a great deal on published sermons and books, which deliberately stress the polemical side of the New Christian Right. LaHaye's *The Battle for the Family* (1982), cited by Hadden (1983), is an excellent example. These polemics frequently state "conservative" positions in the strongest possible terms which, understandably, draw critical comment from "liberal" social scientists; and these, in turn, encourage more counterstatements from NCR authors.

Neglected in these polemical exchanges is the realm of pastoral literature and exhortations, both written and on cassette tapes readily obtainable. Why is this literature important? It is precisely within it that (a) the loving, nurturing, and caring dimensions of the NCR worldview on the family are to be found, as well as (b) a broader understanding of NCR presuppositions implicit in both pastoral and polemical literature.

An important source of popular pastoral material on the family is the work of Tim LaHaye and his wife Beverly. LaHaye is a member of the Executive Board of Moral Majority and the author of a dozen books. While citing LaHaye's polemical treatise, *The Battle for the Family* (1982), Hadden neglects to cite, much less analyze, Tim and Beverly LaHaye's *Spirit-Controlled Family Living* (1978). Another example of pastoral literature from NCR is a 3-cassette "Family Seminar Packet" by Dr. Ed Hindson (1978), director of the Christian Counseling Center at the Thomas Road Baptist Church of which Jerry Falwell is pastor. While polemics are by no means absent from these sources, their overall thrust is toward articulating a theological and pastoral framework designed to be helpful to families and particularly to parents, trying to find a "formula for a successful family" (Hindson's title for the tape series).

The LaHayes open the book by stating flatly that "the family is the most important factor in our lives" (1978:18). Without fulfillment through the family, "nothing else in life really matters" (1978:18). Those attaining success in business, the professions, or the arts in later life, only "to spend their final years in despair," are in such a state because "they become alienated from their families and . . . [have] sacrificed family to gain notoriety (1978:18). The family, too, "is easily the most important single influence" in a child's life. If a child is raised in a family in which "the father rebels against authority," the child will grow up "taking advantage of his fellow man." By contrast, a child growing up "in a loving home, where values are communicated, and laws are respected," will become a productive adult "who makes a significant contribution to society" (1978:19). On the other hand, a "child-centered home" is an aberration. The primary love relationship in the home must be that of husband and wife, from which will emerge an atmosphere in which "any child will flourish" (1978:24).

Supportive relationships in the family are particularly essential today because of the "eight causes for today's family breakdown." These "causes" will sound familiar to many readers because they *are* elements of the more publicized and discussed polemical literature and may be briefly stated as follows: dominance of atheistic, anti-Christian humanism in schools and the media; sexual immorality and promiscuity; legalization of pornography; divorce made too easy; the permissive philosophy of child-rearing promoted in the last generation by Dr. Spock; women in the labor force; the morality of women's liberation; and urbanized living, which makes for uprootedness and is inimical to development of solid community-supported moral norms.

Discussion of these "causes," however, occupies only the book's opening three chapters. The remaining seven concentrate on pastoral theology and counseling themes. In these themes can be seen most clearly the distinctive presuppositions of NCR family ideology. The LaHayes cite six "basic enemies" of home and marriage: (a) anger, hostility, and bitterness as a first cluster; (b) worry and anxiety; (c) selfishness; (d) infidelity; (e) self-rejection; and (f) depression. These enemies of Christian family living "grieve or quench the Holy Spirit and limit His use of our lives" (1978:79). Husband and wife are urged to discuss these when they arise in family life. For each problem area, the basic formula of Spirit-filled family living is to be applied: facing the problem as a sinful area, confessing it, asking God to remove the problem or habit, asking for the filling of the Spirit in one's life, thanking God for assistance and whatever success is achieved, repeating the formula when the problem arises again. Supportive biblical quotations illustrate each discussion of a problem area, together with examples of persons who have achieved success in overcoming these difficulties. (1978:40–46.)

The first of two major presuppositions informs all of the proposed strategies offered for handling these problems: (a) *By exercising personal agency and so choosing, one can change his/her life by seeking spiritual input*. The worldview so portrayed describes the human condition as peopled with responsible agents and a social and/or "spiritual" reality which includes influences other than those attributed to a materialistic this-world view limited to matter-in-motion conceptualizations.

The second presupposition is illustrated by Beverly LaHaye as she discusses the "roles of the wife" within the governing evangelical norm of submission of wife to husband and submission of both to God. Submission, she insists, does *not* mean reduction to slavery or an inferior or unequal status. "She is a subordinate, a vice-president, who serves directly under the head of the household or the president, who is her husband" (1978:82). Yet,

> submission does not involve closing her mouth, shutting off her brain, and surrendering her individuality. The loving husband who is wise will seek the insights of his wife before he makes the final decision. We have found in our own marriage that we repeatedly see things differently and frequently do not agree on how to approach difficult circumstances. Because Tim has allowed me to develop my own thoughts and feelings, thus retaining my uniqueness, he listens respectfully to my counsel and considers it carefully before making the final decision. (1978:83.)

Within the LaHayes' framework the believing wife can develop multiple roles of home manager, lover, attentive mother, and teacher. Unity of husband and wife results in unity "on the teaching and disciplining of their children," with the book of Proverbs—a chapter from which should be read daily by parents—a principal guide (1978:104). An example of the latter is provided by the LaHayes: "And have joy of the wife of your youth. Her love will invigorate you always; through her love you will flourish continually." (Proverbs 5:17–19.)

Tim LaHaye's chapter on "the roles of the husband" emphasizes the headship of the husband and the husband's obligation to assume the role of leader in the home. Decisions are not, however, to be made without hearing and evaluating the wife's views nor without scrutinizing one's motivation. "Always pray for the decision-making wisdom which God promises to provide" (1978:110). In a section entitled "Handling Spirit-filled Disagreements," LaHaye proposes a negotiatory process in settling differences, recommending prayer by both husband and wife, and stating that God "will cause one of us to acquiesce joyfully with the other's point of view, or many times He will lead us to an entirely different decision" (1978:114). Respect for the wife by the husband is essential to maintaining a love relationship in any decision-making context.

A lengthy subsection is devoted to discussion and illustration of the major virtues of love found in 1 Corinthians 13: the husband is to be unselfish, gracious, trusting, sincere, polite, generous, humble, kind, and patient. Love that has "sputtered" is to be countered by mutual discussion of the problems, or "walking together in the Spirit"; by refusing to dwell on "insults, hurts, or weaknesses of your partner" (1978:129) and by "thanking God for ten things about your partner, twice daily for three weeks" (1978:130). The husband as "family priest" will strive to be a "Spirit-controlled man" who regularly reads the Bible, shares his reading with the children and discusses the reading with them, and leads family devotions.

Hindson's tapes, *Formula for a Successful Family* (1978), while stressing the hierarchical structure of the family—obedience of wife to husband and of children to parents—contain much the same kind of practical pastoral advice for mothers and fathers in a context of mutual prayer and reading of the Bible. Hindson urges fathers to be fully and undistractedly present to their wives and children since they will be judged on their performance of these responsibilities rather than on success in their careers.

> The same scriptural passages that command the wife to obey her husband command the husband to *love* his wive! Being a leader is not being a dictator, but a loving motivator who, in turn, is appreciated and respected by his family. Dad, God wants you to be the loving heartbeat of your home by building the lives of your family through teaching and discipline. (Tape 2; emphasis in the original.)

"Teenage rebellion" and a child's self-image are subjects of two tape sides, with parental responsibility stressed again and love urged as the enveloping context in which children must be raised and disciplined. In the final tape, "Learning to Love," Hindson attacks the "myth of perfect compatibility" and urges virtues of forbearance and forgiveness of spouse by spouse; he places this exhortation in the framework, once again, of 1 Corinthians 13, Paul's celebration of love—which is a gift and must be sought in prayer for the benefit of husband and wife and for the sake of the children.

This discussion continues the emphasis identified in the first presupposition—namely, the reality of the Spirit's influence on the human condition—and outlines the basic nature of the second presupposition: *The highest form of love will emerge in relationships in which one willingly submits to true values held by another*. Just as families are to look to the father as head, so too are fathers to look to Christ as head, and all are to be fundamentally concerned about the well-being of one another. Love of others as well as self can flourish only in service to others. The often-cited advice concerning charity by Paul (1 Corinthians 13), applied to fathers, identifies as necessary characteristics of a loving relationship such dimensions as being polite, kind, gracious, and patient. Traditionally the latter have been linked with female roles rather than with the mastery and dominance dimensions typical in masculine roles. Love is not antithetical to dominance. Submissive relations in the family and the Pauline characteristics of Christian love eventually ought to be found in all family members.

Conclusion

The foregoing brief overview of conservative evangelical pastoral theology demonstrates the cogency of Warner's argument that social scientists tend to be blinded by their own presuppositions to central aspects of evangelical spirituality—in this case, the spirituality of the family. Thus, the *verstehen* mode of grasping the inner *Welt* of NCR believers is short-circuited. To be more specific, the primacy of individual choice and the centrality of Western participatory democracy define and illuminate the social scientist's advocacy of a nonhierarchical universe or, at least, the assumption that binding decisions should be a result of the full participation in decision making of all persons affected. Any social institution that allocates decision making to some members and subordination to others is "out of phase" or "out of sync," at the least and, at the worst, an instrument of oppression vis-à-vis classes of persons (women, children) who have a long history of being subordinated.

These suppositions tend to keep social scientists from considering the possibility that hierarchical structures and "external regulation" may be integrated with loving consideration by each spouse toward the other, in which negotiation of conflicting interests frequently occurs. Also obscured is the combining of firm discipline of children with manifestations of love toward them and the fact that this very combination is the condition under which children will develop self-esteem as well as respect for the rights and for the welfare of other persons. In other words NCR advocates seem fully supportive of the democratic ethos in the larger political arena (the polis) but believe firmly that rearing children disciplined in love produces the very kind of adult best prepared (because they respect the rights of others) to participate fully in a democratic society.

Second, social scientists focusing on the macrostructures of modern society and the impact of these structures on the family (a bureaucratized work world, and inflationary economy, a consumer society, etc.) fail to understand NCR's focus on *those macrostructures they consider as having inimical effects:* the school system, the media, "secular" universities, the ERA movement, the Supreme Court, to name but a few. In addition, NCR advocates do not consider these developments as "inexorable" or incapable of being combatted. As the LaHayes have indicated, resistance takes place on two levels—that of counterinstitutions, such as Christian schools and media networks, and a family life imbued with the devotional and pastoral supports cited above.

Third, to the extent that social scientists and other modern commentators are convinced that "commitments" and "self-sacrifice," "attachment" and "restraint" inhibit full individual growth, development, and emotional expression and simply perpetuate subordinate relationships, they are incapable of appreciating the conservative Christian insistence (an ethos shared by many "more liberal" Christians, as well as non-Christians) that love, particularly as it focuses on rearing children, per se involves subordination of one's desires and inclinations; and that this is the case in a loving spousal relationship as well. Individuals can grow and find fulfillment through lifelong attachment to one spouse, a process that indeed may involve resistance to temptations to "find love elsewhere"; but the very resistance is seen as an expression and condition of love and not as a forgoing of possible further growth and development.

Certainly, some social scientists are re-evaluating the "modern conception of love" as stated by Swidler. Yankelovich (1981), quoted approvingly by Scanzoni (1983), strongly criticizes a "me-first, satisfy-all-my-desires attitude" as leading to "relationships that are superficial, transitory, and ultimately unsatisfying" (1981:248). He proposes an "ethic of commitment" which shifts the focus away from self-concern with growth and development "toward connectedness with the world . . . commitment to people, institutions, objects, beliefs, ideas, places, nature, projects, experiences, adventures, and callings" (1981:247). To the extent that this conception gains favor or becomes a "presupposition" of increasing numbers of analysts and commentators, it may well help build a bridge of understanding to the fulfillment-through-commitment orientation of conservative Christians.

Fourth, viewed from the "inside," NCR's vision of the family indeed involves a primary emphasis upon love; upon loving negotiation where conflict is present;

and upon a conviction that human nature indeed requires "controls" because human beings, wounded through Original Sin, are easily susceptible to "going astray." Viewed from the inside, again, a major presupposition not shared by "outsiders" is that scripture, being divinely inspired, is the major reliable guide for human living; furthermore, the hierarchical framework and the differing "natures" of men and women and their consequent asymmetrical relationship are precisely the conditions of human fulfillment, of order and stability in the family, and are maximally conducive to a nurturing, caring atmosphere in which children can be reared with proper values and secure identities intact. Once again, the pastoral sources cited (not the polemical on which social scientists have so heavily relied) make it clear that, even within the evangelical hierarchical framework, compromise, negotiation, and mutual adjustment can take place in husband-wife relationships precisely because the compromise and negotiation take place in a context emphasizing love of God, neighbor, and self (see LaHaye and LaHaye, 1978:chapters 5 and 6). From the "insider" viewpoint terms such as *authoritarian, rigid, conformist* distort a reality that allows for much more flexibility than the strictly normative expressions of scripture would suggest.

None of the foregoing should be taken to mean that social science criticism of NCR family worldviews is without insight or value. The observers cited above point to NCR ideological "blind spots," too. D'Antonio's (1983) strictures concerning NCR support of a free enterprise system, which has given rise to the very forces that undermine the traditional family, deserve serious consideration. This liberal critique, however, can be turned around by NCR advocates who can readily reply that inconsistency is not confined only to conservatives: liberals support "free enterprise" in gender relationships and decry any imposition of authority in this sphere as damaging to individual autonomy, yet are quick to call for government (that is, authority) controls on the free enterprise system within the economy.

Hadden's contention that cause-and-effect relationships are obscured in NCR analysis seems cogent when one considers the LaHayes' lament that so many married women are in the work force, because temptations to infidelity multiply. Furthermore, it is difficult not to agree with critics who see in NCR's definition of the man-woman relationship a sacred legitimation of the continuing relegation of women to second-class personhood and of the cementing of male domination throughout society's institutions.

Thus, whatever "foundations of consensus" the "scientific community" may develop concerning how to view the "social reality" of the family (Thomas and Edmondson, 1986:62), that consensus must include explicit awareness of presuppositions and how to deal creatively with them so that analytical distortion is identified and caricatures avoided. There are woefully few social scientific studies of NCR families from "the inside"; and to this extent our understanding of how they *actually* work, as contrasted with ideal portraits painted by pastoral theologians on the one hand and critical commentary from social scientists on the other, is severely limited. One sociologist (Thomas, 1983) has attempted such an analysis in an "insider's" portrait of the Mormon family experience. One theologian (Cox, 1984) recently has attempted to state the concerns of evangelical and fundamentalist preachers in a sympathetic fashion, yet without forgoing critical comment, making clear his own presuppositions. While the foregoing cannot be offered as ideal models, they are at least initial steps in the right direction. Family theorists are challenged to "go forth and do likewise" in their future studies of the New Christian Right. It is hoped that these studies will allow social scientists and religiously committed family members to understand better their own and each other's presuppositions about familial and religious reality, better aware of the relative strengths *and* distortions inherent in the viewpoint one espouses. Perhaps then we will understand better how family and religion combine to meet the individual's social, emotional, and even eschatological needs in a world not only threatening to families, but whose continued existence may be in doubt.

Bibliography

Alexander, J. C. 1982. *Theoretical Logic in Sociology* (Vol. 1). Berkeley, CA: University of California Press.

Brown, H. I. 1977. *Perception, Theory and Commitment: The New Philosophy of Science*. Chicago: University of Chicago Press.

Cox, H. 1984. *Religion in the Secular City: Toward a Post-modern Theology*. New York: Simon and Schuster.

D'Antonio, W. V. 1983. "Family Life, Religion, and Societal Values and Structures." Pp. 81–108 in W. V. D'Antonio and J. Aldous (eds.), *Families and Religions: Conflict and Change in Modern Society*. Beverly Hills, CA: Sage.

D'Antonio, W. F. and J. Aldous (eds.) 1983. *Families and Religions: Conflict and Change in Modern Society*. Beverly Hills, CA: Sage.

Hadden, J. K. 1983. "Televangelism and the Mobilization of a New Christian Right Family Policy." Pp. 247–66 in W. V. D'Antonio and J. Aldous (eds.), *Families and Religions: Conflict and Change in Modern Society*. Beverly Hills, CA: Sage.

Hargrove, B. 1983a. "The Church, the Family, and the Modernization Process." Pp. 21–48 in W. V. D'Antonio and J. Aldous (eds.), *Families and Religions: Conflict and Change in Modern Society*. Beverly Hills, CA: Sage.

Hargrove, B. 1983b. "Family in the White American Protestant Experience." Pp. 113–40 in W. V. D'Antonio and J. Aldous (eds.), *Families and Religions: Conflict and Change in Modern Society*. Beverly Hills, CA: Sage.

Hindson, E. 1978. *Formula for a Successful Family* (3 cassette tapes). Liberty Family Seminar Series 2. Lynchburg, VA: Thomas Road Baptist Church.

Kuhn, T. 1970. *The Structure of Scientific Revolutions*. Chicago: University of Chicago Press.

LaHaye, T. 1982. *The Battle for the Family*. Old Tappan, NJ: Fleming H. Revell.

LaHaye, T. and B. LaHaye. 1978. *Spirit-Controlled Family Living*. Old Tappan, NJ: Fleming H. Revell.

Marsden, G. 1983. "Preachers of Paradox: The Religious New Right in Historical Perspective." Pp. 150–68 in M. Douglas and S. Tipton (eds.), *Religion and America: Spirituality in a Secular Age*. Boston: Beacon.

Scanzoni, J. 1983. *Shaping Tomorrow's Family: Theory and Policy for the 21st Century*. Beverly Hills, CA: Sage.

Suppe, F. 1977. *Structure of Scientific Theories* (2nd ed.). Urbana, IL: University of Illinois Press.

Swidler, A. 1980. "Love and Adulthood in American Culture." Pp. 120–47 in N. Smelser and E. Erickson (eds.), *Themes of Work and Love in Adulthood*. Cambridge, MA: Harvard University Press.

Thomas, D. 1983. "Family in the Mormon Experience." Pp. 167–288 in W. V. D'Antonio and J. Aldous (eds.), *Families and Religions: Conflict and Change in Modern Society*. Beverly Hills, CA: Sage.

Thomas, D. and J. Wilcox. 1987. "The Rise of Family Theory: An Historical and Critical Analysis." Pp. 81–102 in M. B. Sussman and S. K. Steinmetz (eds.), *Handbook of Marriage and the Family*. New York: Plenum Press.

Warner, R. 1979. "Theoretical Barriers to the Understanding of Evangelical Christianity." *Sociological Analysis* 40:1–9.

Weber, M. 1978. *Economy and Society* (Vol. 1). (Ed. by G. Ross, with C. Wittich.) Berkeley, CA: University of California Press.

Yankelovich, D. 1981. *New Rules: Searching for Self-Fulfillment in a World Turned Upside-Down*. New York: Random House.

16

Developments in Modern Physics and Their Implications for the Social and Behavioral Sciences

Mark A. Schroll

The present article is a brief overview for social and behavioral scientists who are unfamiliar with the modern physics movement and the emerging "new age paradigm." Evidence of the emergence of this new age paradigm is reflected in the plethora of books and articles published throughout the last decade on the modern physics movement and its relationship to the perennial philosophy of the world's great religious traditions (Bohm and Weber, 1982a; Bohm and Sheldrake, 1982b; Capra, 1975, 1983a, 1983b, 1984; Comfort, 1983, 1984; Deikman, 1982; Pelletier, 1978; Valle, 1981; Weber, 1986; Wolf, 1981; Young, 1984; Zukav, 1979; etc.).

Unfortunately this movement is often mistaken as an occult uprising, antiscientific, and a belief in the irrational. Many reasons could be given, and have been (Capra, 1983a; Ferguson, 1980), as to why this area has continued to gain the interest of countless authors and larger audiences. Historian Theodore Roszak has put forth the view that the emergence of these books, articles and

Mark A. Schroll is adjunct instructor of the Physics Department at Kearney State College, Kearney, Nebraska. He has been researching the emerging new age paradigm since 1981. He has been a member of the Association for Transpersonal Psychology since 1984. Most recently he has been invited to become a scholar in residence at the Wittgenstein Institute, Kirchberg/Wechsel (near Vienna), lower Austria, where he plans to continue his multi-disciplinary research on the emerging new age paradigm, the perennial philosophy, and the history and philosophy of science.

the rising culture surrounding them is the indication of a great religious appetite, reaching out into areas that are not traditionally religious in character (Roszak, n.d.).

This same view is held by Ken Wilber, editor of the New Science Library, Shambala Publications. In his introduction to this series, Wilber says that the "New Science Library has come into existence for the purpose of exploring and encouraging the dialogue between the scientific and spiritual views of the world" (1984:2).

My first exposure to what is now generally referred to as "new age thinking" was through Fritjof Capra's *The Tao of Physics* (1975) and an unpublished manuscript, "The Awakening" (Sallach, 1976), which had been greatly influenced by Capra's book. Since then my world perspective has been greatly influenced by the eminent physicist David Bohm, a student of Einstein. Bohm has added significantly to the new physics literature by discussing connections between modern physics and the perennial philosophy of the world's great religious traditions. Bohm's viewpoint is that the empirical evidence stemming from modern physics suggests the need for a new metaphysics. (Bohm and Weber, 1982a; Schroll, 1987a; Weber, 1986.)

According to Bohm, this new metaphysics would rest upon the premise that the universe is an undivided wholeness. This undivided wholeness, this transcendental source-ground is, says Bohm, the fundamental Reality and through a cyclic process of projection, injection, re-projection, this primary Reality gives rise to a secondary reality, the manifest world of sensory phenomena. Bohm's viewpoint counters the present metaphysics of Western science, which rests upon the premise that the domain of manifest sensory phenomena represents the primary and "only" reality.

Furthermore, Bohm believes the present worldview of Western science is maintained through the self-deceptive fragmentary division of subjectivity and objectivity. This division of our self-worldview has been humanity's major source of suffering and confusion.

Believing that Bohm was essentially correct in his plea for a new metaphysics and sensing great confusion stemming from efforts to retain the traditional objective-subjective dichotomy in Western thought, I wondered, could developments in the modern physics movement provide a more adequate philosophical foundation for the social and behavioral sciences?

My research over the past few years and this manuscript provide a possible answer to that question, that "new age thinking" has the potential to generate a new ontological and epistemological metaphysics, providing the possible reconciliation between positivistic science and the perennial philosophy of the major world religious traditions—eliminating the presently existing separation of the sacred and the secular.

The developments of the modern physics movement have already had a profound effect upon the worldview of physics as well as the physicists themselves. Indeed, as the profoundly shocking ontological and epistemological developments of the new physics come to be more fully understood by social and behavioral scientists, their paradigm will also undergo a transformation (Schroll, 1987b). Niels Bohr argues that those who are not at first shocked by quantum mechanics do not understand it.

Contrary to the view of classical science, the ontological position of the new physics is not to prove or disprove the reality of objective phenomena. Rather, the ontology of the new physics cannot be separated from its epistemology, because the purpose of the new physics is to track down, as precisely as possible, the relationship between the manifold aspects of the world of phenomenological events (the observed) and the symbolic construction of these phenomenological events as they are experienced by the observer. (Guillemin, 1968.)

Thus, an important thesis of this article is that emergent phenomenological reality is inextricably entwined with the act of measurement, which implies participation, as opposed to the classical scientific stance of passive observation. Therefore, emergent reality can neither exist apart from nor prior to the act of measurement, but is in fact the act of measurement itself.

The participatory ethos of new age thinking which underscores emergent phenomenological reality can serve to heal the fragmentary metaphysics and methodological reductionism of Western science. However, it should not be seen as a panacea for the ills of humanity. It will be the responsibility of humanity as a whole to help heal the split between the sacred and the secular, and help to bridge the gap between ancient wisdom and modern science.

The Historical Overview of Modern Physics

Some came for the reasons
some came along for the ride
some knew what they needed
others needed time to decide.

The first of a new breed
standing on a new frontier
seeking direction when a voice
came through loud and clear. . . .

Open your eyes up to the ways of the world [universe].
Keith L. Volquardsen
and Phillip C. Potter
musicians, song writers
Lincoln, Nebraska 1983

It is appropriate to begin our historical overview of modern physics with Lord Kelvin, one of the leading theoretical physicists of the nineteenth century, and his view of the state of classical physics as summarized by Bohm:

[Lord Kelvin] . . . expressed the opinion that physics had more or less completed its development. He therefore advised young men not to go into this field because further work would only be a matter of confirming the next few decimal points. He did however mention two small clouds on the horizon. These were the negative results of the Michelson-Morely experiment and the difficulties of understanding quantized [sic, blackbody] radiation. We must admit that Lord Kelvin was able to choose his clouds properly. These were precisely the points of departure for the developments of relativity and quantum theory. (Bohm, 1984.)

The Michelson-Morley experiment, conducted in 1887, was designed to measure the ether breeze. The ether was believed to be a corpuscular web that extended throughout the universe and served as the invisible medium through which light propagated itself (Jeans, 1943).

The ether breeze was thought to be the result of the earth's rotation and movement through space. The Michelson-Morley experiment failed to detect the ether. Various explanations to account for why the ether had not been detected began to emerge. However, it took the bold statement by a young scientist named Albert Einstein to declare eighteen years later than the ether was not detected because the ether does not exist!

During this same time in history, Max Planck (known as the father of modern physics), having been influenced by the writings of Lord Kelvin, believed he would be one of the world's last theoretical physicists. Ironically, it was his work on blackbody radiation that helped to change all this. (Briggs and Peat, 1984.)

For simplicity's sake, blackbody radiation refers to an object that absorbs all the radiation that falls upon it. The word *blackbody* is a bit of a misnomer, as the word *blackbody* also denotes an object capable of turning heat energy into electromagnetic radiation—such as the sun (Gribbin, 1984).

Thus a second seemingly unanswerable problem emerged for nineteenth-century physicists when their predictions of blackbody radiation in terms of classical thermodynamics produced results indicating that blackbodies at very high temperatures and short wavelengths contained infinite amounts of energy. This prediction came to be called the "ultraviolet catastrophe." (Gribbin, 1984.)

Planck's attempt to solve the ultraviolet catastrophe created the anomalous solution (contrary to Thomas Young's experimentally confirmed wave theory of light) that light or thermal radiation is emitted in discrete energy packets or "quanta." Even though this hypothesis helped to explain thermal radiation, Planck was hesitant to accept his own discovery because it contradicted scientific "fact."

Although Planck himself was still doubting the existence of quanta as a physical entity, the existence of light quanta or "photons" were seen to be a necessary condition toward the explanation of the photoelectric effect. This bold conclusion was published in 1905 by the same young physicist who had denied the existence of the ether, Albert Einstein. This also marked the beginning of the many quantum paradoxes. How, physicists began asking themselves, can light and other forms of energy possess the qualities of individual, pointlike particles (such as the photoelectric effect suggested), as well as Young's theory of light as continuous waves?

Although the hypothesis of light quanta or photons appeared to explain the experimental results of the photoelectric effect, Einstein, like Planck before him, balked at his own discovery; this dual personality of light made as much sense to classical physicists as saying that stones are also steam (Briggs and Peat, 1984).

While this controversy was still far from being solved, Niels Bohr was trying to resolve certain peculiarities in Rutherford's model of the atom. Early in the twentieth century, from his research on radioactivity, Ernest Rutherford had proposed that the atom was like a tiny solar system—having a massive central core of protons surrounded by orbiting electrons of lighter density. This model had satisfied and convinced most physicists of the day, but Bohr noticed that based on the electrons' orbital decay, all atoms should collapse in a moment. Bohr asked, why don't they?

His first clue to this question came from optical spectroscopy, the science of studying atomic spectra. When an atom emits energy, light is given off, forming the so-called emission spectrum. When energy is absorbed by an atom, a negative image of the emission spectrum (the absorption spectrum) is formed. Furthermore, this optical spectrum (of a chemical element such as hydrogen) acts as an identifiable pattern—much like a fingerprint. (Briggs and Peat, 1984.)

It was Bohr's insight—to combine the quantized energy concept of Planck and Einstein with spectroscopy and Rutherford's atomic solar system—which birthed a new model of the atom. This hybrid was an immediate success with the physicists of the time, who applauded Bohr's ability to account for the insights of Planck and Einstein by bringing them into accord with the traditional Newtonian framework.

Despite this, the paradox of the dual nature of light had yet to be properly addressed. But the majority of scientists, then as now, were simply going along for the ride and, in the wave of excitement over Bohr's new atomic model, this anomaly was soon forgotten (as anomalies usually are [Schroll, 1987a]). Fortunately for science and humanity, there are those who listen to an inner voice, choosing to march to a different drummer.

Indeed, before the wave/particle paradox of light energy would once again become a topic of debate, another young physicist needed to open his eyes up to the ways of the universe. This healthy young voice of objection came from Werner Heisenberg, who, along with his friend Wolfgang Pauli, began to notice some irregularities in the Bohr atom.

To begin with, technical improvements in spectroscopy had revealed finer spectral lines, producing computational abnormalities in Bohr's atomic model. However, these experimental and computational objections were overshadowed by an insight that was to help produce the next visionary breakthrough. These pliable young minds had realized what senior physicists following classical scientific dogma could not, that "Bohr had grafted the new quantum ideas onto older nineteenth-century notions like planetary orbits. While older physicists felt content with this hybrid, the compromise seemed unsatisfactory to the two [young] students." (Briggs and Peat, 1984:42.)

Social and behavioral scientists have a valuable lesson to learn from scientists such as Pauli and Heisenberg. Unlike Planck and Einstein, they were not afraid to question the scientific dogma of practical realism or positivistic science. Instead they trusted their own intuitive insight.

Following the completion of his thesis on hydrodynamics, Heisenberg took an academic post at the University of Göttingen. It was at this time that Heisenberg turned his full attention to the structure of the atom. But his progress toward finding any sort of solution was impeded as a result of his teaching schedule. Ironically, as a result of a severe hay fever attack toward the end of May 1925, he was freed from his teaching responsibilities for two weeks. To recover from his illness, Heisenberg retired to the pollen-free island of Helgoland. Here, free from interruptions, he made rapid progress. Guided by his inner vision of how things ought to go, he developed an algebraic method based on his observation of atomic spectra to account for the energy fluctuations of electrons in the Bohr atom. This method came to be known as matrix mechanics.

The tremendous exhilaration experienced by Heisenberg from his "seeing" into the heart of atomic structure is best expressed by Heisenberg himself in his autobiographical account:

> I reached a point where I was ready to determine the individual terms in the energy table, or, as we put it today, in the energy matrix.... When the first terms seemed to accord with the energy principle, I became rather excited, and I began to make countless arithmetical errors. As a result, it was almost three o'clock in the morning before the final result of my computations lay before me.... At first, I was deeply alarmed. I had the feeling that through the surface of atomic phenomena I was looking at a strangely beautiful interior, and I felt almost giddy at the thought that I now had to probe this wealth of mathematical structures nature had so generously spread out before me. I was far too excited to sleep. (Heisenberg, 1971:60, 61.)

Returning to Göttingen, Heisenberg spent three weeks summarizing his discovery in a form suitable for publication, which he completed in July 1925. Remarkably, just as with Planck's concept of the quantum which appeared in 1900, "there was no historical precedent for Heisenberg's idea" (Pagels, 1982).

Exhausted from his efforts and still unsure if his paper really made sense, Heisenberg sent a copy to his old friend Pauli, who, after reviewing it, was enthusiastic. Heisenberg then departed for Leyden and Cambridge to give a series of lectures, leaving his paper with one of his former professors, Max Born, "to dispose of as he saw fit." (Gribbin, 1984.) Seeing the importance of Heisenberg's work, Born happily sent the article off to be published.

Initially Heisenberg's matrix mechanics were warmly received by the scientific community, who, lacking Heisenberg's personal intuitive vision, were simply going along for the ride. But the fanfare of Heisenberg's matrix mechanics seemed doomed to extinction a few months later with the publication of a rival theory by the Austrian physicist Erwin Schroedinger in January 1926.

Schroedinger's theory, which came to be known as wave mechanics, had its inception in the Ph.D. thesis of French nobleman (and later prince) Louis Victor de Broglie.

De Broglie's revolutionary ideas had been presented a few years earlier in September 1923, where, reasoning by analogy, he proposed the concept that electrons could exist as both a wave and a particle. De Broglie then "deduced the wavelength of the electron," referring to these ambidextrous electrons as "matter waves." (Pagels, 1982.)

Paul Langevin, an examiner of de Broglie's thesis, later sent a copy to Einstein. It was Einstein who later suggested the heuristic value of de Broglie's ideas to Schroedinger. Originally Schroedinger believed that de Broglie's "matter waves" were real physical entities, which was more appealing to the worldview of classical physicists because it offered a picture of atomic processes—where Heisenberg's matrix mechanics did not.

In support of his work on wave mechanics, Schroedinger received in April 1926 the following letters from Einstein and Planck respectively:

I am convinced that you have made a decisive advance with your formulation of the quantum condition, just as I am equally convinced that the Heisenberg-Born route is off the track (1926).

I read your article the way an inquisitive child listens in suspense to the solution of a puzzle that he has been bothered about for a long time, and I am delighted with the beauties that are evident to the eye (1926). (Quoted in Briggs and Peat, 1984:46).

Later, "when Schroedinger accepted Planck's chair in Berlin, the retiring Planck praised him as the man who had brought determinism back to physics" (Pagels, 1982). To illustrate what fair-weather friends those scientists who go along for the ride can make, Born—who had even contributed to matrix mechanics mathematical formulation—came to believe (like the majority of physicists during that time) that Heisenberg's matrix mechanics would soon be forgotten. But, as history shows, this was not to be the case.

Six months later, in June 1926, Born recanted his position with a new interpretation of Schroedinger's "matter waves," which is generally heralded as "the birth of the God who plays dice and the end of determinism in physics" (Pagels, 1982). This reinterpretation of Schroedinger's "matter waves" came as a result of applying wave mechanics to atoms that had more than one electron. Schroedinger's wave mechanics had given a clear, almost direct representation of "matter waves" when applied to the hydrogen atom that had only one electron.

Contrary to this conceptual clarity, when Schroedinger's classical picture of physical "matter waves" were applied to atoms having more than one electron, Schroedinger's wave equations could no longer be written in three dimensions of space. Thus it became clear that Schroedinger's wave mechanics did not describe physical objective reality at all; rather, wave mechanics had to be "expressed in abstract mathematical space." (Briggs and Peat, 1984.)

Indeed, it was Born's reinterpretation of Schroedinger's "matter waves" that helped to end this conceptual enigma, as it was Born's realization that Schroedinger's "matter waves" were not real physical entities at all; rather, they were waves of probability.

To better understand the statistical nature of Born's probability waves, Pagels provides a very lucid analogy:

> Imagine that an individual atom is a deck of cards and a specific energy level of that atom corresponds to a specific poker hand dealt from the deck. Poker hands have probabilities that can be calculated—using the theory of card playing it is possible to determine precisely the possibility of a given hand's being obtained from the dealer. The theory does not predict the outcome of a particular deal. Demanding this latter kind of determinism requires looking into the deck—cheating. According to Born, the de Broglie-Schroedinger wave function specifies the probability that an atom will have a specific energy level just as the theory of card playing specifies the probability of a certain hand. The theory does not say whether in a particular single measurement the atom will in fact be found in a specific energy level, just as the theory of card playing can't predict the outcome of a specific deal. Classical physics, in contrast to the new quantum theory, claimed to be able to predict the outcome of such specific measurements. The new quantum theory denies that such individual events can be determined. . . . Here we see for the first time the new idea of causality in quantum theory—it is probability that is causally determined into the future, not individual events. (Pagels, 1982: 64.)

A vicious debate arose between physicists who favored Schroedinger's model, with its pictorial benefits, and the Heisenbergian approach based on the experimental observation of atomic spectra. These two approaches were eventually shown to be mathematically equivalent by the transformation theory of British physicist Paul Dirac. Analogy must also be employed to elucidate Dirac's transformation theory. Language and mathematics "are both symbolic means of representing the world; language is richer, while mathematics is more precise." (Pagels, 1982.)

Pagels continues this analogy by saying:

> Suppose someone describes a tree in the English language while someone else describes it in Arabic. The English and Arabic descriptions are different symbolic representations of the same object. If you want to describe the tree, you must pick at least one language or representation. Once you have one representation you can find the others by the rules of translation or transformation. That is how it is in the mathematical description of quantum objects like electrons. Some representations emphasize the wavelike properties, others the particlelike properties, but it is always the same entity that is being represented.... It is by varying the symbolic representations through transformations that we arrive at the notion of *invariants: those deep, intrinsic properties of an object which are just artifacts of how we describe it.... Invariants establish the true structure of an object*. (Pagels, 1982:65–66; italics added.)

Together these two approaches came to be known as quantum mechanics or quantum theory. To this basic structure of quantum theory must be added the Heisenberg uncertainty principle and Bohr's concept of complementarity. The Bohr-Schroedinger debate had failed to solve the conceptual differences between wave mechanics and matrix mechanics. This perplexing polemic weighed heavily on Heisenberg, who in his 1927 discussions with Bohr concerning this issue became nearly overwrought with despair.

Heisenberg struggled to make sense of the absurdities of this quantum paradox, until finally the psychological trauma triggered an insight so prc found scientists today are still discussing the full impact of its implications. In its most simple exposition, the Heisenberg uncertainty principle states:

> The closer we try to measure the position of a quantum object, the more uncertain becomes its momentum. It seems the very act of observation or measurement changes the system. Heisenberg's uncertainty principle showed that the actual properties of objects could no longer be separated from the act of measurement and thus from the measurer himself.... The pre-Heisenbergian scientist is metaphorically seated behind a half-silvered mirror, a spectator to nature, observing things as they really are. With the uncertainty principle, as physicist John

Wheeler was later to put it, the scientist smashed through that imaginary window separating him from nature. (Briggs and Peat, 1984:51.)

Heisenberg's excitement and enthusiasm concerning his new discovery, however, was met with mixed emotions by Bohr. While Bohr agreed with the basic view of the uncertainty principle, he believed this notion was part of a more basic ontology of the cosmos. This notion was referred to as complementarity. Essentially, this view says that the universe cannot be known by, nor does it have, a single ontological picture. Instead, the ontological nature of the universe is only clearly apprehended through complementary views that overlap with each other and may be paradoxical. (Briggs and Peat, 1984.)

Complementarity found itself not only in the wave/particle paradox, but, as Bohr later discovered, in the Chinese philosophy of Taoism and its symbolic representation of complementary opposites known as Yin and Yang; also in Gestalt psychology, specifically the perceptual enigma of the gestalt switch, where the cognitive shift from foreground to background cannot be understood using logic and reason but can only be known through an intuitive process.

These and other differences were finally resolved through what was later to be called the Cophenhagen interpretation of quantum theory:

> Bohr and Heisenberg finally agreed that any property is, to some extent, a result of the act of measurement. As Bohr said, the photon depends on us to exist. And presumably the converse is also true. We also depend on it! There are no separate, independent objects. (Briggs and Peat, 1984:54.)

Thus we have once again returned to the thesis of this article: that the ontology of emergent phenomenological reality is inextricably entwined with the act of measurement itself. That is, reality emerges during the act of measure at the point of contact between the measurer and that which is being measured.

The Ontological and Epistemological Significance of the New Physics

If the present interpretation of the new physics holds up, the philosophy of science may be seeing the beginnings of a reconciliation of the centuries-old argument between idealism and realism. Idealism refers to the ontological stance that physical reality exists only as thoughts and ideas—which reflect a timeless order of external laws or archetypal forms. Therefore, according to the subjective idealist the external world we see and experience is merely a reflection of this timeless order, an illusion created by our linguistic descriptions of a domain we can never truly know except on rare transcendental occasions.

Despite the attempts of competent philosophical argument, this view of reality has never been thoroughly refuted. Nevertheless, classical science has built its foundation upon the bedrock of practical realism or positivism. This ontological stance declares that there does exist an empirical world "out there" independent of our sensory perceptions, whose characteristics are immutable, complete, and ready to be observed. Radical positivists give an even stricter definition, saying that "all we can know is the set of our observations and/or our actions." (d'Espagnat, 1983.) Therefore, it is the purpose of empirical science to objectively inquire and analyze these fixed forms—thus coming to know and understand the ontological nature of the world.

Physicists of this century, however, have realized that it is no longer meaningful to separate the observed object, the observing instrument, the experimental conditions, and the experimental results (Bohm, 1971). Instead, the entire process of the experimental situation must be considered as a whole, as an emergent phenomenon resulting from the participation between the observed object and the observing instrument.

Despite the inseparability of the ontological and epistemological aspects of the experimental situation, the profound significance of the new physics has been much simpler and distinctly unsettling. To summarize the difference between the old and new physics, it is best to refer to the writings of the great physicists themselves, beginning with Sir James Jeans.

> ... from the broad philosophical standpoint, the outstanding achievement of twentieth-century physics is not the theory of relativity with its welding together of space and time, or the theory of quanta with its present apparent negation of the laws of causation, or the dissection of the atom with the discovery that things are not what they seem; it is the general recognition that we are not yet in contact with the ultimate reality. We are still imprisoned in our cave, with our backs to the light, and can only watch the shadows on the wall. (1931) (Quoted in Wilber, 1984b:9-10.)

This reference to Plato's cave image does not end with the former description by Jeans, but we find it in the following statements by Sir Arthur Eddinton and Erwin Schroedinger, who tell us:

In the world of physics we watch a shadowgraph performance of familiar life. The shadow of my elbow rests on the shadow table as the shadow ink flows over the shadow paper.... The frank realization that physical science is concerned with a world of shadows is one of the most significant of recent advances (1929). Schroedinger drives the point home: "Please note that the very recent advance of quantum and relativistic physics does not lie in the world of physics itself having acquired this shadowy character; it had ever since Democritus of Abdera and even before but we were not aware of it, we thought we were dealing with the world itself" (1958). (Quoted in Wilber, 1984b:6.)

With regard to these ontological descriptions (especially those of Jeans and Eddinton), while they may have transcended the illusion that the epistemology of physical science cannot lift the veil of shadow symbols, their descriptions remain essentially dualistic. Dualistic in the sense that Jeans, Eddinton and Schroedinger merely emphasize the symbolic representation of objective observations—that is, their descriptions continue to be those of mere spectators, despite the fact that these physicists realize the need to give an equal amount of emphasis to an aspect of Reality that lies beyond such symbolic representation. Indeed, to fully escape this illusory ontology, we must not only "watch a shadowgraph performance of familiar life," we must become the shadowgraph performance ourselves.

Capra (1983a) addresses this issue—that the act of measurement creates phenomenological reality—by saying:

In atomic physics the observed phenomena can be understood only as correlations between various processes of observation and measurement, and the end of this chain of processes lies always in the consciousness of the human observer. The crucial feature of quantum theory is that the observer [measurer] is not only necessary to observe the properties of an atomic phenomena, but is necessary even to bring about these properties.... We can never speak about nature without, at the same time, speaking about ourselves. (Capra, 1983a:86–87.)

Thus, contrary to classical physics, modern physics stresses an observer-created reality, woven from the symbolic construction of the measurement of phenomenological events, inextricably linking the event-probabilities of nature with the perceptual awareness of human consciousness.

Implications for the Social and Behavioral Sciences

Having explored the recent developments in physics and their implications upon the metaphysical framework used to contruct the scientific nature of Reality, let us turn our attention to the subsequent impact this "new age paradigm" may have upon the social and behavioral sciences.

Many of the characteristics of the emerging new age paradigm and its potential effects upon the social and behavioral sciences have been outlined in an article by Willis Harman, "The New Copernican Revolution." A partial list of these characteristics provided by Harman suggests that

> one of the dominant characteristics will be a relaxing of the subject-object dichotomy. The range between perceptions shared by all, and those which are unique to one individual, will be assumed to be much more of a continuum than a sharp division between "the world out there" and what goes on "in my head." Related to this will be the incorporation, in some form, of the age-old yet radical doctrine, that we perceive the world and ourselves in it as we have been culturally "hypnotized" to perceive it. The typical commonsense-scientific view will be considered to be a valid but partial view—a particular metaphor, so to speak. Others, such as certain religious or metaphysical views, will be considered also, and even equally valid but more appropriate for certain areas of human experience. (Harman, 1972:102.)

To further emphasize the difference between the old and new social science viewpoints, Floyd Matson clearly demarcates these differences in the following discussion:

> It is noteworthy that in his methodological arguments Mannheim was far from seeking to disparage "objectivity" in the name of a radical or ineffable "subjectivity," such as Romanticism had undertaken. What he sought was rather to redefine for social science the fundamental relationship between subject and object which the standard canons of the field had ordained as one of absolute detachment and disinterest [e.g., value neutrality]. Where for the orthodox behaviorist the distance between observer and observed was a vast Newtonian void filled with the ether of indifference, the sociologist of knowledge proceeded on the basis of "relativity," or relationship, by abolishing the ether. The main point was that, with respect to things human, it is not disinterest that makes knowledge possible but its opposite. Without the factor of interest, in the primary sense of concern or care, there can be no recognition of the subject matter in its distinctive human character—and hence no real awareness of its situation and no understanding of its behavior. [Most poignantly] in the development of his sociology of knowledge, Mannheim was very much aware of the quality of complementarity—the alternation of objective and human perspectives—in the study of human affairs. (Matson, 1972b:113–14.)

Thus we can see that contrary to the present methodology of the social and behavioral sciences stressing value neutrality, predictive power, and a cool disinterested objective stance, the new social and behavioral sciences expand this perspective by including value embeddedness, human freedom, subjective/ethnomethodological interpretation of data, transcendence of enculturation and the cultivation of global attitudes.

We should therefore see the emerging new age paradigm as a breaking away from the strict reductionistic stance of Descartes and his separation of the observer (mind) and the observed (body). Furthermore, the new age paradigm rejects the notion of objectivity in the strict Newtonian sense, where Newton envisioned the universe as a multitude of separate objects—atoms in the void—working in accordance with causally determined mechanistic principles. (See Capra, 1983a for a more complete discussion.)

However, despite our overview of the emerging new age paradigm, our full understanding of it will require a much more sustained effort than mere intellectual knowledge can provide. The central problem of our full understanding of the new age paradigm is, says physician Alex Comfort, the problem of "empathy." To quote Comfort:

> By empathy I mean incorporation going beyond intellectual assent. We know the earth is spherical, and many actually have flown around it, but not until astronauts saw it ab extra can its roundness be said to have been empathized. . . . [Hence] empathy has two overlapping aspects: how we feel about the process of making knowledge incorporable affects the content we give to what is incorporable. (Comfort, 1984:xviii.)

Therefore, the development of empathy is for Comfort closely tied to "the proper purpose of metaphysics which is the study of world models. . . . This involves the making of new, and the description of old, world models, and the study of the way such models are formed, with the considerations, mental mechanisms, and other matters which enter into them." (Comfort, 1984:xviii.)

To reiterate Comfort's main message concerning the proper study of world models, we must first begin by consciously realizing that many of the so-called "facts" we use to construct our paradigm are not "facts" at all, but socially constructed shared assumptions, consensus reality, and agendas for research. We adopt these agendas for research through the process of enculturation, that is, cultural amnesia, becoming "hypnotized" by consensus reality and begin acting toward our cultural assumptions as "social facts," which later manifest themselves as social-psychological pressures.

Physician Roger Walsh (1984) discusses the problem of cultural amnesia and its crippling effect upon our psychological growth and understanding in his book *Staying Alive: The Psychology of Human Survival*. In order to free ourselves from the symptoms of cultural amnesia—from our limiting and distorted cultural biases—Walsh suggests the curing process of "de-tribalization." (Walsh, 1984.) Walsh embellished his discussion of de-tribalization during a presentation (1985a) he gave at the 1985 Annual Association for Transpersonal Psychology Conference.

> De-tribalization is the process by which we step outside the distorting beliefs and biases of our own culture and develop perspectivism, the capacity to look at things from other people's point of view. This also requires inner work, some periodic disengagement from the cultural belief system, perhaps some time and reflection, or time in retreat. It is interesting that the historian Arnold Toynbee found the one common characteristic in people who had contributed most to human history was that they withdrew from their culture to go into themselves as deeply as they could to find answers to the existential questions of their time. Once they had done that, they returned to their culture to contribute their understanding. (Walsh, 1985b:6.)

Several examples of such socially constructed "facts" have been presented throughout this article. A resume of these are: the belief in the ether breeze; the belief that the atom is a tiny solar system; the belief that "matter waves" are physical entities; the belief in causally determined individual events; and finally, the assumption that the real empirical world is "out there," whose characteristics are immutable, complete and ready to be observed.

The primary importance of providing these examples, however, does not lie so much within the theories themselves, but in the empathetic understanding, the personal transformation or "quantum leap" that helped to free the pioneers of the modern physics movement from their culturally induced consensus reality, and the resulting revolutionary shift in their conscious perception of the cosmos.

A proliferation of movements resembling the historical revolution that took place in physics during the early part of this century have been going on in the social and behavioral sciences; beginning with the existential-phenomenological movement growing up on European soil, whose development later midwifed the birth of transpersonal psychology and transformational sociology. (See Schroll, 1985; Gilbert, 1985, for a more complete discussion.)

Although the theoretical framework of phenomenology has to a large extent provided the foundation of transpersonal-transformational behavioral science, their methodological approach has become primarily that of the participant observer or ethnomethodological-hermeneutics. Participant observation is the behavioral science application of what I referred to as the act of becoming the shadowgraph performance of familiar life. The act of becoming the shadowgraph performance of familiar life requires the act of measurement and has as its foundation the metaphysical position of emergent phenomenological reality.

Family theorist Patrick McNamara (1985) has suggested the use of participant observation as a method of gaining a more accurate description of the New Christian Right (NCR). McNamara stresses the need to clearly define the methodological presuppositions employed by social and behavioral scientists in an attempt to "analyze the degree to which popular evangelicalism meets cognitive, emotional, and interpersonal needs often unmet in the larger culture or in alternative systems of faith." (Warner, 1978:8; quoted in McNamara, 1985:452.)

This same viewpoint finds support in the work of Darwin L. Thomas and Vern Sommerfeldt, who tell us:

> In addition to making explicit our presuppositions, we see a second benefit accruing from an intellectual milieu surrounding social science analysis characterized by a decline of dogmatism [e.g., the blind acceptance of metaphysical assumptions without empathetic understanding]. We shall call this a reevaluation of the pretense of objectivity. . . . There has been a well-entrenched custom in the social sciences to portray an objective, value-free stance toward the subject matter. . . . However, given our view of scientific knowledge, we suggest that it would be good to move away from the pretense of objectivity, announce our value positions, and present our arguments so they can be more easily evaluated by others. We would then know whether a given analysis was constructed by insiders or outsiders in various religious groupings. (Thomas and Sommerfeldt, 1984:122.)

To sum up, the direction the new age paradigm appears to be taking the social and behavioral sciences is toward a wholistic metaphysics, stressing empathetic rather than strictly intellectual understanding, and toward methods and models that promote a participatory role of the observer in the process of scientific investigation of social-psychological phenomena.

However, despite the participatory ethos of the emerging new age paradigm which underscores emergent phenomenological reality, Wilber suggests the use of caution in a completely uncritical application of this methodological perspective, explaining that:

> For hermeneutics, all religious expressions—indeed all symbolic productions— are to be understood from the inside; verstehenden sociology at its extreme. If you are in the hermeneutical circle, consensual interpretive agreement is validation; if you are outside the circle, you are not allowed a judgment. In neither case can the circle itself be shown to be wrong, or partially wrong, or even just partial. Such theoretical absolutizing of cultural relativity often translates itself, in the field, into exasperation, an exasperation apparently due in some cases, not to incorrect methodological application, but to a more native pre-understanding that not all religious expressions are "true" and that some form of critical appraisal is mandatory. (Wilber, 1983:15.)

Wilber's caution against extreme relativism reflects Walsh's suggestion to develop perspectivism via de-tribalization and Comfort's emphasis on empathetic understanding to help free ourselves from the hypnotic effect of consensus reality. Indeed, only a concentrated effort of questioning, dialogue and sustained reflection will provide the psychological milieu necessary to produce genuine empathetic understanding—leading toward a redefinition of the metaphysical, theoretical and methodological assumptions of the social and behavioral sciences.

Summary

In retrospect, the general notion of this article has been to invoke within the reader a sense of urgency toward the need to begin questioning the metaphysical, theoretical and methodological assumptions—both explicit and implicit—upon which the social and behavioral sciences have been founded. Specifically to focus this process toward a central point, I have discussed the problem of measurement.

We have seen that the new age realization resulting from the development of modern physics is that physics is dealing with shadow-symbols and not

Reality. The result of this profoundly shocking realization has shifted the onto-logical position of physics from attempting to prove or disprove the reality of objective phenomena toward a position of emergent phenomenological reality.

Emergent reality refers to the inseparable relationship between the mani-fold aspects of the world of phenomenological events (the observed) and the symbolic construction of these phenomenological events as they are experi-enced by the observer.

Many new age writers have referred to the adoption of this position as the "death of the spectator"—the termination of the passive observer seated in the audience watching the drama unfold before him. Boldly we have risen from our seat of objectivity in answer to our curtain call, becoming "recast" as actor and director, thus enabling us to see Reality as a divine play, exorcising the shadow-symbols haunting our senses and realizing that these phantoms are creations of our measuring and categorizing cognitive processes.

Indeed this recasting has thrust our ontological view of reality through the epistemological eye of the needle of measurement, weaving the tapestry of emergent reality; whereby the participatory weaving process of emergent phe-nomenological reality has shown us most vividly (if not painfully) that the cosmos cannot be fully comprehended through a single ontological picture (such as realism or idealism). Rather, the cosmos can only be understood and appreciated through overlapping complementary and ofttimes paradoxical worldviews.

Bibliography

Bohm, D. 1971. "On Bohr's Views Concerning the Quantum Theory." *Quantum Theory and Beyond*, T. Bastin, (ed.). London: Cambridge University Press, pp. 33–40.

Bohm, D. 1980. *Wholeness and the Implicate Order*. London: Routledge & Kegan Paul, Ltd.

Bohm, D. 1984. "The Implicate Order: The Holodynamic Model of the Universe." Lecture given at the conference on Science and Mysticism: Exploring the New Realities, at the Harvard Science Center, Harvard University, Cambridge, MA, Sept. 29–30.

Bohm, D. and R. Weber. 1982a. "Nature as Creativity." *ReVision*:5(2), 35–40.

Bohm, D. 1982b. "Morphogenetic Fields and the Implicate Order." *ReVision*:5(2), 41–48.

Briggs, J. and F. D. Peat. 1984. *Looking Glass Universe: The Emerging Science of Wholeness*. New York: Simon & Schuster, Inc.

Capra, F. 1975. *The Tao of Physics*. New York: Bantam Books.

Capra, F. 1983a. *The Turning Point: Science, Society, and the Rising Culture*. New York: Bantam Books.

Capra, F. 1983b. *The Tao of Physics* (updated). Boulder: Shambala Pub.

Capra, F. 1984. "The New Vision of Reality: Toward a Synthesis of Eastern Wisdom and Modern Science." S. Grof (ed.). Albany, NY: State University of New York Press, pp. 135–48.

Comfort, A. 1983. "Sir Thomas Brown's Skull and Schroedinger's Cat." *ReVision*:6(2), 83–88.

Comfort, A. 1984. *Reality and Empathy: Physics, Mind, and Science in the 21st Century*. Albany, NY: State University of New York Press.

Deikman, A. 1982. *The Observing Self. Mysticism and Psychotherapy*. Boston: Beacon Press.

d'Espagnat, B. 1983. *In Search of Reality*. New York: Springer-Verlag.

Ferguson, M. 1980. *The Aquarian Conspiracy: Personal and Social Transformation in the '80's*. Los Angeles: J. P. Tarcher.

Gilbert, C. 1985. "A New Paradigm for Environmental Sociology: Introducing Transformational Sociology." Presented at the Annual Meetings of the Society for the Study of Social Problems, Environmental and Technology Division, in Washington, D.C., August 25, pp. 1–35. (Under publication review.)

Gribbin, J. 1984. *In Search of Schroedinger's Cat: Quantum Physics and Reality*. New York: Bantam Books.

Guillemin, V. 1968. *The Story of Quantum Mechanics*. New York: Charles Scribner's Sons, pp. 218–47.

Harman, W. 1972. "The New Copernican Revolution." *Humanistic Society*, J. F. Glass and J. R. Staude, (eds.). Pacific Palisades, CA: Goodyear Pub. Co., Inc., pp. 99–105.

Heisenberg, W. 1971. *Physics and Beyond*. New York: Harper & Row, Pub.

Jeans, Sir James. 1943. *Physics and Philosophy*. New York: Dover Pub., Inc.

Matson, F. 1972. "The Human Image: Science and the Understanding of Man." *Humanistic Society*, J. F. Glass and J. R. Staude (eds.). Pacific Palisades, CA: Goodyear Pub. Co., Inc., pp. 106–20.

McNamara, P. 1985. "The New Christian Right's View of the Family and Its Social Science Critics: A Study in Differing Presuppositions." *Journal of Marriage and the Family*: May, 449–58.

Pagels, H. R. 1982. *The Cosmic Code: Quantum Physics as the Language of Nature*. New York: Bantam Books.

Pelletier, K. 1978. *Toward a Science of Consciousness*. New York: Delacorte Press.

Roszak, T. n.d. *East Meets West: Alternative Life-styles in California*. British Broadcasting Company, video presentation.

Sallach, D. L. 1976. "The Awakening." Unpublished manuscript. Dept. of Sociology, Washington University, St. Louis, MO.

Schroll, M. A. 1985. "Expanding the Perspectives of Mental Health: The Emergence of Transpersonal Psychology." Presented at the Thirteenth Annual Association for Transpersonal Psychology Conference, Asilomar Conference Center, Pacific Grove, CA, August 4, pp. 1–31. (Under review for publication.)

Schroll, M. A. 1987a. "Scientific Controversies Shaping the Worldview of the 21st Century." In *Reports of the 11th International Wittgenstein Symposium*, P. Weingartner and G. Schurz (eds.). Vienna: Springer-Verlag. In press.

Schroll, M. A. 1987b. Science, Pseudoscience and the Search for the Genuine: The Ontological and Epistemological Foundations of Transpersonal Psychology. (Current work in progress.)

Thomas, D. L. and V. Sommerfeldt. 1984. "Religion, Family, and the Social Sciences: A Time for Dialogue." *Family Perspective*:18(3), 117–25.

Valle, R. S. 1981. "Relativistic Quantum Psychology: A Reconceptualization of What We Thought We Knew." *The Metaphors of Consciousness*, R. S. Valle and R. von Eckartsberg (eds.). New York: Plenum Press, pp. 419–36.

Volquardsen, K. L. and P. C. Potter. 1983. *Rise Up*. Musicians and songwriters, Lincoln, NE.

Walsh, R. 1984. *Staying Alive: The Psychology of Human Survival*. Boulder, CO: Shambala Pub.

Walsh, R. 1985a. "Revisioning Tomorrow: Psychological Understandings for Survival." Delivered at the 1985 Annual Association for Transpersonal Psychology Conference at the Asilomar Conference Center, Pacific Grove, CA. August 3.

Walsh, R. 1985b. "Revisioning Tomorrow: Psychological Understandings for Survival." Association for Transpersonal Psychology Fall Newsletter, pp. 4–6.

Weber, W. 1986. *The Search for Unity. Dialogues with Saints and Sages*. Ed. R. Weber. London: Routledge & Kegan Paul.

Wilber, K. 1983. *A Sociable God: Toward a New Understanding of Religion*. Boulder, CO: Shambala Pub.

Wilber, K. 1984a. "Introduction to the New Science Library." Autumn/Winter Catalog, Boulder, CO: Shambala Pub.

Wilber, K. 1984b. *Quantum Questions: The Mystical Writings of the World's Great Physicists*. Boulder, CO: Shambala Pub. June.

Wolf, F. A. 1981. *Taking the Quantum Leap*. New York: Harper & Row, Inc.

Young, A. 1984. "Are the Foundations of Science Inadequate?" *ReVision*:7(Summer), 97–105.

Zukav, G. 1979. *The Dancing Wu Li Masters. An Overview of the New Physics*. New York: Bantam Books.

17

Families and Religions: An Anthropological Typology

James V. Spickard

Introduction

Religious apologists frequently speak of the important relationship between religion and family life. "The family that prays together stays together" is an oft-cited—though occasionally ridiculed—cultural aphorism. The converse is often conceived to be true as well: strong family structure is supposed to provide an opening to the spiritual life. Despite the historic importance of monastic religion, most Americans believe that religion and traditional family life go together, and are mutually reinforcing.

To cite only a few examples of this cultural assumption:

My local newspaper's "Church Notes" for the week in which I am writing shows that four of the ten or so published sermon topics deal with family issues. This same newspaper quotes state politicians opposing employment protection for gays because "homosexuality goes against both God and family."[1]

James V. Spickard is Research Director at the Cultural Development Institute, and a writer in the social sciences. He received his Ph.D. from Graduate Theological Union, where his dissertation analyzed Mary Douglas's method of relating different belief systems to their social settings. He taught sociology and anthropology for several years at the College of Notre Dame in Belmont, California. His research interests include social influences on religious experience, and relativism in the social sciences.

Howard Ruff, the well-known investment counselor, draws an explicit connection between his Mormon convictions and the centrality of "family values" to his life (Ruff 1983). His financial advice is designed to give the middle class the means to support both family and the church of their choice.

On a more academic note, a chapter entitled something like "The Family in Religious Context" is—or at least used to be—an obligatory part of any introductory text in sociology of religion.[2]

Indeed, the very existence of a conference on "Religion and the Family" implies a connection between religion and family more significant than that between, say, "the Family and Greed" or "Religion and Cheap Sex." Something universal is suggested to us by the first juxtaposition that is lacking in the others.

These are clearly impressionistic data—but that is just the point. The supposed connection between religions and families is an ideological artifact, something that we expect because of our cultural heritage. The significant question, then, is "Does such a connection actually exist?"

This question may be posed in a more sophisticated manner. "How," we may ask, "are religions and families related in each of several cultural milieux?" If, in fact, our cultural ideology proposes that religions and families are mutually supporting (and if in certain segments of our society they *are* supporting) we ought to expect that in other cultures and societies different types of relationships will be culturally expected, and indeed will apply.

We also ought to expect that religion and family will be even more reinforcing for some groups than they are alleged to be among us. For others they will be supportive, but in a completely different mode. And for still others, religion and family will have nothing to do with one another. Such is the cultural variation that anthropology teaches us to anticipate.

An Anthropological Typology

In order to approach this issue we must make use of a typology. We must group together various societies so that their different ways of relating religion and family become apparent. But no purely ad hoc grouping will do, for we hope that the differences discovered here will correlate with cultural differences on other levels. We seek real dividing lines that separate different cultures, and which may prove to illuminate cultural differences within our society as well.

British anthropologist Mary Douglas has spent the last fifteen or so years constructing such a typology—one which relates many elements of culture, including religious belief, to social structure. (Her theory is found in various forms in Douglas, 1970, 1973a, 1973b, 1978, 1982; and Douglas and Wildavsky, 1982. Douglas, 1978 is the key text.)

She calls her system "Grid/Group Analysis" (the name admittedly lacks style). She presents it as a means of sorting various societies and, at the same time, ordering their belief systems. Society and cosmology, she says, vary *together*. Social forms come packaged with beliefs in such a way that "most values and beliefs can be analysed as part of society instead of as a separate cultural sphere" (Douglas, 1982:7). Religion and social structure—for our interests, religion and the kin-system—can be analyzed in one motion. Douglas claims to be able to predict the kind of relation between these two elements from the position a given society takes in her scheme.

Douglas presents several forms of her typology, about which I have written elsewhere (Spickard, 1984). In the typology's most defensible form she distinguishes between three basic kinds of social organization. These she labels "ascribed hierarchy," "individualism," and "factionalism/sectarianism." (Douglas, 1982:4.)

Ascribed hierarchy portrays a social unit in which the group is apparently the focus of all activity, and in which hierarchical roles and prescriptive rules govern almost all behavior. The individual is enmeshed in a net of expectations that govern a great part of his or her behavior. Examples of this social type are the Hindu caste system (in its more rigid manifestations) and medieval monastic Catholicism.

Individualism portrays just the opposite[3] kind of social system: one in which individuals and individual activity are the focus of social life, and in which there are few or no specified roles and rules to which the individual must conform. Here the basis of social life is the individual-centered network rather than the group. Within this social type, individuals choose their own companions, negotiate the terms of their interactions with one another, and compete for the possession of whatever their society values.

"Factional/sectarian" societies are somewhat different, possessing both an extreme attachment to group life and a lack of the internal role differentiation that might make that life go smoothly. Individuals lack guidelines on how to regulate their behavior—a situation which Douglas claims produces conflict and competition among them. But competition is neither allowed overt expression (as among the individualists), nor is it forced into socially sanctioned channels (as among the hierarchists). The result is covert conflict, which periodically erupts into social strife. Douglas's examples include central African witchcraft movements (she did her fieldwork among the Lele of Zaire) and, interestingly, academic departments. She remarks that the latter, with their developed consciousness of the boundaries between their own and other academic disciplines, and with their putative (but not actual) internal egalitarianism, are prime social grounds for covert infighting and periodic "witchhunts." (1973a:168–69.)

Each of these social types, Douglas argues, exhibits a distinctive cosmology—ofttimes religious—that proves functional to the conduct of its life. Different types of society typically encounter differing organizational problems, which their cosmologies may mediate or even solve. (Douglas and Wildavsky, 1982.)

Hierarchical organizations, for example, suffer from the difficulty of getting many people with differing skills and interests to agree on any undertaking, even on living together for great lengths of time. To counter this, the hierarchist's cosmology will emphasize the group above the individual and will promote multiple goals, thus satisfying everyone enough to keep the group going. Nepalese Hindu polytheism, as we shall soon see, conforms to this model.

Individualism, on the other hand, suffers from an inability to see long-term projects through to completion, and from an inability to weigh the long-term or cumulative effects of individual actions. This is counteracted—though at the same time sustained—by a cosmology that sees universal, impersonal forces regulating the effects of individual decisions for the benefit of all. The "invisible hand" of free-market economists is the most famous example, though the extent to which this hand actually helps solve the individualist's organizational problems is very much in doubt. Nepalese Buddhist conceptions of merit, which I shall examine later, do a better job.

The way beliefs arise from and affect "factional/sectarian" societies is more complicated, and is best considered in conjunction with my example of the Coast Miwok, below.

I shall first illustrate Douglas's typology by describing the relationship between religion and family in three non-Western societies.[4] Then I shall use it to examine some of the recent religious developments in North America. For both endeavors we shall have to free ourselves from any too-limited definition of religion, and indeed from any too-American definition of family. Instead, we must frame our analysis in terms of wider kin relations and the general shape of relations with the spiritual world.

Nepalese Hindus

Nepalese Hindu culture, as studied by Haimendorf (1979), Hitchcock (1966) and others, generally corresponds to Douglas's hierarchical model.

Castes are a dominant attribute of Nepalese Hindu life. Though in India castes include a multitude of people not directly related to one another, in a Nepal village caste is a more kin-like institution. A given caste (such as the Chetri or Magars) regards itself as having entered the area at a particular point in history from a given location, and is made up of a specified number of lineages, each with a corporate organization. Caste, lineage, and family form a hierarchical nesting of family or family-like ties.

Hierarchy also dominates intercaste relations, though the prohibitions against intercaste contact are less among Nepalese than they are among Hindus of India (Hitchcock, 1966:chapter 7). Various types of Brahmans rank above other "twice-born" castes, who in turn are ritually superior to Magars, Ghartis, Metalworkers, Leatherworkers, Tailors, and so on. The specific castes vary from place to place, but in every case different castes exhibit differing— and hierarchically graded—behavior and styles of life. Deference to those of a higher caste is an enforced norm.

These kin-centered people see conformity as a moral ideal. In Nepalese caste society, Haimendorf notes, the individual is not an independent agent but belongs to a tightly organized community, and must constantly act for that community's welfare. For example, the Chetris, a high-caste group, pre-occupy themselves with caste rules, striving always to avoid pollution and to maintain their ritual status. "Their ideal is the man who lives strictly according to the rules of his caste and never undertakes any action which endangers the purity of his status or arouses unfavorable comment among his caste-fellows." (Haimendorf, 1979:169.)

This tight caste organization is paralleled in family life by a developed patriarchalism. Fathers retain authority even over their grown and married sons, and women are subject to the authority of men throughout their lives, first fathers, then husbands. To dishonor one's family is the chief sin; to honor it requires obedience in all things.

Ritual pollution incurred by the living, for example, can even affect the status of one's departed ancestors. Were a man to marry a woman who had been previously betrothed, his kinsmen who have already reached heaven might have to leave it and descend to hell. (Haimendorf, 1979:173.) One can scarcely imagine a greater stimulus to conformity.

But this corporate concern stops at a group's boundaries. Other than intercaste deference, it simply does not matter to Nepalese Hindus what the members of other families and other groups do. Hinduism, says Haimendorf, does not present a single moral law to which obedience is required of all persons, as do Western religions.

Hindu society generally, says Haimendorf, is dominated by a notion of ethical relativity. Action appropriate to one caste or group is inappropriate to another. Aside from responsibility for the behavior of one's kin and caste-fellows, one is not concerned with the activities of others; one's responsibility is focused on one's own people.

Likewise, Hinduism allows different groups to have different gods, goddesses, and godlings to whom they pay homage in various ways. Hitchcock (1966:chapter 3) details the numerous and changing deities of the Magars, a mid-level caste, and notes that many are specific to particular locations, particular lineages, and even particular households. Religion is family-centered, and as people respond to the demands of their own family and not others, so they respond to their own family's gods. The spiritual world is fragmented much like the social. Gods, like people, possess a hierarchy, and their behavior may be influenced differently depending on their godly social position.

Douglas's theory roughly predicts this parallel between social and cosmological structure, at least for hierarchically organized societies. And because the chief problem of this kind of society is how to let many different kinds of people live in relative peace together, a mutual tolerance in the moral sphere and a fragmentation of deities in the religious realm both make good organizational sense. Peace is maintained by recognizing that different people have different goals and must meet different (supernatural) demands.

At the same time, the Nepalese agricultural situation requires a strong kin and lineage system. Nepalese cultivators exploit a limited amount of arable land, and need strict rules to prevent either the fragmentation of that land into unfarmable plots or its concentration into only a few hands. A strong family keeps land ownership stable, so that subsistence can be maintained. Pollution beliefs emphasize the group and draw tight boundaries between groups that might compete for similar resources. Though caste hierarchy divides labor, it turns much of the potential competitiveness of these groups into reciprocal interdependence.

This interdependence becomes symbolized in the religious sphere. As Hitchcock (1966:34) remarks, "the gustatory godlings are emblems of two ideas: the idea of reciprocity and the idea of scarcity. . . . [and] express the inevitable ambiguities of [the Magar] situation." Supporting this analysis is the fact that taboos on intercaste contact are less developed in areas where there is less pressure on the land. There the necessity of group solidarity vis-à-vis outsiders is not so great (pp. 41–42).

In sum, for Nepalese Hindus religion and family go together, but not as our culture expects: within each caste and lineage we find great conformity, but great toleration of other groups' gods and other ways of living. In this hierarchical society, religious notions parallel kin relations. Social unity is maintained through diversity.

Buddhist Sherpas

The situation is quite different among Nepalese Buddhists, especially the Sherpas studied by Haimendorf and by Michael Thompson.[5] The sense of corporate kinship so central to Hindu society is generally lacking. A kin-system clearly exists, but individual families are relatively independent of wider kin obligations. Haimendorf (1964:39) argues that this is a consequence of the Sherpa economy: migratory herding rewards self-reliance and discourages stringent kinship obligations.

Though Sherpas have loose clan affiliations, and there are some rudimentary caste-like distinctions, these by no means approach the hierarchism of the settled Hindu populations. Instead, they approximate the American discrimination against those "from the wrong side of the tracks." Sherpas possess what Haimendorf calls an "open society" in which individual initiative is more important than family position. Group boundaries are generally low, and generations of immigrants have been able to make themselves a place.

While every society must find itself a means of social control, Sherpa society has made that control less onerous than many: it is basically egalitarian, and whatever authority exists is vested in the totality of its inhabitants. This authority is delegated to elected officials whose privileges are strictly defined.

Much activity falls outside of their scope and is unregulated. (Haimendorf, 1979:182.)

Unlike Hindu villages, Sherpa villages lack corporate councils for dispute resolution. Instead, every village has one or two men who are skilled in mediation. These men neither hold office nor possess any authority over others, but attempt to defuse conflict by meeting with the quarrelers—usually over beer—and seeking agreement. "The peace-maker gains social esteem and religious merit, but does not get any material reward for his efforts and the expenditure he has incurred" (Haimendorf, 1964:182).

Families, too are independent. As soon as a couple marries, it establishes its own household (to which, as is well known, a second husband may later be added). The family's economy is independent of others', though there is some unorganized sharing for the benefit of the poor. Because of the altitude, the growing season is short, and a family must engage in other activities to make ends meet. Usually this involves trading—either bringing goods up from the lowlands or bringing goods across the Himalayas from Tibet (though this latter opportunity is now closed). Lately it has involved work for mountaineers—an occupation that requires the same self-reliance and ability to be gone from home for long periods that trading previously demanded. (Thompson, 1982.) Families must often make do with absent men—a factor which has probably contributed to the acceptability of polyandrous marriage among these people.

Compared to Hindus, kin-group control over the individual is extremely low. While Hindu marriages are arranged and relations between the sexes are severely regulated, Sherpas decide their own marital fates and casual sex prior to marriage is the norm. And considering the fact that a girl's amorous liaisons take place in the same room where her parents are sleeping, a blind eye and a deaf ear to others' behavior must be culturally valued. Parents are not authoritarian; in fact Haimendorf lists one of their chief sins as being "to threaten children or make them cry . . . whatever the reason" (1979:187).

But there are areas of life where collective activity is necessary, though extremely difficult for an individualist society to carry off. Mountain travel depends on a network of trails and bridges, which demand constant upkeep; yet there are no public organizations which make it their business to perform this work. Nuclear families are certainly not up to the task, and communal work cannot be compelled by any wider group.

Here the Sherpas' Buddhism has its effect. The Sherpas' moral system is based on the belief that every act of virtue adds to an individual's store of merit, whereas every morally negative action or sin diminishes this valuable commodity. They place special emphasis on meritorious activities which benefit the general public and even complete strangers. This demonstrates one's total selflessness, for one's efforts will not benefit one's kin and friends more than others. Providing for the construction of bridges, the maintenance of trails and so on, as well as the sponsorship of religious and secular festivals, provide scores of good marks for anyone interested in improving their chances in the afterlife. Economic surplus is expended not only in the support of religious institutions (and the manufacturers of the famous prayer-wheels), but also in the provision of secular good works. (Haimendorf, 1979:182ff.) After death a person's good and bad deeds are counted up, and the balance of good or bad marks determine a man's fate.

Sherpas do not believe their deities punish them or demand sacrifices of them. They see serving the deities as a possible source of merit, but not the only source available. Their concept of sin centers on infringements upon the dignity of persons or animals rather than on offenses to gods. Sins against persons will weigh most against them at the end of their lives—though to the extent that spirits are persons, they deserve good treatment too. The model of ideal action vis-à-vis others is extended to the gods rather than the other way around. Ethics lie at the center of religious life.

Unlike Hindus, who spend a great deal of time trying to placate spirits, Sherpas' notions of the highest powers in life are almost mechanical. Merit is a calculable substance, attainable through specified and commonly known channels. Sin—or demerit—is calculable as well, and is something that is almost unavoidable in the course of day-to-day existence. So the goal of life is to accumulate enough merit (while avoiding enough demerit) to help one later on.

Clearly, on Douglas's terms, this cosmology is functional to the Sherpa social organization. The society is individualistic, probably as a response to a difficult ecological situation, and as a result is unable to carry out certain civic activities necessary for its survival. So, the religious orientation of the people—likewise individualistic—provides the means by which these activities can be carried out. Through religion the weaknesses of the social sphere are overcome.

But this religion is not family-centered, and individuals are on their own vis-à-vis the supernatural world. Douglas's schema predicts this individualism, because, in her view, cosmology reflects social life. Contrary to our own cultural stereotype, a weak family structure does not mean a weak religion—just a different one.

Coast Miwok Sorcery

Our third case, as promised, is more complex. The Coast Miwok Indians of central California were a settled village people exploiting a relatively rich environment.[6] Their location just to the north of San Francisco Bay (prior to the Spanish conquest) gave them access to acorns, shellfish, waterfowl, roots, deer, rabbits, buckeyes, and other foodstuffs in relative abundance. They were organized into tightly bounded exogamous lineages which "owned" these resources, each family group (*lineage* and *family* being synonyms for these people) holding gathering rights to certain tracts for each of the major resources. There were no interlineage work groups and no village-wide institutions for the redistribution of surplus. Most of the time they did not need any. Each extended family was self-sufficient, and, in general, lived well in a relatively stable environment.

Residents of rural California, however, know something about this purported "stability." The mountains in which the Miwok lived are dominated by a series of micro-climates. Weather in this area varies considerably from year to year, and the variation from valley to valley and hillside to hillside is even greater.

This variation had a particularly important impact on the acorn crop—the staple of the California Indian diet. While in a given year the oaks owned by one lineage might bear prolifically, those owned by another might prove barren. The same was true of buckeyes and seeds—the replacement staples. Hunting with the small bows available at the time was notoriously difficult, and this left shellfish as the sole more-or-less dependable resource. And if the members of a given lineage became sick and unable to gather, their ability to feed themselves was in jeopardy.

Of course, common sense suggests that if one family's resources failed, that family should be able to get help from others. In south-central California, for example, the village headman functioned as a center for redistribution—in other words, taxing the rich to give to the poor. But this was not the Miwok headman's role. Though some redistribution did occur, it was not so regularly institutionalized as elsewhere. Instead, because the boundaries between lineages and those between villages were so great, cooperation across them was next to impossible. So, for those whose resources had failed, all that kept them going was their savings from the past and the fact that the next year the resources would succeed—while some other lineage would get the short end of the stick.

To see what happened in this situation, we need only enter into the mental framework of the Miwok and see the universe from their point of view. The Miwoks knew nothing of science, had no conception of natural causality, and in particular could not explain why one oak grove would bear in a given year and another would not. It would have been one thing if all families' resources had failed, but they did not. Only a few did so, and only a few were struck by disease, while others had plenty to eat and were healthy. Their reasoning was sensible: mystical effects must come from mystical causes. Obviously, they thought, if one family is fat while another is starving, then a sorcerer must be at work.

Sorcery fears were rife among the Miwok and their neighbors. Sorcerers never came from one's own lineage (in pre-contact times), but from the lineages of one's enemies. One had always to be on guard against them—much as today we are on guard against reckless drivers when we cross a busy street. If one were to let a bit of one's hair, one's nail parings, one's feces, or the like fall into the hands of a sorcerer, then one would be in grave danger. These very substances—boundaries of the body, symbolically speaking—could be used to penetrate a person's own bodily boundaries, and cause one to sicken and die.

I do not want to detail Miwok sorcery beliefs, for they are not at issue here.[7] My point is that Miwok cosmology, as best I have been able to reconstruct it, involved a perception of mystical danger to members of families—both at the hands of other families and from usually neutral (though sometimes maleficent) spirits. It is not quite correct to say that the Miwoks had a religious pantheon, for the only beings equivalent to gods were active at the beginning of and the renewal of the world, and, furthermore, these gods did not take an interest in people's day-to-day affairs. The entry of the supernatural into the human realm took place at the time of misfortune, and usually wore human robes.

This cosmology was a product and a reflection of a particular kind of family structure—one in which kin groups did not cooperate with one another. On the one hand, the relatively rich environment made this lack of cooperation possible (had the environment been less rich the innate selfishness of the system could never have prevailed); on the other hand, that same environment's occasional failures presented a practical problem that demanded solution. The cosmology that resulted both explained environmental failures and expressed the underlying social hostilities in a particularly direct way.

Given all this tension, one might ask how such a society survived with any stability for over a thousand years. How were lineages—being exogamous—able to reproduce, given a generalized uncooperativeness periodically erupting into hostility? One answer is that the level of inter-lineage tension was not always high; though the environment was not stable enough for sorcery fears ever to dissipate entirely, resource-failure was not a yearly recurrence. In addition, by trading women (and men) repeatedly, specific lineages became informal marriage providers. Until a child was born to a couple, the in-marrying partner was looked upon with some suspicion, but after the birth of one or two children, the spouse as well as his or her lineage was regarded as relatively safe. This tended to focus sorcery fears away from certain lineages and toward others, and provided a path for material assistance to flow in time of need.

Just as important, however, was a third option: expulsion. Because certain lineages developed such bad reputations for sorcery over a long period of time, and were so cut off from their neighbors, the neighbors would expel them from the village. Although the records I consulted revealed that this was a rare occurrence, it was, nevertheless, possible, and therefore could defuse a particularly volatile situation.

Like Nepalese Hindus and Sherpas, the Miwoks' cosmology reflects their family structure. Trapped in tightly bounded lineages that lacked interfamily ties, they saw anything outside themselves as threatening. The typical response to such threat was to draw closer to those one could trust, exacerbating the family's isolation. Society and cosmology reinforced one another, and were themselves reinforced by an environment that failed at random—lending credence to the perceived supernatural menace.

Unlike the Hindus and Sherpas, however, Miwok cosmology did not solve their social problems. Though one would expect social isolation to be overcome by sharing, sorcery fears stood in the way. Family-centeredness in this faction-ridden society did not promote tolerance, but aggression. Had their environment failed more frequently, it is doubtful that their society could have survived.

North American Parallels

I have summarized the foregoing in Table 1 which lists the primary attributes of each of the three social types in Douglas's model, along with the religious cosmologies that accompany them and some suggested examples. Her basic principles—that cosmology reflects social structure, and often proves functional to its continuance—should be clear.

Unfortunately, I cannot take up these examples here in any greater detail. Instead, without pushing things too far, I would like to point out some possible North American parallels—religious groups on which Douglas's typology might just shed some light.

Douglas asks us to look for a set of social relations that may be correlated with a religious cosmology. Since ours is a complex society, we would expect to find all three of her social types present in it.

Although we do not find hierarchies on the Hindu scale among us, some parts of our society are clearly more hierarchical than others. For example, the so-called "Eastern Establishment"—the wealthier, old-line, New England-centered denominations—is perhaps the closest thing to hierarchism left in this nation. It is in this Establishment, I expect, that we can find the tolerant, family-centered religions that best approximate the Hindu model. (The term *Boston Brahmin* becomes culturally interesting here.)

In this subculture there is considerable church-going as a family activity. But with this habit is an attitude that considers the actual content of religious devotion (within a certain range) less important than its mere existence. Religion is seen as a private, family matter, and excessive preoccupation with things spiritual is not well regarded. That is, some religiousness is expected from all, but it should not take over all of one's life and certainly should not create barriers between people.

Though I did grow up with people like this, and have certainly met many of them in my adult life, I am not sure to what extent such a subculture still exists in America. The shifts in political and social power in the last few decades (see Bensman and Vidich, 1971) lead me to believe that this group is certainly much less influential than it once was, and is not the wave of the future for

TABLE 1. COSMOLOGY AND FAMILY STRUCTURE

	Family Type		
	Hierarchical	Individualist	Factional/Sectarian

Social attributes	Group-centered
	Internal ranks/many
	  linked groups
	Fixed roles
	Inequality
		Person-centered
		  networks
		
		Flexible roles
		Equality
			Group-centered
			High group
			  boundaries
			(Role rigidity varies)
			Internal equality

Chief social problem	How to stay together	How to do common tasks	Keeping group unity

Religious attributes	Polytheism
	In-group
	  conformity/out-
	  group tolerance
	Group defines
	  doctrine
	Rituals central
		Pluralism
		Tolerance
		
		Individual defines
		  doctrine
		Ethics central
			In-group monotheism
			Bigotry
			
			Group defines
			  doctrine
			Group membership
			  central

Cosmology's
structure
	Parallels society
	  (hierarchical)
		Parallels society
		  (individualist)
			Parallels society
			  (emphasizes
			  boundaries)

Cosmology's function	Helps accept group
	  differences
	Aids division of labor
		Frees individual
		Aids tolerance
		Aids public works
		Encourages charity
			Defines the group
			  against others

Examples	Nepalese Hindus
	
	Establishment
		Nepalese Buddhists
		  (Sherpas)
		"New-Age" religions
			Coast Miwok
			
			Fundamentalists/
			  Sectarians

American religion. But as a theorist rather than a church sociologist, I will leave it to others to check out my suppositions.

I suspect the other two types will be of greater future importance.

While the factionalism of the Miwok does not have a complete American parallel, on the so-called "Religious Right" there is both a clear concern for family issues, along with an intolerance for alternative points of view that clearly does not fit with either the Hindu or the Buddhist models. While I would not be as willing as Douglas to identify all religious sectarians with the factional social type,[8] there is some truth to this association. Certainly if one looks at the proliferation of fundamentalist groups over the last century or so of American history, the combination of religious and social conservatism with a desire for factional purity stands out (Marsden, 1980).

The standard sociological description of the supporters of this religious right portrays them as being left out of the dominant cultural and economic developments of recent years.[9] Urban sophistication, lax upper-middle-class morality, the lack of patriotism and traditional values perceived among the educated and the jet-set—all these are focal points for political resentment that wears a religious mask. Like the Miwok, the members of these classes, so the explanation goes, act out their social frustrations in a religious idiom, and a particularly intolerant one.

The key here is the moral distinction made between "them" and "us"—a division that is also found among certain of the "new religions" such as the Unification Church or the People's Temple. On Douglas's theory the high external barriers erected by these groups go hand in hand with a dualistic cosmology which serves to reinforce group identity—that is, to maintain the very barriers which make the group unique. Of course these barriers also isolate the group, encouraging social conflict—as in the Miwok case.

Most important is a religious dualism paralleling the social. Unlike the Establishment, sectarians emphasize the cosmic struggle between Good and Evil. The key question, both religious and political, is "Whose side are you on?" Only one answer is allowed. "Family," "traditional values," and so on have become code words for in-group membership. The modern religious right seeks to recast all of society in its image.

What is the future of this intolerant sectarianism? Secularization theory sees it as a response to modernity, and believes that as we become used to our new way of life, fundamentalism will fade away. On Douglas's model we would disagree. Her theory predicts that any time a society becomes factionalized such aggressive, dualist cosmologies will emerge.

But not all of the new religious sectarians are rightist, or even Christians. Much of America's new spirituality has affinities with the eastern religions, and "new-age" sects seemingly spring up everywhere. Even the mainline denominations have altered much of their ministry from traditional families to youth work, urban outreach, and so on. Ministry by women, "marriages" of homosexuals, Zen in the chancel—many of the trends that the religious right-wing abhors are an ever-expanding part of the American scene.

Rather than moralize, Douglas's theory would have us look to the social relations that support this change. I think we can find a parallel to the Sherpa case here.

Economically speaking, the family is much less important to survival in America than it once was. With the decline of family-centered enterprises, including farming, the rise of salaried employment, and particularly the growth of national firms at the expense of local businesses (and the resulting necessity of job mobility), the maintenance of a family has become a luxury that some cannot afford. At the same time, cheap and effective means of birth control free those who want sex but not children from the necessity of having a spouse as well. Like the Sherpas, economic mobility and easy sexuality go hand in hand with both a restriction on the importance of kin ties, and with an individualization of religion. The relationship between a person and the spiritual world can now be a matter of the individual heart.

Theologically, these individuals see God, life, or some other all-encompassing end as something to be actively sought, not passively awaited. Thus the growth of various kinds of meditation, the popularity of the ecstatic experience of the divine among both Catholics and Protestants, the resurgence of liberal Quakerism as a religion of experiencing—all are indications of a cultural move toward individualism in religious life.

But as in the Sherpa case, with the decline of the family, all is not sin and degradation. As Buddhism is for the Sherpas a religion of ethics, and one which is functional to the wider social situation, so ethics are at the center of this new religious development. "Do your own thing" goes hand in hand with "do unto others . . . " Social philanthropy is alive and well, and the church's outreach to those traditionally excluded from its life does much to alleviate the condition of the casualties of modern living.

Individualism in religion, and the centrality of both ethics and an active spiritual striving both seem to me to be correlated with a society in which, at least for major sectors of the population, extended and even nuclear families have become economically irrelevant, and even difficult to maintain. The decline of the group and the increasing autonomy of the individual, while causing great psychological strains, place both the burden of the pursuit of social justice and the pursuit of God—key elements of our Judeo-Christian heritage—squarely on the individual's shoulders. Thus, it is up to the individual—not the family or the church—to carry this burden. And if individual experience becomes the touchstone of spirituality, the proliferation of paths that these individuals take in their spiritual pursuits will probably continue.

If the foregoing is valid and if current socioeconomic trends continue, Douglas's theory predicts that American religion will become more individualized, more tolerant of disparate religious paths, and even more concerned with ethical action toward others.[10]

I must admit, however, that I find it disturbing to be able to explain by sociological means the kind of spirituality toward which I am most drawn, and which I see as being the most appropriate path toward an appreciation of Deity.[11]

Notes

1. *Watsonville Register-Pajaronian*, February 11 and 16, 1984.

2. For example: Benson (1960), Hoult (1958).

3. Declaring that "individualism" and "ascribed hierarchy" are opposites betrays a peculiarly Western cultural bias of which Douglas seems to be unaware. This is the source of one of my criticisms of her theory (Spickard, 1984:chapter 15), but it does not vitiate my use of her typology for the quite limited purposes of this essay.

4. Michael Thompson, in an unpublished paper written for the International Institute for Applied Systems Analysis of Laxenburg, Austria, suggests the applicability of Douglas's types to Nepalese Hindus and Buddhists, though he puts her typology to very different use than do I. (He discusses their differing attitudes to risk [Thompson, 1983].) The application of Douglas's work to the Coast Miwok is my own (Spickard, 1974).

5. Haimendorf (1964, 1975, 1979); Thompson (1982). Cf. Peissal (1979).

6. See Spickard, 1987, for sources for and an extended discussion of the following.

7. The symbolism of these beliefs first interested me in Douglas's theories (Spickard, 1974).

8. Comments to this effect may be found in Douglas (1970, 1973a, 1982) and in unpublished remarks made before the 1983 convention of the American Academy of Religion in Dallas.

9. See Bensman and Vidich (1971:148ff). For other views see Marsden (1983) and Anthony and Robbins (1983).

10. Anthony and Robbins (1983) argue that only one trend among the "new religions" moves in this direction. The other trend, typified by such groups as the Unification Church and the People's Temple, moves in their eyes toward a reestablishment of a "civil religion," but in sectarian terms (see Bellah, 1967, 1975). On Douglas's model, the manichaean worldview of these groups seems more akin to right-wing fundamentalism than to the old-style civil religion of which Bellah speaks.

11. This essay was written for the Twelfth Annual Family and Demographic Research Institute Conference on Religion and the Family, held at Brigham Young University in February, 1984. I am indebted to John Sorenson of the Anthropology Department at Brigham Young University for comments and criticism.

Bibliography

Anthony, D. and T. Robbins. 1983. "Spiritual Innovation and the Crisis of American Civil Religion." In M. Douglas and S. M. Tipton (eds.) *Religion and America: Spirituality in a Secular Age*, pp. 229–48. Boston: Beacon Press.

Bellah, R. N. 1970. "Civil Religion in America." *Daedalus*, 1967. Reprinted in *Beyond Belief*, pp. 168–89. New York: Harper & Row.

Bellah, R. N. 1975. *The Broken Covenant*. New York: Seabury Press.

Bensman, J. and A. J. Vidich. 1971. *The New American Society: The Revolution of the Middle Class*. Chicago: Quadrangle Books.

Benson, P. H. 1960. *Religion in Contemporary Culture: A Study of Religion Through Social Science*. New York: Harper & Brothers.

Douglas, M. and A. Wildavsky. 1982. *Risk and Culture: An Essay on the Selection of Technical and Environmental Dangers*. Berkeley: University of California Press.

Douglas, M. 1970. *Natural Symbols: Explorations in Cosmology*. London: Barrie & Rockliff. Simultaneously New York: Pantheon (1st American edition).

Douglas, M. 1973a. *Natural Symbols*, 2nd revised edition. London: Barrie & Jenkins. Simultaneously New York: Vintage Books/Random House.

Douglas, M. 1973b. "Self-Evidence." The 1972 Henry Myers Lecture. *Proceedings of the Royal Anthropological Institute*, 1973:27–44. Reprinted in *Implicit Meanings: Essays in Anthropology* by M. Douglas, pp. 276–318. London: Routledge & Kegan Paul, 1975.

Douglas, M. 1978. *Cultural Bias*. London: Royal Anthropological Institute. Reprinted in *In the Active Voice*, by M. Douglas, pp. 183–254. London: Routledge & Kegan Paul.

Douglas, M. (editor). 1982. *Essays in the Sociology of Perception*. London: Routledge & Kegan Paul.

Haimendorf, C. F. 1964. *The Sherpas of Nepal*. Berkeley: University of California Press.

Haimendorf, C. F. 1975. *Himalayan Traders*. London: John Murray.

Haimendorf, C. F. 1979. *South Asian Societies: A Study of Values and Social Controls*. New Delhi: Sterling Publishers Pvt. Ltd. Originally published as *Morals and Merit*. London: Weidenfeld & Nicolson, 1966.

Hitchcock, J. T. 1966. *The Magars of Banyan Hill*. New York: Holt, Rinehart and Winston.

Hoult, T. F. 1958. *The Sociology of Religion*. New York: The Dryden Press, Publishers.

Marsden, G. M. 1980. *Fundamentalism and American Culture: The Shaping of Twentieth-Century Evangelicalism: 1870–1925*. New York: Oxford University Press.

Marsden, G. M. 1983. "Preachers of Paradox: The Religious New Right in Historical Perspective." In M. Douglas and S. M. Tipton (eds.), *Religion and America: Spirituality in a Secular Age*, pp. 150–68. Boston: Beacon Press.

Peissal, M. 1979. *Zanskar: The Hidden Kingdom*. New York: E. P. Dutton.

Ruff, H. J. 1983. *Middle Class Financial Survival*. Pleasanton, CA: Target Publishers.

Spickard, J. V. 1974. "Coast Miwok Witchcraft Symbolism." Unpublished manuscript.

Spickard, J. V. 1984. "Relativism and Cultural Comparison in the Anthropology of Mary Douglas: An Evaluation of the Meta-Theoretical Strategy of Her 'Grid/Group' Theory." Ph.D. dissertation, Graduate Theological Union, Berkeley, CA.

Spickard, J. V. 1987. "Environmental Variation and the Plausibility of Religion: A California Indian Example." *Journal for the Scientific Study of Religion*, 26/4.

Thompson, M. 1982. "The Problem of the Centre: an Autonomous Cosmology." In M. Douglas (ed.), *Essays in the Sociology of Perception*, pp. 302–27. London: Routledge & Kegan Paul.

Thompson, M. 1983. "Institutionalized Styles and Political Regimes." Unpublished paper prepared for the International Institute of Applied Analysis, Laxenburg, Austria.

18

Types of Religious Values and Family Cultures

Horst J. Helle

The Problem

One of the basic premises of this paper is that the number of different family cultures is limited. While on the *micro* level of social psychology *individual* preferences tend to lead to an infinitely large variety of family styles, I shall assume only *four* stable family cultures to exist on the *macro* level. Those four culture types are theoretically constructed according to Max Weber's methodology of ideal types. For the sake of brevity I will call them, H, M, F, and P culture respectively. In our typology H stands for HUNTER, M for MOTHER, F for FATHER, P for PARENT. Table 1 presents the basic typology.

After dealing first with the four types of religious value systems, we will look at sexual norms (including different forms of the incest taboo and varied mating rules and forms of marriage among the four different cultures), and, finally, comparative types of kinship organization.

Horst J. Helle is Professor of Sociology, Ludwig-Maximilians University, Munich, West Germany. Previous professorships include RWTH Aachen, Germany, and University of Vienna, Austria. He was visiting professor in Leuven, Belgium; in Calgary, Alberta, Canada; and in Zurich, Switzerland. His research focuses on Georg Simmel, sociology of religion, and family sociology.

TABLE 1. TYPOLOGY OF FAMILY CULTURES

	HUNTER	MOTHER	FATHER	PARENT
Religious value system defining the origin and sustaining source of life	animal deity	female deity: fertility goddess	male deity: fertility god	Christian dogma: trinity plus virgin mother
Sexual norms and mating rules, forms of marriage	male bands exchange each other's 'sisters'	individual males 'borrow' each other's sisters	female chastity as basis for fatherhood	monogamy: marriage means merging two clans into one
Organization of kinship solidarity: what makes us relatives?	to eat from one animal body: local group and allies	to descend from one common mother (lineage)	to descend from one common father (lineage)	to descend from one married couple: nuclear family!

This paper shows how these three levels of analysis interlink, and what this theoretical scheme, if applied in empirical research on the family in modern industrial society can explain as a heuristic tool.

Religious Value Systems

Methodology

Orienting family and sexual behavior toward collectively held values causes a large proportion of modern confusion and anxiety; the confusion can be attributed to the difficulty people have in recognizing which separate values match into one consistent set and which ones are incompatible. Therefore, I present different types of values as coherent sets in a developmental perspective, assuming that older forms were superseded by and integrated into more recent forms. According to Bakan, "there is at least heuristic value in thinking about development as taking place in stages. Each stage in a developmental sequence is the aim of earlier stages and the precondition of subsequent stages. Moreover, earlier stages in a developmental sequence never disappear entirely but continue to exist, at least in some form." (D. Bakan, 1979:25.)

Each stage that can be shown to embody other, presumably earlier, stages is comparatively complex. Thus the various types of value orientation can be described and evaluated according to their respective levels of complexity. To better understand the stability of such sets of values and their relationship to innerworldly experiences, future empirical research can be designed.

H Religion: The Animal-Deity

The least complex level of human religion focuses on the animals man needed to hunt and kill for his own survival. There is reason to assume that humans developed their "role-taking" skills enough to include the animal species they needed as meat. If the animal (as an alter ego) would not let itself be hunted and eaten, human beings would die from starvation. Man therefore correctly viewed the animal as the source of life, and his earliest concept of a deity took the image of an animal. This deity was either the animal that served as food or the predator that was admired and often feared for its superior hunting ability. Thus hunters like the lion and the eagle could become deities as well as the mammoth, the bear, and the buffalo whose flesh became food. Walter Burkert in his remarkable contribution to the history of religion, has shown that relics from hunting culture can be traced as far as the sacrificial rites of early ancient Greece (W. Burkert, 1972).

M Religion: The Female Deity

Embedded in the most recent layers of the paleolithicum, archeologists have found figurines that are apparently indications of religious attention focused on female fertility. These prehistoric Venus statues have been discovered in Eastern Europe "only inside of residential structures. . . . From that we gain the insight, that, consequently, only those tribes of the recent paleolithicum, who had become sedentary to a high degree, had figurines of women. Throughout the vast territory of the Venus figurines the stationary hunting culture can be ascertained." (F. Hancar, 1939:40–148, translation mine.)

By transforming the image of the life-giving deity from an animal to a female human being, mankind shifted toward a stable new feature of its culture. This change of religious worldview reflects a change in life-maintenance: In migratory hunting the central source of survival is the animal; life depends on whether it permits itself to be killed by the hunters. In late sedentary hunting, and certainly in the agrarian cultures, survival of the tribe depends on the fertility of its mothers. These dramatic changes cannot possibly be explained only in terms of material living conditions. Rather, they result as well from the evolution of both new forms of religious values and new forms of family life. The concept of the mother-goddess gives divine authority to child-care as well as to fertility. And since these early cultures have no notion of fatherhood it is left entirely to the women to be fertile in the sense of having offspring.

The continuity of the mother-goddess religion reaches as far as Old Testament times. About Abraham, who later was to become a symbol of fatherhood, the Bible tells us: "When he was about to enter Egypt, he said to his wife Sarai: 'I know well how beautiful a woman you are. When the Egyptians see you, they will say: She is his wife! Then they will kill me, but let you live. Please say, therefore, that you are my sister, so that it may go well with me on your account and my life will be spared for your sake.' When Abraham came to Egypt, the Egyptians saw how beautiful a woman she was; and when Pharaoh's courtiers saw her, they praised her to Pharaoh. So she was taken into Pharaoh's palace. On her account it went well with Abram, and he received flocks and herds, male and female slaves, male and female asses, and camels." (Genesis 12:11–16.)

This remarkable quotation could be dismissed with the comment that in an extreme emergency it would certainly be acceptable for a wife to pose as a sister. But the end of the report shows the shortcoming of such an interpretation, because Sarai was in fact taken to Pharaoh's palace, and Abram was generously rewarded for her being there. This report is more plausible if read in the tradition of one prince sharing his sister with another prince. After, in connection with their special calling the two have their names changed from Abram to Abraham and from Sarai to Sarah, respectively; they travel in the land of Gerar, where, for the same reasons as in Egypt, Abraham "said of his wife Sarah, 'She is my sister.' So Abimelech, king of Gerar, sent and took Sarah.... 'I was afraid,' answered Abraham, '... besides she is in truth my sister, but only my father's daughter, not my mother's; and so she became my wife.'... Then Abimelech took flocks and herds and male and female slaves and gave them to Abraham; and after he restored his wife Sarah to him, he said,... to Sarah...: 'See I have given your *brother* a thousand shekels of silver....'" (Genesis 20:2–16.)

Our thesis is that these documents contain collective memories of the mother-goddess religion. Authors belonging to a more complex culture-context would have been too preoccupied with the possibility that Abraham might be misunderstood as a pimp and Sarah as a prostitute. Therefore, they would have shied away from recording such events as Sarah's stay with Pharaoh or her visit to Abimelech's palace.

F Religion: The Male Deity

The Ten Commandments of the Old Testament are the charter of the patrilineal family. The father's fear of disloyal or even rebellious offspring is answered by the words: "Honor your father and your mother, that you may have a long life. . . . " (Exodus 20:12.) This commandment is repeated elsewhere more explicitly: "Whoever strikes his father or mother shall be put to death. . . . Whoever curses his father or mother shall be put to death." (Exodus 21:15, 17.) The authority of the mother, apart from having firm foundations in less complex family types, could rest on the small child's physical dependence. The father's authority depends more on religious and legal support. Therefore these threatening verses help stabilize the institution of fatherhood. The source of these commands, Israel's God, himself appears as a father. He also forbids adultery, because it is an attack against the basis for the institution of fatherhood: female chastity.

Abraham then becomes the pioneer of a father-culture by recognizing in god the fertility-deity El Shaddai, and by receiving from that deity, whom he makes his personal god, the promise of fertility for himself, a man. Male fertility, which among pastoralists had been known merely as a physical reality, is thus defined as a sacred gift. This development of a religiously founded concept of fatherhood out of and yet in the continuity of the mother-deity was later forgotten and repressed in Israel's long periods of strife with heathenish cults. In consequence, one of the most fascinating chapters in the history of religion remains obscure and unresearched.

P Religion: The Christian Synthesis

New and more complex value-systems have no stability and enduring force if they simply negate all previous forms. They may just provoke a powerful swing of the pendulum of history toward the less complex faith that seemed to have been defeated. Only what has been integrated has in fact been overcome. In our hypothetical reconstruction of the metamorphosis of religious value-systems we assumed an animal-deity, that gave food as the basis of life to the male band, a mother-goddess that granted fertility to the human woman, and finally a father-god, who made his covenant with a human male Abraham, granting him countless offspring.

We started our typology of religious values with the animal-deity of a pre-family stage. The males formed a band of hunters, asked the deity to help them supply food for their women and children and to protect them from any harm. They felt united not by ties of kinship, but by eating from the same body of the animal they had killed. Even at their much more complex level of culture evolution the Israelites met in groups large enough to eat one lamb.

At the stage of the mother-goddess a female deity bestowed fertility on the human woman, made conception, pregnancy, birth, and motherhood mani-festations of her divine powers, and laid the foundations of family values. This form of religion, however, left human males outside the family context. They prayed to the lord of hosts to lead them in their military expeditions; he was the god of war and victory, strong and powerful, but not yet a father. The fatherly god who bestows fertility on a man and makes him responsible for his personal wife and children, is a sensational form of revelation, only about four thousand years old. The form had its beginnings with Abraham, but was later to be resumed and intensified in the words of Jesus: "He who sees me, sees the father."

The Christian religious value system consists of statements on family val-ues and relations which are integrated into a typical complex of beliefs. The creator-god, originally one person, is differentiated into the Trinity. He embod-ies the loving relationship between father and son, thereby having a patrilineal principle built into the deity itself. In Catholic and Orthodox Christianity the Virgin Mary continues the sanctification of motherhood given by the mother-goddess.

"The idea of Christ being the second person in the Trinity and the Son of God the Father, whose Holy Spirit impregnated Mary, divides the Godhead into three separate roles and thus saves Christianity from worshiping, what is in effect an incestuous god" (W. Lloyd Warner, 1961:304, 305).

The concept of the creator-god contains all the qualities of previous stages. He incorporates both the "tremendum," or unlimited power, and the love of a father. The final synthesis is in his being the Son of God and at the same time the son of Mary. Thus he represents the solution to any imaginable tension or contradiction inside the Christian synthesis of less complex value systems.

Sexual Norms and Mating Rules

H Sexuality: Exchange of "Sisters" Among Bands

Hunting such large animals as the mammoth or the buffalo required lasting and highly efficient cooperation. Intimate solidarity among the men in the local group became possible by eliminating sexual rivalry. Thus the least complex variety of the incest taboo may have been tabooing the women in the local group for the men in that group. Consequently, sexuality was banned from inside that group whose members had grown up together and regularly shared their meals.

However, this form of the incest taboo caused the problem of fertility and of channeling sexual drives. Therefore, relationships of cooperation and solidarity must have been established also with at least one other neighboring group, in order to give the hunters peaceful access to sexual mates. This mutual interest in forming alliances was supported in the area of food supply: When a band had killed a mammoth, they had more meat available than they and their own people could eat. They would then invite the neighboring group to eat from the same animal body. Thus the participants would have the sacred experience of transcending the boundaries of their local group of everyday life: they would eat the meat of their deity together. At another occasion the guest band would kill a mammoth and thus host their allies. This elementary potlach would also be the elementary form of a "marriage" feast, in the course of which the men of one band would impregnate the women of the other. Later, in more complex hunting cultures, the women would stay with their mates, but even with the adoption of a virilocal "marriage" each "spouse" retained his or her totem: "marriage" did not affect clan membership (as it often does not in modern industrial societies).

M Sexuality: Exchange of Sisters Among Males

When the religious value system is dominated by the fertility goddess, it is the women's responsibility to be fertile and have offspring. A close male, to whom she is taboo because both come from the same group, may assist her in finding an appropriate mate. It is against this background that such events as Sarah's stay with Pharaoh or her visit to Abimelech's palace become meaningful. But still this is a striking remark: Abraham himself says that Sarah was *only of the same father* and therefore a possible spouse to him. This shows a strictly matrilineal version of the incest taboo; the physical fact of fatherhood is known but not considered culturally relevant. Before it could become a central religious concept, applicable in defining father-son, father-daughter or sibling relationships, it was necessary to introduce yet another institution, without which fatherhood could not exist, marriage as the exclusive right of one man to have sexual relations with his spouse.

F Sexuality: Female Chastity

The oldest passages of the Bible show traces of marriage institutionalized originally in the matrilineal context. "That is why a man leaves his father and mother and clings to his wife and the two of them become one flesh" (Genesis 2:24). Here, being of one flesh means belonging to the same family, being blood-relations. This well-known decree from Genesis assigns the husband membership in his wife's clan, thereby introducing marriage and fatherhood as institutions into the matrilineal context.

But for men even to want to be fathers in the patrilineal sense, they had to overcome this fear: Had their wife been true to them, and was the child they were raising really their own? This issue concerned the male band as a whole. It was thinkable that some of them raised their own children as fathers with the assistance of their wives, while others continued the simpler custom of having offspring the matrilineal way through their sisters and without marriage. Any tolerance of matrilineal values would have meant the collapse of the patrilineal culture. Those who had no ambition to be fathers but preferred to continue being uncles, would probably have had affairs with other men's wives. The resultant jealousy would have weakened the band to the point at which enemies could have easily overpowered the whole people. This is precisely what the book of Judges describes as happening to the chosen people again and again.

The God of the people of Israel appears as a father who forbids adultery, because it attacks the basis of fatherhood. His indictment of adultery can also be read as the men's pact not to take each other's wives away. Thus on a more complex level we see the reduction of sexual rivalry achieved at the band level. Besides, if a man has intercourse with another man's wife, it will be uncertain whose child she is to give birth to. However, the patrilineal family depends on that very certainty. Therefore the future husband must also insist on the virginity of his bride. How else could he be sure that she had not previously conceived of someone else? It becomes clear then, that a population seeking to establish a firm basis for fatherhood must accept a rather complex system not only of religious values but also of norms to restrict sexual spontaneity.

P Sexuality: Monogamy

Parenthood as shared fertility of mother and father is the basis for the bilateral kinship system. The P-type family culture forms a synthesis of the M and the F types. Since, however, the fundamental interest in establishing fatherhood is carried over practically unchanged from the F-level system, sexual norms and mating rules remain just as strict and repressive. It appears, then, that the increasing liberalization of sexual behavior in modern societies makes neither the F- nor the P-type family viable.

Whereas H- and M-type cultures ban sexuality inside the family, F- and P-type sexualities take the form of erotic married life inside the nuclear family. The increasing difficulty of leading sexual lives in an F or P culture context makes it more and more unlikely that sexual behavior will be limited to intrafamilial married activities.

Types of Kinship Organization

H Solidarity: "We All Eat from the Same Canteen"

We have used a colorful array of materials from pre-historic speculation, from cultural anthropology, and from the history of religion mainly to inspire and guide our theoretical endeavor: the construction of ideal types of family cultures. At the end of this article I sketch a few possibilities for their application to family research.

In modern industrial societies it seems questionable whether kinship and the family are relevant concepts to the individuals involved. This is true particularly in the occupational world. The more work tends to be the center of existence rather than just a means to an end, the more family ties fade in significance. To adolescents their relatives may seem far less important than their peers. For some this orientation would be simply a phase in their maturation, but it might become a stable and lasting attitude with others.

Such a person's answer to the question, "Who are your relatives?" would not tell us much about the persons closest to him or her. Empirical research on the family should first of all investigate the problem of modern man's increasing or decreasing inclination to organize meaningful interaction around concepts of kinship. We cannot simply deny the ability to form close associations of solidarity to those segments of our populations to whom family orientations are remote. Rather, their most meaningful social ties may be organized around nonfamilial forms of creativity such as in the work world or in intellectual life in general. They are geared toward making a living rather than toward having a family. To them, solidarity is sharing the economic source of sustenance, of eating from the same canteen.

It follows from our scheme that the three levels of (a) religious value systems, (b) sexual norms, and (c) organization of solidarity are mutually dependent. Accordingly, we would be able to formulate hypotheses (to be tested in empirical research) that would take such interdependence into consideration. For members of the H-type culture we would predict a high flexibility in their sexual norms, however, with a tendency to attach a sexual taboo on members of their own closely knit in-group. They would not consider marriage a desirable state. Children are socialized in the mother-child dyad which is often but loosely integrated into the peer group. Moreover, we would predict little affinity to any personal deity regardless of whether it be conceived as male or female.

M Solidarity as Absence of Fathers

A member of the M-type culture would name as relatives those who descend from the same mother, grandmother, or great-grandmother. The striking increase of births out of wedlock in the United States is reason to predict an increase in the membership of the M-type: In the USA

> between 1970 and 1982, the number of one-parent families headed by never-married women rose by a startling 367 percent. The highest rate of out-of-wedlock births was among women between the ages of 20 and 24. But the number of illegitimate births among teenagers jumped from 199,900 in 1970 to 271,801 in 1980—even as the number and rate of births among teenagers declined. The racial differences are striking: among white teenagers, 33 percent of all births were illegitimate, while among black teens, 86 percent were out of wedlock. Experts

attribute the increase to greater sexual activity among teenagers. (*Newsweek Special Report: A Portrait of America*, January 17, 1983:27.)

Obviously, then, the number of persons who grow up with relatives from their mother's side only will steadily increase. Following our three-level scheme, we should predict among the M-type population strict observance of an incest taboo between mother and son and among siblings from the same mother, but an increased likelihood of sexual activities among siblings from the same father but different mothers, and among father and daughter. All these forms of incest can be attributed to the decreased significance of fatherhood as a culture concept. Sexual norms in general will be flexible or—to use a widespread terminology in our field—"liberal." Already the position of the husband is comparatively weak, and in divorce the children stay with the mother, while the father is simply dismissed. We would also have to predict a decreasing inclination to accept a male deity.

F Solidarity: The Model of Japan

Among Protestants and Jews, acceptance of a religious value system dominated by a male god will be relatively high. Among these groups we can expect a large percentage of members of the F-type culture. However, the absence of female figures within the religious value system suggests that these groups will produce the highest percentage of feminists. The question "who are your closest relatives?" will evoke a list of cousins and in-laws from the father's side and also attribute more significance to the father's parents and siblings than to those of the mother. The patrilineal kinship system is characteristic of modern Japan. Its followers favor female chastity: virginity of at least the woman prior to marriage, and fidelity during it. It is far more acceptable for one man to have more than one woman, than for one woman to have more than one man. In a marriage the husband tends to dominate, and in divorce the children will stay with their father.

P Solidarity: The Dream of Little Children

While a matrilineal lineage as well as a patrilineal lineage can be kept alive and be the basis for kinship solidarity across many generations, the principle of descending from one parent couple emphasizes the nuclear family. Lines of descent can be traced back only either in the male or in the female line. Any attempt to consider both with equal attention must lead to a family tree with four grandparents, eight great-grandparents, and so on, with the number of ancestors doubling from generation to generation. The resulting confusion focuses attention to the nuclear family.

In the P-type culture people feel as close to relatives from their mother's side as to those from their father's side. Marriage means that the families of both spouses unite into one clan. The P-type culture generates more resistance to divorce than any of the other types. Sexual norms are even more restrictive than in the F-type culture, because under P-type conditions absolute monogamy is a prerequisite for the maintenance of the kinship system. Due to its high level of complexity this culture type does not have a good chance of acceptance. It has never been an empirical reality on a large scale, but it probably produces ideal conditions for the socialization of small children. (Berger and Berger, 1983.)

Bibliography

Bakan, D. 1979. *And They Took Themselves Wives. The Emergence of Patriarchy in Western Civilization*. San Francisco: Harper & Row.

Berger, B. and Berger, P. L. 1983. *The War over the Family. Capturing the Middle Ground*. Garden City, New York: Anchor Press/Doubleday.

Burkert, W. 1972. *Homo Necans. Interpretationen altgriechischer Opferriten und Mythen*. Berlin, New York: Walter de Gruyter.

Hancar, F. 1939-40. *Zum Problem der Venusstatuetten im eurasiatischen Jungpal aeolithicum*. Praehistorische Zeitschrift, 30./31. Bd. S. 85–156.

Warner, W. L. 1961. *The Family of God*. New Haven: Yale University Press.

V. Conclusion

19

Future Prospects for Religion and Family Studies: The Mormon Case

Darwin L. Thomas

The increased emphasis in a variety of disciplines in the social sciences on the study of religion, along with more studies analyzing multiple institutions simultaneously such as religion and family (Abrahamson and Anderson, 1984; Thomas and Henry, 1985), and a social science encouraging more open dialogue from disciplinary adherents (Thomas and Sommerfeldt, 1984), argue for an optimistic view of the future of religion and family studies. We do not expect to see a return to the widespread neglect of religious studies that characterized the social sciences in the second, third, and fourth decades of this century (Thomas and Henry, 1985; Bergin, 1980; Beit-Hallahmi, 1974). In addition to the foregoing, we see a growing trend of religious organizations calling upon social science researchers to help them better understand the opportunities and challenges that churches face in helping individuals and families. Many of these social scientists are receiving recognition for their work (Howery, 1986).

Our optimistic projections must be tempered with an acknowledgment of the low status that family and religion studies carry in our contemporary social sciences. Universities by and large do not allocate large portions of available funds to encourage the study of religion and the family. Our conclusion of low status is based on the perception that the social sciences in general take their cues from the larger social order in determining the significant problems which deserve the major portions of available resources. Within the social sciences the study of religion and family have not competed effectively for an equal share of available resources. Similarly, the dominant institutions in society uniformly see family and religion as low-status entities. Even though 80 percent of the nation's businesses are family owned and generate 50 percent of the G.N.P. (Meyer, 1987), business schools do not organize curriculum to focus on family businesses nor do they offer much by way of studying churches as businesses. Impressive legal careers are not made by becoming specialists in domestic law. Medical schools do not place training for the study of family medicine as a high priority specialty. A psychologist does not become president of the American Psychological Association by becoming a nationally known family psychologist or psychologist of religion. The list could go on, but these suffice to illustrate the low status of religion and familial emphases in the contemporary social order. We do not see radical change here.

In summary, we see increased activity in two areas, religion and family, which have traditionally been underfunded in the social sciences. We expect this increased activity to continue into the future for two basic reasons. One is the recognition by the social sciences of the remarkable staying power of both religion and family. The earlier dire predictions of the demise of both religion and the family coming from general theories of social change as well as specific theories of secularization have now been shown to be false (Hadden and Shupe, 1986; Roberts, 1984; Hout and Greeley, 1987; Bahr and Chadwick, 1985). As these researchers have noted, it is now past time for the social sciences to begin to ask questions about what it is in the contemporary American social order that sustains a belief and involvement in religious institutions as well as conviction that family life offers some of the most meaningful experiences for children and adults. Is the staying power of one institution related to the staying power of the other? The time is right for the social sciences to address such issues.

The second reason for our expectation of increased research activity is our conviction that research funded by religious organizations will make significant contributions to our understanding of the religion and family interface. Examples of such studies completed and currently under way are numerous. Hoge and Roozen's study (1979) entitled *Understanding Church Growth and Decline*, and the multiple reports coming from the currently ongoing Notre Dame Parish study, are only two in a growing number.

Recent American research identified fifteen religious denominations that have ongoing research organizations which, taken together, are conducting hundreds of research projects. These include the Catholic, Jewish, Mainline Protestant, Mormon,[1] and many smaller denominations. (Anderson and Weed, in press.) An important development in encouraging research of this type is the Lilly Foundation's research funding program which stipulates that the social science researchers work in cooperation with the churches in designing and conducting the research. In addition to these ongoing research organizations, most of the denominations encourage research conducted by and for their seminaries. In combination, the above represents an impressive amount of research information generated by and for the churches, which we think will add measurably to the social science knowledge base about religion and the family.

Potential Areas of Significant Contribution

Writing in 1984, we identified five areas of possible benefit from increased study of religion and the family. They were:

(1) Increase our understanding of the role of religion and family in social change.

(2) Better understand these two institutional influences on personal well-being.

(3) Encourage more social-psychological studies of religion as opposed to institutional analysis.

(4) Encourage a greater appreciation for the role of spiritual influences in the lives of people.

(5) Encourage a discussion of the role of presuppositions in the social scientist's work. (Thomas and Henry, 1985.)

Our judgment is that the research published since 1984 corroborates the utility of this formulation. Indeed, the chapters in this book make important contributions to each of the above areas. For instance, the chapters in the section titled "Religion and Family in the Changing Social Order" address fundamental questions of the impact of the social order on Catholic, Jewish, Mormon, Protestant, and Amish families and raise questions about reciprocal influence discussed in Thornton's chapter. Hynes's chapter on Ireland adds a historical dimension to the issues of religion, family, and social change. The chapters in the socialization section, along with Stack's chapter on suicide, increase our understanding of the social-psychological dimensions inherent in religion and family studies as well as the impact of both religion and family upon the child in those families.

With more studies linking parental religious belief systems to child-rearing attitudes and behavior, such as Clayton's chapter and research reported by Barber and Thomas (1986a and b), we may begin to understand better the impact of an individual's religious orientation on socialization practices. This is a much-neglected area of study. The chapters by McNamara and Schroll make important contributions to our understanding of how presuppositions in the scientific process are related to both the nature of the questions we ask and the answers that are suggested by the particular approaches we use. The chapters by Spickard and Helle illustrate how different perspectives lead to very different typological systems of families and religions.

One additional payoff needs to be added to the above list. We believe that studies of religion and family will make important contributions to our understanding of the human conditions by generating more comparative studies of religion and family. We along with others (Bahr and Forste, 1986a and b; Alston, 1986; D'Antonio and Aldous, 1983) see the need for comparative studies. The best comparative studies will be done when we have sufficient information about the religion and family connection within each religious orientation to make and test theoretical formulations about how religion and family influence each other.

Thus, our plea for future studies is that they carefully document the important relationships between religion and family within one religious denomination and then carefully assess the degree to which those relationships hold or are modified across religions. For example, Scanzoni, in her discussion of the religion and family connection from a Protestant woman's point of view, discusses gender roles. The Mormon teachings and doctrines about marriage and family life may be unique in the Christian tradition (Marciano, 1987:306). How much does the unusual Mormon theology influence what occurs in the family along gender role lines? Heaton believes that Mormons are different from other religious groups in the emphasis given to the father's authority, but his evidence is sketchy at best. There is clearly room for alternative interpretations of the effect of Mormon teachings on gender roles (Thomas, 1983; Smith, 1986). Even Heaton's discussion raises the possibility that Mormonism, if it is taken to be the nearest thing to an ideal type as Marciano (1987) has argued, has countervailing influences.

For Mormons who participate in temple marriage, certain blessings in this life and the world to come are promised to the husband and wife unit, rather than to either singly. In addition, Mormon fathers are encouraged not only to have large families but also to be involved in the lives of their children. For instance, in large Mormon families there is an increase in affection whereas in other families there is a decline in affection as family size increases (Wilkinson and Tanner, 1980). Thus, we need better information about what is happening within Mormon families and how the countervailing influences of emphasizing father's authority gets played out among religious teachings which also encourage increased involvement in the lives of family members. Once we know that, we could then compare those relationships in families from other churches. We would then be closer to understanding religion's impact of gender roles both in and out of the family.

Fertility is the second example of comparative studies adding to our understanding. As Brodbar-Nemzer's discussion indicates, fertility has become a significant concern in the contemporary American Jewish family. The consistent fertility decline in American Jewish families has raised discussion about having enough children to maintain present population levels. When this pattern is contrasted with fertility for the Mormon family, it becomes readily apparent that the two religious traditions are very different even though they are similar on many family characteristics. Both value children and place a high premium on family life. Mormons have maintained a significantly higher fertility rate than the society within which it is imbedded. Why? Heaton believes that the Mormon case illustrates how religious teachings influence fertility patterns (Heaton, 1988). Are there specific aspects of Jewish theology that encourage Jewish parents to have few children, or is the Jewish fertility pattern at base influenced by secular forces?

Careful studies of belief structures, particularly about the meaning of this world's existence as well as postmortal expectations, would need to be effectively carried out in order to understand these very different patterns and the religion and family influences. Once careful studies comparing Mormons and Jews were carried out, other significant religious groups such as the Catholics could also be studied. Heaton implies that there is a difference between religions which emphasize the value of children by valuing and encouraging the advent of children as contrasted with a religion which influences fertility by disapproving of contraceptive use, such as the Catholic church. While such speculations might make sense, we obviously need careful social-psychological studies to know how meaning systems interface with fertility decisions.

Aside from the above substantive-oriented issues that comparative studies of religion and family could illuminate, there is one additional potential pay-off. This is the issue raised by McNamara and Schroll in their chapters, in which they discuss the role of presuppositions in a scientist's work. Schroll convincingly makes the case that developments in physical sciences have implications for social science endeavor. McNamara argues convincingly that the presuppositions which guide a particular social scientist's analysis will influence not only the kinds of questions that are asked but also the answers that are generated from the research evidence.

We are convinced that not only comparative studies are needed but comparative studies done by both insiders and outsiders, since the presuppositions they bring to their work will likely differ. As Alston (1986), an outside observer of Mormonism, notes, work done by "professional anti-Mormons make [him] nervous." He is also made nervous, but to a lesser extent, by the religious "specialist." If Alston is nervous over work done by both of those groups, one wonders what type of researcher would not make Alston nervous. We assume that in Alston's scheme of things there is an unnamed third group that he sees as more "objective" than either "professional anti" or the "specialist." We are not convinced that degrees of objectivity will necessarily generate solutions, given our view of the nature of scientific inquiry. Our position is simply that work needs to be done by both insiders and outsiders and that the consumers of the research have the right to know which group is represented.

We have previously argued that the social sciences ought to reject the methodological pretense of objectivity (Thomas and Sommerfeldt, 1984; Thomas and Wilcox, 1987). Social scientists in general, we believe, recognize that their own presuppositional system influences both the questions asked and answers suggested (McNamara, 1985). The postpositivist position, which emphasizes the constructed and social consensual nature of human knowledge and was first developed in the physical sciences (Thomas and Wilcox, 1987; Schroll 1988), rejects the notion that it is even possible to describe in an objective fashion the world that is taken to exist independent of the observer. Thus, the analysts need to identify their own presuppositions, especially as they relate to religious belief and commitment, since that is the very institution that is coming under their scrutiny. This would allow the reader to judge the adequacy of the information presented. McNamara's (1985, 1986; Goettch, 1986) discussion of the consequences of differing presuppositions of insiders' and outsiders' analyses of conservative Christian churches is a persuasive example of the need to address presuppositional influence in scientific discourse.

Mormon Case

As indicated above, we believe research encouraged and funded by religious organizations will continue to make an important contribution in the area where research in general is "underfunded and understaffed" (Alston, 1986:123). The research discussed below is presented with the intent of illustrating the contributions that such research can make in four of the above listed areas of potential payoff; namely, social change, well-being, social-psychological studies, and spiritual influences. While the research is not comparative by nature, it is a necessary first step in attempting to clarify the nature of the religion and family interface within one denomination. Once this connection is understood, comparative research could be undertaken to determine to what degree the relationships discussed in this research hold for other denominations.

In the spirit of identifying presuppositions, we note that this research, conducted by Mormons for the Mormon church, was conceived, designed, and carried out by insiders. The advantages are that the researchers have greater insight into those social-psychological realities of meaning, intention, and personal belief that tend to be underemphasized or ignored by outsiders (McNamara, 1985). This is significant, since the Mormon teachings about religion and family are the nearest thing to a unique set of teachings in Christendom (Marciano, 1987). By the same token, we recognize that outsiders may see a different set of meanings and relationships in the data discussed here. The competition between alternative explanations is all a necessary part of scientific inquiry.

The Study

Questionnaire data was collected in 1985 from a sample of age 18 years and older men and women of The Church of Jesus Christ of Latter-day Saints residing in the continental United States. The response rate of 57 percent produced usable data from a sample of 1100 females and 996 males. The questionnaire gathered considerable information on the religious life and practice of the people as well as information about family composition and practices. The analysis reported here comes from a subsample (780) of those respondents who had been married and had children old enough to enable them to answer the questions in the questionnaire detailing child-rearing attitudes and behavior. The Appendix lists the items used to measure the variables included in the LISREL[2] model depicted in Figure 2.

Theoretical Model

Figure 1 presents the theoretical model that was developed from a review of literature. We cannot present in detail the research and theory base underlying this theoretical model. We can, however, for the interested reader, identify the literature that allows us to make each of the links in the model. Each propositional link appearing in the model has a number identifying that link, and Table 1 presents a list of the studies from which each link was derived.

The general theoretical orientation depicted in Figure 1 argues that some characteristics of the family of orientation will influence both the religious and the family characteristics in the family of procreation. The family of orientation variables are closeness to parents and parents' religious practice. As can be seen in Figure 1, closeness to parents is theorized as influencing both marital satisfaction and one's religious belief and practice. Parents' religious practices are seen as influencing the adult religious belief and practice, but there is no body of literature or well-developed theory which indicates that parents' religious practice would influence either marital satisfaction or satisfaction with parenting. Note also that the theory argues that there is no direct effect of these family-of-orientation variables upon adult well-being. The effect of the closeness-to-parent variable is seen as being mediated through both the religious belief and practice and the satisfaction with the husband/wife relationship.

The theoretical formulation argues that religious belief and practices are best conceived as antecedent in their effect upon satisfaction with the husband/wife relationship and the parent/child relationship. But the religious variables in the family of procreation are also seen as having a direct effect upon adult well-being as well as indirect effect through both parental and marital satisfaction. This theoretical formulation allows us to pull apart some of the sources of influence between religion and family variables that have often

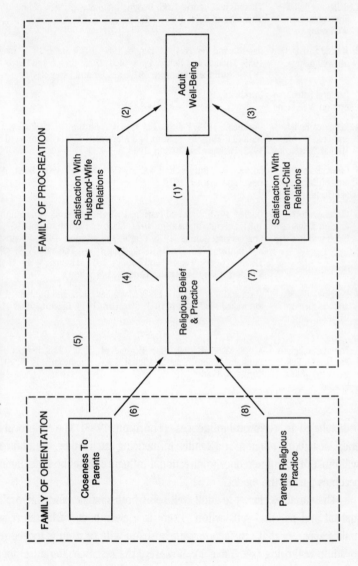

Figure 1. Proposed Causal Model of the Connection Between Religious Variables and Family Variables and Their Theorized Relationship to Well-Being.

FAMILY OF PROCREATION

FAMILY OF ORIENTATION

Adult Well-Being

Satisfaction With Husband-Wife Relations

Satisfaction With Parent-Child Relations

Religious Belief & Practice

Closeness To Parents

Parents Religious Practice

(1)*
(2)
(3)
(4)
(5)
(6)
(7)
(8)

* These numbers refer to the order of theoretical links as they are listed in table 1.

TABLE 1. Research and Theory Sources Used in Deriving the Theoretical Links in the Proposed Model (Figure 1) of Religion and Family Influences on Adult Well-Being.

Theoretical Link	Sources
1. Religious Belief and Practice on Well-being	Thomas and Henry, 1985; Bergin, 1980; Stack, 1985; Aldous, 1985; Thomas and Kent, 1985; Durkheim, 1915; Erikson, 1969
2. Marital Satisfaction on Well-being	Bateson and Ventis, 1982; Bergin, 1980, 1983; Stark, 1971; Stack, 1985; Thomas and Henry, 1985; Judd, 1985; Brown and Harris, 1978; Pearlin and Johnson, 1977; Kessler and Essex, 1982
3. Parental Satisfaction on Well-being	Durkheim, 1915
4. Religious Belief and Practice on Marital Satisfaction	Durkheim, 1915; Babchuk, et al., 1967; Shrum, 1980; Hartley, 1978; Hunt and King, 1978; Kunz and Albrecht, 1977; Schumm, et al., 1982; Filsinger and Wilson, 1984
5. Closeness to Parents on Marital Satisfaction	Locke, 1947; Burgess and Wallen, 1953; Stryker, 1964; Dean, 1966; Lewis and Spanier, 1979
6. Closeness to Parents on Religious Belief and Practice	Dudley, 1978; Hoge and Petrillo, 1978; Hoge, Petrillo, and Smith, 1982; LoSciuto and Karlin, 1972; Clark and Worthington, 1987; Chartier and Gohner, 1976; Pearlin and Johnson, 1977; Wilkinson and Tanner, 1980; Landis, 1960; Weigert and Thomas, 1979; Thomas, Gecas, Weigert, and Rooney, 1974; Thomas, Weigert, and Winston, 1984; Barber and Thomas, 1987a and b
7. Religious Belief and Practice on Parental Satisfaction	Clark and Worthington, 1987; Glass, Bengston, and Dunham, 1986; Vinovskis, 1987; Slater, 1977; Stannard, 1975; Clayton, 1988
8. Parents' Religious Practice on Religious Belief and Practice	Acock, 1984; Weiting, 1975; Hoge, et al., 1982; Glass, Bengston and Dunham, 1986; Greeley and Rossi, 1966; Himmelfarb, 1977, 1979; Cornwall, 1988

been labeled as "reciprocal influences" (Thornton, 1985). The reciprocal influence idea (both religion and family influencing each other simultaneously) will most of the time reduce to directional influence once the time dimension becomes part of the model.

The variables closest to adult well-being both spatially and temporally are marital and parental satisfaction. There is a clear body of literature which makes apparent that satisfaction with husband/wife relation is indeed related to adult well-being (see Table 1). However, the research literature does not really support the link between parental satisfaction and adult well-being. That link is made on the basis of the theoretical formulations coming from Durkheimian social integration formulations which argue that satisfaction in important social orders will be related to a sense of well-being. We assume that satisfaction with parent/child relations, since the role of children is such a central part of Mormon theology (Heaton, 1988), will predict adult well-being. To our knowledge there is no research which clearly supports this link.

Each of the variables in the model is best conceptualized as a block of variables, and the purpose of this analysis was to include enough information about the respondents' religious and family life that important dimensions within each of these blocks of variables could be measured and analyzed.

The literature on which this general model is based is general social science literature, and only a few of the cited studies report data from Mormon respondents. Thus, we are not sure to what degree this theoretical model will or will not be confirmed in the data for Mormons. That is the central purpose of the particular analysis reported here.

Findings

Figure 2 presents a test of the model using LISREL analysis. The standardized coefficients are reported here such that the size of the coefficients can be compared one with another. Since this is a causal model, the larger the coefficient on any one of the arrows indicates a greater amount of influence that that particular variable has on other variables in the model. The overall fit of the model is fairly good. The Goodness of Fit Index of .93 and the root mean square residual of .04 are well within the suggested limits for models of this type. Also, this model explains a sizeable proportion of variation in the measures of well-being (57 %).

While the overall fit of the model to the data is good, a number of very important and surprising findings emerge in this analysis. First, it confirms some of the general theoretical propositions outlined at the beginning. The experiences in the family of orientation (closeness to parents and parents' religious attendance) are related to measures of religiosity and dimensions of family functioning (marital and parental satisfaction) as well as adult well-being. The closeness to parent variable is considerably more important than is parents' religious attendance in accounting for variation in the model. Second, as was theorized, dimensions of religiosity are best conceptualized as antecedent variables to marital and parental relationships. Of the two religiosity dimensions,

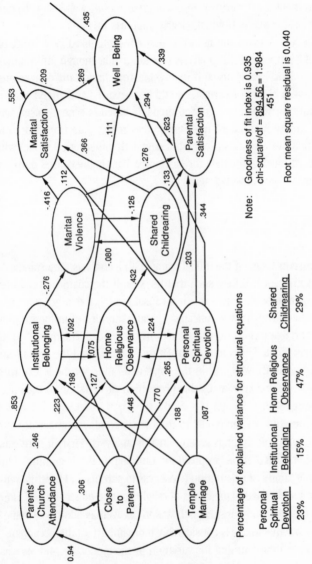

Figure 2. The Effect of Religion Variables and Family Variables on Well-Being (N = 780) (Male and Female)

Percentage of explained variance for structural equations

Personal Spiritual Devotion	Institutional Belonging	Home Religious Observance	Shared Childrearing
23%	15%	47%	29%

Conflict Resolution	Marital Satisfaction	Parental Satisfaction	Well - Being
11%	45%	38%	56.5%

Note: Goodness of fit index is 0.935
chi-square/df = 894.56 = 1.984
451

Root mean square residual is 0.040

Total Coefficient of determination for structural equations is 0.526

personal spiritual devotion is significantly more important in terms of its effect on well-being as well as its effect on marital and parental satisfaction.

When we computed the total effect for each of the variables on well-being, personal spiritual devotion emerged as the single most important influence on adult well-being. This is a positive relationship, meaning that the higher the individual scores on the measure of personal spiritual devotion the higher the well-being. It has a sizeable direct effect on well-being but it also has one strong indirect effect through parental satisfaction to well-being and the other weaker one through marital satisfaction to well-being. Thus, our second finding is that personal spiritual devotion is very important for Mormon well-being. This finding argues persuasively for the conceptualization that religious commitment is positively related to well-being. This is currently being debated in the social science literature (Bergin, 1980; Stack, 1985; Thomas and Henry, 1985). The data argue convincingly that for Mormons, personal well-being is very much influenced by an individual's attempts to live a Christlike life, seek the influence of the Holy Ghost, and be forgiven.

The third most important finding from this research is the significant influence of parental satisfaction upon well-being. This was not anticipated as the original model was developed. As was indicated, there was no well-established body of research literature which indicated that parental satisfaction would be strongly related to well-being. The connection was made on the basis of theoretical formulations developed by Durkheim years ago as he tried to understand the religious institution. In Durkheim's formulations, integration into dominant social spheres, be they religion or family, equipped an individual to live better. In Durkheim's words, the religiously integrated individual is a person "who is *stronger*" (italics in the original, Durkheim, 1915:464).

It is important to realize that these data say that satisfaction with one's parental experiences in the family has a very strong and independent effect upon well-being, both independent from the effects that other religious variables have on well-being and independent from the effect that satisfaction with the conjugal relationship has on well-being. To our knowledge this is the first research to identify clearly the independent influence of parental satisfaction on well-being. This is a strong effect. The analyses indicates that parental satisfaction (.34) is second to personal spiritual devotion (.46) in the strength of its effects on personal well-being.

The fourth most important finding is the effect of closeness to parents in the family of orientation on well-being. After the effect of personal religious devotion and parental satisfaction on well being, the next single most important variable is closeness to parents (.33). While it only has a small direct effect (.11) on well-being, it influences virtually all of the other variables in the model, namely, the religiosity dimensions and marital and parental satisfaction. Thus, it can be seen as an important variable in understanding adult well-being among Mormons.

The last finding discussed is the importance of shared child-rearing for marital satisfaction and the relationship of shared child-rearing to home religious observance and temple marriage. The general theoretical formulation (Figure 1) was not specific enough to anticipate a number of the important relationships that emerged in the data between home religious observance, shared child-rearing, marital satisfaction, and temple marriage. The second most important variable in accounting for marital satisfaction among Mormons is the degree to which husband and wife share in the child-rearing duties and responsibilities. The single strongest influence on shared child-rearing is the degree to which Mormons engage in home religious observance, and the single most important influence on home religious observance is whether or not the husband and wife were married in a Mormon temple.

Our interpretation of these relationships is that, for Mormons who are married in the temple, (1) they are more likely to engage in home religious observance, (2) both husband and wife are more likely to share in child-rearing duties and responsibilities, and (3) they will in turn experience a greater amount of marital satisfaction. Shared child-rearing also influences parental satisfaction, but the influence is not nearly as strong as it is on marital satisfaction. The role of shared child-rearing in Mormon families adds important information and clarification to the whole discussion of gender roles (Heaton, 1988; Scanzoni, 1988; Brinkerhoff and MacKie, 1985).

As was indicated in the earlier discussion, Mormonism has traditionally been seen as a religion which emphasizes the authority of the father. However, these data allow us to specify what are the countervailing influences operating within the Mormon family. The influences from temple marriage and home religious observance lead to increased shared child-rearing roles. This more egalitarian participation in child-rearing in turn has a significant impact on marital satisfaction, which affects adult well-being.

These data clarify a trend noted by a number of researchers that when it comes to gender role ideology, Mormons emphasize both separation of roles and authority of the fathers, whereas when Mormons respond about who does what, they score relatively high on measures of egalitarian role performance (Heaton, 1988; Brinkerhoff and MacKie, 1985; Thomas, 1983; Bahr, 1982; Smith, 1986). These data now allow us to specify that, contrary to some proposed explanations which see the egalitarian role performance of Mormons as coming from larger societal influences on Mormon parents, these findings illustrate that some religious variables (temple marriage) and family religious activities (home religious observance) are important sources of egalitarian role behavior in the child-rearing domain. These patterns appear plausible when paired with Mormon theology which teaches that husbands and wives enter an order of the priesthood when they are married. All blessings are promised to the couple jointly, not singly. Parents together have mutual responsibility for teaching and caring for children born to that union. The family unit has an ontological reality that transcends mortal existence. (McConkie, 1964; Heaton, 1988; Thomas, 1983.) This theology apparently encourages shared child-rearing role performance, which impacts marital satisfaction and well-being.

Summary

This chapter began by arguing for the utility of more studies focusing on religion and family. A number of possible payoffs were identified and then data were presented from a study of Mormon adult men and women focusing on family and religious influences on their sense of well-being. The data illustrated the importance of measuring multiple dimensions of religious belief and practice as well as multiple dimensions of family functioning in order to see more clearly what is happening in Mormon families. In order to understand well-being among adult Mormon men and women, the impact of both religion and family must be analyzed.

The data underscore the very important role of personal spiritual devotion in the lives of these adult Mormons. The social sciences have tended to neglect this dimension in studies of religiosity, especially in studies that deal with religion and family. Recent observers have called for more studies of social-psychological dimensions of meaning, intentionality, or future expectational states in the study of religion and family (D'Antonio, Newman, and Wright, 1982; McNamara, 1985; Thomas and Henry, 1985). These findings corroborate that plea. One would have a hard time understanding what is occurring in Mormon families without establishing the degree to which men and women are committed to and attempt to seek spiritual guidance in their lives.

Mormon theology depicts Mormonism as a restoration of spiritual gifts existing in Christ's church in his day. Ordinances are performed in which the Holy Ghost is conferred upon those who believe. Additional covenants are made by Mormons in church and temple ceremonies which underscore the importance of spiritual direction in daily living. These data indicate that this personal spiritual devotion is important for these Mormon respondents. The importance of personal spiritual devotion in these data corroborate Moberg's (1979) early efforts to call attention to the study of the spiritual dimension in sociological studies of religion. Clearly, for these Mormon respondents, religion provides a significant source of meaning for not only their family relationships but also their own personal sense of well-being.

The final dominant impression coming from these Mormon data is the tremendous impact of parent-child relations for adult well-being. The feeling of closeness to parents in the family of orientation influences virtually all variables in the model. Satisfaction with parenthood is the single most important influence on well-being. Given these relationships, comparative research should now attempt to investigate the meaning of parent-child relations in other religions. Our own predictions lead us to believe that closeness to parents will show similar effects on the social and emotional well-being of adults for most religious groups. The nature of the human being and the socialization process lead us to this conclusion. We tend to see the strong relationships between parental satisfaction and well-being as perhaps more characteristic of Mormon families when compared to other religious groups. The distinctiveness of Mormon theology which ties conjugal to parental dimensions in the view of the human condition in this and the other world underlies our prediction that the link between parental satisfaction and well-being will be stronger for Mormons.

Our prediction of a stronger relationship is consistent with research in other areas. For example, Christensen (1962, 1976) concludes that the Mormon faith is more successful than other faiths in limiting premarital sexual activity. Smith (1976) shows that Mormon sexual attitudes remained relatively constant during the sexual revolution. Stott (1988) shows that the influence of parents on children is generally stronger for Mormons than for Baptists. Future comparative research will have to test the expectation that parental satisfaction is more strongly related to well-being for Mormons than it is for other denominations.

The major findings reported in this chapter have important implications for any attempt to understand the social-psychological dimensions of adult functioning in our contemporary society. The Mormon data confirm the wisdom of those social scientists who have repeatedly called for more social-psychological studies. Such studies will undoubtedly add to our understanding of religion and family influences in various analyses of social change. Those concerned about the contemporary adult's feelings of well-being will need to include religion and family influences in their analysis to more correctly identify important sources of influence. Lastly, those who would analyze the religious connection to well-being cannot ignore the spiritual dimension of religious experience. This chapter, as well as this volume, argues convincingly that social scientists must focus on the religion and family interface if they wish to more fully understand the human condition. The best research and theory will be that which analyzes the two institutions simultaneously. The prospects for increased knowledge from future research are encouraging.

Notes

1. Mormon is a nickname commonly used to refer to The Church of Jesus Christ of Latter-day Saints.

2. LISREL is a general computer program designed to analyze the linear structural relations existing in a set of data. It allows the researcher to test both the adequacy of the measurement model and the theoretical model (the set of structural equations representing the theorized relations among variables) in causal analysis.

Appendix. List of Items Used to Measure Each Construct in the LISREL Model with Reliability Coefficients

Well-Being (alpha = .8166):

Life.suc: Life achievement perceived by respondent (alpha = .7211)

Q40. For each pair of opposites below, circle the 'x' on the scale that would be most really true for you (5 point scale).

1. I would like to live my life very differently vs. I would want to live it just the same.
2. Made no progress vs. progressed to complete fulfillment in achieving life goals.
3. If I should die today I would feel that my life has been completely worthless vs. very worthwhile.

Q42. For each pair of statements below, please circle the 'x' on the scale that is closest to your feelings (5 point scale).

    5. I feel guilty all the time vs. I don't feel particularly guilty.

N.depress: Beck's depression scale (alpha = .8989)

Q40. For each pair of opposites below, circle the 'x' on the scale that would be most really true for you (5 point scale).

    4. My life is filled with conflict and despair vs. filled with peace and joy.

    5. My life is out of my hands and controlled by external factors vs. my life is in my hands and I am in control of it.

    6. Facing my daily tasks is an unpleasant and boring experience vs. a source of pleasure and satisfaction.

    7. In life I can see no meaning in the trials I experience vs. purpose and meaning in the trials I experience.

Q42. For each pair of statements below, please circle the 'x' on the scale that is closest to your feelings (5 point scale).

    1. I do not feel sad vs. I am so sad or unhappy that I can't stand it.

    2. I feel that the future is hopeless and that things cannot improve vs. I am not particularly discouraged about the future.

    3. I am dissatisfied or bored with everything vs. I get as much satisfaction out of things as I used to.

    4. I am disgusted with myself vs. I do not feel disappointed with myself.

    6. I feel guilty all the time vs. I do not have any thoughts of killing myself.

    7. I can't make decisions at all anymore vs. I make decisions about as well as I ever could.

    8. I don't get more tired than usual vs. I am too tired to do anything.

Marital Satisfaction: (alpha = .8849)

Mar.sat: Marital satisfaction (alpha = .9569)

Q22. All things considered, how would you describe your marriage? For each pair of opposites below, circle the 'x' that is closest to your feelings.

    1. I feel distance between my spouse and me vs. I feel extremely close to my spouse.

    2. I am very unhappy in my marriage vs. I am very happy in my marriage.

    3. My marriage is less satisfying than most marriages vs. my marriage is more satisfying than most marriages.

    4. If I had to do it over again, I would marry someone different vs. if I had to do it over again, I would marry the same person.

    5. My spouse and I are just two people who live in the same house vs. my spouse and I are like a close knit team.

Problems: Marital Problems (alpha = .8546)

Q23. Even in cases where married people are mostly happy, they sometimes have problems getting along with each other. Please indicate to what degree the following are problems in your marriage. Respondent categories: (1) not a problem to (5) a major problem.

    1. We do not spend enough time together as companions.

2. We do not agree on where to spend our money.

3. Marriage makes me feel trapped.

4. Our sexual relations are unsatisfying.

5. We disagree about child-rearing practices.

6. We don't understand each other very well.

7. There isn't enough romance in our marriage.

Parental Satisfaction (alpha = .7652):

Par.sat: Parenting Satisfaction (alpha = .8111)

Q26. Given the rewards and difficulties that one encounters in rearing children, how do you feel about your parenting experiences up to this point? Please indicate how well each of these statements describes your feelings.

1. I feel I have been a good parent.

2. In general I would say that the work involved in rearing children is more satisfying than working in a job.

3. I have often felt guilty about the way I fulfill my role as a parent.

4. My experience in rearing children has been very frustrating.

5. I feel I am capable of dealing with the challenges parents have to face in today's world.

6. The demands of being a parent have often been so overwhelming that I have wished for a way out.

7. For me, rearing children has been an exciting and growing experience.

Harmony: Harmony in family (alpha = .8709)

Q25. To what extent do the following things occur in your family, that is, with you, your children, and spouse (if married)? If your children are no longer at home, respond to these statements for the time when your children were at home. Respondent categories: (1) to a very little extent to (5) to a very great extent.

1. Family members help and support one another.

2. The children respect me.

3. We fight in our family.

4. Family members lose their tempers.

5. We really get along well with each other.

6. There is a feeling of togetherness in our family.

7. Family members criticize each other.

8. The children and I have quality time together.

9. The children are responsible and independent.

Marital Violence (alpha = .7837):

Q24. No matter how well married couples get along they sometimes have disagreements, get annoyed at each other, or just have spats or fights. This may be due to stress, tiredness, or other reasons. They also use many different ways of trying to settle their differences. These may include some of the things listed below. How often has your spouse done any of the following during the past year?

4. Insulted you or swore at you?

5. Stomped out of the room or house or yard?

6. Threw, smashed, hit, or kicked something?

7. Pushed, grabbed, or shoved you?

8. Kicked, bit, or hit you?

Shared Child-rearing (alpha = .6855):

Q28. The activities listed below take place in different amounts in different families. When the activities have occurred in your family, which parent is (or was) more involved? (Mostly mother or mostly father = 1; mother more or father more = 2; mother and father about the same = 3.)

3. Having informal discussions with your children about gospel principles.

5. Planning and holding a family night with your children.

8. Helping children to read and do well in school.

9. Disciplining children when necessary.

10. Seeing that children's chores and duties are assigned and completed.

Institutional Belonging (alpha = .7876):

Q20. Sometimes members feel they do not fit the church picture of the ideal LDS family. Some may not be married, some may not have children, some may have a spouse who is not LDS or not active, etc. Whatever your family situation may be, please indicate how often the following situations have occurred in your experience in the church. Respondent categories: (1) rarely or never to (5) very often.

2. I have found the people in my ward or branch ready and willing to make friends with me.

4. I have NOT felt left out of some ward or branch social activities.

5. I have felt that some church leaders and members really seem to understand my situation.

8. I have felt that some people think there is something wrong with me.

Home Religious Observance (alpha = .7330):

Famscrip. How frequently in the past six months have you had family scripture study? Respondent categories: (1) not at all to (5) about daily. (Recoded from q38.4.)

Fampray. How frequently in the past six months have you had family prayer together? Respondent categories: (1) not at all to (5) about daily. (Recoded from q38.2.)

Q38.7 How frequently in the past six months has your family held or attended family home evening? Respondent categories: (1) not at all to (5) about once a week.

Personal Spiritual Devotion (alpha = .8939):

Q36. How often do the following statements describe your personal experiences, feelings, and beliefs? Respondent categories: (1) Doesn't describe me at all to (7) describes me very well.

5. I work very hard at seeking forgiveness and overcoming my weaknesses.

6. In my life, seeking spiritual goals always comes first.

7. I am strongly committed to being like Christ.

9. I frequently feel prompted by the Holy Ghost.

10. I always seek God's guidance when I have important decisions to make.

Parents' Church Attendance (alpha = .7912):

Q48.1 How often did your father attend religious services when you were a child? Respondent categories: (1) rarely or never to (5) once a week.

Q48.2 How often did your mother attend religious services when you were a child? Respondent categories: (1) rarely or never to (5) once a week.

Close to Parents (alpha = .5954):

Q49.1 How close did you feel towards your father (or male guardian) when you were growing up? Respondent categories: (1) not at all close to (5) extremely close.

Q49.2 How close did you feel towards your mother (or female guardian) when you were growing up? Respondent categories: (1) not at all close to (5) extremely close.

Temple Marriage:

Temple It's a dummy variable where 0 = is not married in temple and 1 = married in temple.

Bibliography

Abrahamson, M. and W. P. Anderson. 1984. "People's Commitments to Institutions." *Social Psychology Quarterly* 47(4):371–81.

Acock. A. C. 1984. "Parents and Their Children: The Study of Inter-generation Influence." *Sociology and Social Research* 68:151–71.

Aldous, J. 1985. "Theoretical Perspectives on the Religion and Family Connection with Personal Well-being." Paper presented at the Theory Development Workshop, National Council on Family Relations annual meeting.

Alston, J. P. 1986. "A Response to Bahr and Forste." *Brigham Young University Studies* 26(1):123–26.

Babchuk, N., H. J. Crockett, and J. A. Ballweg. 1967. "Change in Religious Affiliation and Family Stability." *Social Forces* 45:551–55.

Bahr, H. M. 1982. "Religious Contrasts in Family Roles." *Journal for the Scientific Study of Religion* 21:201–17.

Bahr, H. M. and R. T. Forste. 1986a. "Toward a Social Science of Contemporary Mormondom." *Brigham Young University Studies* 26(1):73–121.

Bahr, H. M. and R. T. Forste. 1986b. "Reply to Alston." *Brigham Young University Studies* 26(1):127–29.

Bahr, H. M. and B. Chadwick. 1985. "Religion and Family in Middletown, USA." *Journal of Marriage and the Family* 47(May):407–14.

Barber, B. K. and D. L. Thomas. 1986a. "Dimensions of Adolescent Self-esteem and Religious Self-evaluations." *Family Perspective* 20(2):137–50.

Barber, B. K. and D. L. Thomas. 1986b. "Dimensions of Fathers' and Mothers' Supportive Behavior: The Case for Physical Affection." *Journal of Marriage and the Family* 48(3):783–94.

Batson, C. D. and W. L. Ventis. 1982. *The Religious Experience: A Social-Psychological Perspective.* New York: Oxford University Press.

Beit-Hallahmi, B. 1974. "Psychology of Religion in 1880–1930: The Rise and Fall of a Psychological Movement." *Journal of the History of the Behavioral Sciences* 10:84–94.

Bergin. A. E. 1980. "Psychotherapy and Religious Values." *Journal of Consulting and Clinical Psychology* 48(1):95–105.

Bergin, A. E. 1983. "Religiosity and Mental Health: A Critical Re-evaluation and Meta-analysis." *Professional Psychology: Research and Practice* 14(2):170–84.

Brinkerhoff, M. B. and M. MacKie. 1988. "Religious Sources of Gender Traditionalism." *The Religion and Family Connection: Social Science Perspectives.* Provo, UT: Religious Studies Center, Brigham Young University.

Brodbar-Nemzer, J. 1988. "The Contemporary American Jewish Family." In D. L. Thomas (ed.), *The Religion and Family Connection: Social Science Perspectives.* Provo, UT: Religious Studies Center, Brigham Young University.

Brown, G. W. and T. Harris. 1978. *Social Origins of Depression: A Study of Psychiatric Disorder in Women.* New York: Free Press.

Burgess, E. W. and P. Wallin. 1953. *Engagement and Marriage.* Chicago: J. B. Lippincott.

Chartier, M. R. and L. A. Goehner. 1976. "A Study of the Relationship of Parent-Adolescent Communication, Self-esteem and God Image." *Journal of Psychology and Theology* 4:227–32.

Christensen, H. T. 1962. "A Cross-cultural Comparison of Attitudes Toward Marital Infidelity." *International Journal of Comparative Sociology* 3:124–37.

Christensen, H. T. 1976. "Mormon Sexuality in Cross-cultural Perspective." *Dialogue* 10(2):62–75.

Clark, C. A. and E. L. Worthington, Jr. 1987. "Family Variables Affecting the Transmission of Religious Values from Parents to Adolescents: A Review." *Family Perspective* 21(1):1–22.

Clayton, L. 1988. "The Impact of Parental Views of the Nature of Humankind upon Child-rearing Attitudes." In D. L. Thomas (ed.), *The Religion and Family Connection: Social Science Perspectives.* Provo, UT: Religious Studies Center, Brigham Young University.

Cornwall, M. 1988. "The Influence of Three Agents of Religious Socialization: Family, Church, and Peers." In D. L. Thomas (ed.), *The Religion and Family Connection: Social Science Perspectives.* Provo, UT: Religious Studies Center, Brigham Young University.

D'Antonio, W. V. and J. Aldous. 1983. *Families and Religions: Conflict and Change in Modern Society.* Beverly Hills, CA: Sage Publications.

D'Antonio, W. V., W. M. Newman and S. A. Wright. 1982. "Religion and Family Life: How Social Scientists View the Relationship." *Journal for the Scientific Study of Religion* 21(3):218–25.

Dean D. 1966. "Emotional Maturity and Marital Adjustment." *Journal of Marriage and the Family* 28:454–57.

Dudley, R. L. 1978. "Alienation from Religion in Adolescents from Fundamentalist Religious Homes." *Journal for the Scientific Study of Religion* 17:389–98.

Durkheim, E. 1915. *The Elementary Forms of the Religious Life.* Translated by Joseph Ward Swain. New York: The Free Press.

Erikson, E. H. 1969. *Gandhi's Truth.* New York: W. W. Norton.

Filsinger, E. E. and M. R. Wilson. 1984. "Religiosity, Socioeconomic Rewards, and Family Development: Predictors of Marital Adjustment." *Journal of Marriage and the Family* 46(3):663–70.

Glass, J., V. L. Bengston, and C. C. Dunham. 1986. "Attitude Similarity in Three-generation Families: Socialization, Status Inheritance or Reciprocal Influence?" *American Sociological Review* 51(5):685–98.

Goettsch, S. L. 1986. "The New Christian Right and the Social Sciences: A Response to McNamara." *Journal of Marriage and the Family* 48:447–54.

Greeley, A. M. and P. Rossi. 1966. *The Education of Catholic Americans*. Chicago: Aldine.

Hadden, J. K. and A. Shupe (eds.). 1986. *Prophetic Religions and Politics: Religion and the Political Order*. New York: Paragon House.

Hartley, S. F. 1978. "Marital Satisfaction Among Clergy Wives." *Review of Religious Research* 19:178–91.

Heaton, T. B. 1988. "Four C's of the Mormon Family: Chastity, Conjugality, Children, and Chauvinism." In D. L. Thomas (ed.), *The Religion and Family Connection: Social Science Perspectives*. Provo, UT: Religious Studies Center, Brigham Young University.

Helle, H. J. 1988. "Types of Religious Values and Family Cultures." In D. L. Thomas (ed.), *The Religion and Family Connection: Social Science Perspectives*. Provo, UT: Religious Studies Center, Brigham Young University.

Himmelfarb, H. S. 1977. "The Interaction Effects of Parents, Spouse, and Schooling: Comparing the Impact of Jewish and Catholic Schools." *Sociological Quarterly* 18:464–71.

Himmelfarb, H. S. 1979. "Agents of Religious Socialization Among American Jews." *Sociological Quarterly* 20:447–94.

Hoge, D. R., G. Petrillo, and E. Smith. 1982. "Transmission of Religious and Social Values from Parents to Teenage Children." *Journal of Marriage and the Family* 44:569–80.

Hoge, D. R. and D. A. Roozen. 1979. *Understanding Church Growth and Decline: 1950–1978*. New York: The Pilgrim Press.

Hoge, D. R. and G. H. Petrillo. 1978. "Determinants of Church Participation and Attitudes Among High School Youth." *Journal for the Scientific Study of Religion* 17:359–79

Hout, M. and A. M. Greeley. 1987. "The Center Doesn't Hold: Church Attendance in the United States." *American Sociological Review* 52(June):325–45.

Howery, C. B. 1986. "Researching the Church from Within." *Footnotes* 14(19):7.

Hunt, R. A. and M. B. King. 1978. "Religiosity and Marriage." *Journal for the Scientific Study of Religion* 17:339–406.

Hynes, E. 1988. "Family and Religious Change in a Peripheral Capitalist Society: Mid-nineteenth-century Ireland." In D. L. Thomas (ed.), *The Religion and Family Connection: Social Science Perspectives*. Provo, UT: Religious Studies Center, Brigham Young University.

Judd, D. K. 1985. "Religiosity and Mental Health." Unpublished master's thesis, Brigham Young University.

Kessler, R. C. and M. Essex. 1982. "Marital Status and Depression: The Importance of Coping Resources." *Social Forces* 61(2):485–507.

Kunz, P. R. and S. L. Albrecht. 1977. "Religion, Marital Happiness and Divorce." *International Journal of Sociology of the Family* 7:227–32.

Landis, J. T. 1960. "Religiousness, Family Relationships, and Family Values in Protestant, Catholic, and Jewish Families." *Marriage and Family Living* 22:341-47.

Lewis, R. A. and G. B. Spanier. 1979. "Theorizing About the Quality and Stability of Marriage." Pp. 268-94 in W. R. Burr, R. Hill, F. I. Nye, and I. L. Reiss (eds.), *Contemporary Theories about the Family* (Vol. 1). New York: Free Press.

Locke, H. J. 1947. "Predicting Marital Adjustment by Comparing a Divorced and Happily Married Group." *American Sociological Review* 12:187-91.

LoSciuto, L. A. and R. M. Karlin. 1972. "Correlates of the Generation Gap." *The Journal of Psychology* 81:253-62.

Marciano, T. D. 1987. "Families and Religions." Pp. 285-315 in M. B. Sussman and S. K. Steinmetz (eds.), *Handbook of Marriage and the Family*. New York: Plenum Press.

McConkie, B. R. 1967. "The Eternal Family Concept." Devotional address given at the Second Annual Priesthood Genealogical Research Seminar, Brigham Young University, Provo, Utah, June 23.

McNamara, P. H. 1985. "The New Christian Right's View of the Family and Its Social Science Critics: A Study in Differing Presuppositions." *Journal of Marriage and the Family* 47(May):449-58.

McNamara, P. H. 1986. "A Reply to Goettsch." *Journal of Marriage and the Family* 48:453-54.

Meyer, A. 1987. "Copykids." *Mature Outlook* 4(3):29-37.

Moberg, D. O. (ed.). 1979. *Spiritual Well-being: Sociological Perspectives.* Washington, D.C.: University Press of America.

Olshan, M. A. 1988. "Family Life: An Old Order Amish Manifesto." In D. L. Thomas (ed.), *The Religion and Family Connection: Social Science Perspectives*. Provo, UT: Religious Studies Center, Brigham Young University.

Pearlin, L. I. and J. S. Johnson. 1977. "Marital Status, Life-Strains and Depression." *American Sociological Review* 42:704-15.

Roberts, K. A. 1984. *Religion in Sociological Perspectives*. Homewood, IL: The Dorsey Press.

Scanzoni, L. D. 1988. "Contemporary Challenges for Religion and the Family from a Protestant Woman's Point of View." In D. L. Thomas (ed.), *The Religion and Family Connection: Social Science Perspectives*. Provo, UT: Religious Studies Center, Brigham Young University.

Schroll, M. A. 1988. "Developments in Modern Physics and Their Implications for the Social and Behavioral Sciences." In D. L. Thomas (ed.), *The Religion and Family Connection: Social Science Perspectives*. Provo, UT: Religious Studies Center, Brigham Young University.

Schumm, W. R., S. R. Bollman, and A. P. Jurich. 1982. "The 'Marital Conventionalization' Argument: Implications for the Study of Religiosity and Marital Satisfaction." *Journal of Psychology and Theology* 10:236-41.

Shrum, W. 1980. "Religious and Marital Instability: Change in the 1970's?" *Review of Religious Research* 21:135-47.

Slater, P. G. 1977. *Children in the New England Mind: In Death and in Life*. Hamden, CT: Archon Books.

Smith, J. E. 1986. "A Familistic Religion in a Modern Society." Pp. 273-97 in Kingsley Davis (ed.), *Contemporary Marriage*. New York: Russell Sage Foundation.

Smith, W. E. 1976. "Mormon Sex Standards on College Campuses, or Deal Us Out of the Sexual Revolution!" *Dialogue* 10(2):76-81.

Spickard, J. 1988. "Families and Religions: An Anthropological Typology." In D. L. Thomas (ed.), *The Religion and Family Connection: Social Science Perspectives*. Provo, UT: Religious Studies Center, Brigham Young University.

Stack, S. 1985. "The Effect of Domestic Religious Individualism on Suicide, 1954-1978." *Journal of Marriage and the Family* 47(May):431-47.

Stannard, D. E. 1975. "Death and Puritan Child." Pp. 9-29 in D. E. Stannard (ed.), *Death in America*. Philadelphia: University of Pennsylvania Press.

Stark, R. 1971. "Psychopathology and Religious Commitment." *Review of Religious Research* 12(3):165-76.

Stott, G. 1988. "Familial Influence on Religious Involvement." In D. L. Thomas (ed.), *The Religion and Family Connection: Social Science Perspectives*. Provo, UT: Religious Studies Center, Brigham Young University.

Stryker, S. 1964. "The Interactional and Situational Approaches." In H. T. Christensen (ed.), *Handbook of Marriage and the Family*. Chicago: Rand McNally.

Thomas, D. L. 1983. "Family in the Mormon Experience." Chapter 11 in W. V. D'Antonio and J. Aldous (eds.), *Families and Religions: Conflict and Change in Modern Society*. Beverly Hills, CA: Sage Publications.

Thomas, D. L. and J. E. Wilcox. 1987. "The Rise of Family Theory: An Historical and Critical Analysis." Pp. 81-102 in M. B. Sussman and S. K. Steinmetz (eds.), *Handbook of Marriage and the Family*. New York: Plenum Press.

Thomas, D. L. and R. Kent. 1985. "Theoretical Perspectives on the Religion and Family Connection with Personal Well-Being." Paper presented at the Theory Construction Workshop, National Council on Family Relations annual meetings, Dallas, Texas, November 4-5.

Thomas, D. L. and G. C. Henry. 1985. "The Religion and Family Connection: Increasing Dialogue in the Social Sciences." *Journal of Marriage and the Family* (May):369-79.

Thomas, D. L. and V. Sommerfeldt. 1984. "Religion, Family, and the Social Sciences: A Time for Dialogue." *Family Perspective* 18:117-25.

Thomas, D. L., A. J. Weigert, and N. Winston. 1984. "Adolescent Identification with Father and Mother: A Multi-national Study." *Acta Paedologica* 1:47-68.

Thomas, D. L., V. Gecas, A. Weigert, and E. Rooney. 1974. *Family Socialization and the Adolescent*. Lexington, MA: Lexington Books.

Thornton, A. 1985. "Reciprocal Influences of Family and Religion in a Changing World." *Journal of Marriage and the Family* 47 (May):381-94.

Vinovskis, M. A. 1987. "Historical Perspectives on the Development of the Family and Parent-Child Interactions." Pp. 295-312 in J. B. Lancaster, J. Altmann, A. S. Rossi, and L. R. Sherrod (eds.), *Parenting Across the Life Span*. New York: Aldine de Gruyter.

Weed, S. L., and D. Anderson. Forthcoming. "Applied Research in Religious Institutions: 1987 in Review." *Journal of Religious Research*.

Weigert, A. J. and D. L. Thomas. 1979. "Family Socialization and Adolescent Conformity and Religiosity: An Extension to Germany and Spain." *Journal of Comparative Family Studies* 10(3):371-83.

Weiting, S. G. 1975. "An Examination of the Intergenerational Patterns of Religious Belief and Practice." *Sociological Analysis* 36:137–49.

Wilkinson, M. L. and W. C. Tanner III. 1980. "The Influence of Family Size Interaction, and Religiosity on Family Affection in a Mormon Sample." *Journal of Marriage and the Family* 42(2):297–304.

Index